Inside Windows Storage

Inside Windows Storage

Server Storage Technologies for Windows® 2000, Windows® Server 2003, and Beyond

Dilip C. Naik

✦✦Addison-Wesley

Boston • San Francisco • New York • Toronto • Montreal
London • Munich • Paris • Madrid
Capetown • Sydney • Tokyo • Singapore • Mexico City

Many of the designations used by manufacturers and sellers to distinguish their products are claimed as trademarks. Where those designations appear in this book, and Addison-Wesley was aware of a trademark claim, the designations have been printed with initial capital letters or in all capitals.

The author and publisher have taken care in the preparation of this book, but make no expressed or implied warranty of any kind and assume no responsibility for errors or omissions. No liability is assumed for incidental or consequential damages in connection with or arising out of the use of the information or programs contained herein.

The publisher offers discounts on this book when ordered in quantity for bulk purchases and special sales. For more information, please contact:

U.S. Corporate and Government Sales
(800) 382-3419
corpsales@pearsontechgroup.com

For sales outside of the U.S., please contact:

International Sales
(317) 581-3793
international@pearsontechgroup.com

Visit Addison-Wesley on the Web: www.awprofessional.com

Library of Congress Cataloging-in-Publication Data

Naik, Dilip C.
    Inside Windows storage : server storage technologies for Windows® Server 2003, Windows® 2000, and beyond / Dilip Naik.
        p.   cm.
    Includes bibliographical references and index.
    ISBN 0-321-12698-X (alk. paper)
    1. Microsoft Windows server. 2. Operating systems (Computers) 3. Computer storage devices. I. Title.

    QA76.76.O63N345 2004
    005.7'13769—dc21

                                                        2003050298

Pearson Education, Inc.
Rights and Contracts Department
75 Arlington Street, Suite 300
Boston, MA 02116
Fax: (617) 848-7047

ISBN: 0-321-12698-X
Text printed on recycled paper
1 2 3 4 5 6 7 8 9 10—CRS—0706050403
First printing, July 2003

Dedicated to
Riti, Nihar, and Varsha

Contents

Introduction

Gordon Moore, Intel's cofounder, once observed that the density of transistors per square inch was doubling every year. Subsequently, the pace dropped a little and the doubling was perceived to be once every 18 months instead of once every 12 months. According to industry analysts, however, the enterprise storage industry is still beating Moore's law in its growth.

One estimate is that in the next few years, more data will be generated than has been created since the dawn of known history! Regardless of the exact details, one must concede that Windows servers play an important role in the enterprise storage industry. Therefore, knowledge of the storage aspects of the Windows operating system will prove to be invaluable. This book is a humble attempt to meet this perceived need.

A word or two about the conventions used in this book would be helpful. The book uses the phrases "Windows NT" and "Windows Server family" interchangeably. Both are used when a feature that is common across all of Windows NT 4.0, Windows 2000, and Windows Server 2003 is being discussed. When necessary, a particular version of the operating system is mentioned—for example, Windows 2000 or Windows Server 2003—and these terms refer to particular versions of the operating system rather than to the operating system in a generic sense.

This book has been written for those who are somewhat conversant with computer systems and the IT industry and who are looking to further their knowledge of the storage industry in general and of Windows NT architecture details as they apply to storage devices. To be clear, this book is about enterprise storage, and consumer storage details are described cursorily, if at all. The book attempts to strike a balance between catering to the software professional who knows nothing about storage and the professional who is somewhat conversant with storage but looking for good insights into Windows NT storage architecture.

If the reader comes away with just one idea after reading this book, it should be a deep appreciation of the steady acceleration of enterprise storage–related features that each succeeding release of the Windows NT operating system has brought and will bring to market.

This book attempts to strike a balance among the following aspects:

- Making information available in a timely manner.
- Providing detailed information and respecting intellectual property rights. The book covers several software development kits (SDKs) that are available only on a nondisclosure agreement (NDA) basis. Hence the coverage of these kits has been necessarily limited to what is already publicly available information. I have erred on the side of caution, preferring to provide only information that I know is publicly available, but I have added value to this often cryptic and hard-to-find information by providing the necessary explanations.
- Providing information on upcoming Windows NT releases and not just "stale" information about past Windows NT releases. Such forward-looking information is necessary for a proper appreciation of the clear focus that Microsoft has devoted to enterprise storage in the Windows NT operating system. The obvious risk is that plans are subject to change. The book clearly mentions when a particular aspect is related to forthcoming Windows NT releases.

A word of caution is in order here. This book makes some forward-looking statements in the form of expected features in forthcoming releases of the Windows NT operating systems. Microsoft has repeatedly made it clear that the only guaranteed way of identifying features in an operating system release is to look for them after the actual release. No matter what is said in venues such as trade shows and seminars, there is no guarantee that features tentatively discussed will ever ship, let alone ship with a particular version of the operating system. No material plans of any kind should be based on these guesses.

Any reader who does not appreciate the "Safe Harbor statement" nature of the previous paragraph is highly encouraged to study (and not just read) it again.

The book begins with an overview of Windows NT architecture, including the Windows NT I/O subsystem and storage driver architectures. Chapter 1 is an attempt to condense the vast amount of information purveyed in the excellent *Inside Windows NT* books (Microsoft Press), and it is intended for readers who do not have the time to peruse the book in its entirety.

Chapter 2 describes direct-attached storage, which was historically the first choice for storage.

Chapter 3 describes network-attached storage, the next major milestone in enterprise storage. The Windows NT network stack is explained in detail, from the point of view of the storage professional.

Chapter 4 describes Fibre Channel storage area networks, a technology that is perceived to be rapidly maturing now and still holding its own in the face of upcoming new technology in the form of iSCSI and InfiniBand.

Chapter 5 covers the basics of backup and restore, and the new volume shadow copy service (also popularly referred to as snapshots) in Windows Server 2003.

Chapter 6 covers file systems and disk virtualization, with particular reference to Windows NT. Cluster file systems are also discussed.

Chapter 7 discusses storage management in general and the various storage management solutions as they apply to Windows NT.

Chapter 8 covers new technologies in storage, particularly IP storage (which attempts to meld storage and IP networks), as well as InfiniBand.

Chapter 9 discusses Windows Server 2003 and Windows 2000 natively supported solutions to provide high-availability services (including failover, failback, and load balancing) using multiported dual host bus adapters (HBAs) in a Windows NT server. The chapter also discusses more mundane high-availability and high-performance solutions, such as RAID.

Although the rest of this book is organized into chapters based on technologies, Chapter 10 is organized by Windows NT releases. Irrespective of the storage technology that is being discussed, Chapter 10 traces the storage features as they appeared in Windows NT 4.0, Windows 2000, Windows Server 2003, and expected features in Windows releases to come.

So read on, and I hope, enjoy.

Please send all feedback to **dilipn@niriva.com**.

Dilip C. Naik
Redmond, Washington
dilipn@niriva.com

Acknowledgments

An endeavor of this magnitude is never accomplished in isolation. I am deeply indebted to a number of people, notably:

- My editors Karen Gettman and Emily Frey. They believed in me to begin with and held their belief through thick and thin, as I made my sometimes successful attempts at keeping to a schedule and as I struggled to get my ideas across in a consistent and proper fashion.
- Tom Clark, who was instrumental in helping me sell the idea for the book and rendered other invaluable assistance as well.
- The technical reviewers—James Anderson, Ellen Beck Gardner, Robert Griswold, Varina Hammond, Milan J. Merhar, Bob Snead, and Richard Wheeler—who appreciated the diamond in the rough and helped me polish the contents until they were often unrecognizable from the raw content with which I had begun.
- Developmental editor Laurie McGuire.
- Copy editor Stephanie Hiebert.
- Jeff Goldner and Karan Mehra at Microsoft, who provided invaluable feedback and encouragement.
- And last, but not least, my family. My wife Varsha, who for months on end put up with typing away on my lap, my IBM Thinkpad. My son Nihar and my daughter Riti, who put up with the odd dad who brought a laptop to soccer and basketball games and practices.

Thank you, all of you!

CHAPTER 1

Introduction to Windows NT and Windows NT Storage Device Drivers

This chapter introduces the novice reader to Windows NT device drivers in general, filter drivers, and the Windows Server family storage device driver stack in particular. The discussion is intended to provide only enough background to enable the novice reader to understand the intricacies of the Windows NT I/O subsystem and gain a better understanding of storage drivers. The emphasis is on building a base understanding of how the storage-related features described in this book—such as multipath I/O, Single Instance Storage in Remote Installation Services, Windows NT reparse points, and Windows Remote Storage Services—are designed.

To be clear, this chapter is *not* intended to be the sole reference that will completely prepare the reader for writing Windows NT device drivers, nor is it a complete overview of the Windows NT operating system. The reader is encouraged to peruse the references listed at the end of the book to become completely knowledgeable about Windows NT and to be able to write various kinds of drivers, including file system filter drivers.

Further, this chapter will adhere specifically to Windows NT and driver architecture as it applies to storage devices. Windows NT features and driver architecture as they apply to non-storage-related topics or devices are discussed very briefly, if at all.

Sections 1.1 and 1.2 discuss some terminology that will be used frequently throughout this book. Included are the terms *kernel mode, user mode*, and *process context*. After these preliminaries the chapter will launch into a description of the Windows storage stack detailing the various layers of the stack, including the file system, volume management, class, and port layers. Filter drivers are also described briefly. The chapter closes by describing a typical I/O request and how it is handled at each layer of the storage I/O stack.

1.1 Windows Kernel Mode and User Mode

This book uses the terms *kernel mode* and *user mode* regularly. Before we see how they are defined, a bit of background is in order.

Windows NT has been designed as a portable operating system with all processor- and hardware-dependent code isolated in a module called the *hardware abstraction layer (HAL)*, which is described in Section 1.3.1. Although Windows NT did indeed once run on multiple processors, including PowerPC and Alpha, it is now supported only on Intel and Intel-compatible processors. Some basic details of the Intel x86 architecture are presented here so that the details of Windows NT presented later can be appreciated. This section does not attempt to describe all the features of the Intel x86 architecture, but explains only what is immediately relevant.

The Intel x86 architecture supports four modes of operation: real mode, virtual x86 mode, system management mode,[1] and protected mode.

In **real mode**, every process has access to the lower 1MB of memory address space with no restrictions. On power-up, the processor always starts in real mode. We can easily switch the processor to protected mode by setting a bit in a control register, and we can switch it from protected mode to real mode by clearing this bit. Windows NT uses real mode for initialization, but it switches to protected mode well before applications are started. Throughout the Windows NT family of products, the trend has been toward reducing the amount of work done in real mode and switching more quickly to protected mode. Once the processor is in protected mode, Windows NT never switches it to real mode.

Virtual x86 mode provides the ability to execute multiple real-mode applications while the processor is in protected mode. Windows NT 4.0 supports this with a subsystem called the NT Virtual DOS Machine (NTVDM). The requirement that DOS-based applications must run easily on the Windows Server platform has gradually been

---

1. System management mode is not used by Windows NT.

decreasing in importance. Hence the importance of the NTVDM subsystem has also been decreasing.

Protected mode is the mode that Windows NT uses most heavily. Protected mode offers four levels of operation, as shown in Figure 1.1. At level 0 (or ring 0), often called **kernel mode**, processor instructions and features to facilitate memory protection and virtual memory are available. Privileged instructions, such as instructions to manipulate control registers within the processor, are also available at level 0. Windows NT does not use levels (rings) 1 and 2. The lowest privilege level—level 3, or **user mode**—offers the greatest protection in terms of restricting one process from accessing memory or code owned by another process.

Here are some concrete examples of the functionality provided by Windows NT using the x86 architecture:

- All memory is manipulated (allocated, read, written) in units called *pages*. See Section 1.3.3.6 (Virtual Memory Manager) for more details.
- Each memory page has an associated tag defining whether it can be read or written and what privilege level is needed to do so. The intent is to protect user processes from each other and to protect

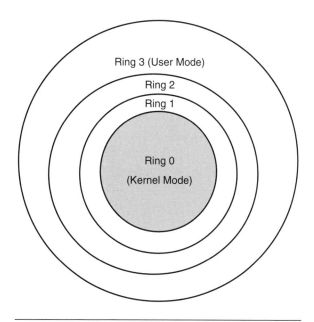

Figure 1.1 Intel x86 Architecture Privilege Levels

system code and data from user processes. Note that system code (running in kernel mode) is not protected in any way from other code running in kernel mode.

- Memory pages containing code (as opposed to data) can be marked as nonwritable by user processes and kernel mode code.

Applications running in user mode access Windows NT kernel services by executing a special instruction that allows a controlled transition into kernel mode and then back into user mode once the kernel mode request has been completed.

1.2 Processes, Process Context, and Threads

A **process** is an in-memory image of an executing program. A process is assigned a memory region that it owns for the duration of its existence. It may share code (dynamic link libraries) or data (shared memory regions) with another process. A process is described by a process object maintained by the Object Manager. Data maintained within the process object includes virtual memory address space details, process priority, file handles, and memory allocation details, to name just a few.

In Windows NT, multiple processes can exist at the same time; however, only one of them is executing at a given moment on any CPU. Note that the drivers in general and the storage drivers in particular do not create a process of their own. The operating system creates some processes for its own purposes and other processes in response to user commands—for example, when the user launches an application such as Microsoft Word or Microsoft Excel. When a driver is called while a particular process is executing, the driver is said to be running in the context of that process.

Process context may be defined as all the state information needed to track a process. This information includes the virtual memory used by the process, the CPU register values, and the various file and object handles, as well as various security tokens associated with the process. Process context is extremely important because a lot of data structures and resources, such as file handles and memory pointers, are relative to a particular process. For example, a file handle created in one process is invalid in another.

A **thread** is a subunit of a process; a process may have one or more threads. A thread shares the global data structures and address space of the process, but a thread also has its own private data. Switching between processes is an expensive task that involves saving the processor state to a process-specific data structure while also changing memory and CPU control registers. Switching between threads is very efficient because less data has to be saved.

Each thread has an associated thread object maintained by the object manager. Information contained within the object includes processor affinity (in a multi-CPU system, the CPU on which a thread prefers to run), thread state (e.g., whether the thread is running, is ready to run, or is blocked on an I/O,), and other thread features.

A thread may be a user mode thread or a kernel mode thread. Kernel mode threads can be created only by kernel mode entities, such as device drivers, and they always execute in kernel mode. A user mode thread usually executes in user mode, except when executing in kernel mode as a result of requesting an NT service, as mentioned in Section 1.1.

1.3 Windows NT Architecture

Windows NT has been designed with a modular, layered architecture that allows for efficiency and extensibility. The architecture allows for easy addition of support for new devices or new functionality, such as encrypting file systems. The architecture also allows for adding support for applications based on a different operating system—for example, OS/2 or POSIX. Of course, both of these have been historically more important than they currently are, but they are still good examples of the modular extensible architecture.

Figure 1.2 shows the high-level architecture of Windows NT. As explained in the Introduction, the term *Windows NT* is used in a generic sense to refer to all versions of the operating system based on the NT code, which includes Windows NT 3.X, Windows NT 4.0, Windows 2000, Windows XP, and also Windows Server 2003.

Sections 1.3.1 through 1.3.6 explain the various entities in Figure 1.2, from the bottom up. Note the line dividing kernel and user modes in Figure 1.2. The importance and meaning of the two modes have already been explained earlier in this chapter.

Kernel mode hosts all privileged processes running at ring 0 of the Intel x86 architecture. Windows NT kernel mode consists of three primary subsystems:

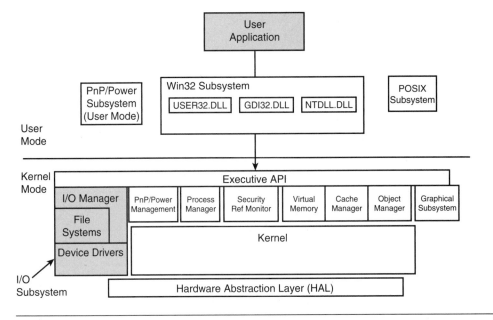

Figure 1.2 Windows NT Architecture

1. Hardware abstraction layer
2. Windows NT kernel
3. Windows NT Executive

Sections 1.3.1 through 1.3.3 look at each of these in turn.

1.3.1 Hardware Abstraction Layer

The **hardware abstraction layer** (**HAL**) provides protection by controlling access to hardware resources. This is the sole part of Windows NT that has hardware-dependent code (or processor-dependent code) and possibly some assembly language code as well. In general, the HAL provides an abstraction for the purposes of the higher-level components so that they can be shielded from hardware-dependent details. The functionality that the HAL provides includes

- A timer service interface shielding the Windows NT Executive from the specifics of the underlying timer hardware.
- I/O support in terms of bus and DMA (direct memory access) operation support. The HAL translates between external bus and

Windows NT addressing information, and it provides support for bus configuration information.

■ Interrupt support by mapping the external interrupts to Windows NT interrupt request (IRQ) levels and providing masking/unmasking services for interrupts.

1.3.2 Windows NT Kernel

The Windows NT kernel is the next layer above the HAL and provides functionality that enables the Windows NT Executive (described in Section 1.3.3), as well as other subsystems. Here are the main services provided by the kernel:

■ Synchronization assistance
■ Scheduling of threads and processes
■ Handling of interrupts and exceptions
■ System recovery from exceptions—for example, a power failure

The kernel always resides in memory; it is never paged out to disk as user applications' memory may sometimes be. The kernel cannot be preempted, meaning that execution of code in the kernel can never be suspended in favor of other code unless the kernel voluntarily yields to enable other code to run. The kernel is built as an object-oriented system that uses two classes of objects:

1. **Dispatcher objects**, which dispatch threads and processes and also synchronize different threads and processes. Dispatcher objects include mutexes, semaphores, and timers. Mutexes are synchronization objects that provide synchronization between two entities. (*Mutex* is short for "mutual exclusion.")
2. **Control objects**, such as asynchronous procedure calls (APCs) and interrupt service routines (ISRs), both of which are described in more detail in Section 1.5.

1.3.3 Windows NT Executive

The Windows NT Executive provides very important functionality, including APIs that enable threads in Windows NT user mode to communicate with the Windows NT kernel to request services. Like the Windows NT kernel, the Windows NT Executive cannot be paged out of memory. The Executive manages multiple operations, including I/O, security, interprocess communication, memory, processes, Plug and Play support, power management, file systems, objects, and graphical devices. All of the Windows NT Executive is located within a single file called ntoskrnl.exe. The Executive creates very few threads to accomplish its work. Typically, a user mode process will request some system services, and the Executive will simply be invoked in the context of this process. One example of a thread created for the Executive is the lazy writer thread that flushes pages to disk.

The Windows NT Executive itself consists of the following components:

- Object Manager
- Security Reference Monitor
- Process Manager
- Plug and Play subsystem
- Power Manager
- Virtual Memory Manager
- Cache Manager

Each of these is described in Sections 1.3.3.1 through 1.3.3.7.

1.3.3.1 Object Manager

The Windows NT Object Manager provides services to the rest of the Windows NT operating system, including the Windows NT Executive (of which it is a part). The Object Manager provides services to name, create, destroy, manipulate, and share objects. The Object Manager interacts heavily with the Security Reference Monitor as a means of ensuring that only authorized processes and users are allowed appropriate access to appropriate objects. The qualifier *appropriate* refers to the fact that even when access is granted, it is enforced as a type of access, such as read-only access. Every object created by the Object Manager has an associated access control list (ACL). An ACL is really a group of objects specifying what rights are explicitly or implicitly granted to a particular user or group; the ACL may also have objects specifying what rights are denied.

In addition, the Object Manager assigns a handle to every object it creates. It ensures the uniqueness of handles and can internally transform a handle into a reference to a unique object. However, Object Manager clients (which use the services of the Object Manager) treat the handle simply as an opaque token without any structure. Some examples of the types of objects that the Object Manager deals with include file, directory, port, process, thread, semaphore, and event objects.

1.3.3.2 Security Reference Monitor

The Security Reference Monitor performs access checking and logging for resources. The access checking is done at a highly granular level, including not only whether access is permitted, but also what type of access is permitted—for example, read-only or read/write access. The functionality of the security subsystem is enabled by the object-oriented nature of Windows NT. When an object is accessed, the Security Reference Monitor simply checks the ACLs associated with the object against the security token of the process before deciding to allow or disallow the access. ACLs are of two types: one that implicitly or explicitly allows a particular access, and another that implicitly or explicitly disallows a particular type of access. The Security Reference Monitor is heavily used by other Executive subsystems, such as the Object Manager.

The Security Reference Monitor also provides similar services for user mode applications. It provides a facility to generate a token (per process) that can be used for security and access checking, as well as for generating audit logs.

1.3.3.3 Process Manager

The Process Manager facilitates creation, deletion, and manipulation of processes and threads. It does not maintain a hierarchy; for example, it does not track parent–child process relationships. That is left to the entity that creates a process. As an analogy, think of a file manager that provides a facility to create a file, but the user of the file manager is responsible for linking the file into a directory structure. The Process Manager uses the services of the Object Manager, as well as the security subsystem, to accomplish its goals. For every process that is started, there are at least two calls to the Process Manager—the first one to create the process, and the second one to create a thread within the process because every process must have at least one thread.

1.3.3.4 Plug and Play Subsystem

Figure 1.2 shows the power management and Plug and Play (PnP) subsystems in a single box. This is simply to keep the figure from becoming too complicated. In fact, the two subsystems are distinct, though closely related.

Plug and Play is a term used to describe functionality implemented by hardware and software that allows a Windows-based system to dynamically recognize hardware and provide the software support that is needed to operate the device properly. In particular, this software support is responsible for

- Correctly detecting the hardware identity.
- Correctly detecting when hardware is dynamically plugged in or removed.
- Allocating and configuring resources to operate hardware properly.
- Correctly locating and loading the proper device drivers.
- Providing a notification mechanism to detect the arrival and removal of hardware; this notification mechanism can be used by both kernel mode software and user mode software.

The PnP subsystem consists of both user mode and kernel mode components. The user mode component provides applications with a way to accomplish device management, including a registration mechanism by which they can be notified about device arrival and removal.

The PnP subsystem plays an extremely important role in device discovery, device enumeration, device initialization, and device addition/removal. In particular, the PnP subsystem is responsible for generating an important IRP (I/O request packet) called IRP_MN_QUERY_DEVICE_RELATIONSHIPS and sending it to bus drivers. This IRP is often referred to as QDR in Microsoft presentations. This QDR functionality is important because it is used to enumerate devices and build a device stack. Filter drivers are sometimes written to watch for QDR functionality and modify the device list being reported. As will be described in Chapter 6, the Partition Manager is a filter driver that exhibits such functionality.

1.3.3.5 Power Manager

The Power Manager plays an extremely important role in providing power-saving features such as spinning down disks, CD-ROM and DVD drives, and video monitors. Obviously the Power Manager is more important in notebook computers than on servers, but even on servers, the Power Manager has a role to play with hot-swap devices and with monitoring the management of standby power supply devices for servers. The Power Manager also provides APIs for the benefit of higher-level applications.

1.3.3.6 Virtual Memory Manager

The Virtual Memory Manager (VMM) provides memory functionality so that processes can use larger amounts of memory than the amount of physical memory in a system. Application requests for memory allocation are checked by the Virtual Memory Manager. If insufficient memory is left, the VMM tries to move other pages of memory to disk in order to make room for the new allocation to succeed. If an application tries to access a page of memory that is not physically present, the VMM makes room in physical memory before moving the requested pages back from disk to RAM. This functionality is commonly referred to as **paging**.

The area on disk used to hold pages that do not fit in physical memory is called a **swap file**. The operating system creates and protects this swap file automatically. An administrator can change the size of the file. This file is also sometimes referred to as a **paging file** because memory is moved to and from the file in multiples of pages.

With Windows NT 4.0, the total addressable space of 4GB is evenly divided between 2GB in user mode and 2GB in kernel mode. The top 2GB is allocated to Windows NT kernel mode and the bottom 2GB to user mode. With Windows 2000 Advanced Server, a boot-time switch can reallocate the addressable space into 1GB for the kernel mode and 3GB for the user mode. The user mode applications need to be rewritten to take advantage of this extra 1GB of virtual memory. Of course, with 64-bit versions of Windows NT, this restriction does not apply.

The Virtual Memory Manager provides APIs for allocating and freeing memory, as well as for locking down and unlocking memory. *Locking down memory* refers to functionality that prevents the memory that is being manipulated from being swapped out to disk. This functionality is often mistaken to mean that the physical address of the memory cannot change. Although this is true in the present Windows NT implementation, it may not remain true in future versions of Windows NT. Drivers directly use this API and request pageable or nonpageable memory depending on the particular need.

1.3.3.7 Cache Manager

The Cache Manager is an integral part of the I/O subsystem and works closely with file system drivers and the Virtual Memory Manager. The Windows NT Cache Manager is file system oriented and thus closely coordinated with the file system drivers. This is a change from the Windows 95 caching strategy, which was disk sector oriented. The Cache

Manager handles all file systems, local as well as remote, using a single pooled cache. The Cache Manager can cache multiple data streams per file. Data streams are a feature of the NT file system (NTFS) and are explained in Chapter 6, the file systems chapter.

All file I/O appears to be paging I/O because of how the interaction between the Cache Manager and the Virtual Memory Manager is designed. When a file I/O operation is requested, the file system first checks with the Cache Manager to see if the Cache Manager has the required data. If the Cache Manager finds that the requested data is not available, it calls the file system driver to read the data. This is really a circular loop, since the file system asked the Cache Manager for the page and the Cache Manager asked the file system for the page. The difference is that the Cache Manager marks the I/O differently, causing the file system driver to read the data and not bother checking for cached data a second time.

1.3.4 I/O Subsystem

The I/O subsystem is responsible for handling all input/output requests and is designed to accomplish the following:

- Provide extremely fast I/O response on single- and multiprocessor systems.
- Provide asynchronous I/O. Synchronous I/O is actually done as an asynchronous I/O request followed by a blocking wait for that I/O to complete.
- Support multiple file systems—for example, CDFS, NTFS, UDFS.
- Provide a modular architecture that supports addition of new file systems and devices.
- Provide for devices (and their associated drivers) to come and go, on the fly, without requiring a reboot (really implemented in Windows 2000 and subsequent Windows NT products).
- Provide for advanced features such as caching and memory-mapped files. Memory-mapped files are a feature that offers the ability to have a file's contents mapped into a specified memory location in the process address space. To access or modify the contents of the file, the application simply reads or writes from the specified address space.
- Provide for protection of resources that are shared across various processes.

To achieve these goals, the I/O system is built as a modular system (like the rest of Windows NT) consisting of the following modules:

- I/O APIs
- I/O Manager
- File system drivers
- Other drivers (such as disk drivers or keyboard drivers)

These modules are described in Sections 1.3.4.1 through 1.3.4.3.

1.3.4.1 I/O APIs

The term *I/O APIs* refers to functionality provided by the I/O Manager for the benefit of upper layers of Windows NT, as well as kernel mode components to accomplish I/O Manager–related operations. All the I/O API names are in the form "IoXXXX," where "XXXX" is a string followed by parameters. (See the Driver Development Kit for complete details.) Some good examples of APIs involved here include

- **IoCreateDevice**, to create a new device object. Device objects are described in Section 1.4.2.
- **IoCallDriver**, to send an I/O request packet to a driver (I/O request packets are described in Section 1.4.3).

1.3.4.2 I/O Manager

The I/O Manager is part of the core NT kernel Executive and provides a variety of functions, including the following:

- Building I/O request packets (IRPs) and directing them to the appropriate driver, as well as routing IRPs between drivers.
- Deleting or freeing IRPs when the I/O operation is complete.
- Interfacing with the Cache Manager and other parts of the NT Executive system.
- Interfacing with the Virtual Memory Manager to provide memory-mapped I/O for file systems.
- Keeping track of which file systems are loaded and invoking them as needed.
- Providing support for synchronous and asynchronous I/O. Asynchronous I/O is particularly important for storage applications; for

example, a backup application will want to use asynchronous I/O
to queue multiple requests so that it can keep the tape device busy.
- Managing buffers for an I/O operation.

1.3.4.3 File System Drivers

Windows NT implements file system functionality using kernel mode
drivers. Windows NT ships with the following file system drivers:

- NTFS (NT file system)
- UDFS (universal disk file system)
- CDFS (CD-ROM file system)
- FAT (file allocation table)

Network file system drivers are covered in Chapter 3. File system
drivers are implemented via the Windows NT DDK and an add-on product that Microsoft sells, called the *Windows NT Installable File System
Kit*. This kit documents the various APIs needed to write file system drivers and also contains sample code that implements a FAT and a UDFS
file system.

File system drivers behave like other drivers in the sense that they
interact with the I/O Manager and deal with I/O request packets. File
system drivers are logical drivers in that they do not directly deal with
hardware; for example, a file system does not care whether it is getting
data from a SCSI disk or an ATA (also referred to as IDE) disk. However,
file system drivers are also different from other drivers. Here are some of
the differences:

- File system drivers are always called in the context of the thread
  that requests the I/O operation.
- File system drivers interact heavily with the Cache Manager and
  the Virtual Memory Manager, simply using these two modules to
  implement its data buffering. For example, the file systems use the
  Cache Manager services to cache file system metadata such as
  locations of files or directories on disk to avoid generating a heavy
  overhead of repeatedly fetching the same metadata.
- File system drivers are the only drivers that implement a method
  of I/O that is not IRP based. This method is called *Fast I/O* and
  consists of some entry points within the driver. The I/O Manager
  calls these entry points to do an I/O operation in the hope that the
  data is cached and can be handled quickly. The file system driver

can make the call fail if appropriate, and the I/O Manager will simply reissue the same I/O request using the regular IRP method.

Closely associated with the notion of file systems is the notion of file system filter drivers. File system filter drivers are used to implement a wide range of important functionality, such as encrypting file systems and Remote Storage Services. The different types of functionality are discussed in the appropriate chapters.

1.3.5 Graphical Subsystem

Given that the focus of this book is enterprise storage, Figure 1.2 depicts the graphical subsystem in kernel mode even though a portion of it is also in user mode. Windows 2000 moved a considerable amount of graphical subsystem code from user mode to kernel mode primarily to improve performance. For the purposes of this book, the graphical subsystem can be thought of as containing all the code that pertains to windowing and using video devices, scanner devices, printer devices, and so on.

1.3.6 Win32 Subsystem

The Win32 subsystem is one of the most important elements of Windows NT, especially for programmers. It provides the Win32 APIs for the benefit of the programmer. The Win32 APIs are also the platform upon which other subsystems, such as the POSIX subsystem, build.

The Win32 API set can be broadly divided into three categories:

1. Windowing and window messaging APIs are implemented in a dynamic link library called user32.dll. This DLL is then linked with applications that use any API exported by this file. Multiple applications that link with this file and are running will share a single copy.
2. Graphical drawing APIs are implemented in a dynamic link library called gdi32.dll, which is then linked with applications that call any API exported by this library. In Windows NT versions prior to Windows 2000, gdi32.dll acted as a client and contacted the Win32 server process (described later) because the functions were implemented in the Win32 server process. The Win32 server would then call on the kernel mode component of the graphical subsystem as needed. In Windows 2000, gdi32.dll directly calls the kernel mode graphical subsystem as needed.

3. Base functionality APIs such as APIs to open a file (CreateFile), read a file (ReadFile), and write a file (WriteFile) are implemented in a dynamic link library called ntdll.dll. This library makes a call to the kernel mode Executive as needed. To make this call, the library uses one of the 256 interrupts defined by the Intel x86 architecture. In particular, it uses the interrupt 46 (decimal 46, hexadecimal 0x2E). The interrupt handler[2] validates the API requested (by a simple table lookup) and the parameters passed for that API. If all parameters pass validation tests, the handler then calls the appropriate Executive subsystem to perform the requested operation.

Applications are written with the Win32 APIs and other support mechanisms described in the software development kit (SDK). In some senses, even the POSIX subsystem is an application tool, developed to support UNIX applications. Although the POSIX subsystem is not as important as it once was, it still provides a good example of the Windows NT modular and extensible architecture.

1.4 Windows Device Driver–Related Data Structures

Before we consider the details of Windows NT device drivers, it will be advantageous to understand some important data structures that these drivers use. Every Windows driver, including storage drivers, must deal with three major types of objects: driver objects, device objects, and I/O request packets. These objects are described in Sections 1.4.1 through 1.4.3.

1.4.1 Driver Objects

A **driver object** is created by the Windows NT Executive when a driver is loaded. The driver object is allocated from nonpageable memory. A driver object contains important information, such as the driver dispatch table that identifies addresses for various driver routines. Each driver has only one driver object, even when the driver is controlling multiple devices. Even when a driver runs on multiple CPUs on a multiprocessor

---

2. Strictly speaking, this is not just an interrupt handler, but the details are not relevant here and hence it is referred to as simply an interrupt.

Windows NT system, there is only one driver object in memory. Although the driver object is created by the Windows NT Executive, it is the responsibility of the driver writer to fill out some details, such as the routine addresses in the driver dispatch table. This requirement applies only to drivers that export a driver object; therefore minidrivers that rely on the class or port driver's object are not required to enter these object details.

1.4.2 Device Objects

A **device object** represents a physical I/O device (e.g., host bus adapter, disk, or tape device) or a logical device (e.g., a virus-checking filter driver). Each device can have only one device object. A device object contains a pointer to the driver object that handles processing of this device. A device object also describes physical characteristics of the device—for example, the largest amount of I/O that can be done in a single operation, or the unit on which the buffer supplied to a device must be aligned.

The three kinds of device objects share the same basic device object structure, but they differ in device object extensions and in how they are used. The three kinds of device objects are

1. The **physical device object** (**PDO**), which represents a device on a bus. PDOs are typically created by a bus driver (bus drivers are explained in Section 1.7.1). A PDO is required to communicate with the device. Examples of data kept in the PDO are device power state and device identity—for example, SCSI bus identifier, SCSI target identifier, and SCSI logical unit number (LUN). These SCSI terms are explained in Chapter 2. For now, suffice it to say that to uniquely identify a SCSI device, you need to specify three values: bus, target, and LUN identifiers.

2. The **functional device object** (**FDO**), which is typically created by a class or port driver (class and port drivers are discussed in Sections 1.7.2 and 1.7.3). Use of a device requires an FDO. Examples of data kept within an FDO include details of disk organization—for example, a disk partition table and, if the disk is a DVD, the region information about a DVD.

3. The **filter device object** (**DO**), which represents a device to a filter driver.

Figure 1.3 shows some significant parts of a driver object.

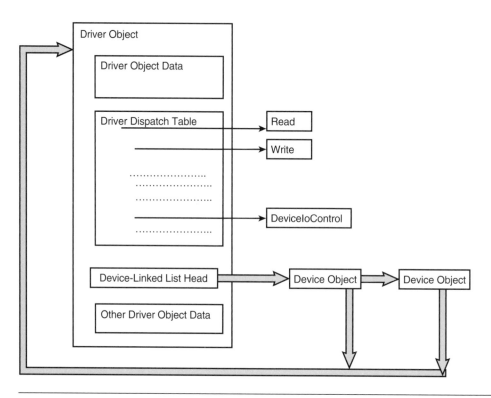

Figure 1.3 Windows NT Driver Object

One important part of the driver object is the driver dispatch table. The driver dispatch table defines various standard functions that a driver implements. Depending on the exact nature of the driver, some of these functions *must* be implemented by the driver, and some *may* optionally be implemented by the driver. Figure 1.3 shows only the Read, Write, and DeviceIoControl functions, but there are many more, and curious readers may obtain more details from the Windows Driver Development Kit.

Devices for which a driver implements functionality are described by device objects (PDO, FDO, or DO), and all the devices for which a driver provides functionality are kept in a linked list. The head of the linked list is kept in the driver object, as shown at the bottom left of Figure 1.3. Note that because device objects (PDOs, FDOs, DOs) contain a pointer to the driver device object, one can walk the data structure, locate the driver object, and from the dispatch table inside that driver object, invoke the appropriate driver function.

1.4.3 I/O Request Packets

Windows NT is a layered operating system that uses a packet-based interface to communicate with kernel mode drivers. These packets, which are used to communicate with drivers, are referred to as **I/O request packets**, or **IRPs**. The communication with a driver could come from another driver or from the I/O subsystem.

IRPs are allocated from nonpageable memory. Nonpageable memory is a precious system resource. IRPs are allocated and maintained on a thread-specific queue. Windows NT maintains some IRPs ready and allocated on a lookaside list[3] so that they may be quickly assigned to a driver or the I/O Manager when requested.

As Figure 1.4 shows, IRPs have a fixed-size header and a variable number of I/O stack locations. The I/O stack locations represent data structures for individual drivers that will process the IRP. That is, each driver that processes an IRP gets its own private data area in the IRP stack. When an IRP is allocated and sent to a driver, sufficient stack locations are needed for each driver that will handle the IRP. A driver attempting to access a nonexistent IRP stack location will cause a system error. Thus an IRP that works for one driver stack chain may or may not be reused for another driver stack chain.

As shown in Figure 1.4, the IRP header consists of various kinds of information, such as

- Whether the request is synchronous or asynchronous
- Whether the request is a paging I/O operation or an operation that should be done with no intermediate caching
- A buffer pointer for I/O operations
- An I/O status block representing the current status of the IRP, which changes as the IRP is handled by various drivers
- Information needed to handle IRP cancellation, in case an I/O operation specified by an IRP is canceled (for example, because of a timeout or because the user decides it is taking too long)
- An indication of whether the I/O request originated in user mode or kernel mode

---

3. The term *lookaside list* is a generic phrase used to refer to a situation in which something of importance (e.g., an IRP) is maintained in a separate list and may be readily moved from that list to another list (e.g., the list of IRPs attached to a particular thread).

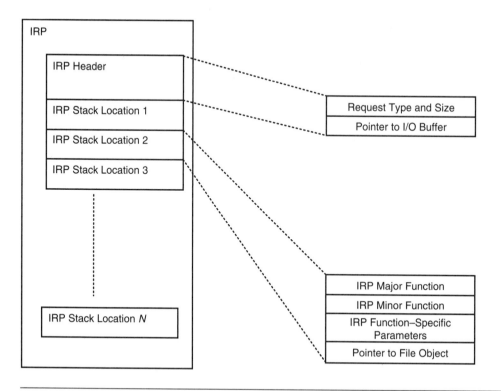

Figure 1.4 IRP Structure

Figure 1.4 also shows that each IRP stack location consists of information that is specific to a particular driver. Here are some examples of information within the stack location:

- Major function code (such as read, write, and device control operation)
- Minor function code that specifies more precisely what needs to be done and that is applicable for only some major function codes
- Function-specific parameters such as parameters for device control
- Pointer to file object

The IRP structure contains an element that indicates which is the current IRP stack location. A driver is responsible for manipulating this element before passing the IRP to the next driver in the chain. Each active IRP is put on a thread-specific queue that contains the IRPs associated with I/O initiated by that IRP.

A driver may create secondary IRPs in response to an IRP that it receives. The advantage is that the secondary IRPs may be simultaneously handled, in a somewhat parallel fashion, thus speeding up the I/O process. Of course, there are limitations here; for example, write operations to a tape device cannot be broken into multiple write operations that are handled in parallel.

1.5 Anatomy of a Windows Device Driver

All Windows device drivers have a similar structure. Each driver has a driver object that is created by the I/O Manager when the driver is loaded. Section 1.4 discussed structures related to the device driver, including driver objects. This section discusses the routines that a driver implements, as well as some other characteristic behavior of a storage device driver.

A Windows device driver implements a variety of standard routines, some of which are mandatory and some of which are optional. The definitions of *mandatory* and *optional* depend on the nature of the driver. These standard routines include the following:

- A mandatory **initialization routine**, by which a driver performs its housekeeping and initializes and configures device objects (including attaching them to the appropriate driver stack chains) as required. This routine is called by the I/O Manager when a driver is loaded.
- A mandatory set of **dispatch routines** to accomplish specific functionality, such as read, write, create, and close. These routines are called by the I/O Manager and are passed an IRP as a parameter.
- An optional **startup routine** (**StartIO**) that initiates the I/O to a physical device. Obviously only drivers that deal with a physical device (and not necessarily all such drivers) will need this.
- An optional **interrupt service routine** (**ISR**). Drivers that control a physical device may have this. ISRs are described in Section 1.5.1.
- An optional **deferred procedure call** (**DPC**), which drivers may use to handle postprocessing of an ISR. DPCs are described in Section 1.5.2.
- An optional **completion routine** that is called by the I/O Manager (as a notification mechanism) when a lower-level driver completes an IRP. Because all I/O is handled as asynchronous I/O, the

completion routine is required quite often, especially for higher-level drivers that always depend on a lower-level driver to complete an IRP.

- A mandatory **unload routine** that is called by the I/O manager to unload a driver.
- An optional **cancellation routine** (**CancelIO**) that is called by the I/O manager to cancel an outstanding operation.
- A mandatory **system shutdown notification routine** that is called by the I/O Manager to notify a driver that it must quickly complete any essential housekeeping when the user requests the system to be powered down.
- An optional **error-logging routine**.

When processing an IRP, a driver may behave in one of many different ways, depending on the nature of the driver and the nature of the I/O request in the IRP. Here are some examples of driver behavior:

- Performing the requested operation and completing the IRP.
- Performing part of the operation and passing the IRP to a lower-level driver.
- Simply passing the IRP to a lower-level driver.
- Generating multiple IRPs to a lower-level driver in response to a single IRP. For example, in response to a file open request received by the NTFS file system driver, the driver may need to read some file system metadata to locate the directory and succeeding subdirectories under which the file is located.

Drivers typically access the IRP stack location, as well as the IRP stack location for the next driver. The lowest driver in a stack chain accesses only its own IRP stack location. A driver is responsible for manipulating a pointer in the IRP that points to the stack location that the next driver should be looking at.

Note that the same driver code may be running simultaneously on different CPUs within the same Windows NT system. The driver code needs to be able to synchronize access to critical data from code running on different CPUs. For example, if a driver has a linked list of work items, the code to pull an item off the queue or to add an item to the queue must be such that it will work correctly even when running the same code is being attempted simultaneously on different CPUs. Executing the same request twice can be disastrous at times—for example, writing the same record twice to tape.

1.5.1 The Interrupt Service Routine

An **interrupt service routine** (**ISR**) is normally executed in response to an interrupt from a hardware device and can preempt any code executing with a lesser priority. An ISR must do the bare minimum to service the interrupt so that the CPU can be available for servicing other interrupts. The ISR collects the bare minimum of information that it needs and queues a deferred processing call (DPC) to finish servicing the interrupt. The DPC is scheduled to run at an unspecified time, which may be immediately or a little later, depending on what other processing is required.

To ensure that ISRs are always available to service the interrupt, they are never swapped out to the disk. An ISR can be interrupted by a higher-priority ISR, but it can never be preempted by anything else, such as a DPC.

ISRs are typically required for drivers that own a piece of hardware such as a tape or disk driver, but typically a driver that implements only some software functionality, such as a file system driver or a filter driver, will not have an ISR.

1.5.2 The Deferred Processing Call

When an ISR is executing, it needs to accomplish its task quickly and efficiently. Thus an ISR does the bare minimum and then queues a request to a **deferred processing call** (**DPC**) to accomplish the remaining work at a lower privilege level (these levels are sometimes referred to as IRQ levels, or IRQLs). DPCs may also be queued from code other than ISRs. The queue request creates a new DPC object (via the services of the Object Manager). After the queuing, a hardware request for a DPC interrupt (IRQ level 2) is generated.

Here are some important points about DPCs:

- A DPC can be interrupted by another ISR, but it can never be preempted by user mode code.
- A DPC cannot cause page faults, so all memory that a DPC accesses must be locked down in physical memory.
- A DPC may not take any action that causes it to block—for example, causing I/O.
- A DPC is similar to an ISR in that it needs to execute quickly and it needs to be passed control quickly and efficiently. To minimize the overhead of scheduling a DPC, Windows NT saves the bare

minimum state before passing control to a DPC. After the DPC has finished executing, the overhead of restoring state is also minimized because very little state was saved in the first place. As a result, a DPC will execute in the context of an arbitrary process. For example, if Excel is running as a process and Excel initiates an I/O, the resulting DPC (if any) may be called in the context of a Word or PowerPoint process (rather than the Excel process).

- Each processor has its own queue of DPCs. Thus a four-CPU Windows NT server will have four separate DPC queues. DPCs can have high, medium, or low priority; the default is medium. A driver can change the priority setting. High-priority DPCs are inserted into the beginning of the queue. Low- and medium-priority DPCs are inserted at the end of the queue.

- DPCs typically run on the same CPU as the ISR, but a driver can change this behavior.

- If a driver already has a DPC queued, the next request to queue a DPC object is simply ignored. When a DPC is run, it needs to figure out if it has multiple work items—for example, if the interrupt happened multiple times and each interrupt queued up a work item.

- A DPC may be queued on another CPU if the DPC queue on a particular CPU exceeds a certain maximum value. The Windows NT kernel periodically attempts to run DPCs by generating software interrupts.

- DPCs cannot be paged out to virtual memory.

1.5.3 The Asynchronous Procedure Call

Asynchronous procedure calls (**APCs**) share similarities with DPCs, but they also have some significant differences. Like DPCs, APCs are executed at a privilege level that is higher than that of the regular code. Unlike DPCs, APCs are always executed in the context of particular processes, as compared to DPCs that are executed in the context of a random process. Thus, APCs are not as lightweight as DPCs, because a lot of context may need to be saved and restored. If you are familiar with UNIX, think of APCs as being somewhat similar to UNIX signal handler routines.

There are two types of APCs: kernel mode and user mode. Kernel mode APCs are associated with drivers or other kernel mode code. Kernel mode APCs are typically used for data transfer—for example, for copying data from a kernel buffer to the user buffer. Recall that the user buffer needs to be accessed in the context of the process that owns the buffer.

User mode code can also have an APC, which can be queued via the QueueUserAPC API documented in the Platform SDK). The user mode APC is delivered only when the thread is a state that allows the APC to be alerted—for example, blocked as the result of a WaitForSingleObject or WaitForMultipleObject API call. Details of these APIs can be found in the Platform SDK. Suffice it to say that these APIs allow a thread to achieve synchronization.

APCs may block—for example, for specific I/O. They are queued per thread, implying that there are multiple APC queues.

1.6 Drivers and I/O Buffers

This section elaborates on I/O buffers, introduced earlier in this chapter. Drivers have to deal with buffers for their I/O and I/O control (IOCTL) operations. For this purpose, drivers specify a method of I/O that they prefer via their driver object. There are three types of I/O that a Windows NT driver may support: Buffered I/O, Direct I/O, and Neither I/O. These are described in Sections 1.6.1 through 1.6.3.

1.6.1 Buffered I/O

Buffered I/O is typically used for smaller data transfers because it involves some data copy operations. When an application makes an I/O request, the I/O Manager validates the request to ensure that the application has appropriate access to the buffer it passed in with the I/O operation (in this case *appropriate access* means that the application has the necessary read or write privilege and access to the required size of the buffer as specified in the I/O operation). The I/O Manager allocates a buffer from a nonpageable pool of memory, and for a write request it copies the data from the application buffer to this newly allocated buffer. This buffer is passed to the driver.

The driver does not need to worry about thread context because this buffer in the nonpageable pool is valid under any thread or process context. The driver performs the desired I/O. For a read operation, the driver copies the data into the buffer it received. The driver can assume that this buffer is contiguous in terms of virtual address, but like any other buffer in Windows NT, a virtually contiguous buffer does not necessarily dictate a physically contiguous buffer.

The driver would complete the IRP at this point, and it is the responsibility of the I/O Manager to copy the data from the nonpaged pool buffer back into the application's buffer. This copy operation needs to be done in the context of the original process that made the I/O request. It is also the duty of the I/O Manager to free the nonpaged pool buffer used.

1.6.2 Direct I/O

Direct I/O is a little more involved than Buffered I/O, but more efficient for I/O operations involving larger amounts of data. The I/O Manager performs some basic checks, such as verifying that the application has appropriate access to the buffer over the entire desired amount of I/O. The memory buffer is described to the driver by means of a data structure called a **memory descriptor list**, or **MDL**. An MDL is a data structure that describes a buffer in a process-independent manner. The buffer address is specified as a systemwide virtual memory address.

Windows NT provides routines for drivers to access various fields on the memory descriptor list, and driver writers are encouraged to treat the MDL as an opaque entity and are referred to the Windows NT DDK to get details of the MDL-related routines provided by the DDK. The routines, which are described in the DDK, include functionality to

- Lock and unlock the application memory buffer
- Map the locked buffer into a virtual address that is accessible from any arbitrary thread context
- Collect required information to perform a direct memory access (DMA) I/O to or from the buffer that is really a series of potentially physically separate pages

Direct I/O is the type of I/O most often used by storage drivers. For example, the disk and tape class drivers perform Direct I/O.

1.6.3 Neither I/O

Neither I/O eliminates the overhead associated with Buffered I/O (data copy operation and buffer allocation/deallocation) and with Direct I/O (setting up and tearing down of the memory descriptor list), but at the cost of limiting the situations in which this type of I/O can be used. With Neither I/O, the driver is directly passed the virtual address of the requesting application's data buffer. Astute readers will quickly deduce that since a virtual address makes sense only in the context of a particular process or thread, the driver must be called in the context of the requesting application. Further, the driver must perform the operation in the same context (that is, the driver cannot queue a request that could execute in an arbitrary context).

This constraint limits the situations in which this I/O method is used, and most storage drivers do not use this I/O method. File system drivers typically use Neither I/O. File system drivers are always called in the context of the process that initiates the I/O. In addition, Neither I/O facilitates the copy between the cache and data buffers because no buffer management (e.g., address mapping) is required.

The impression that a driver must choose only one of these methods is incorrect. A driver that performs an I/O control (IOCTL) operation can use one I/O method for regular IRPs, but a different I/O method for the IOCTL operations that are privately defined between it and the communicating application. Of course, even a driver that is down the stack chain and unsure of the context in which it is being called may not necessarily use Neither I/O in its privately defined IOCTL.

While we're on the topic of private IOCTLs, it is worthwhile noting that Microsoft actively discourages their use, especially when better alternatives exist. The big problem with private IOCTLs is that one cannot easily test the robustness of the driver code by deliberately passing bad buffers to the IOCTL operation to verify that the driver correctly handles the case. To pass bad buffers, one needs to have an idea of the valid buffer size, alignment, and boundary conditions expected by the IOCTL code, and these parameters are different for each private IOCTL operation.

1.7 Storage Driver Hierarchy and Driver Types

As explained briefly in the preceding sections, Windows NT has an architecture that layers multiple drivers into a hierarchy. The advantage is that the architecture is extensible, and new drivers can easily be introduced anywhere in the hierarchy. Thus, by layering drivers one on top of another, we can create complex functionality. From the point of view of the Windows NT Executive, all drivers have similar structures and driver functionality can be invoked in a similar manner, no matter what driver is being invoked to provide a particular functionality.

This section presents an overview of the Windows NT storage driver stack. Note that this is an overview of just the basic drivers involved and not a comprehensive review of all storage-related drivers. For example, the Remote Storage Services–related drivers are presented in Chapter 7 and omitted here, in the interest of keeping things simple.

Figure 1.5 shows the Windows NT storage driver stack. Note that the figure depicts the architectural layering of the drivers, but depending on the situation, one or more layers may or may not be relevant. For example:

- All layers are relevant when I/O is done to a physical disk such as an IDE or SCSI disk. The class and port layers are needed here, as are the file system and volume management layers. All of these layers are explained later in this section.
- The volume management and file system layers are not relevant when I/O is done to a tape device.

Sections 1.7.1 through 1.7.7 explain the bus, port, and class, volume management, file system, and filter drivers shown in Figure 1.5.

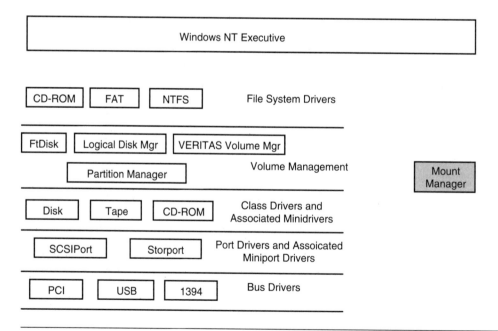

Figure 1.5 Windows NT Storage Driver Stack

1.7.1 Bus Drivers

A Windows NT **bus driver** exposes functionality provided by a bus for the benefit of other drivers. The term *bus* is used here in a fairly generic sense, being defined as any device, either virtual or physical, onto which other devices are connected. Bus drivers are required to have enumeration routines that can be called by the Plug and Play (PnP) manager to enumerate the devices connected to the bus. Bus drivers are also required to provide code to handle PnP, as well as power management IRPs. Microsoft provides bus drivers for all physical buses that a PC-based computer typically has (e.g., SCSI, PCI, 1394, USB), although independent hardware vendors can also provide a bus driver if needed. A bus driver creates a physical device object (PDO) for each device that it enumerates on its bus.

1.7.2 Port Drivers

A **port driver** implements device-specific functionality and insulates a class driver from the specifics of the hardware. A port driver *must* implement a set of specified functionality for the benefit of the class driver and *may* implement additional functionality. A port driver receives IRPs and passes SCSI request blocks with embedded command descriptor blocks to a miniport driver that is dynamically linked to the port driver. Miniport drivers do not create a device object and simply use the device object created by the port driver. As described in Section 1.4.2, port drivers create a device PDO that is required to communicate with the device.

Windows NT ships with some predefined port drivers, including SCSIPort and 1394. Windows Server 2003 ships with an additional port driver called the Storport driver. For now, suffice to say that whereas the SCSIPort driver caters to older SCSI-2 and earlier devices, the Storport driver is intended to cater to newer SCSI-3 and Fibre Channel devices. More details about the Storport driver can be found in Chapter 2.

Port drivers in turn, typically have miniport drivers that are implemented by independent hardware vendors. Miniports provide the vendor-specific device-level functionality not provided by the port driver. Miniport drivers are written with the Windows NT Driver Development Kit.

1.7.3 Class Drivers

A **class driver** implements general device-independent support for a range of devices. A class driver depends on either miniclass drivers or miniport drivers to provide device-specific functionality. Storage class drivers in particular are used to handle both SCSI and non-SCSI devices. Among other functions, a class driver does the following:

- Creates a device FDO. An FDO is needed to use a device. Examples of data in the FDO include details of disk organization (partition table) and the DVD region.
- Validates I/O request parameters.
- Retries failed requests.

In particular, a storage class driver also does the following:

- Splits large read or write requests (received via IRP_MJ_READ and IRP_MJ_WRITE IRPs, respectively) into smaller multiple requests as needed to meet the capacity of the underlying HBA adapter.
- Receives IRPs and translates them into appropriate SCSI request blocks (SRBs) that contain embedded command descriptor blocks. These SRBs are then sent to the next driver in the stack chain, which can be a filter driver or a port driver. The SRBs are incomplete in the sense that the class driver does not fill out the addressing information in the SRB and depends on a lower-level driver to do this.
- Plays an important role in power management, adding and removing devices, and setting timeout values for I/O on devices. In other words, storage class drivers are heavily involved in implementing PnP and power management.

Class drivers interact with port drivers at the next lowest level in the storage stack. The interface between class driver and port driver consists of a private IOCTL interface, as well as the exchange of SRBs. Some parts of the SRB are used only for class or port interface, and some are meant to be used by the port driver.

Examples of storage class drivers in Windows NT include disk, tape, and CD-ROM class drivers; these can deal with various types of devices, including SCSI, IDE, USB, and 1394 devices.

From the point of view of the I/O Manager, a storage class driver is just like any other driver, so the storage class driver must follow all the requirements, such as having I/O startup, unload, and completion routines, and so on.

A storage class driver often behaves like a bus driver, enumerating child devices. A good example is the disk class driver (disk.sys) that reads the partition table on the disk and creates a device object for each disk partition that it finds.

Some class drivers define a miniclass driver interface. A miniclass driver, typically written by an independent hardware vendor, is simply a kernel mode DLL that interfaces with the class driver, typically provided by Microsoft. The miniclass driver registers its hardware adapters with the class driver, and the class driver creates a device object for each registered adapter. The miniclass driver does not have a device object and simply uses the device object of the class driver. Miniclass drivers typically help fill out details of the SCSI request blocks that the class driver builds. A good example is the tape miniclass driver.

Interestingly, with Windows 2000, Microsoft introduced a new library called **ClassPnP**. This library implements all PnP functionality common across class drivers. Some functionality is implemented entirely within the class library. For other functionality, the driver using the class library needs to provide callback routines that the class driver can invoke as needed. All of the Microsoft-provided class drivers (disk, tape, and CD-ROM class drivers) use the services of the ClassPnP library (implemented in the file classpnp.sys). This situation remains true for Windows XP and Windows Server 2003 products as well.

1.7.4 Windows NT Device Tree for Storage Devices

The description of various layers in Figure 1.5 is still incomplete. However, before the discussion of the volume management and file system layers, it will be useful to deviate a little and understand the device tree built up by the operating system. A good understanding of the device object tree will make it easier to understand storage-related topics such as high-availability multipath I/O (described in Chapter 9) and reparse points (described in Chapter 6). This discussion will make more sense while the information presented about device objects, class drivers, and port drivers in the preceding sections is still fresh.

As stated earlier, PnP plays a major role in device enumeration. PnP loads bus drivers one at a time and initiates device enumeration on these buses. As devices are detected, PnP plays a role in loading the appropriate drivers. In particular, device enumeration starts with a virtual bus driver called the **root**. The root driver is responsible for enumerating legacy drivers, and typically it also enumerates the PCI bus. Drivers loaded by the root driver are often referred to as *root-enumerated*. The MPIO bus driver (described in Chapter 9) is one such example.

As drivers load and enumerate the devices for which they are responsible, they report the devices to PnP. PnP builds a tree linking the various driver objects in a proper fashion to show their logical and physical relationships. Note that PnP can only build a tree; it cannot support a device graph. That is, with PnP, a child node can have only a single parent; a node can never have multiple parents.

Figure 1.6 shows a simple configuration in the top left-hand corner. A Windows NT server with a single host bus adapter (HBA) and a single storage disk connected to that HBA. In the interest of keeping things simple and relevant, we will ignore other peripheral devices that would typically be connected to this Windows NT server.

Figure 1.6 shows a detailed overview of just some parts of Figure 1.5. In particular, Figure 1.6 does not show the volume management and file system layers. Figure 1.6 shows just the port and class driver layers corresponding to Figure 1.5. Starting from the bottom right-hand corner of Figure 1.6, the series of steps in building the device tree is as follows:

Step 1: The Windows NT Executive (Plug and Play Manager in particular) creates a PDO (physical device object) for the PCI bus driver.

Step 2: The PCI bus driver in turn creates an FDO (functional device object) for the PCI bus and attaches it to the PDO.

Step 3: The PCI bus driver also enumerates adapters and finds the SCSI (storage) adapter. Upon discovering the SCSI adapter, the PCI bus driver creates a PDO for it. For the sake of simplicity, we do not consider other adapters that the PCI bus driver may discover.

Step 4: The Plug and Play Manager loads the SCSIPort driver, and after this driver has initialized, calls it at its AddDevice entry point and passes it the PDO created by the PCI bus driver. The SCSIPort driver creates an FDO for the HBA device. The port driver attaches the newly created FDO to the PDO created by the PCI bus driver.

Step 5: As discussed earlier, a driver can show multiple examples of driver-type behavior and the SCSIPort driver now acts as a bus driver, enumerating devices it finds on its SCSI bus. It finds the disk and reports this to the Plug and Play Manager, which loads the disk class driver (disk.sys). The disk class driver, after it has

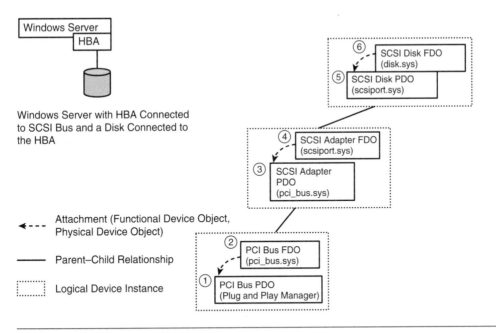

Figure 1.6 Driver Device Tree

initialized, is called at its AddDevice entry point, with the PDO created by the SCSI driver as a parameter.

Step 6: The disk class driver creates an FDO for the disk that is connected to the HBA and attaches it to the PDO created by the SCSIPort driver. In reality, the HBA is more likely to be connected to a fabric switch, and the HBA will enumerate a lot more devices. This example is deliberately kept simple. In addition, the device stack does not end here. In the interest of keeping the discussion focused and simple, the device stack farther up into the volume management and file system layers is discussed later and shown in Figure 1.7.

Notice that two drivers cooperate to create a logical device instance such as the PCI bus driver and the SCSIPort driver. This is logical (as Spock would say), because the device interfaces to the PCI bus on one end and exposes a SCSI interface at the other end. Thus a single device has characteristics of PCI at one end of the card and SCSI at the other end, so it needs processing by both the PCI bus driver and the SCSIPort driver.

1.7.5 Volume Management Layer

We can now return to Figure 1.5 and discuss the volume management layer. Volumes are a logical entity created to facilitate storage management. Physical disks—for example, an IDE or SCSI disk—may be logically divided into entities called *partitions*. A partition is simply a set of physically contiguous sectors on a disk. Partitions are then combined in some fashion to construct a volume. The advantage is that this combination can result in some enhanced functionality; for example, multiple partitions may be concatenated to construct a volume that is larger than any of the physical disks. Another example would be creating a mirrored volume by constructing a volume out of two partitions of exactly the same size. Volumes are explained in more detail in Chapter 6. For now, the topic at hand is to understand how volume-related functionality is implemented in Windows NT by a software device driver.

Windows 2000, Windows XP, and Windows Server 2003 support three different volume managers: FtDisk, Microsoft Logical Disk Manager, and VERITAS Volume Manager. All three are described in detail in Chapter 6. For now, the example will take the simplest of the three, the Microsoft FtDisk Manager. A device tree with the other volume managers is presented in Chapter 6. To keep things simple, the device tree in Figure 1.7 pertains to a situation in which there is a single SCSI disk, organized into two partitions, and the two partitions are concatenated to form a single volume.

To understand how volume managers work, consider Figure 1.7, starting from the bottom right-hand corner. The PnP subsystem and PCI bus drivers cooperate to create the PDO and FDO for the PCI bus. Next the PCI bus driver enumerates devices on the PCI bus and creates a PDO for the SCSI adapter. The SCSIPort driver creates the FDO for the SCSI adapter. Next the SCSIPort port driver and disk class drivers create a PDO and an FDO for the one disk that is present in the system configuration. Until now, the description of Figure 1.7 has simply summarized the description for Figure 1.6.

The Partition Manager is an upper-level filter driver (filter drivers are described in Section 1.7.7) that registers with the Windows NT PnP subsystem requesting notifications for new device objects created by the disk class driver. The Partition Manager was newly introduced in Windows 2000 and is also present in Windows XP and Windows Server 2003 products. The Partition Manager communicates with the volume managers in general (and FtDisk in particular in Figure 1.7) using a private interface and forwards notifications of device creation to the Partition Manager.

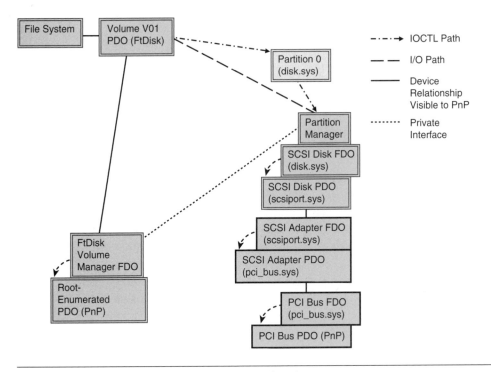

Figure 1.7 Device Object Tree for a Volume Stack

When the volume manager finds that it has all disk partitions that collectively constitute a volume, it creates a device object representing the volume. The Partition Manager also ensures the notification to PnP of partition or device object destruction (e.g., when deleting a partition). The Partition Manager communicates with the FtDisk driver to inform it about partitions that dynamically come and go.

Newly introduced in Figure 1.7 (as compared to Figure 1.6) is the Partition Manager. The Partition Manager watches the IRPs go by and ensures that it is in the I/O path for IRP completion. When the Partition Manager sees a QDR (IRP_MN_QUERY_DEVICE_RELATIONSHIPS) request being completed, it quietly removes all details of devices discovered—in this case the device objects for partition 0, created by the disk.sys disk class driver. Hence the device object partition 0 is never discovered by the PnP subsystem at all. That's why the device object for partition 0 is shaded differently from the other device objects in Figure 1.7.

The Partition Manager passes details of the device objects it discovers (and "steals") to registered volume managers. For now, the discussion is limited to cases with just one volume manager. Chapter 6 discusses a similar situation, but with multiple volume managers involved. The volume manager inspects the devices represented by the device objects "stolen" by the Partition Manager and either claims or rejects ownership. In the example, the FtDisk driver claims ownership of these device objects. The FtDisk manager then inspects the volume configuration and determines that the volume has a single underlying partition, as well as ownership of the relevant partition. At that point the FtDisk driver will create a device object to represent the volume (called "Volume V01" in Figure 1.7). The file system can then be mounted on this volume. Details of operations involved in mounting a file system are described in Chapter 6.

What is noteworthy here is that there are actually two separate device stacks. One stack represents the logical entity, the volume; the other stack encompasses the physical devices in the system, such as the PCI bus, the SCSI adapter, and the disk drive. The volume manager acts as a bridge between the two stacks.

In Figure 1.7, the FtDisk driver sends all IRPs that it understands directly to the disk class driver. Of course, the FtDisk driver also transforms volume relative offsets to disk relative offsets before it does so. These I/O operations are shown with the thick dashed lines. The thin dotted line shows the private interface between the volume manager and the Partition Manager. In addition, the FtDisk driver sends I/O controls that it does not understand directly to the partition device object. This is shown with dashed-dotted line in Figure 1.7.

1.7.6 File System Drivers

File system drivers are Windows NT device drivers that implement file system functionality. Although the file systems reside on physical media such as a disk or CD, the file system drivers themselves are considered logical drivers that do not directly manipulate any hardware. File system drivers rely on class and port drivers to do the actual I/O to disk. A file system driver typically receives IRPs to perform a request and takes one of two actions:

1. It fills in the next IRP stack location with necessary information to complete the I/O. Then it sends the IRP on to the class driver.
2. It builds a series of associated IRPs to accomplish the requested I/O.

A file system driver has metadata on the media. The metadata includes things such as file system access permissions and a file allocation table (location on disk). The file system driver receives the IRP that specifies a particular operation relative to a file, reads metadata if needed, and issues an IRP request that is now relative to a disk block rather than to a file. Windows NT ships with several file system drivers, including

- NTFS
- UDFS
- FAT file system

Writing file system or file system filter drivers was a black art with Windows NT 3.X. Subsequently, Microsoft made available the Installable File System Kit, which provides necessary header files, some documentation, and samples for writing file system and file system filter drivers.

Both file system and file system filter drivers need to implement support for PnP IRPs, including power management, removal of media, and removal of the storage device itself, such as an external USB floppy.

1.7.7 Filter Drivers

Filter drivers are drivers that layer themselves over some device objects and perform preprocessing and/or postprocessing of I/O requests in order to modify the system behavior. Filter drivers are typically used for the following reasons:

- To provide modularized functionality—for example, CD-ROM audio filter driver
- To add functionality such as CD-ROM burning/writing to a device
- To add functionality to a file system—for example, file system encryption filter drivers, reparse point filter drivers, and Single Instance Storage filter drivers (all of which are described in Chapter 6)
- To add functionality such as AGP support and ACPI BIOS extensions support, both done through filter drivers, to a bus
- To adjust I/O for hardware functionality quirks such as breaking up I/O into smaller chunks

Filter drivers always create a device object that is attached to either a functional device object or a physical device object (both described in

Section 1.4.2). This object is essential to the ability of the filter driver to receive I/O requests and perform pre- and/or postprocessing on the I/O request. Some filter drivers create a secondary device object, often called a control device object (CDO) because it is used to send control/management information to the filter driver from an accompanying management applet. Filter drivers that attach to the FDO created by a class driver are called **upper filter drivers**. Filter drivers that attach to the PDO (which is lower down in the stack) created by port drivers are called **lower filter drivers**.

Lower filter drivers are much more difficult to write than upper filter drivers. One technical issue is related to deciding which errors should be propagated and from which particular I/O operations. Another problem is that all of the available samples relate to upper filter drivers, and hence no samples are available for lower filter drivers. In the rare instances that lower filter drivers are used, they provide protocol converter functionality or functionality to work around a particular device limitation.

Filter drivers have existed in Windows NT since the first commercial release of the operating system. The Windows NT Installable File System (IFS) Kit (http://www.microsoft.com/ddk/IFSKit) documents the filter driver architecture and is a good reference for developers.

Starting with Windows 2000, a significant change has been made in the way filter drivers are loaded. Previously, the person writing the filter driver had to do some extra work to make sure that the driver was loaded at the correct time. If the driver is loaded too early, the device to which the filter driver wants to attach will not yet have been created. If the driver is loaded too late, the device to which the driver wants to attach may already be claimed and attached to by another driver, forcing the filter driver to attach itself higher up the driver stack than it would like. With Windows 2000, the driver writer specifies whether the filter driver is above or below a particular functional or physical device object, and the Plug and Play Manager loads the driver at the correct time.

Ironically, Microsoft may have made creating a filter driver too easy. The driver stack chain is becoming a bit crowded, with implications for performance and memory hits (each IRP needs more stack locations, and IRPs are allocated out of nonpaged memory). Consider the known filter drivers already being loaded (these are discussed later in the book):

- Encrypting file system (EFS) filter driver
- Hierarchical Storage Management/Remote Storage Services filter driver

- Single Instance Store (SIS) for Remote Installation Services (RIS) filter driver
- Reparse point filter drivers that other vendors may have written
- Virus-checking software filter drivers

On the other hand, writing a filter driver is also rather difficult. Consider a driver that wants to do some very simple encryption on data as it is written to disk and read from disk. All this driver really wants is to have a facility that allows it access to buffers before they are written and after they have been read. But the driver writer does not have a facility for simply registering a callback that accomplishes the desired functionality quickly. The driver writer needs to deal with all kinds of overhead, including handling canceled IRPs.

1.8 A Typical Storage Application I/O

At this point it will be helpful to put everything together and consider a typical storage application in an end-to-end scenario, exploring the various Windows NT entities that we have encountered in this chapter and seeing how they are all used.

The application that we'll consider is a simple one that reads data from a file. The file is on a volume managed by the FtDisk volume manager. Because this configuration is identical to the configuration for Figure 1.7, the device object tree will be similar. Figure 1.8 shows a simplified version of the device object tree for the configuration in Figure 1.7. Again, in the interest of keeping things simple, file system and Cache Manager interactions are ignored; that is, it is assumed that the file is not cached.

With reference to Figure 1.8, the sequence of operations can be summarized as follows:

Step 1: An application—for example, a backup application—issues a read request. After some basic checking, the I/O subsystem forwards the request via an IRP to the relevant file system.

Step 2: The file system determines that it needs to get the data from the volume. The file system driver prepares the IRP with the required parameters, including volume-relative offset from where the read operation must be accomplished and the size of

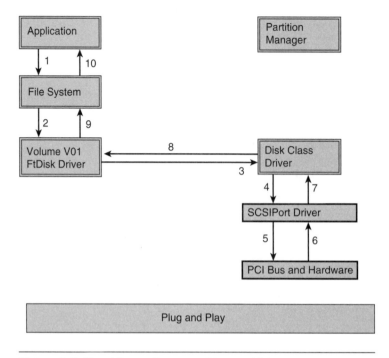

Figure 1.8 Read Operation on a Storage Volume

the read operation. The file system driver also specifies an I/O completion routine. The file system driver then sends the IRP to the volume manager.

Step 3: The volume manager translates the volume-relative offset to a disk-relative offset, fills out the IRP appropriately, and then invokes the services of the I/O Manager to send the IRP to the disk class driver.

Step 4: Upon receipt of the IRP, the disk class driver fills in a completion routine in its own IRP stack location. Typically the disk class driver builds another IRP called an associated IRP to accomplish the I/O. The disk class driver fills out the required information in the associated IRP with a SCSI request block (SRB) read request. Note that the SRB is simply the data portion of the IRP, so the basic data structure that is relevant is still an IRP. The disk class driver sends the IRP to the port driver, using the services of the I/O Manager.

Step 5: The SCSIPort driver queues the I/O with some assistance from the miniport driver that controls the SCSI adapter. At this point the IRP is marked as pending and then returned. Typically, the I/O Manager processes the IRP in reverse order of what was just described—that is, port driver followed by class driver followed by volume manager followed by file system. At each stage, the IRP is marked as pending. For the sake of simplicity, this is not shown in Figure 1.8. At some point the I/O will be sent to the physical device via the PCI bus.

Step 6: At some point the I/O operation completes. Again, in the interest of keeping things simple, it is assumed that the I/O operation was successful. An interrupt is raised to indicate that the I/O operation is complete.

Step 7: The ISR runs and queues a DPC to complete the I/O processing. The DPC is scheduled and runs. The SCSIPort driver marks the IRP as completed and calls the I/O Manager to process the IRP further. The I/O manager processes the IRP and calls the completion routine for the next driver up the stack chain, which is the disk class driver.

Step 8: The I/O Manager calls the disk class driver completion routine. The disk class driver completion routine does the necessary housework and calls the I/O Manager to process the IRP further. The I/O Manager takes processing one more step up the stack chain, in this case to the volume manager FtDisk driver.

Step 9: The FtDisk driver completion routine is invoked, and it does its own processing. When done, it calls the I/O Manager indicating that it is done with the IRP. The I/O Manager walks up the stack and invokes the completion routine for the next driver, which is the file system driver.

Step 10: The file system driver completion routine is called. It does the necessary housekeeping and invokes the I/O Manager. The I/O Manager schedules an APC. The APC is scheduled and copies the necessary data and status code to the backup application user mode buffers. The I/O operation is now complete.

1.9 Practical Implications

The storage I/O stack of the Windows Server family has been described in some detail. Beware, though, that the storage stack does not yet cater to multiprotocol devices.

In an effort to improve Windows reliability and security, the Microsoft model for signing and certifying drivers is continuously evolving. Vendors are advised to keep abreast of the updates in this area by certifying drivers. The Microsoft Web site in general and http://www.microsoft.com/hwdev/driver/drvsign.asp in particular are good starting points.

1.10 Summary

Windows NT has been designed as a layered and extensible operating system, especially with regard to the storage and I/O subsystem. We can easily add new devices by writing a driver of the appropriate type (such as a SCSI miniport driver or a Storport minidriver).

It is fairly easy to add functionality to Windows NT by adding a storage device driver that is a filter driver. Microsoft itself has written such a driver as part of its Hierarchical Storage Management application.

Writing Windows NT drivers requires a fair amount of specialized knowledge and access to the appropriate development kits.

CHAPTER 2

Direct-Attached Storage

Storage systems were first developed for mainframe computers, and most were proprietary. Standards such as SCSI were developed to work with the minicomputer. With the advent of the PC, server standards such as SCSI and IDE started to flourish.

This chapter describes direct-attached storage—that is, storage devices directly connected to a Windows NT server. Chapter 1 described the Windows NT storage I/O stack in detail. This chapter explains developments in the Windows NT storage I/O stack designed to improve the handling of newer Fibre Channel and SCSI devices that appear to the Windows NT server as direct-attached devices.

2.1 SCSI

SCSI stands for "Small Computer System Interface," a title that is now a misnomer, given that SCSI devices are usually found in high-performance servers and are the dominant storage choice for large multi-CPU data center servers. The SCSI standards are defined by the T10 Technical Committee (http://www.t10.org), a body of the InterNational Committee for Information Technology Standards (INCITS), which in turn operates under the purview of the American National Standards Institute, or ANSI (http://www.ansi.org).

2.1.1 Standards

The SCSI bus was initially defined as a parallel architecture in which the data is sent, in parallel, over a data bus that is 8 or 16 bits wide. Serial SCSI architectures have also been defined and adopted. Serial Storage Architecture (SSA) and 1394 are just some examples. To some degree these architectures (especially SSA) were developed independently and later folded into the SCSI-3 draft standards, a fact that sometimes causes confusion. Neither SSA nor 1394 has been widely adopted in the enterprise storage market, although 1394 is used in consumer storage devices.

The SCSI standards have evolved remarkably over the years, and there are a bewildering number of them. These standards are differentiated by the following features:

- The width of the data bus.
- The speed of the data bus.
- The number of devices that can be supported on the bus.
- The electrical and mechanical characteristics of the bus.
- The maximum length of the bus.
- The nature of the bus architecture—serial or parallel. Although SCSI has historically been associated with parallel buses, the industry seems to be moving toward a serial architecture, and the SCSI standards are no exception.

Note that SCSI is now not a single standard, but a collection of standards. Some standards define mechanical and electrical characteristics; others define command sets implemented by devices. These standards have been implemented by other devices as well, such as Fibre Channel devices.

Table 2.1 summarizes the various defined SCSI standards and their characteristics.

The older standards, such as SCSI-1, are pretty much obsolete. The latest standard is SCSI-3, which is really not a single specification, but a family of specifications that continues to evolve. Thus the SCSI standard should now be thought of as a standard defining the command set and a series of other specifications dealing with specific physical implementations, such as wire. The significance is that one can now take just a particular specification and implement it over a different medium. A good example is the trend to implement the SCSI command set over Fibre Channel and SSA. The most popular devices currently available are Ultra SCSI and SCSI-3 devices.

2.1.2 Functions and Characteristics

Another important point is the trade-off between the distance at which the SCSI device can reside from the host bus adapter (HBA) and the number of SCSI devices on the bus. A higher number of devices dictates a shorter length for the SCSI bus; a lower number permits a longer length. The maximum bus length also depends on electrical characteristics of the

Table 2.1 SCSI Standards and Characteristics

SCSI Type[a]	Bus Width (bits)	Bus Speed (MB/s)	Maximum Number of SCSI IDs	Maximum Bus Length (meters)
SCSI-1	8	5	8	6 or 25
Fast SCSI (SCSI-2)	8	10	8	6 or 25
Wide SCSI (SCSI-2)	16	10	16	6 or 25
Fast Wide SCSI (SCSI-2)	16	20	16	6 or 25
Ultra SCSI (SCSI-3 SPI-1)	8	20	8	1.5 or 25
			4	3
Wide Ultra SCSI (SCSI-3 SPI-1)	16	40	16	25
			8	1.5
			4	3
Ultra2 SCSI (SCSI-3 SPI-2)	8	40	8	12
			2	25
Wide Ultra2 SCSI (SCSI-3 SPI-2)	16	80	16	12
			2	25
Ultra 3 SCSI or Ultra 160 (SCSI-3 SPI-3)	16	80	16	12
Ultra 320 (SCSI-3 SPI-4)	16	320	16	12

[a]The SCSI standard on which the type is based is shown in parentheses.

bus. Note that this discussion pertains strictly to SCSI. Newer implementations such as iSCSI (discussed in Chapter 8) significantly change the distance limitations in that they pass SCSI commands and command results over geographical distances using Internet Protocol as a transport protocol.

SCSI devices are connected in a daisy chain fashion. Each SCSI device on the bus is assigned a unique identifier. SCSI identifiers are not assigned arbitrarily, because they also indicate a relative priority that the device enjoys when contending for the bus with other devices.

SCSI devices are backward compatible, and some are even capable of operating in multiple SCSI modes. There are caveats here, though, and the details are beyond the purview of this book. The curious reader is directed to the references at the end of the book.

High-speed storage devices alone are not sufficient to ensure high performance and throughput. When we're evaluating a server, it is important to match the speed and bandwidth capacity of the storage to the speed and bandwidth capacity of the server's internal busses. Most high-end servers use multiple SCSI HBAs, which connect to multiple fast PCI (Peripheral Component Interconnect) buses to make sure that the PCI bus itself does not become a performance bottleneck.

2.1.3 Terminology and Commands

To accomplish a given I/O, one device on the SCSI bus will act as an **initiator**, and another device will act as the **target**. For example, the SCSI controller in a Windows NT server acts as an initiator, and a disk device or tape device acts as the target.

Although it is probably unusual for a device to be deployed as both a target and an initiator, most HBAs can be used as either one (depending on whether or not the firmware has the support turned on). iSCSI might be the best example of a dual target/initiator: One box can serve as a target as it exports its own local disks and as an initiator when using the disks of a remote iSCSI target.

The initiator sends a command to the target, and the target accomplishes the requested functionality and then sends an appropriate response. A SCSI target is passive until it receives a command from an initiator. Once a valid command has been received, the target arbitrates for control of the bus before responding to the command—for example, when sending back the requested data. The initiator and all other devices on a shared bus play a role in bus arbitration.

When a Windows NT server boots up, its SCSI controller (often called a host bus adapter, as explained later) issues a SCSI command to each SCSI device that it finds on the bus. This is the **Report LUNs** command, which causes the target device to return an inventory of all logical unit numbers (LUNs) that it controls. See Section 2.5 for an explanation of LUNs.

The SCSI **Reserve** and **Release** commands also are important. When multiple initiators are present, an initiator may want to ensure that it has sole access to a target device. A good example is when an initiator wants to ensure that it has sole access to a tape device. Having two initiators take turns writing to a tape device would cause the tape reel to have useless data. The Reserve and Release commands facilitate this access control.

There are two different forms of SCSI Reserve and Release commands. One form is called *nonpersistent* because a reset of the target device will cause the reservation to be voided. Another form, called a *persistent* reservation, will cause the reservation to continue to be enforced even when the target device is reset. Target devices may need to be reset if the initiator device encounters problems after the reservation is made. Another command allows the initiator to reserve the target device on behalf of another device, called a *third-party reserve*. Reservations are expected to be released by the device that made them or by the third-party device on whose behalf the reservation was made.

The **Extended Copy** command allows an initiator to send a command to a target SCSI device requesting that the target device perform a copy between two sets of SCSI devices. The devices between which the copy is performed may be, but need not be, distinct from the device that receives the Extended Copy command and acts on it. An accompanying command, **Receive Copy Results,** collects the status from execution of the Extended Copy command, which can be used to determine the nature of any errors that were encountered during execution of the Extended Copy command.

SCSI-3 defines some additional commands. The sets of commands defined for SCSI include block-oriented commands, graphics commands, and changer commands.

Windows NT requires applications to use an interface called the *SCSI pass-through interface* to send commands to SCSI devices. Actually the interface is used to send commands to Fibre Channel devices as well, since they also implement the SCSI command set. An application uses the DeviceIoControl API with the IoControlCode of IOCTL_SCSI_PASS_THROUGH or IOCTL_SCSI_PASS_THROUGH_DIRECT. Applications must first acquire a file handle for the SCSI device using the CreateFile API. Starting with Windows 2000, Microsoft tightened security by requiring applications to specify read/write access in the CreateFile API and allowing only limited user accounts to have write access. Thus the CreateFile API will return an error for most users other than those that the system administrator chooses to allow.

Although this interface does work, on reflection one can see that the architecture is not quite consistent. On one hand, the operating system reflects a philosophy of "anything I see, I own," including resources such as disk drives. On the other hand, the operating system is not even aware when an application reserves a storage device and releases it. A better architecture is one in which an application asks the operating system to perform the necessary function and the operating system either denies the request if it cannot be satisfied or performs the requested operation and returns the appropriate status to the application. Whether or not a future version of Windows moves in this direction is something only time will tell.

2.2 IDE, EIDE, and ATA

IDE devices are the most common storage devices in the PC world, especially for the consumer segment. *IDE* stands for "Integrated Drive Electronics," *ATA* for "AT attached," where the *AT* refers to the historical IBM PC AT. Both refer to the same disk drive standard. The basic idea is to have a disk drive with the disk controller integrated into the disk drive itself—hence the name *Integrated* Drive Electronics. The IDE/ATA standard specifies a 16-bit bus.

Just as SCSI has evolved through several standards revisions, so has IDE/ATA. The original standard specified use of programmed input/output (PIO) mode, where the main CPU plays a role in every disk I/O. Later revisions switched to using direct memory access (DMA), where the I/O happens without any assistance from the main CPU.

IDE/ATA cabling supports two disk drives at most, with one drive acting as a master and the other as a slave. At any given time, only one drive may be active. A later standard, called EIDE (Extended IDE), supports four disk drives by having a single EIDE controller that behaves like two IDE controllers. A truly multitasking operating system like Windows NT can take advantage of EIDE by issuing two simultaneous I/Os on the two IDE "channels."

The highlights of the various ATA specifications can be summarized as follows:

- ATA-1 specified the use of programmed input/output (PIO).
- ATA-2 was defined as an ANSI standard in 1996. ATA-2 specified the use of faster PIO modes and allowed for the use of direct memory access (DMA). ATA-2 also allowed for Plug and Play possibilities by defining an "identify drive" command that returns details of the drive geometry.
- ATA-3 was defined in 1997 and can be considered to be a minor upgrade to ATA-2 that improved reliability for faster transfer modes. The biggest feature of ATA-3 was defining SMART

(Self-Monitoring, Analysis and Reporting Technology), a standard for monitoring the health of disk drives. SMART can be used with both SCSI and ATA drives.

■ ATA-4/ATAPI introduced support for new devices such as CD-ROM drives and Jazz drives. *ATAPI* stands for "AT Attachment Packet Interface." Support for Ultra DMA, which can move twice the data per clock cycle that regular DMA moves, was also introduced.

ATA devices are still evolving and are starting to narrow the performance and reliability gap with SCSI devices while attempting to retain a price advantage. Further, with the increasing reliability of hardware overall, and with the advent of software to ensure higher reliability (such as software RAID, described in Chapter 9), ATA may someday play a bigger role in the enterprise. That debate is outside the scope of this book.

2.3 Mini IDE Driver Model

Windows Server 2003 ships with a new mini IDE driver model that is meant to replace the existing IDE driver model. The new port driver supplied by Microsoft is faster, caters to multiple channels, and allows desegregation of channel interfaces and control interfaces. The new driver model provides more flexibility to disk vendors; for example, the vendor-written miniport driver may alter the timeout request value and also choose whether the I/O will be accomplished with DMA or PIO on a per-request basis. Microsoft appears to recognize that ATA devices may play a more important role in the future and is evolving the driver model for ATA devices. Hopefully a future edition of this book will provide more details as the new driver models become public knowledge.

2.4 The Emergence of HBAs

Originally, storage devices such as disk or tape units were connected directly to the server. The storage units would be either within the server cage itself or housed in external units, yet directly attached to the server via the server I/O controller. The server I/O controller could be either in an add-on card or on the motherboard itself. Over the years, the term *HBA*, or *host bus adapter* (an adapter that interfaces with the I/O bus on the host), came to be used for controllers.

Figure 2.1 shows a server with an I/O controller card and several devices connected to the controller card via a SCSI bus. Direct-attached storage works well for small isolated LANs (local area networks), such as a small departmental LAN, but does not scale well at all. One obvious problem is the limitation on the number of storage units that can be used. The other problem is the fact that all I/O must be accomplished through the single SCSI bus.

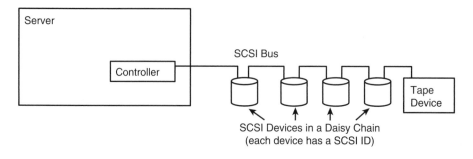

Figure 2.1 Direct-Attached SCSI Storage

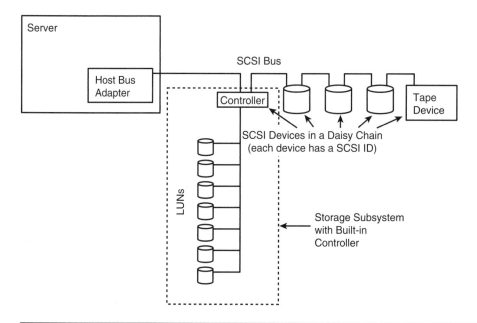

Figure 2.2 Intelligent Storage Subsystem

The next thing the storage industry developed was a storage subsystem with its own I/O controller (see Figure 2.2).

The storage subsystem added some complexity, as well as increased functionality, and caused some rethinking in terms of the terminology. The system in Figure 2.1 has only one I/O controller, which is connected to the server. The system in Figure 2.2 has two controllers, resulting in potential confusion as to which one is being referred to. If more storage subsystems were present, each with its own controller, things would be even more confusing. The terminology adopted was to call the controller card connected to the server a *host bus adapter*, or *HBA*. An HBA may provide connectivity to a SCSI or IDE bus or a Fibre Channel network.

2.5 LUNs

The storage units, located behind the controller in the storage subsystem depicted in Figure 2.2, need to be accessed in some fashion. These units are called *LUNs*, which is short for "logical unit numbers." As far as a storage application or Windows NT is concerned, three separate identifiers work together to uniquely identify each LUN. Note that SCSI literature uses the phrase "per SCSI target." I prefer to use "per SCSI identifier" because a SCSI device can be both a target and an initiator. This distinction will become even more important with the advent of iSCSI, where a SCSI device can be an initiator in one case, but can itself be the target in another case.

A SCSI command is directed at a SCSI device that is uniquely identified by a set of triple values:

1. **The SCSI bus** (an HBA may support multiple buses, or a Windows NT server may have multiple HBAs installed). Windows NT supports up to 8 buses per HBA.
2. **The SCSI device identifier on the bus**. Windows NT supports up to 128 SCSI identifiers per bus.
3. **The SCSI LUN identifier**. Windows NT SP4 and higher versions of Windows NT support up to 254 LUNs per SCSI identifier. This is sometimes referred to as Large LUN support. Prior versions of Windows NT supported up to 8 LUNs per SCSI identifier. SCSI-2 specifies 8 LUNs per SCSI identifier. SCSI-3 specifies a 64-bit LUN value per SCSI identifier, but the actual number supported depends on the device implementation.

Support for this larger number (more than 8) of LUNs depends on the HBA driver that is providing the support, as well as the SCSI devices that are properly implementing the Report LUNs (SCSI) command. Newer drivers support the higher number by default. Older drivers may not support LUNs at all, or they may require Windows NT registry changes to support this feature. Windows NT discovers the presence of these devices by sending a Report LUNs command to each initial LUN (LUN 0). To enable Windows NT to work with more LUNs, the device must respond properly to this Report LUNs command.

2.6 Storport Driver

Chapter 1 described the Windows NT storage I/O stack. In particular, one important component of the storage I/O stack is the SCSIPort driver (written by Microsoft), which works in close cooperation with a vendor-written miniport driver that is specific to the storage device. Prior to Windows Server 2003, storage devices of various types—such as older SCSI devices, newer SCSI-3 devices, and Fibre Channel devices—all had a device-specific miniport driver that was linked with the SCSIPort driver. This scenario has several shortcomings:

- The model assumes that Fibre Channel devices have capabilities similar to those of SCSI devices—an assumption that is just not true!
- The SCSIPort driver follows a single threading model without any support for full duplex communication. This means that requests cannot be completed while a request is being queued and vice versa. When the miniport was servicing an interrupt, it could neither accept a new request nor indicate completion of a request that had already been satisfied. Having a multi-CPU Windows machine made the problem worse, not better!
- The port driver has some information that it does not pass to the miniport, but instead requires the miniport to collect laboriously via multiple calls. In particular, this is true for scatter/gather lists.[1]
- Out of sheer frustration, Fibre Channel device vendors resorted to ignoring the SCSIPort driver (written by Microsoft) and writing

---

1. *Scatter/gather list* is a generic term applied to the situation in which I/O is initiated into multiple buffers simultaneously.

either a monolithic driver (encompassing the functionality of both the port and the miniport drivers) or their own miniport as well as port driver. Because this process involved reverse-engineering the functionality of the port driver, the attempts, at best, have worked with some degree of problems. At the very least, situations in which two devices from two different vendors can no longer co-exist on the same Windows NT server are likely to arise.

With Windows Server 2003, Microsoft has introduced a new driver model with a Storport port driver (Figure 2.3). The Storport driver is meant to be used by vendors of newer and higher-performance devices, such as SCSI-3 and Fibre Channel devices. It is meant to supplant the older SCSIPort driver. Although the SCSIPort driver was not totally removed, it is meant to be used only for older, less capable storage devices.

HBA vendors are now expected to write miniport drivers that link with the Storport driver rather than the SCSIPort driver. To keep this effort to a minimum, Microsoft has kept the Storport model backward compatible with the SCSIPort model. So vendors who want to put in minimal work may easily reap some (but not all) of the advantages of the new model. To take complete advantage of the new model, these vendors will have to do some more work beyond a simple recompile and relink.

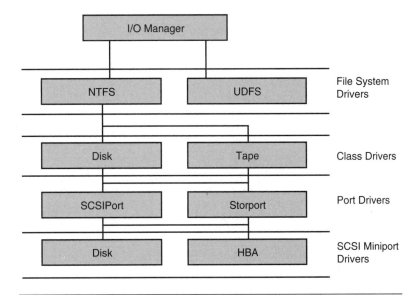

Figure 2.3 Storport Driver in the Windows Server 2003 Driver Hierarchy

The new architecture provides for a remarkable improvement in performance, which is accomplished in several different ways:

- The new driver model allows for a full duplex model in which new requests can be queued to the driver at the same time that outstanding I/O requests are being completed. The new model allows for more work to be accomplished in the vendor-written miniport driver with interrupts enabled. Note that this efficiency is gained at the cost of making the miniport driver a little more complex because the miniport now has to deal with synchronization issues. SCSIPort miniports, though they were half duplex and not as efficient, did not have to worry about synchronization issues because all synchronization was handled by the port driver.
- The new model minimizes the calls from the miniport to the port driver. For example, in the old model, the miniport driver made multiple calls (to the SCSIPort driver) to collect the scatter/gather lists.

In addition to the improvement in performance, the Storport model offers some other advantages—for example:

- The Storport model allows for better communication between the port and miniport drivers. SCSIPort never explicitly allowed the port driver to signal busy conditions. The Storport model allows the miniport to signal the Storport driver to pause, resume, or signal an adapter as being busy.
- The new architecture provides for sophisticated error management. SCSIPort simply attempted to reset the bus, which is very costly and disruptive. With the appropriate support from the independent hardware vendor in the miniport driver code, the Storport model allows for resetting the logical unit, followed by resetting the device and, only as a last resort, resetting the bus. Another improvement in error handling is that the new Storport model allows for a wider range of errors to be reported as compared to SCSIPort. The advantage is that the new errors reported by newer SCSI-3 devices can be handled in a better manner with Storport, whereas SCSIPort would mask those errors to the older range of errors it understood.
- All of the new features are provided in as minimally disruptive a fashion as possible because Storport is literally backward compatible with SCSIPort. Vendors can choose to recompile and relink their

existing code to work with Storport (instead of SCSIPort) with very little effort. They will benefit from the new model but will not reap all the advantages if they adopt this minimal-effort path.

■ The new architecture provides an interface that removes the requirement to create a "ghost device." The SCSI model does not allow an application to query capabilities if no unit is mounted. The Storport model removes the requirement to create a ghost device by supporting query capabilities even when no miniport unit has yet been mounted.

■ The new architecture also improves the interface to meet requirements of high-end storage vendors, particularly Fibre Channel and RAID vendors. For example, the old SCSIPort model allowed for very little in terms of queue management. Newer devices need sophisticated management. The Storport model allows for 254 outstanding requests per logical unit per adapter. The maximum number of outstanding queues per adapter is limited simply by the number of logical units per adapter, as depicted in Figure 2.4.

Another advantage of the hierarchy with the Storport driver is that it adds a manageability interface for configuration and management of high-end storage devices. This interface is WMI (Windows Management Instrumentation) based and is used by other Windows components, such as the management command-line interface. WMI is described in Chapter 7. The WMI management interface defines four different WMI classes:

1. **An adapter/HBA class**. A host system may have multiple such adapters installed, and an instance of this class would be created for each adapter.

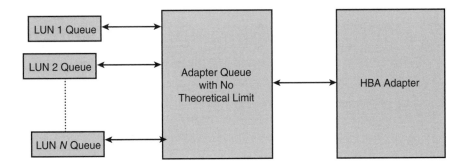

Figure 2.4 Storport Queuing Model

2. **A channel class**. Each adapter may have one or more channels that connect the adapter to the physical disks it owns.

3. **A disk array class**. Each channel may have zero or more disk arrays.

4. **A physical disk class**. Each adapter may have zero or more physical disks attached.

2.7 Practical Implications

The new Storport driver model provides a lot of efficiency, including optimizing I/O and driving throughput. However, system administrators and IT procurement officials would be well advised to note that the Storport driver model applies only to the Windows Server 2003 platform. IT procurement officials who have settled on the Windows platform would be well advised to investigate the plans of their storage device vendor to adopt the Storport model and meanwhile investigate the same vendor device support on the Windows 2000 platform, including details of how the vendor implemented the driver on the Windows 2000 platform.

Specifically, they should investigate whether the system throughput is adequate with the soon-to-be-legacy SCSIPort model driver if that's what the vendor is using. They should also investigate whether the vendor has developed its own solution that does not use the SCSIPort driver at all and whether that solution has been certified and is supported by all relevant parties. Finally, they should investigate whether the vendor will provide a smooth migration path from the current Windows 2000 solution to a Storport-based solution on Windows Server 2003.

2.8 Summary

The SCSI standard has been evolving over the years, and several standards exist. SCSI standards have evolved remarkably in terms of higher data transfer speeds. The user needs to compromise between having a higher number of SCSI devices connected to a bus and having fewer devices that may exist farther away. SCSI standards have also evolved in terms of defining more advanced commands, such as the Extended Copy command.

ATA/IDE standards, performance, and reliability have also evolved and are still evolving.

LUN masking in Windows NT may be accomplished in the HBA driver written by the HBA vendor.

Windows Server 2003 introduces a new Storport driver that augments the older SCSIPort driver. The newer Storport driver is meant for use by higher-performance/capability devices such as SCSI-3 and Fibre Channel devices. Compared to the older SCSIPort driver, the Storport driver provides remarkably higher performance, improved manageability, and improved error handling. Vendors may get all benefits of the newer Storport model by rewriting their driver or may get some benefits of the newer Storport model by doing minimal work and relinking their existing driver with Storport (instead of with SCSIPort).

The industry evolved from servers with direct-attached storage to a client/server paradigm with multiple servers on the LAN. In the latter scenario, some servers were dedicated to applications such as running a database application, while other servers were dedicated to serving storage needs. These servers dedicated to serving storage needs were dubbed network-attached storage servers, and that is the focus of the next chapter.

CHAPTER 3

Network-Attached Storage

The previous chapter discussed direct-attached storage, wherein storage devices are connected directly to a server. Regardless of whether the devices are within the server cage or external, only that particular server has access to that storage. This chapter looks at the next iteration of storage: network-attached storage (NAS).

We begin with a brief history of NAS, followed by an overview of the Windows Server family networking stack. Following that, some details of Common Internet File System (CIFS) and Network File System (NFS) are presented. Next follows a brief discussion about the technical issues involved in having a NAS device serve clients with various different operating systems and various different kinds of file systems. The chapter closes with a discussion of the role of Windows as a NAS device operating system.

3.1 The Emergence of NAS

After the appearance of direct-attached storage, several factors resulted in a situation in which multiple servers with direct-attached storage were deployed. The storage was accessed via a network file system, typically NFS, at least in the mid-1980s. One relevant factor was that in the 1980s, the client/server era had begun, following the eras of the mainframe and the minis. Client/server computing was widely accepted in commercial enterprises.

In addition, storage was still relatively expensive, yet storage needs were growing. The bottleneck in deploying more storage was the fact that a server could have only a limited number of direct-attached storage devices (typically only seven or eight addresses were allowed, and the host took one address, before advances in SCSI allowed more). This constraint meant that more storage could easily be deployed only if more servers were deployed. Finally, the bottleneck with I/O operations was (correctly) perceived to be the storage I/O bus. Deploying more servers meant reducing the load on each server bus.

Vendors took advantage of the prime conditions and started pushing the concept of network-attached storage, or NAS. As Tom Clark points out in his book *Designing Storage Area Networks*, NAS is more a marketing term than a technical term. NAS devices were touted as easy to use, easy to manage, and easy to deploy. NAS devices were also described as specialized for optimum storage device I/O throughput. Although in some cases this was true—that is, the NAS operating system had really been honed down to the bare minimum required—in other cases NAS devices were simply thinly disguised general-purpose servers. Even the term *NAS device* has implications of a specialized device and not a general-purpose server that happened to have some large amounts of storage attached to it.[1]

A NAS device consists of some server software that runs with the aid of an operating system. Further, as shown in Figure 3.1, the NAS software stack builds on the normal server file system plus I/O system stack by adding the network server code, network protocol stack, and network file system stack, which provides elements of distributed file systems such as caching and coherence. These three additions are shown shaded in Figure 3.1.

In general, the network-related portions of a NAS device are shown on the left-hand side of Figure 3.1, whereas the local file system and storage-related stack are shown on the right-hand side. In the interest of simplicity, only a TCP/IP network stack is shown and discussed here. In reality, several different network protocols, such as UDP/IP or Netware IPX/SPX, may be used.

In Figure 3.1 the NAS server software posts a TCP/IP listen request, waiting for a client to send it a request. When a client sends a request, the listen completes and a TCP/IP session is started. Once the TCP/IP session is established, the client can authenticate and then send requests to open files and read or write files via the SMB/CIFS or NFS network file system protocols (described later in this chapter). Once the NAS server

---

1. Note that the storage local to a NAS device is typically of the direct-attached storage type, discussed in Chapter 2.

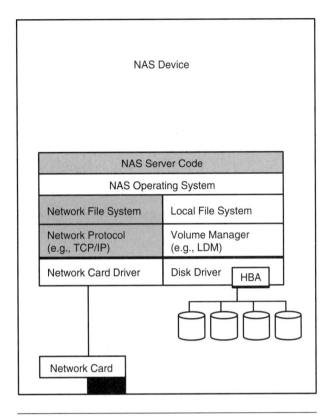

Figure 3.1 NAS Device I/O Stack

software receives a file I/O request, the NAS server uses the services of the local file system to accomplish the I/O operation. The results of the I/O operation (read data or write status) are sent back to the client via the network file system and network device protocol stack.

NAS vendors have adopted various different strategies for developing the operating system and file system needed for the NAS devices:

- Using a standard operating system such as Windows NT or UNIX
- Developing their own operating system and file system—for example, Network Appliance
- Buying an operating system and file system from another vendor

3.2 The Windows NT Network Stack

Understanding the Windows NT network I/O stack is important for several reasons. A Windows NT client uses this network I/O stack to access resources controlled by a server and for data communications. In addition, with network-attached storage a situation often arises in which one server accesses resources controlled by another server. A good example is a Windows NT Web server application that, in response to a request from a client, makes a database call to retrieve some data and the database is running on a separate Windows NT SQL server. The Web server application accesses the SQL server using the Windows NT network I/O stack.

Figure 3.2 shows the Windows NT network I/O stack. Sections 3.2.1 through 3.2.6 describe the various components, starting from the bottom of the figure (and the I/O stack).

The networking card is typically operated and controlled by an NDIS (Network Driver Interface Specification)–compliant driver. NDIS is architecture for decoupling network card drivers from higher-level network protocol stacks. The next layer up is the TCP/IP stack. The term *TCP/IP* (which stands for "Transmission Control Protocol/Internet Protocol") is used loosely to refer to all the various components that play a

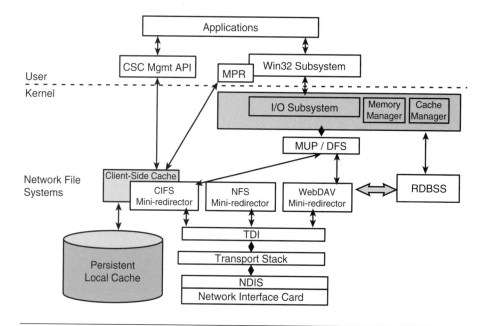

Figure 3.2 Windows NT Network Stack

role in networking and data communications, such as IP, DHCP (Dynamic Host Configuration Protocol), or TCP. The TCP/IP stack is not the focus of the discussion here. The next layer up is the Transport Driver Interface, described next.

3.2.1 Transport Driver Interface

Moving up a layer from the TCP/IP network protocol stack, one encounters the Transport Driver Interface (TDI). TDI defines an efficient kernel mode interface for network applications to request and receive services from network transports. It is implemented as a library that the kernel mode drivers link with. TDI allows for efficient network communication and attempts to reduce the number of times data is copied around—for example, to/from an application buffer to/from a network transport protocol.

For example, TDI allows an application to register a callback, and when the application receives a data packet, the callback procedure specified is invoked. The callback procedure may simply look at the data packet, especially if it is short, and indicate that it is done with the data packet (and the transport may treat the packet as having been successfully delivered). If necessary, the client may cause the data packet to be copied into a buffer where it can look at it later.

3.2.2 Redirected Drive Buffering Subsystem

The next layer up is the Redirected Drive Buffering Subsystem, or RDBSS. As the name implies, RDBSS is responsible for providing buffering code for all redirectors. The RDBSS handles intricacies of interacting with the Windows NT Cache Manager on behalf of all network file systems. The RDBSS was first introduced with Windows 2000. Prior to that, all network file systems had to implement a full-fledged driver that also dealt with routine operating system interactions.

3.2.3 Mini-redirectors

Mini-redirectors implement functionality specific to a network file system or protocol and use the services of the RDBSS to handle routine interactions with the Windows NT operating systems. Several mini-redirectors ship with Windows 2000 and Windows XP:

- The **CIFS mini-redirector** ships with Windows 2000, Windows XP, and Windows Server 2003. Earlier versions of Windows NT implemented a monolithic redirector. The RDBSS code that is common to all mini-redirectors is implemented independently by each redirector vendor. CIFS is explained in detail in Section 3.3.

■ The **WebDAV** (short for "Web Distributed Authoring and Versioning") **mini-redirector** supports HTTP 1.1 and the WebDAV extensions for reading and writing Web documents. It provides an ability that allows drive letters to be mapped to a server, no matter whether the server is an HTTP server or a CIFS server. Corporate firewalls are often set up to allow HTTP access, but they may not be set up to allow CIFS protocol requests and responses to pass through. Thus the WebDAV mini-redirector provides support for accessing HTTP servers through firewalls where the CIFS mini-redirector may fail. With XML and HTTP playing an ever increasing role, the importance of the WebDAV mini-redirector should only increase in the days to come. Note that WebDAV is a strictly client-to-server protocol and plays no role in server-to-server communication.

■ The **Windows NT Services for UNIX** (**SFU**) product ships with a mini-redirector that implements the NFS protocol. NFS is described in Section 3.4.

3.2.4 Multiple Universal Naming Convention Provider

Windows provides a Universal Naming Convention (UNC) for accessing remote files. UNC support dates from MS-DOS 3.3 days, well before the advent of Windows NT. With UNC, an application can address a file relative to a server and a share (recall that a single server may have multiple shares). The UNC format is

\\ServerName\Share\SubDir1\......\SubDirN\FileName

The various versions of Windows differ in UNC support in terms of

■ The maximum length of a UNC path
■ The maximum length of each subcomponent—for example, the subdirectory name
■ The maximum size of the server name

To allow applications and utilities to use the services of network resources accessed via UNC style pathnames, Microsoft has built the Multiple UNC Provider (MUP).

Because Windows NT supports multiple network file systems, the MUP acts as a router, routing the request to the correct network file system, or more correctly, to the mini-redirector implementing that particular network file system. The routing is accomplished in one of two ways:

1. The MUP cache is checked to see if the server in question has been connected to before. In this case the same mini-redirector that provided the previous connection is used.
2. Each mini-redirector is polled in a defined order for UNC connections not in the cache.

3.2.5 Multi-provider Router

The multi-provider router (MPR) provides functionality similar to the MUP, routing application requests to the appropriate mini-redirector, but with two differences:

1. The MPR code runs in user mode rather than kernel mode.
2. The MPR provides functionality for applications that do not use UNC pathnames. One example is providing functionality for applications that use the WinINet APIs. *WinINet* stands for "Windows Internet," an application programming interface that provides an abstraction layer for applications to use standard Internet protocols such as HTTP, FTP, and Gopher.

The MPR is a dynamic link library provided by Microsoft with a well-defined interface at its bottom edge to which the vendor of the mini-redirector writes. This library is installed when the redirector is installed.

3.2.6 Client-Side Caching

The Windows 2000 CIFS mini-redirector implements a feature called *client-side caching* that allows for frequently used files to be cached locally within the client. The files cached could be documents like a Microsoft Word or Excel file, or they could be executable files—for example, executable files associated with Microsoft Office applications. The caching is initiated in one of two ways:

1. The user explicitly requests caching.
2. The mini-redirector initiates caching when a file is opened.

Client-side caching provides for performance, scalability, and robustness. Clients can continue to work even when the server is unavailable because of problems at the server or within the network. The load on the servers is reduced, and a single server can cater to more clients. The client application runs faster because retrieving a file from a local disk is much faster than retrieving a file from the network.

Not just any file can be cached. Only files that are stored on a share (resource) that is explicitly marked cacheable (by the server administrator) can be cached. This information is conveyed to the CIFS mini-redirector in a Server Message Block (SMB) response. The SMB protocol was modified to convey information to the client indicating whether the files on the share are cacheable or not, and if cacheable, the exact nature of the caching the client should employ. This caching can be of three different types:

1. Shares where caching is enabled for documents only
2. Shares where caching is enabled for programs only
3. Shares where no caching of any kind is allowed

At press time, only Microsoft CIFS clients implement client-side caching. Non-Microsoft clients also cache files, but only when the client has a live connection to the server, and then only for files that the client has actively opened on the server. Client-side caching as implemented by the Windows client caches files even when the client is disconnected, and it caches files that have been opened in the past, but these files need not be actively open. Indeed, this cache of files on the client is accessible even when the client is disconnected from the server.

Windows 2000 client-side caching is designed to provide seamless functionality to Windows applications; that is, the caching is transparent to the application. Although the caching is also intended to be generally transparent to the user, the user is not isolated and needs to get involved with the synchronization and error handling required by client-side caching. In other words, when multiple clients have made conflicting changes to the same document in their respective caches, the user is notified of the conflict, and it is up to the user to take corrective action.

The various components that collectively provide the functionality include:

- The CIFS mini-redirector.
- An API supported by the CIFS mini-redirector and the associated user mode components that allow applications to administer and use the features offered.

- A user mode component that drags data from the server and writes it out to the locally cached file.
- A local database that tracks what is cached locally and its current state. An entry is created in this database for each share to which the client connects (that is marked cacheable), for each cacheable file that the client opens, and for any intervening directories between the file and the share. For each entry created in the database, the associated security information for the user and the guest user on the client is copied from the CIFS server. The database acts as a file system for locally cached files.

When a program file is first cached, it is marked as sparse and the local copy is gradually filled in as the application requests data from the server. When a document file is cached, it is also marked as sparse. All write commands are sent to the remote document first and also reflected in the local cached copy. A user mode agent runs in the background and gradually drags data from the share to the local cached copy. When a file is fully copied, the sparse marking is removed and the file may henceforth be used instead of the copy on the share.

If multiple clients may cache documents and edit them while in a disconnected state, the question arises as to how coherence is maintained between multiple clients. One simple way out is not to allow cached documents to be edited. However, Microsoft has not taken this easy way out, and instead, cached documents may indeed be edited.

Offline changes made to a file are preserved and synchronized. In the case of conflict during synchronization, the user is notified and asked to deal with the conflict.

3.3 Common Internet File System and Server Message Blocks

The Common Internet File System (CIFS) has its roots in the Server Message Block technology first introduced in the days of MS-DOS 3.3. Server Message Block is popularly referred to as *SMB*. SMB defines a protocol for a client to send file system–oriented requests (open file, read, write, lock, and close) to a file server.

Before we dive into the technical details of CIFS and SMB, a small digression explaining the political difference between the two is in order.

Originally there was only SMB technology, used as a client/server file system protocol in the PC world. In the mid-1990s Microsoft rechristened its implementation of SMB as *CIFS* and positioned CIFS as a competitor to both WebNFS and NFS. Microsoft provided an informational RFC (Request for Comments) to the Internet Engineering Task Force (IETF)[2] and subsequently let it expire without ever attempting to move the RFC onto any kind of IETF specifications track.

Independently of Microsoft's work, network-attached storage vendors started a movement to create a CIFS specification and organized CIFS trade shows and plug fests. The Storage Networking Industry Association (SNIA) took on the task of publishing a CIFS specification. Microsoft also made available a CIFS specification (called "Common Internet File System File Access Protocol") on a royalty-free basis (see the reference list at the end of the book).

The SNIA CIFS specification and the Microsoft CIFS specification are fairly similar, and both cover the protocol used by Windows NT 4.0 clients to interact with Windows NT servers. Neither specification covers new SMBs used by newer versions of Windows (such as Windows 2000 client-side caching, described in Section 3.2.6), and neither covers all the server-to-server communications protocols. The newer SMBs, not included in the specification that is available without any royalty, are covered in an SMB specification that Microsoft has voluntarily made available on a royalty basis as part of its legal proceedings with the EU and the United States government. See the reference titled "Microsoft Settlement Program: Communications Protocol Program" on the Microsoft Web site (http://www.microsoft.com/legal/protocols) for further details.

To summarize, Microsoft now appears once again to be referring to its own implementation as *SMB*, a proprietary protocol that is a superset of the industry standard CIFS.

It is also worth noting the historical association between SMB/CIFS and NetBIOS. NetBIOS is a session-layer network application programming interface that is now relegated to historical significance. The API provides an abstraction, allowing an application to run with a variety of network protocols, such as TCP/IP, NetWare, or the now historical transport protocol XNS (Xerox Network System). The need for an API that provides the ability to write network-aware applications in a transport-independent manner still exists. However, this need is now largely filled

---

2. Yours truly was a coauthor of the RFC.

by the sockets interface in general and, in the Windows world, the Winsock interface in particular.

Microsoft originally used NetBIOS for name resolution (resolving a server name to a network address), but now it uses the industry standard Domain Name Service (DNS) for this purpose.

The original Microsoft implementation did not use TCP/IP as the transport protocol beneath the NetBIOS layer. Microsoft next moved to using TCP/IP as the transport protocol, but it also continued to use NetBIOS, though the dependence on NetBIOS was reduced. With the assignment of a TCP/IP port for SMB file servers, the dependence on NetBIOS was finally eliminated, at least as far as the core protocol was concerned. However, the situation was confusing because some secondary services used by Windows clients and servers remained NetBIOS based. A good example is how servers announce their presence and the services they offer and how other servers amalgamate these announcements for the benefit of clients. Over a period of time, these services were redesigned, and the dependence on NetBIOS was finally eliminated altogether with Windows 2000.

Finally, the SMB roots can be seen in the fact that every CIFS request and response must begin with "0xFF", followed by the ASCII characters "SMB."

3.3.1 CIFS Flavors

There really is no concrete definition of a CIFS standard. Various flavors of SMB protocols are referred to as *dialects*. Here are just a few:

- A flavor used by DOS and Windows 3.X clients
- A flavor used to connect to non-Windows servers
- A flavor used by Windows NT clients

In general, a client sends out a negotiate request to the server and lists all the flavors it implements. The server picks the implementation with the highest functionality it can support and sends an appropriate response. Depending on the flavor negotiated, certain requests and their corresponding responses may or may not be legal. To make things even more confusing, the flavor negotiated does not completely define the implementation. Certain bits can be turned on or off in the response to indicate whether or not a particular functionality is supported. In other words, even with a certain protocol negotiated, variations exist. For example, one bit indicates whether or not long file names are supported.

As defined by Microsoft in the informational RFC[3] (which, according to the IETF's rules, technically is now out-of-date), the CIFS protocol defines client and server interaction for file access and manipulation. Other functionality, such as printing and server announcements, is outside the purview of CIFS.

SNIA is working on providing a CIFS specification. SNIA also holds an annual CIFS conference and hosts several interoperability events that include CIFS interoperability.

SMB has been an Open Group standard since 1992 (X/Open CAE Specification C209). The Open Group defined SMB as a specification for the purpose of proving interoperability among DOS, Windows, OS/2, and UNIX.

3.3.2 CIFS Protocol Description

CIFS requests and responses have a basic structure that is well defined. The fields within the SMB themselves are well defined, with some variations depending on the CIFS dialect negotiated and the capabilities implemented by the client and the server.

Table 3.1 shows the overall structure of an SMB. Note that only the parts that are present in all SMBs are shown. The details of each individual SMB are outside the scope of the discussion.

Some of the fields in Table 3.1 bear more explanation than what is provided in the "Description" column of the table.

The command field is 1 byte long and indicates the nature of the request, and the server faithfully copies this value into the response, allowing the client to analyze the response. The CIFS specification lists the values and definitions for this 1-byte field. The commands specified allow for operations such as opening a file, reading a file, writing a file, and locking a byte range in a file. All of these operations are initiated in response to an application request.

In addition, CIFS client requests (and their corresponding server responses) are initiated by the redirector code without any explicit participation by the application. Examples are caching and opportunistic locking, which is explained in Section 3.3.5. The CIFS RFC and SNIA specification, as well as the Open Group specification, defines the values and semantics for the 1-byte CIFS command code.

---

3. Yours truly was a coauthor of the RFC.

Table 3.1 SMB Header Structure

Field	Size	Description
0xFFSMB	4 bytes	Always set to value 0xFFSMB.
Command	1 byte	Indicates the nature of the request.
Status	4 bytes	32-bit error code (preferred; generated by Windows NT servers and returned as a 32-bit error code to clients that understand 32-bit Windows NT–style error codes)
		OR
		For the benefit of older clients that do not understand 32-bit error codes, the error is mapped to an old-style error structure consisting of ■ An 8-bit error class indicating success or the nature of the error—that is, whether the error is an error reported by the server operating system, an error reported by the server, a hardware error, or an SMB protocol error ■ 8 bits ignored ■ 16-bit error code that is meaningful only if the error class indicates an error of some kind)
Flags	1 byte	Semantics explained in Table 3.2.
Flags2	2 bytes	Semantics explained in Table 3.3.
Pad/Signature	12 bytes	Pad/Signature; described in the text.
Tid	2 bytes	Used to identify the share/server resource that the request is for; established via the TreeConnect SMB request.
Pid or Process Id	2 bytes but can optionally be 4 bytes	Set by the client; indicates the client process that is making the request; used by the server to track file open mode and locks; echoed back by the server and, together with Mid, uniquely identifies which one of multiple outstanding requests the server response is for.
Mid or Multiplexer Id	2 bytes	Set and used by the client; server faithfully echoes Mid in response; the client uses Mid and Pid to identify which one of multiple pending requests the response is for.

continued on page 72

Table 3.1 *(continued)*

Field	Size	Description
Uid	2 bytes	Assigned by the server once the client has been authenticated; the client needs to use this in all requests.
Parameters	variable	Consists of a 16-bit word count that indicates the number of 16-bit words that follow. For each SMB command, this count is usually a fixed entity with one word count for the command and a second word count for the response. This word count is usually a small number, less than 5 words or so.
Data	variable	Consists of a 16-bit count indicating the number of bytes (8-bit bytes) of data that follows. Compared to the Parameters field, the data field can be a much larger amount—for example, in the kilobyte range or even more. For example, for a read or write SMB, this data is the actual file data that is being read and written.

Keep in mind that new values and semantics for this byte field *may* appear without notice as the protocol evolves with future versions of Windows.

There are multiple commands to achieve the same basic operation; for example, multiple commands exist for opening a file as well as reading and writing a file. Some are no longer used, in other cases, different commands may be used, depending on the protocol dialect negotiated.

Examples of the range of functionality specified by this command field include

- Negotiating an SMB dialect.
- Establishing a session.
- Traversing a directory and enumerating a file or directory.
- Opening, creating, closing, or deleting a file.
- Byte range locking and unlocking.
- Multiple flavors of read and write operations.
- Printing operations.
- File and directory change notifications.
- Transaction operations in which data, parameters, and a transaction operation are specified. The CIFS server performs the requested operation and returns the result, data, and parameters.

Examples of transaction operations include, but are not limited to, a distributed file system (Dfs) referral and manipulation of extended attributes.

Table 3.2 describes the functionality of the Flags field listed in Table 3.1.

The Flags2 field in Table 3.1 indicates even more optional functionality. This functionality is summarized in Table 3.3.

The Pad/Signature field originally started out being just pad bytes. Over the years, this field has evolved. The Pad field *can* consist of the following:

- 2 bytes of a Process Id in order to allow a 32-bit Process Id
- 8 bytes used for storing the signature when SMB signing (see the Flags2 description in Table 3.3 and Section 3.3.3) is turned on
- 2 unused bytes

3.3.3 CIFS Security

CIFS enforces security at the server. An administrator can disable this security if so desired, but this is hardly ever done and the default option enforces security.

Older CIFS dialects allowed a plain-text password to be sent by a client, but that is now strongly discouraged. CIFS allows for a resource at the server to be protected by a user-specific password (called **user-level security**). This is the preferred method of security. For backward compatibility, CIFS servers also allow for a resource to be protected by a

Table 3.2 Flags Field Semantics

Value	Description
0x01	Reserved; used by obsolete requests
0x02	Reserved; must be zero
0x04	Indicates that pathnames and file names should be treated as case sensitive
0x08	Reserved
0x10	Reserved; used by obsolete requests
0x20	Reserved, used by obsolete requests
0x40	Reserved; used by obsolete requests
0x80	Indicates that this is an SMB response

Table 3.3 Flags2 Field Semantics

Value	Description
0x0001	Client understands long file names; server may return long file names
0x0002	Client understands OS/2 extended attributes
0x0004	SMB signing is turned on
0x0008	Reserved
0x0010	Reserved
0x0020	Reserved
0x0040	Any path name in the request is a long name
0x0080	Reserved
0x0100	Reserved
0x0200	Reserved
0x0400	Reserved
0x0800	Indicates extended security, which is described in Section 3.3.3
0x1000	Pathnames in the request should be resolved with Dfs
0x2000	Paging I/O indicating that reads should be allowed if client has execute access
0x4000	Indicates 32-bit error code being returned; if clear, indicates old DOS-style error
0x8000	If set, indicates that pathnames in SMB are Unicode; if clear, pathnames are ASCII

single password that is the same, irrespective of the user. Because the resource in question is deemed to be offered as a "share" by the server, this is referred to as **share-level security**. Share-level security is highly discouraged and in fact has been removed from Windows 2000 Server. The first SMB that a client sends to a server is always the SMB_NEGOTIATE_PROTOCOL SMB, which is used to negotiate the CIFS dialect to be used. The response to the SMB_NEGOTIATE_PROTOCOL SMB indicates whether the server has been configured in user-level or share-level security.

Starting with Windows 2000 and Windows NT4 SP3, Microsoft offered the capability to place a digital signature on SMBs exchanged between a client and a server. A server may be configured to require that the client implement this; otherwise the client will be denied access. The signing does place an overhead on both the client and the server, but that is the price one must pay for security. Note that this signing and verification is two-way; that is, the client signs the SMB requests it sends, the server verifies this signature, the server signs each SMB response it sends, and the client verifies this signature. Referring back to Table 3.1, the Pad/Signature field of the SMB header is where the signature is carried in each SMB.

Again, the SMB_NEGOTIATE_PROTOCOL SMB response is used to convey information (by the server to the client) about

- Whether or not the server can support SMB signing
- Whether or not the server requires SMB signing

3.3.4 CIFS Authentication

The CIFS protocol provides for security negotiation between the client and the server. A server may be configured to reject a client offer to negotiate a level of security deemed unacceptably low.

CIFS offers some authentication mechanisms that a server can use to authenticate a client. CIFS optionally also provides the means for a client to authenticate a server. At the simplest level of authentication, a client can supply a user identity and password in plain text. For obvious reasons, this approach is highly discouraged. Indeed, a server can be configured to prohibit access to clients that send cleartext passwords.

The authentication can be accomplished via a mechanism called **Challenge/Response protocol**. When a client sends an SMB_NEGOTIATE_PROTOCOL SMB to negotiate the CIFS dialect to be used, a flag bit value in the server response indicates whether or not the server supports the Challenge/Response protocol. If the server does support the Challenge/Response protocol, the 8-byte challenge is included in the response to the SMB_NEGOTIATE_PROTOCOL SMB. The challenge is simply a random value with a very low probability of being repeated. Both the client and the server derive a key from the user password. They both then encrypt the challenge, using the key and a DES (Data Encryption Standard) algorithm. The client sends its response to the server, which compares the response with its own computed value. If the two match, the client has demonstrated knowledge of the password and has thus authenticated itself.

CIFS also supports an authentication mechanism called **Extended Security**. (No prizes for guessing that the capability to perform Extended Security is indicated by the server in its response to the SMB_NEGOTIATE_PROTOCOL SMB.) Extended Security provides a means of supporting arbitrary authentication protocols within CIFS. When Extended Security is negotiated, the first security blob is in the SMB_NEGOTIATE_PROTOCOL response. Security blobs are opaque to the

CIFS protocol. CIFS relies on a mechanism at the client and the server to generate and interpret these blobs. Subsequent blobs may be exchanged with further SMB traffic.

Using Extended Security, Microsoft has introduced support for Kerberos in Windows 2000 and later products. The Windows 2000 Kerberos implementation introduces some Microsoft proprietary wrinkles. In particular, Microsoft uses some fields in Kerberos tickets to pass security information about the groups to which a client belongs. The Microsoft Kerberos implementation allows for mutual authentication, meaning that not only can the server authenticate the client, but the client can also authenticate the server.

Microsoft defines another way, called **Netlogon**, for a client to negotiate a session with a server using machine credentials (as opposed to user credentials). Netlogon is used to establish a secure RPC (remote procedure call) session, and the protocol is a little richer in that it supplies user access tokens that the CIFS-defined logon does not. Netlogon is typically used for server-to-server communication (one server acts as a client to another). The expired Microsoft CIFS RFC does not document Netlogon.

Finally, a CIFS server need not implement the authentication mechanisms itself. CIFS also allows for pass-through authentication, whereby the server can simply request a challenge from another server, pass the challenge to the client, and pass the client challenge response to the authentication server. In addition, if the authentication server responds positively, it will allow the client the desired access. This is known as *pass-through authentication*.

3.3.5 CIFS Optimization Features

CIFS defines several features that provide for efficient optimized communication. Sections 3.3.5.1 and 3.3.5.2 describe these features.

3.3.5.1 The CIFS AndX SMB

CIFS defines a way to chain requests in a dependent manner, allowing for optimizations in that two operations are achieved with a single round-trip between client and server. This feature is called **AndX**; NFS version 4 introduces a similar feature in the form of the COMPOUND procedure. An example is a CIFS client sending an OpenAndRead request to a server or a client sending a WriteAndClose request to a CIFS server. The idea is that instead of sending two requests—for example, Open followed by Read—and receiving two responses, a single OpenAndRead request is sent and a single response is received. This is particularly useful when a high round-trip latency time is involved.

3.3.5.2 Opportunistic Locking

CIFS supports a performance enhancement feature called *opportunistic locking*. Opportunistic locks are also referred to as **oplocks**, which distinguishes them from regular locks. There are two basic goals behind opportunistic locking.

The first goal is to lock a file when possible and start caching the file locally at the client. When the lock conditions can no longer be maintained, the protocol allows a "grace period" within which the client needs to flush its cache. The locking and unlocking happens transparently to an application; all the work is done within the CIFS implementation at the client and the server. The application need not be modified to take advantage of the resulting enhanced performance.

Consider an application that opens a file on a network server for read/write access and writes 128-byte records to the file. Without oplocks, each 128-byte write would cause network traffic to flow. With oplocks, the client would cache the file locally, and multiple write operations would be coalesced into a single write operation that flowed across the network. For example, assume that the client uses 4,096-byte buffers and that the client writes 128 bytes at a time in a serial fashion. The first buffer would accommodate data from 32 write operations (4,096 ÷ 128 = 32), and all of the data from the first 32 write operations would flow across the network via a single write request. If the write operation could not be cached, 32 write operations (instead of one) would be flowing across the network. The reduction of network traffic from 32 write operations to a single write operation provides a lot of efficiency and optimization.

The second goal of opportunistic locking is to increase the number of scenarios in which it can be applied. When oplocks can be applied, caching efficiency can be improved. Increasing the number of scenarios in which opportunistic locking can be achieved thus provides a distinct advantage. Assume that an instance of an application opens a file (on a network server) for read/write access and an oplock is requested and granted. The client-side code can cache file writes. Assume that another instance of the same application is run from a different client. One way to deal with this is to break the oplock and have both applications use network I/O to immediately commit any file write requests done by the application. Another way to deal with this is to delay the oplock break until the second instance of the application actually attempts a write operation. Very often the application may not attempt a write operation at all.

When conditions at the server change, the server sends an oplock break notification to the client. Examples of the situation when a server sends an oplock break include when another client requests access to a file or when a client writes to a file. The server implements logic to time out and clean up the server state (including closing the client session) if a client does not respond to an oplock break request. The client requests an oplock only when it is desirable; for example, if the application requests that the file be opened for exclusive access, there is no point in requesting an oplock.

Specifically, oplocks are implemented in three scenarios:

- Exclusive oplock
- Batch oplock
- Level II oplock

These scenarios are described in the sections that follow.

Exclusive Oplock

An exclusive oplock is requested by the CIFS mini-redirector when an application opens a file with read or write access. The server grants the oplock if the file is not yet opened by any other client. The sequence of operations is illustrated in Figure 3.3.

To begin with, the first client sends a file open request, also asking for an exclusive oplock. The server performs the checks and grants the oplock. The first client happily starts caching the file, performing read-ahead and write-behind operations. Sometime later, another client—say, client 2 (not shown in Figure 3.3)—sends an open request for the same file. The server notices that client 1 has an exclusive oplock on the requested file and sends an oplock break notification to client 1. Client 1 flushes its buffers, sending write and lock requests as appropriate. Once all the state has been flushed, client 1 sends an indication that it is done with its oplock break notification processing. At this point, the server sends an open response to client 2, allowing it, too, to open the file. Client 1 continues, taking care not to cache the file locally. The assumption here is that client 1 opened the file in a mode indicating a willingness to let other clients open the file as well.

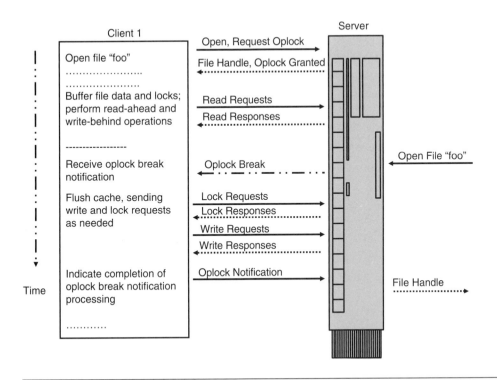

Figure 3.3 Exclusive Oplock Exchange Sequence

Level II Oplock

Very often clients open a file in read/write mode and never write to the file before closing it. Level II oplocks are designed to facilitate sharing and caching of files in this situation. Exclusive oplocks and batch oplocks (described in the next section) are always acquired because of a request by a client. A level II oplock, however, is never requested by a client. A client starts off by requesting an exclusive oplock. If that is granted, the server may, under the circumstances to be described here, demote the exclusive oplock to a level II oplock.

Consider Figure 3.4. Client 1 starts off requesting an exclusive oplock and starts caching the file locally. In particular, client 1 does read-ahead caching and also caches locks locally. Remember, in this case clients do not write to the file. At some point, client 2 (again client 2 is not shown in the figure) requests access to the same file. The server sends client 1 a notification indicating that client 1 should demote itself from an exclusive oplock to a level II oplock. Client 1 flushes its locks and indicates that it has finished processing the oplock notification. At that point

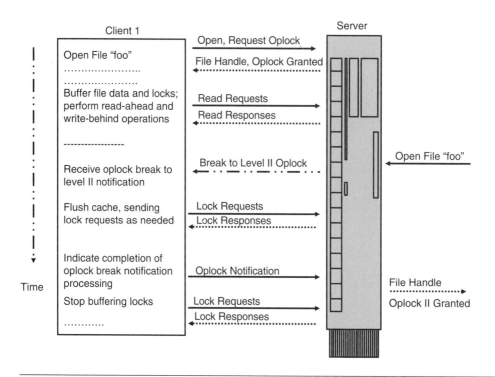

Figure 3.4 Level II Oplock

the server sends a successful open response to client 2 and also grants it a level II oplock. Again, the assumption is that client 1 opened the file indicating that it was willing to let other clients open the file at the same time.

With a level II oplock, clients are not allowed to buffer locks. The advantage in this scheme is that implementing coherence at the server is simplified and clients can still buffer read data, cutting down on network traffic. When any client writes, the server breaks the level II oplocks to no oplocks at all. Because all clients are not buffering locks while they have a level II oplock, a successful write implies that the write was done in a region of the file that no other client had locked. When level II oplocks are broken, clients can no longer buffer read data.

Batch Oplock

Batch oplocks are used to optimize performance while batch files are being executed. The batch command processor typically opens a file, seeks to the proper position within the file, reads a command line, closes the file, and executes the command line. Next it opens the file, seeks to the next line, closes the file, and executes the next line. This cycle is continued until the processing ends.

Figure 3.5 shows the sequence of operations. Client 1 opens a batch file and requests a batch oplock. Assume that the server grants the batch oplock, since nobody else is writing to the batch file. Client 1 seeks to a particular position in the file and performs a read operation. The batch command processor executes the line it read. Then the batch command processor closes the file. The CIFS mini-redirector takes no action on the close request (essentially doing a delayed close). The batch command processor opens the file, and the CIFS mini-redirector takes no action, other than canceling the delayed close that it has queued up. The batch command processor reads the next line by doing a seek and read. The CIFS mini-redirector sends the seek and read requests.

The advantage is that network traffic is reduced (there are fewer close and open requests). Server resources are also optimized because the server does not have to process a close request immediately followed by a request to open the same file it just closed.

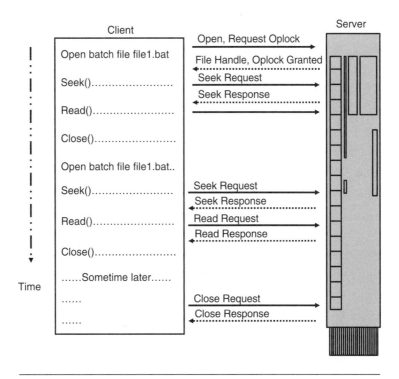

Figure 3.5 Batch Oplock

3.4 Network File System

Whereas CIFS is the dominant network file system for Windows clients, the Network File System (NFS) is the dominant network file system for UNIX clients. In addition, NFS was the first widely deployed network file system, dating back to the early to mid-1980s. But even though the overall objective of both NFS and CIFS is the same—namely, to provide network file system functionality that allows clients to access resources on servers—the two have remarkably differing philosophies. With the introduction of NFS version 4, these differences are being somewhat reconciled.

Whereas CIFS is a state-based protocol—that is, the server retains a state associated with each client—NFS versions up to version 3 have a stateless protocol because the NFS server does not maintain any kind of state associated with any client. As will be discussed later, NFS version 4 introduces state.

An NFS client does not negotiate a session with an NFS server. Security can be implemented on a session or on every exchange between a client and a server. The latter approach is too costly. So NFS takes an easy way out by insisting that all security be implemented at the client. The server assumes that any user ID on the client is the same as the user ID on the server (and that the client checked credentials before allowing somebody to log on at the client with that user ID). NFS does implement some security by controlling the file systems that a client can mount. Whereas a CIFS client opens a file and receives a handle (yet another state that the server must maintain—the file handle) and uses that handle for doing read or write operations on the client, an NFS server implements a lookup call to the server that returns a file handle. This file handle was opaque to a client in NFSv3 and NFSv2. A client could cache this file handle and expect that it would always refer to the same file.

For readers who are familiar with UNIX, the file handle typically consists of the inode number, inode generation count, and a file system identifier associated with the disk partition. For readers who are unfamiliar with UNIX, suffice to say that an inode is an extremely important data structure used in UNIX file system implementations. Enough information is kept to invalidate handles cached by clients if the underlying file is changed to refer to a different file. For example, if a file were deleted and another file copied over with the same name, the inode generation count would change and the file handle cached by the client would be invalid. NFSv4 introduces variations here that are explained in Section 3.4.2.

Some NFS clients implement client-side caching on disk, similar to the CIFS client-side caching. Some NFS clients also dynamically change timeout values by measuring server response times and adjusting the timeout value to be higher for slower servers and lower for faster servers.

NFS is designed to be transport independent and originally used UDP (User Datagram Protocol) as the transport protocol. Variations of NFS implementations that use TCP and other transport protocols have also appeared.

Sections 3.4.1 and 3.4.2 provide some noteworthy highlights of NFSv3 and NFSv4. This discussion is not intended as a substitute for the excellent references listed at the end of the book.

3.4.1 NFSv3

NFSv3 improves performance, especially for large files, by having the client and server dynamically negotiate the maximum amount of data that can be sent in a read or write protocol unit. NFSv2 had a limit of 8K per protocol unit; that is, the client could send a maximum of 8K in a write request and the server could send a maximum of 8K data in a read response. NFSv3 also redefines the file offsets and data sizes to be 64 bits wide instead of the 32 bits that NFSv2 specified.

Here are some of the highlights of NFSv3:

- NFSv3 file handles specify variable length and can be up to 64 bits wide.
- NFSv3 allows the client and server to negotiate the maximum sizes of file names and pathnames.
- NFSv3 specifies the errors that a server can return to a client and requires the server to return either one of these specified errors or none at all.
- NFSv3 allows a server to cache data sent by a client and respond to the client write request before writing the data to disk. NFSv3 adds a COMMIT request that the client can send to the server to ensure that all of the data sent by the client has been committed to disk. This feature balances the needs of performance and ensuring data integrity.
- NFSv3 reduces the number of round-trip operations between the client and the server by returning file attribute data with the original request. NFSv2 required the client to get the file names, and for each file, to acquire a handle and then acquire the file attributes.

3.4.2 NFSv4

NFSv4 has apparently totally changed the NFS philosophy and adopted a lot of features from CIFS, rather to the dismay of some NFS purists. Perhaps a better way to look at the situation is to remember that NFS was widely deployed first, SMB benefited from observing the strengths and weaknesses of NFS, and now, at least in the client space, CIFS/SMB enjoys a wider adoption and NFS is simply benefiting from the strengths and weaknesses of CIFS/SMB. In general, NFSv4 adds features for performance, security, and CIFS interoperability, as described here:

- NFSv4 introduces COMPOUND requests whereby multiple requests can be packed into a single request and the responses themselves are also packed into a single response. The idea is to improve performance by minimizing network protocol overhead and eliminating round-trip time delays on the network. If this sounds very similar to the CIFS AndX SMB feature (see Section 3.3.5.1), it's probably not a coincidence.
- NFSv4 borrows some features from Sun's WebNFS. In particular, NFSv4 subsumes some secondary protocols into the core NFS specification in order to make NFS firewall friendly. NFSv3 and earlier clients had to use a mount protocol to mount a share exported by the server onto their local file system. Because the mount protocol daemon did not have a TCP or UDP port assigned to it, the client would first have to request a port mapper daemon on the server to obtain the port on which the mount daemon would be listening. So besides NFS, a mount protocol and a port mapper protocol are involved here. Further, since the mount daemon could be using any arbitrary port, it is hard to configure firewalls to allow this access. NFSv4 does away with the mount protocol and the necessity to invoke the services of the port mapper. Locking has also been fully integrated into the core NFS protocol, and the Network Lock Manager protocol used by prior NFS versions is obsolete.
- NFSv4 mandates the use of a transport protocol that provides congestion control. This implies that NFS clients or servers will gradually migrate to using TCP instead of UDP, which is typically used with NFSv3.
- NFSv2 and NFSv3 allowed for the use of either the U.S. ASCII character set or the ISO Latin I character set. This led to problems when a client using one locale (character set) created a file and

that same file was accessed by a client using a different locale. NFSv4 uses UTF-8, which can compactly encode 16-bit and 32-bit characters for transmission. UTF-8 also stores enough information that the proper action can be taken when a file is created via one locale and accessed through another locale.

- NFSv4 requires the client to treat file handles differently. With NFSv3, a client could simply treat the handle as an opaque entity that it could cache, and then it could rely on the server to ensure that the handle always referred to the same file. NFSv4 now defines two kinds of file handles. One of them is *persistent file handles*, which have the same functionality as NFSv3 handles. The other one is called *volatile file handles*, in which the handle is invalidated after a certain time period or event. This functionality is meant for servers with file systems (e.g., NTFS) that cannot easily provide a persistent handle to file mapping.

- NFSv4 adds an OPEN and CLOSE operation with semantics that allow interoperability with CIFS clients. The OPEN command creates a state at the server.

- NFSv4 extends the protocol to include an OPEN request that a client can use to provide semantics that are similar to a file open request made by a Windows application. The semantics include a way for the client to specify whether it is willing to share the file with other clients or whether it wants exclusive access to the file.

3.4.2.1 NFSv4 Security

NFSv4 has introduced features to enhance security. In particular, NFSv4 adds support for more types of attributes on files. One of these attributes is Windows NT–style ACLs. This allows for better interoperability and better security as well.

Whereas NFSv3 and NFSv2 simply recommended security, NFSv4 mandates it. NFSv4 mandates that security be implemented via the RPCSEC_GSS (Generic Security Services) API in general and use Kerberos 5 or LIPKEY in particular. Note that RPCSEC_GSS simply acts as an API and a transport for the security tokens and information. NFSv4 allows for the possibility of using multiple authentication and security schemes, as well as for a way to negotiate which scheme will be used.

Taking some time to understand LIPKEY is worthwhile. LIPKEY uses a combination of symmetric and asymmetric cryptography. The client encrypts the user identity and password with a randomly generated

128-bit key. This encryption is done via a symmetric encryption algorithm, meaning that exactly the same key needs to be used for decryption. Because the server needs this key to decrypt the message, this randomly generated key needs to be sent to the server. The client encrypts the key (which it generated randomly) using the server's public key. The server decrypts the data using its private key, extracts the symmetric key, and decrypts the user identity and password.

Clients can authenticate servers using the server certificate and a certificate authority's services to authenticate that certificate. One popular method that hackers use is to capture some packets and replay them later. While using Kerberos, NFS puts a timestamp on each packet. The server "remembers" timestamps it has received in the immediate past and compares those with timestamps on new RPC packets it receives. If the timestamp is an older one that the server has already seen before, the server can detect a replay attack and ignore those packets.

3.5 Multiprotocol Access Problems

Several vendors offer server solutions that provide simultaneous support for CIFS, NFS, and other NFS clients. These vendors have gone to a lot of effort to deal with some tough technical problems arising from the fact that the clients and the servers may be running different operating systems and different file systems. Note that the problems, if any, most likely occur with the file metadata and not the core data itself. An extremely simple test of where a problem lies is to copy a file from the server to the client and then back to the server (or vice versa). After the file is back at its original location, is the metadata still the same? Have the file access permissions changed? Do some groups that previously had no access have some kind of access now? Are all the timestamps on the files the same?

Here are some examples of the technical issues involved:

- Providing for mapping between the different ways in which user and group accounts and permissions are tracked on different operating systems.
- Providing for differences between file opening and locking semantic differences between different operating systems and file systems.
- Providing for differences between file naming conventions. Different file systems have different ideas about maximum file name

lengths, file name case sensitivity, and the characters that are valid for use in a file name.

- Providing for file system differences in data and data structures; for example, one file system may track two times, whereas another may track three times (file last accessed, file last modified, and file creation). Even when the two file systems track the same times, the units of measurement may be different. Another example is units while measuring file offsets. Whereas some file systems may have 32-bit offsets, others may have 16- or 64-bit offsets.

- Addressing lock-mapping problems. A CIFS server enforces locks on a file; that is, if one client has locked a range of bytes, any write operation to any portion of that byte range by another client means that the second client will get an error. NFS servers, however, do not enforce locking. So a choice needs to be made about whether the locking will be enforced, causing an error to be sent to an NFS client.

3.6 Windows and NAS

Microsoft offers a commercial package often referred to as the Server Appliance Kit (SAK) for the benefit of original equipment manufacturers (OEMs) wishing to develop a network-attached storage appliance. The SAK is simply a version of Windows in a modular form, along with some development tools. The modular form of Windows allows an OEM to pick and choose (within reason) the Windows components that it wishes to include with its offering. The idea is to pare down Windows to the bare bones required for running the network protocol stack, a file server, and a local storage stack. The development tools allow OEMs to develop some quick administration tools and brand their offerings.

The SAK also has some components that are not part of the regular Windows server offerings. A good example is the reliability framework that monitors drivers for memory leaks and silently restarts critical components as needed. Several vendors offer NAS devices that use Windows NT as their operating system. One advantage of using Windows within NAS devices is the reduction in cost and time to develop such an offering. The CIFS and NFS protocol stacks are readily available from Microsoft. Probably the biggest advantage is that one gets all the new SMB enhancements that Microsoft builds without having to do any major development and reverse engineering.

Another advantage is that the Microsoft Server Appliance Kit provides for a quick and easy way to build customization into the offering. The SAK includes some management features (e.g., remote management features) and data protection features (such as a snapshot capability). (See Chapter 5 for an explanation of snapshot technology and its uses.)

On the other hand, some OEMs have developed their NAS offerings without using the SAK. Some CIFS and NFS stacks are freely available. The open-source phenomenon does have its appeal, and if one is willing to spend the resources, the advantages of working with source code that one can modify also has its benefits, such as ensuring that the operating system layer is as thin and efficient as possible. A market study of the two approaches is beyond the scope of this discussion.

3.7 Microsoft Exchange 2000 and NAS

Microsoft Exchange 2000 is the latest released version of the popular enterprise messaging system from Microsoft and forms a key part of the BackOffice family of products. The architecture of Microsoft Exchange 2000 is significantly different from that of Microsoft Exchange 5.5, the previous version of the product. Although Microsoft Exchange 2000 introduced a lot of new features, the one big drawback, especially from the point of view of NAS vendors, is that Exchange 2000 cannot be used with NAS storage devices. The present discussion is limited to the parts of Microsoft Exchange 2000 that directly contribute to this limitation.

Figure 3.6 shows the relevant part of the architecture for Microsoft Exchange 2000. Note that what is discussed here is a subset of Microsoft Exchange 2000. A full description is outside the scope of this discussion and would require a complete book by itself. The protocol engine shown in Figure 3.6 provides server functionality for mail-related protocols such as IMAP, POP3, and SMTP. The Exchange store (ESE) is based on the Jet database engine and provides functionality to store and retrieve various objects that collectively constitute an e-mail message. The Exchange Installable File System (ExIFS) provides some important functionality:

- An extremely efficient interprocess communication mechanism between the Exchange store (ESE) and the Exchange protocol engine.
- A cross-protocol Windows NT file handle cache. A handle created

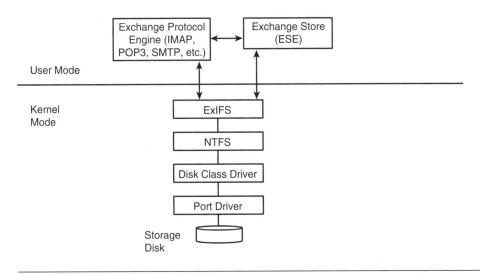

Figure 3.6 Microsoft Exchange 2000 Storage Architecture

by one protocol (e.g., POP) can be reused by another protocol (e.g., DAV).

■ Functionality to minimize data conversion back and forth—for example, storing messages in native MIME format.

Although ExIFS provides this functionality, it is also the culprit as far as NAS vendors are concerned. The reason is that when an Exchange server uses a NAS device for the Exchange store, the ExIFS is not in the I/O path, as Figure 3.7 illustrates.

Notice in the figure that when requests from the Exchange store or the Exchange protocol engine go to some Exchange files stored on a local drive, they flow through the protocol stack on the left-hand side of the diagram. For example, a read request goes from the Exchange store to ExIFS, from there to NTFS, from there to the disk class driver, and from there to the port driver. However, when requests are made to a file stored on a NAS device, the ExIFS driver is not in the I/O path, so they flow through the network stack on the right-hand side of the diagram. Thus the flow would be from Exchange store to CIFS redirector to TCP/IP protocol stack and from there to the network card, completely missing the ExIFS driver altogether.

Note that the architecture shown in Figures 3.6 and 3.7 applies only to Microsoft Exchange 2000 and not to Microsoft Exchange 5.5. Thus the issue described here does not apply to Microsoft Exchange 5.5.

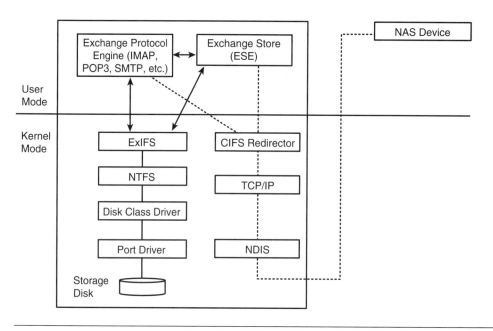

Figure 3.7 Microsoft Exchange 2000 with Local Storage and NAS Storage

3.8 Practical Implications

Starting with Windows 2000, Microsoft introduced a new minidriver model for the benefit of vendors wishing to write a network file system. The vendors need only write a minidriver that deals with the specifics of the network file system protocol of their choice. The interactions common to all network file systems (with the Windows operating system and Cache Manager) have been encapsulated into a driver library. Microsoft has built minidrivers for CIFS, NFS, and WebDAV.

CIFS is now a de facto industry standard for Windows clients communicating with a server. Several operating system platforms running a network file server implement CIFS. Microsoft licenses a royalty-free CIFS specification, and so also does the Storage Networking Industry Association (SNIA). Several dialects are available for CIFS. Both of the royalty-free CIFS specifications referred to earlier correspond roughly to the protocol implemented by a Windows NT 4.0 client. Microsoft also implemented a for-royalty licensing program for the SMB client in the post-Windows NT 4.0 time frame.

Microsoft is competing with NAS appliance vendors built on non-Windows platforms by offering a customized Windows product to NAS OEMs. Only time will determine the degree to which this effort will be successful, though it appears that Microsoft has succeeded in grabbing at least a measurable share of the NAS market with this offering.

Microsoft Exchange 2000 does not work with NAS devices. In the longer term, Microsoft is expected to eventually build a version of Microsoft Exchange that will use SQL Server for its storage needs. Given that the new version of SQL itself is not yet commercially available, that day, if indeed it is to come, is way off in the unpredictable future. In the meantime, can or will Microsoft do something to alleviate the problem that Microsoft Exchange 2000 cannot run with NAS devices? Keep in mind the realities of market adoption rates and time lags. Even though Microsoft Exchange 2000 has been available for some time, some customers are still running on Microsoft Exchange 5.5. Probably the situation will be similar when the next version of Microsoft Exchange is released.

3.9 Summary

Network-attached storage (NAS) is an industry term applied to a class of storage devices that has storage disks, a network card interface, and a host CPU running a file server protocol. NAS devices are typically tuned for performance (thin operating system) and relatively easy to administer. The problem of storage administration is replaced by a better-understood problem: server administration.

NAS devices are typically accessed by clients. Note that *client* is a relative term here. A NAS device client may very well be a database server. Clients use either the CIFS/SMB protocol or the NFS protocol. Whereas Windows clients typically use the CIFS/SMB protocol, UNIX clients typically use the NFS protocol. Both Microsoft and SNIA have a CIFS specification that covers the protocol as implemented by Windows clients accessing Windows NT 4.0 servers. The SMB protocol enhancements for Windows 2000 and Windows Server 2003 may be licensed from Microsoft on a for-royalty basis.

NAS devices that serve both NFS and CIFS/SMB clients have some serious technical problems to solve for interoperability and preserving file metadata.

CHAPTER 4

Introduction to Fibre Channel Storage Area Networks

This chapter is an introduction to storage area networks (SANs) in general and Fibre[1] Channel (FC) storage area networks in particular. Although storage area networks can and will be built with technology other than Fibre Channel, the vast majority of storage area networks are and will continue to be Fibre Channel based for quite some time. Accordingly, this chapter describes Fibre Channel in detail. Storage area networks based on other technologies, such as iSCSI, are discussed in Chapter 8.

Fibre Channel is an interconnectivity technology that merges aspects of high-speed input/output and networking. As this book goes to press, FC SANs have speeds of 1 Gbps (gigabits per second), and commercial deployment of SANs with speeds of 2 Gbps is growing.

Devices in Fibre Channel terminology are called **nodes**. Again, this is similar to the terminology of a node in an IP (Internet Protocol) network. A Fibre Channel node can have multiple ports, just as an IP node can have multiple IP addresses. The difference is that whereas each FC port is a physical entity, each IP address is a logical entity. Each FC node has a unique 64-bit World Wide Name (WWN) assigned by the manufacturer. This is similar to the unique MAC (Media Access Control) address assigned by Ethernet network interface card manufacturers. Each port in a switched-fabric FC SAN has a 24-bit port ID. The ports in an arbitrated-loop FC SAN have an 8-bit address. When the arbitrated loop is connected to a fabric environment, the fabric switch makes the 8-bit

---

1. The spelling was changed from *Fiber* to *Fibre* in an attempt to denote the fact that Fibre Channel can operate over copper as well as optical (particularly fiber-optic) media.

address appear to be a 24-bit address. Both these 24-bit and 8-bit port IDs and addresses are dynamically assigned. The concept of ports and their various different types is explained in Section 4.5.

The need for Fibre Channel is explained next. Following that discussion, SANs are compared with network-attached storage, which was covered in Chapter 3. Then the chapter takes a top-down approach that introduces Fibre Channel topologies, moves on to discuss the underlying protocols, and finally describes the various building blocks (including devices) that constitute a Fibre Channel SAN.

4.1 The Need for Fibre Channel

In general, Fibre Channel is an attempt to combine the best of both worlds: channels and networks. **Channel** is a term that was first used in the mainframe world and denotes a structured, defined mechanism for accomplishing data transfer. In most cases the data transfer is between a computer system and a peripheral, such as a disk or tape unit. Well-known examples of channels include SCSI (Small Computer System Interface) and HIPPI (High-Performance Parallel Interface). Channels are typically implemented mostly in hardware.

Compared to a channel, a **network** is a much more general-purpose mechanism for accomplishing data transfer, and it is much less structured. A network can also typically operate over a much longer range and interconnect many more devices than a channel. Unlike channels, networks are implemented much more via functionality in the software layer than in the hardware layer.

One approach to bringing together the storage and networking worlds is to take a network-centric view and extend the technology to add value and overcome the deficiencies. In general, this is the approach taken with the IP storage technologies described in Chapter 8.

The other approach is to take a storage-centric (channel-centric) view and try to extend the technology. This is the approach taken by Fibre Channel. One big advantage of Fibre Channel over IP storage is that Fibre Channel technology–based products have been shipping for almost a decade, whereas IP storage–based commercial products are a relative newcomer.

Given that Fibre Channel is an attempt to take a channel-centric view, reviewing the deficiencies of one of the most famous channel protocols, SCSI, will be useful. SCSI's deficiencies are as follows:

- It has a maximum data transfer rate of 80MB per second (subsequently raised to 320MB per second, but only after the advent of Fibre Channel), which is not enough for high-volume data storage.
- It allows a maximum of 16 devices per adapter, which is simply not enough.
- One of its greatest strengths is also one of its limitations. SCSI has evolved over the years to meet growing demands, yet SCSI vendors have also managed to build in backward compatibility. The problem is that this places a requirement on administrators to ensure that no older SCSI devices are around, because if they are, the bus reverts to the least common denominator.
- It supports a cable length that can be measured at the most in terms of tens of meters. This is simply not enough for clustering, geographical separation of clusters, and the like.
- Other alternatives to SCSI, such as Serial Storage Architecture (SSA), do exist, but these have not really taken off in the Intel architecture servers or as an open standard at all.

4.2 Comparison of Network-Attached Storage and Storage Area Networks

Chapter 3 described network-attached storage (NAS) in some detail. It is worthwhile comparing NAS and SAN basics before learning about the details of Fibre Channel SANs. Table 4.1 summarizes the similarities and differences between the two.

4.3 Advantages of Fibre Channel

Before diving into the details of Fibre Channel, let's look at the advantages of deploying Fibre Channel–based storage area networks. Although the advantages discussed in Sections 4.3.1 through 4.3.7 are currently accurate, keep in mind that none of these features are permanent and they need to be continuously reevaluated, especially in view of technological advances and adoption patterns.

Table 4.1 Comparison of Network-Attached Storage and Storage Area Networks

Network-Attached Storage	Storage Area Networks
NAS provides access to files over a network. Because users are aware of the existence of files—for example, Microsoft Excel spreadsheet files or Word user document files—NAS devices are intuitively easier to understand.	SANs provide access to disk blocks over a network. Users are typically aware of the existence of files. A file system maintains the abstraction between files and disk blocks as to which particular disk blocks are used to store which particular files and so on.
NAS uses network file access protocols such as Common Internet File System (CIFS) or Network File System (NFS). CIFS and NFS typically are the payload of TCP/IP, which itself is typically the payload of Ethernet.	SANs provide access to disk blocks typically using Fibre Channel protocol, which has SCSI as its upper-layer protocol.
NAS devices appear to be servers from which clients access files.	Devices on a SAN appear to be storage units that are accessible to initiators.
NAS devices can be fairly easily plugged into an existing LAN. NAS does not imply adding more network complexity, but at the cost of leaving all traffic on an existing LAN.	A SAN implies creating a new network architecture that is typically FC based. The new network relieves network congestion and allows new applications such as LAN-free backup.
Adding NAS devices to a LAN is not costly.	Adding SAN to an existing LAN-based network is costly.
NAS typically works on Ethernet at 100 Mbps (megabits per second) and also at gigabit speeds when the LAN is based on Gigabit Ethernet.	Fibre Channel SANs typically work at a rate of 1 Gbps or 2 Gbps.

4.3.1 Scalability

SANs are highly scalable in terms of the volume of data and throughput they can handle. One can simply add switches as needed and grow from a departmental loop that connects multiple loops to a backbone that cascades a hierarchy of switches. Of course, IP networks are also scalable, and that is one reason why IP storage (described in Chapter 8) is also developing rapidly.

4.3.2 Segregation of Storage

When properly configured and managed, SANs offer the best of both worlds: The data storage is decoupled from the application server, yet data storage can be segregated to ensure data privacy and integrity. For example, data may be segregated on a departmental basis, yet exist in a common storage pool.

4.3.3 Centralization and Management of Storage

SANs allow storage to be consolidated, used optimally, and managed more easily. The biggest advantage is that a lot of data duplication that happens without SANs is avoided. Another big advantage is storage allocation, avoiding situations in which one particular server has too much storage while another starves. Efficient storage allocation also minimizes costs that are needlessly incurred to add storage to the server that is starved (of storage). For example, if all disks are centrally administered, storage may be reassigned from a server that has too much to a server that has too little. Another example would be storage needed to create a temporary snapshot for backup purposes. In the classical way, each server would have its own dedicated snapshot disk. With a SAN, all the servers can share a couple of disks that are used for creating temporary snapshots.

4.3.4 Legacy Device Support

SANs offer the ability to protect existing investment in legacy devices— for example, SCSI storage—or even, from an ultramodern point of view, to support legacy devices such as loop hubs. Bridge devices that provide connectivity between older devices and FC are often the backbone of legacy device support. Of course, not all legacy devices can be supported.

4.3.5 Support for More Devices

SANs provide support for more devices. Whereas an arbitrated loop can support a theoretical maximum of 127 ports (up to 15 in typical installations, and a practical maximum of about 50 in terms of realistic latency problems), a fabric SAN can *theoretically* support approximately 15 million (2^{24}) ports.

4.3.6 Distance

SANs allow storage to be located at increasingly greater distances from the hosts (servers or workstations) that access them. Whereas SCSI can support distances of only a few tens of meters, with FC we're typically talking about distances of tens of kilometers.

4.3.7 New Functionality Enabled

FC enables some brand-new functionality. One example is LAN-free backup, in which all backup traffic is routed onto the SAN, leaving the LAN free for clients or servers to access the storage. Another example of new functionality is that data can be moved directly between two storage subsystems without first having to be moved to a server. Yet another example is SAN file systems (described in Chapter 6) that allow multiple servers to directly access and simultaneously share the same file system volumes.

4.4 Fibre Channel Topologies

Sections 4.4.1 through 4.4.3 describe the different topologies that enable interconnection of all the various elements that constitute a Fibre Channel SAN. From least to most complicated, the three different topologies are point to point, arbitrated loop, and switched fabric.

4.4.1 Point to Point

Fibre Channel may be configured with a point-to-point topology. In this case typically a server is connected to a dedicated storage subsystem. There is no data sharing. Figure 4.1 illustrates a point-to-point network.

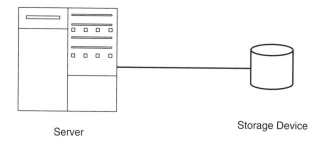

Server   Storage Device

Figure 4.1 Fibre Channel Point-to-Point Topology

To implement a Fibre Channel point-to-point topology, the minimal equipment needed consists of a server, a Fibre Channel adapter (called a *host bus adapter*) and a storage device (e.g., disk or tape) with a Fibre Channel interface.

4.4.2 Arbitrated Loop

A **loop** is simply a logical connection of devices such that data flows in a logical ring fashion around the loop. An **arbitrated loop** is one in which a protocol specifies how a node may seek permission to accomplish data transmission. A Fibre Channel arbitrated loop (FC-AL) can be implemented with various storage devices (such as disk and tape), servers, HBAs, and an interconnect device. This interconnect device can be a Fibre Channel hub or switch. Both of these are described in Section 4.7.4. For now, suffice it to say that the interconnect device plays an important role in the cabling, as well as in the operations and management, of the loop.

Figure 4.2 shows an FC arbitrated loop. The configuration is analogous to a physical star and logical ring, just as in the token ring LANs. And also just as in token ring LANs, data flows in only one direction

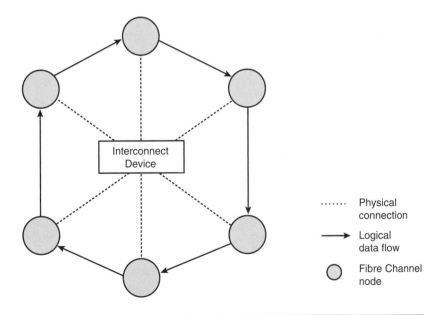

Figure 4.2 Fibre Channel Arbitrated-Loop Topology

around the loop. Unlike token rings, however, a device requests permission to communicate from the hub, rather than wait for an empty token to come around.

Fibre Channel commands enable negotiation and access to the loop for transmission purposes. Commands are also available to assign arbitrated-loop port addresses (AL-PAs) to the various nodes in the loop. Each node on the FC-AL loop has bypass circuitry to take itself out of the loop and maintain loop continuity in cases of errors.

FC-AL loops can address up to 127 ports (of the NL variety; see Table 4.2 later in this chapter) by the way AL-PA addresses are specified. One of these ports is reserved for connection to a fabric switch (described in Section 4.7.4.3), leaving 126 possible addresses that can be assigned to nodes. For practical performance reasons, however, typical loops contain 12 or fewer nodes, and after 50 or so nodes the performance drops to a point at which using fabric switches becomes highly desirable. Arbitrated loops were used as a means of getting the advantages of FC at a lower cost. But with the cost of FC switches also dropping rapidly, the switched-fabric approach has become much more appealing.

Sections 4.4.2.1 through 4.4.2.3 describe some important concepts pertaining to FC-AL: loop initialization, loop arbitration, and different types of loops—that is, public and private loops.

4.4.2.1 FC Loop Initialization

The Fibre Channel protocol for loop initialization follows a finite state machine. Loop initialization happens in the following cases:

- When the loop is first installed and started
- When a new device is plugged in
- When an existing device is removed or restarted

Loops are initialized by means of some special control frames. During initialization, the following activities occur:

- A loop master is elected for the duration until the next loop initialization is needed. One important function of the loop master is to play a role in assigning addresses to the various ports on the loop.
- Loop address assignment is accomplished. The address to which a device is assigned is important because the address value decides which device gets priority when multiple devices wish to transfer

data simultaneously. Fabric switches have the highest priority; they can claim a particular address of their choice. Ports are allowed to claim an address they previously owned.

4.4.2.2 FC Loop Arbitration

When a port needs to communicate with another port, it must first arbitrate for loop ownership. To do this, a port sends a special frame called the *ARB* (short for "arbitration") *primitive*, which includes the loop address of the port seeking control of the loop. When the downstream port receives the ARB primitive, it simply forwards the primitive if it does not seek to do any communication. If the receiving port itself wishes to communicate, it compares the address in the ARB primitive with its own. If the port finds that it has a higher priority—that is, its own address has a lower value—it sends an ARB primitive with its own address. Otherwise it simply sends the ARB primitive that it received. At some point a port receives back its own ARB primitive. At that point it has control of the loop.

The port that won arbitration next sends an *OPN* ("open") *primitive* targeted at the port with which it wishes to communicate. This primitive is simply passed on by intermediate ports until it arrives at the target port. The target port responds with a different ARB primitive, and once that is received by the initiating port, communication can begin. When the initiating port is done sending its communication, it sends a *CLS* ("close") *primitive*. However, the target port may continue sending frames to complete its communication, and the initiating port must be ready to receive these frames even though it already sent a CLS primitive. When the target port is done sending, it responds to the CLS primitive by sending a CLS primitive of its own. At this point the loop is ready for a new communication.

Fibre Channel specifies an optional algorithm to prevent lower-priority devices from getting starved because higher-priority devices continuously wish to communicate. This optional algorithm prevents a higher-priority device from contending for arbitration once it has successfully communicated until lower-priority devices have had a chance to communicate.

4.4.2.3 Public and Private Loops

A **private loop** is a Fibre Channel arbitrated loop that stands alone—that is, is not connected to a fabric (which is described in Section 4.4.3). A **public loop** is an arbitrated loop that is connected to a fabric through a fabric switch. In this case, the fabric switch has to work hard to provide compatibility. Here are some examples:

- The fabric switch needs to ensure that addresses on the fabric and loop are unique and also map between three byte addresses on the fabric and a single byte address on the loop. This process is often referred to as *address spoofing*.
- The fabric switch needs to make devices on the fabric visible to devices on the loop as if they were simply present on the loop.
- Device discovery is essential for public and private communication. Fabric-aware Fibre Channel devices register themselves with the Simple Name Server (SNS, described in Section 4.4.3.1), but FC devices on a loop do not. It is the responsibility of the switch to probe each device in the FC loop and add its characteristics to the SNS for the benefit of the fabric-aware FC devices.

These are simple and not exhaustive examples of the problems involved in supporting a public loop.

4.4.3 Switched Fabric

In Fibre Channel switched-fabric topology, each device has a logical connection to any other device. Note the use of the qualifier *logical* in the previous sentence. It would be extremely difficult and costly to provide any-to-any connectivity via direct physical connections because for N devices, you would need N^2 ports and physical connections. Hence each device is connected to a switch, and the switch implements logical connections among all the ports it has.

Figure 4.3 shows the simplest possible Fibre Channel switched-fabric topology. Multiple nodes (storage devices and computer systems) are connected to a Fibre Channel fabric switch. The switch is a high-speed device that can implement an any-to-any connection and handle multiple simultaneous connections. The switch also implements services such as Fabric Login, which is described in Section 4.4.3.6. Switches may be connected in a cascade or mesh fashion to build a more complex network. Very often a three-tier hierarchy is built with some FC-AL loops at the lowest level, some of which are connected via a lower-end switch and then in turn are connected via extremely high speed/high traffic–capable high-end switches.

There may also be multiple switches that can be connected to each other. A fabric topology uses a 3-byte (24-bit) identifier to uniquely identify

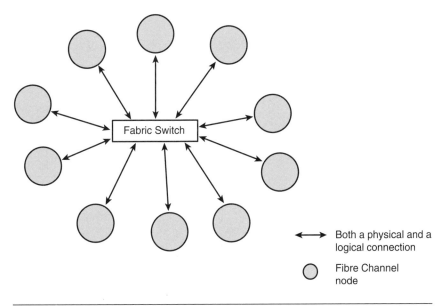

Figure 4.3 Fibre Channel Switched-Fabric Topology

each device and *theoretically* provides any-to-any connectivity among up to 2^{24} (approximately 15 million) devices. In practice, of course, SANs have a much lower number of devices deployed.

Because of the high number of potential devices, it is essential that Fibre Channel SANs offer services for address management as well as other services; otherwise it would be impossible to maintain SANs with manual management. Dynamic address management that is handled by the inherent infrastructure (as opposed to requiring manual intervention) is essential, given the large address space and the fact that the mapping between FC and upper-layer protocols such as SCSI is maintained by the nodes themselves.

A fabric topology is implemented with a fabric switch that is described in Section 4.4.3.5. Besides providing the any-to-any connectivity, the fabric switch provides services such as Simple Name Server, Registered State Change Notification (RSCN), Fabric Address Notification, IP-over-FC Broadcast Server, Principal Switch, and Fabric Login. Sections 4.4.3.1 through 4.4.3.6 briefly describe these services. Note that these services have a client/server model, and that although the fabric switch implements the server component, the client component needs to be implemented in devices such as HBAs and RAID controllers.

4.4.3.1 Simple Name Server

The Simple Name Server (SNS) is a database implemented within a fabric switch that tracks two things:

1. Device name and address information
2. Upper-layer protocols being supported

SNS allows an initiator of communication—for example, a server HBA—to query the name service and discover what storage devices are available. The basic idea here is to let the topology manage addresses by itself, which is highly desirable, given that switched-fabric SANs provide for a 3-byte address that can have up to 15 million unique addresses.

When a fabric-capable device initializes, it sends a login primitive (called *FLOGI* in FC terminology) to the well-known address 0xFFFFFE. The login request is filled with a zero value for address, indicating that an address is being requested.

Once a device has logged in to the fabric, it initiates another request (called a *PLOGI* primitive) to the Simple Name Server. The address for the Simple Name Server is fixed, always 0xFFFFFC. The device sends over information, such as its World Wide Name, port type, fabric address, upper-layer protocols (e.g., SCSI) that it supports, and other service parameters.

Some devices do not send all their information to the SNS. Some switch implementations send targeted probe requests to the device and update the appropriate field entries in the SNS data structures.

4.4.3.2 Registered State Change Notification

The Registered State Change Notification (RSCN) service allows a device to register for notifications when devices of interest join or leave the fabric. For example, a server could register for notifications that are triggered when a storage device joins or leaves the fabric. Thus, RSCN complements the SNS: Whereas SNS allows an FC entity (e.g., a host) to discover another entity (e.g., a storage unit), RSCN allows the host (FC entity) to register for notification of changes to FC entities.

RSCN packets may interrupt data transfer. RSCN frames are used by receivers to update their routing tables. Some vendors provide features in switches to suppress the transmission of RSCN packets widely. Although this suppression is good, the danger is that a device that really needs to see the RSCN may never see it, because of a bad configuration.

4.4.3.3 Fabric Address Notification

The basic idea here is to provide functionality for devices to ensure that their ongoing transactions are still valid. This functionality is typically useful when a loop initialization interrupts ongoing communication between two FC entities.

4.4.3.4 Broadcast Server

Because FC supports upper-layer protocols, it is essential that the needs of upper-layer protocols are met. One of the upper-layer protocols supported is Internet Protocol (IP). Because one of the secondary protocols supported in IP networks is Address Resolution Protocol, in which IP devices issue a broadcast to resolve addresses, it is essential that FC support similar functionality.

4.4.3.5 Principal Switch

When an FC SAN has multiple fabric switches, we need a protocol to select one of them as the principal switch. This principal switch acts as the switch that has the address 0xFFFFFE and ensures that the devices in the FC SAN have unique and nonconflicting addresses.

4.4.3.6 Fabric Login

Fabric-aware devices always attempt Fabric Login, by sending a special frame called an *FLOGI* frame to the well-known address 0xFFFFFE. The FLOGI primitive has a field for the address of the sending device, which can be set to zero to indicate that an address is being requested.

Fabric Login accomplishes some important functions, including

- Retrieval of information about fabricwide parameters—for example, the class of services supported
- Address assignment
- Buffer credit initialization for flow control

4.5 Fibre Channel Port Types

Fibre Channel defines several port types based on the topology of the SAN and the device on which the port exists. The various different types of ports are summarized in Table 4.2.

To simplify life for SAN administrators, device vendors typically build

Table 4.2 Fibre Channel Port Types

Port Type	Device on Which It Can Exist	Description	Port Types That Can Connect to This Type
F	Fabric switch	Fabric-capable only. Never a source or destination for data; acts as middleman to allow two devices to communicate.	N
FL	Fabric switch	Can connect to loop only. Provides connectivity between a Fibre Channel loop and a fabric-switched network. Never a source or destination for data.	NL
E	Fabric switch	Expansion port used to connect fabric switches to other fabric switches. Never a data source or destination; simply acts as a middleman.	E
N	HBA or storage device	Not loop-capable. Always a data source or destination. Exists in either point-to-point or switched-fabric networks.	F or N
NL	HBA or storage device	Similar to N, but loop-capable. Always a data source or destination.	NL or FL
U		Universal port that is simply a port that is not yet used. Once it is used, it can become an E, F, or FL port.	none
L		Generic term used to refer to NL or FL port.	
G		Can be either an E or an F port.	E or N

logic to let the port configure itself. The order in which such configuration is attempted is as follows:

1. The port first attempts to initialize as a loop (FL) port. If the initialization succeeds, the port is configured as an FL port.
2. If the loop initialization fails, the port attempts to initialize as an E port; that is, it checks for connectivity to a fabric switch.
3. If the initialization as an E port fails, the port attempts Fabric Login. If the login succeeds, the port initializes as an F port.

One should not assume that all device vendors are equal in their capability to dynamically configure any port as any kind of port. Some devices have this capability built in and can reconfigure a port on the fly without a reboot or power cycle, but some devices need firmware upgrades or swapping of option cards for the particular port that may require a power cycle.

4.6 Fibre Channel Protocol

Fibre Channel is a set of standards developed by the American National Standards Institute (ANSI). Fibre Channel provides a high-performance serial link between host computers and storage units, as well as between storage units themselves. The standard allows for high-speed data transfers in a point-to-point or a loop network. Moreover, Fibre Channel provides all this with complete error checking.

The Fibre Channel standard defines five functional levels: FC-0 through FC-4. These are described in Sections 4.6.1 through 4.6.5. Note that in practical terms, most of the vendors provide for layers FC-0, FC-1, and FC-2 in silicon.

4.6.1 Layer FC-0

Layer FC-0 defines the physical characteristics of the interface and media. In particular, FC-0 defines the signaling, media, and receiver/transmitter specifications. FC-0 allows for several interfaces, to accommodate a variety of speeds and physical media. Examples of the physical media include copper, single-mode cable, and multimode cable. The transmission speed ranges from 12.5MB to 106.25MB per second. For those familiar with the ISO OSI 7 layer model for networking,[2] one can confidently say that FC-0 exists at the equivalent of layer 0 of the ISO OSI 7 layer model.

4.6.2 Layer FC-1

Layer FC-1 defines the encoding and decoding of data, signal, and special characters, as well as error control. FC-1 also plays a role in link maintenance.

FC-1 uses an encoding scheme called *8B/10B*. The scheme is designed to

- Allow easy synchronization
- Allow for enhanced error detection
- Allow for easy detection of control characters
- Simplify the design of the receiver/transmitter hardware

The 8B/10B encoding scheme transforms each 8 bits into two possibly different 10 bits of rendering. These 10 bits are presented in the form "Ann.m," where

- A = *K* to indicate command or *D* to indicate data
- nn = the decimal value of the last 5 bits of the byte
- m = the decimal value of the first 3 bits of the byte

The two possible different values arise from the fact that the specification chooses one of the two as the encoding to be transmitted on the basis of the immediate past history. The idea is to ensure a minimum number of state transitions (between 1 and 0) and therefore to ensure good transmission efficiency. This immediate past history is called *running disparity*.

As stated already, all data is encoded with 10 bits. Some of the unused 10-bit characters (from a data point of view) are used for frame delineation and signaling, including signaling to indicate that a port is ready to receive data, as well as other types of signaling. The emphasis is on error detection and correction during transmission. FC always transmits data using groups of 4 bytes called **transmission words**.

---

2. *ISO* stands for "International Organization for Standardization," and *OSI* stands for "Open Systems Interconnection."

4.6.3 Layer FC-2

Layer FC-2 defines how data is transferred from one node to the next, in essence defining the transport mechanism. To state this differently, the FC-2 layer assembles frames, defines classes of service, and defines services for fabric or port login. Conceptually, FC-2 can be thought to be at the equivalent of the Media Access Control (MAC) layer of the ISO OSI 7 layer model.

The FC-2 layer defines

- The Fibre Channel transmission hierarchy, consisting of ordered set, frame, sequence, and exchange
- Fibre Channel flow control
- FC-2 protocols
- FC-2 classes of service

These entities are described in Sections 4.6.3.1 through 4.6.3.7. Before we consider them in more detail, it will be useful to understand how the various building blocks of the transmission hierarchy are put together.

Data is exchanged in Fibre Channel via an entity called a **frame**. A frame is the Fibre Channel equivalent of a TCP/IP packet. Frames are built of **ordered sets** and data characters. Multiple frames are grouped together to make a **sequence**, and multiple sequences together constitute an **exchange**. This relationship is shown in Figure 4.4.

Now that the overall view of the transmission hierarchy is clear, in Sections 4.6.3.1 through 4.6.3.4 we'll look at the individual components—that is, ordered sets, frames, sequences, and exchanges.

4.6.3.1 FC Ordered Set

Ordered sets are simply 4-byte transmission sequences that represent special characters or special link signals. Examples of ordered sets include

- **Frame delimiters SOF (start of frame) and EOF (end of frame)**, which are analogous to the Ethernet packets SOF and EOF in functionality. Unlike Ethernet, in Fibre Channel multiple SOF or EOF ordered sets are defined because FC-1 uses an encoding scheme that can have multiple representations for each character transmitted.
- **Two primitive signals to indicate port status:**
  1. **Idle** indicates that a port is ready for transmission and reception.

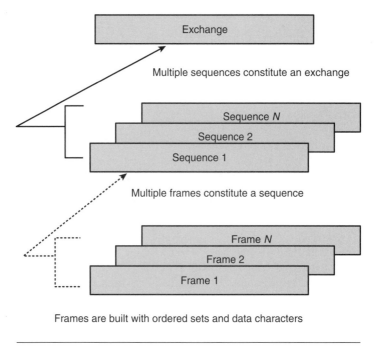

Figure 4.4 Fibre Channel Transmission Hierarchy

2. **Receiver Ready** indicates that an interface buffer (on an interconnect device) is ready for reception of data.

- A **primitive sequence** that is simply an ordered set transmitted continuously to denote special conditions at a port. These special conditions include

- **Not Operational** (**NOS**), which is used only in point-to-point and fabric topologies (i.e., not in arbitrated loops), to indicate a link failure or error.

- **Offline** (**OLS**), which is transmitted when a port is initializing or when it receives a NOS primitive; that is, a port transmits an OLS as the response to a NOS primitive.

- **Link Reset** (**LR**), which is used to indicate that a link reset is desired.

- **Link Reset Response** (**LS**), which is used to indicate that the LR primitive has been received and acted upon.

4.6.3.2 FC Frame

Just as the basic building block for Internet Protocol (IP) is the IP packet, a frame is the basic building block for Fibre Channel. In general, there are three kinds of frames:

1. **Link control frames** to send link commands
2. **Link data frames** to send data needed for link control
3. **Device data frames** that carry data for higher-level protocols—for example, data read off a disk

Figure 4.5 shows the Fibre Channel frame header. The frame is designed to be able to transmit 2,048 bytes of data and an optional 64-byte header. The large size of the frame means that a large amount of data can be transmitted rapidly with very little overhead (about 1.5 percent). On the other hand, another node that needs to transmit will have to wait until the large frame completes, implying a higher latency.

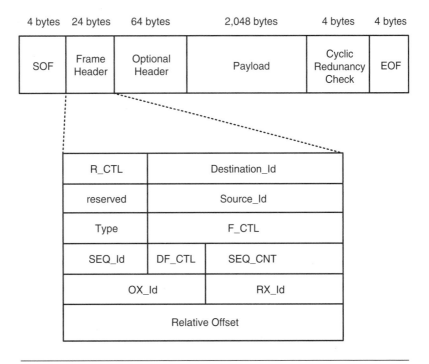

Figure 4.5 Fibre Channel Frame Header

Compare this with ATM (Asynchronous Transfer Mode), in which the frame size is 53 bytes with a protocol overhead of about 10 percent providing for a lower latency, but potentially higher transmission time at the same bit rate.

Every frame begins and ends with a special delimiter, just as in other network protocols. These are the SOF and EOF delimiters, respectively. Every frame also has a header. The header has several purposes. One is to provide source and destination addresses to facilitate switching. Another is to carry information to control the link, including controlling the transfer of data.

The other fields in the Fibre Channel frame header are described as follows:

- The Destination_Id field is used to route the frame. In the point-to-point and loop topologies the routing may be trivial, but not in a switched-fabric topology. The Source_Id field is useful for reporting errors and avoiding routing loops.
- The R_CTL and Type fields are jointly used to distinguish various different FC-4 frames when they arrive at the destination. That is, together these fields tell whether a frame that has just arrived contains SCSI data, IP data, or other data. The values for the Type field are summarized in Table 4.3.
- The R_CTL field is used to indicate what the contents of the frame are. These could be data or link control frames and, in the case of link control frames, could consist of solicited or unsolicited frames.
- The F_CTL field is used to denote frame information such as first sequence or last sequence.
- The DF_CTL field identifies the presence or absence of optional headers.
- The SEQ_Id and SEQ_CNT fields uniquely identify a sequence count within an exchange (see Section 4.6.3.3).
- The OX_Id (originator exchange identifier) field is used to associate a frame with a specific exchange at the originating port.
- The RX_Id (responder exchange identifier) field is used to associate a frame with a specific exchange at the responding port.
- The Relative Offset field identifies the relative displacement of the first byte of the payload from the base address.

Table 4.3 Values for the Type Field in Fibre Channel Frames

Value	Description
0x00	Basic link service
0x01	Fibre Channel port—extended link service
0x02	Memory port
0x03	Memory initialization
0x04	IEEE 802.2
0x05	Internet Protocol
0x06	IPI (Intelligent Peripheral Interface) slave
0x07	IPI master
0x08	SCSI initiator
0x09	SCSI target
0x0A	HIPPI
0x0B	Single-Byte Command Code Sets (SBCCS)
0x0C	Futurebus
0x10	Reserved
0xD0	Vendor unique
0x F0	Direct channel

4.6.3.3 FC Sequence

A sequence is simply a series of frames transmitted from one port to another. To facilitate error recovery, each frame contains a unique sequence count. The error recovery is done by a higher-level protocol, typically at the FC-4 layer. Note that all the frames in a sequence are transmitted in one direction (and are not bidirectional). Figure 4.4 shows how frames, sequences, and exchanges are related.

4.6.3.4 FC Exchange

Multiple sequences make up an exchange. The sequences are a mixture of sequences in each direction; that is, even though a particular sequence is always unidirectional, the sequences that make up an exchange will flow in either direction. In each exchange, only one sequence can be active at any given moment. However, because different exchanges can be active at the same time, different sequences constituting those different exchanges can also be active at the same time.

Each Exchange performs a single function—for example, implements a SCSI command such as Read.

4.6.3.5 FC Flow Control

Fibre Channel end nodes communicate directly with each other and do not make session connections with intervening nodes. They are unaware of the fabric switch and hub. Of course, fabric switches and hubs do exchange flow control packets with these devices.

A flow control mechanism is required to ensure that the sending port does not send frames faster than the receiver can take care of them. Fibre Channel ports have buffers to store the frames temporarily and process them later, processing being defined as either forwarding the frame to another port or passing the frame to an upper-layer protocol. The flow control scheme used by FC is similar to the sliding-window protocol used by TCP/IP. A window representing the number of frames that can be sent, but not acknowledged, is negotiated. This negotiation is binding and cannot be changed. For every frame that is sent, the window size is effectively decreased by one. For every frame that is acknowledged, the window size is effectively incremented by one. Flow control can be implemented in one of two ways: end-to-end and buffer-to-buffer. These are not mutually exclusive, and they are both required.

End-to-end flow control is between two endpoints: a data source such as a server, and a data sink such as a storage unit. End-to-end flow control always occurs between two N ports (there may be intervening nodes between them). The two N ports perform a login with each other, during which each port establishes how many buffers the other port has reserved for it. This amount is called the **buffer credit**. The sender can send at most this many frames. The receiver sends an **ACK** (positive acknowledgment) frame for each frame successfully received and processed, and the sender, upon receipt of the ACK frame, may increment the credit count by one for each ACK frame received. The receiver can also acknowledge successful receipt of multiple frames or an entire sequence, and the sender needs to increment the number of frames it can now send without waiting for acknowledgments.

Buffer-to-buffer flow control occurs between two adjacent nodes that either are intermediate nodes or are between an end node and an intermediate node. Thus, buffer-to-buffer flow control occurs either between N ports or between an F port and an N port. As already explained, the ports exchange values that indicate the number of buffers reserved by each node. These can be different; for example, one port may reserve two buffers while the other reserves four buffers. Frame receipt is acknowledged by means of a Receiver Ready frame rather than an ACK frame in end-to-end flow control.

4.6.3.6 FC-2 Protocols

Fibre Channel standards define protocols for managing data transmission and link control. Additional standards are also defined as needed to cater to higher-level protocols defined in FC-4. The protocols include the following:

- **Fabric Login protocol**, which defines the exchange of parameters between a port and the fabric. Fabric Login is described in more detail in Section 4.4.3.6.
- **Port Login protocol**, which requires that, no matter what the topology (point to point, arbitrary loop, or fabric switch), two ports need to perform a mutual login before they can communicate with each other. The mutual login is accomplished with a special frame called the *PLOGI* frame. Port Login accomplishes some important functionality, including the following:
  - The ability to learn about the N port to which the login is being performed. An example of the knowledge gained is the class of services that the N port supports.
  - Buffer credit initialization for end-to-end flow control. Note that for a direct connection, end-to-end flow control is the same as buffer-to-buffer flow control.
- **Data Transfer protocol**, which defines how upper-layer protocol (defined in FC-4) data is transferred via the flow control schemes defined in Section 4.6.3.5.
- **Arbitrated Loop protocol**, which defines loop initialization and arbitration.

4.6.3.7 FC-2 Service Classes

Fibre Channel was designed to cater to a wide variety of data transmission needs. The various services defined differ in one or more of the following characteristics:

- Orientation of the service connection—that is, like TCP or connectionless, similar to UDP?
- Whether or not multicast is supported
- Whether the service provides notification of delivery and non-delivery
- Whether the service guarantees delivery of frames in the same order they were sent

- The nature of special services provided—for example, reservation of bandwidth per connection if the service is connection oriented
- The nature of flow control mechanisms

To provide for a wide variety of transmission needs, the following different classes of service are defined:

- **Class 1** service defines a dedicated connection, similar to a TCP/IP connection. Just as in TCP, Class 1 guarantees that frames are delivered in the same sequence as they were sent. Class 1 service is useful for transmitting large amounts of data where the time spent to set up the connection is negligible compared to the amount of time required to transmit the data.
- **Class 2** defines a connectionless (datagram-like) service in which frames can potentially be delivered out of sequence (implying that a higher-level protocol must take care of receiving frames out of order and resequencing them). As in networking protocols, Class 2 service makes sense when the amount of data to be transmitted is rather small and the overhead of setting up a connection is comparable to the overhead of the actual data transmission itself. The receiver of a Class 2 frame is expected to send an acknowledgment upon successful receipt of the frame.
- **Class 3** is also a connectionless service, similar to Class 2. The main difference is that the successful receipt of frames is not acknowledged. This is analogous to an IP datagram, where the transmission is sometimes referred to as "send and pray."
- **Class 4**, also called **Intermix**, is an optional service. In this service, Class 1 frames are guaranteed a certain transmission bandwidth, and the remaining bandwidth, if any, is used for Class 2 and Class 3 frames.
- **Class 6** is a unidirectional connection-oriented service that provides multicast capabilities. (Class 5 is a reserved class.)

Table 4.4 summarizes the information about FC service classes.

Note that most vendors support all of Classes 1, 2, and 3 in their implementations. To minimize silicon costs, some vendors support only connectionless service (Classes 2 and 3).

Table 4.4 Fibre Channel Service Classes

	Class 1	Class 2	Class 3	Class 4	Class 6
Nature of service	Connection	Connectionless	Connectionless	Connection	Connection
Multicast support	No	No	Yes	No	Yes
Delivery confirmation	No	No	Yes	No	Yes
Bandwidth used	Full	No guarantee	No guarantee	Partial	No guarantee
Flow control used	End-to-end	End-to-end	Buffer-to-buffer	Buffer-to-buffer	End-to-end
Frame delivery	Guaranteed to be in order	May be out of order	May be out of order	Guaranteed to be in order	Guaranteed to be in order

4.6.4 Layer FC-3

Layer FC-3 defines common services, including services for management and common transport. Whereas FC-3 is common across all ports that a node may have, the FC-0, FC-1, FC-2, and FC-4 layers are on a per-port basis. This arrangement supports the ability of different ports to have different configurations in use, as Figure 4.6 illustrates. For example, one port may be transporting SCSI data while another port is transporting ATM data.

Further, note that whereas the bottom three layers—FC-0, FC-1, and FC-2—are on a per-port basis, the FC-3 layer is on per-node basis. The FC-4 upper layer is also on a per-port basis. Figure 4.6 shows a node with four ports and two upper-layer protocols—namely, SCSI and IP. If there were more upper-layer protocols, there would be more FC-4 boxes for the respective mapping functionality.

Some examples of common functionality that can be implemented at the FC-3 layer include

■ **Trunking** or **striping**, in which parallel links and ports are "collapsed" to provide a thicker, fatter pipe between two nodes.

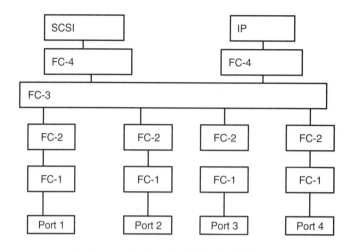

Figure 4.6 Fibre Channel Layers

- **Multicast**, in which a single transmission can be delivered to multiple ports. Multicast is implemented via a registration service in the fabric switch by which nodes can register or deregister for a multicast group. The notion of multicast here is similar to the notion of multicast in Internet Protocol (IP). Note that a multicast could be to all ports on the fabric; that is, a multicast could also be a broadcast.

- **Hunting**, in which multiple ports have the same alias. This is similar to a company acquiring multiple telephone lines, all with the same number, and when a consumer dials the company number, the consumer is simply directed to one of the free lines. The obvious advantage is that the chances of reaching a free port are higher with hunting implemented.

Brocade is one example of a vendor that has implemented trunking, although Brocade prefers to call it Inter Switch Link (ISL) Trunking. The name is intended to convey the fact that Brocade promotes its high-end switches as being extremely high-speed switches that are intended to form the backbone of a switched fabric and are primarily intended to connect to other switches rather than to servers and storage devices. Note that other vendors may also have implemented trunking.

4.6.5 Layer FC-4

Layer FC-4 defines mapping of upper-level protocols to Fibre Channel. FC-4 defines mappings for the following protocols, and more will probably follow:

- SSCI
- Internet Protocol (IP)
- Intelligent Peripheral Interface (IPI)
- High-Performance Parallel Interface (HIPPI)
- IEEE 802.2
- SBCCS (Single-Byte Command Code Sets)
- ATM Adaptation Layer for computer data (AAL5)
- Link Encapsulation (FC-LE)

Note that a single Fibre Channel link can simultaneously carry multiple upper-layer protocols.

4.7 SAN Building Blocks

Sections 4.4 and 4.6 provided an overview of Fibre Channel topologies and the Fibre Channel protocol. Continuing with the top-down approach, it is time to consider the various different devices and elements that are used to construct a Fibre Channel SAN. These elements, referred to as the *building blocks* of a Fibre Channel SAN, are

- Host bus adapters
- Fibre Channel cables
- Connectors
- Interconnect devices, which include hubs, switches, and fabric switches

All of these are described in Sections 4.7.1 through 4.7.4. Note that all addressable entities on a Fibre Channel SAN have unique World Wide Names. These are analogous to the unique MAC addresses for Ethernet interfaces. In Fibre Channel, the World Wide Name is a unique 64-bit number, typically written as "XX:XX:XX:XX:XX:XX:XX:XX." The IEEE assigns each manufacturer a range of addresses. The manufacturer is responsible for allocating its assigned addresses in a unique way to its devices.

4.7.1 Host Bus Adapters

A **host bus adapter** (**HBA**) is simply an adapter that plugs into a computer system and provides connectivity with storage devices. In the Windows PC world, HBAs are typically PCI (Peripheral Component Interconnect) based and can provide connectivity to IDE (Integrated Drive Electronics), SCSI, or Fibre Channel devices. The HBA is operated and controlled via a device driver, which in the Windows PC world is typically a SCSIPort or Storport miniport driver.

When an HBA port is initialized, it logs into the fabric (whenever a fabric is available) and registers various attributes that are stored within the fabric switch. Applications can discover these attributes, typically using either switch vendor–specific APIs or HBA vendor–specific APIs. The Storage Networking Industry Association (SNIA) is working on defining a standardized API that will work across all vendor APIs.

For robust SANs that have high availability requirements, some HBA vendors offer additional capabilities, such as automatic failover (to another HBA). These solutions, along with additional architecture, are described in Chapter 9.

In an arbitrated loop, only two devices can be simultaneously communicating. Assume that one of these devices is an HBA in a host system, and that the HBA is receiving data from a storage device. However, if this HBA is connected to switched-fabric SAN, it could send multiple read requests to multiple storage units. The responses to those requests could arrive in any order and in an interleaved fashion. To make matters worse for the HBA, the fabric switch typically provides a round-robin service for the ports, and hence it is more likely that the packets will arrive in such an order that succeeding packets will be from different sources.

HBAs deal with this problem in one of two ways. One strategy, called *store and sort*, simply stores the data in host memory and then lets the HBA driver use host CPU cycles to sort the buffers. Obviously this approach is expensive in terms of host CPU time, and the total time taken is on the order of a few tens of microseconds for each context switch. The other strategy, called *on the fly*, provides extra logic and silicon on the HBA itself to accomplish context switching without using the host CPU cycles. Typical context-switching times with this strategy are on the order of a few seconds.

As explained in Section 4.6.3.5, *buffer credit* is a term defined as part of the FC standard. One credit allows the sender to send one FC frame. Before the next frame can be sent, a Receiver Ready signal must be received by the sender. To keep the FC pipe busy, one must have multiple frames in flight, but that requires multiple credits, which means more memory available for frame reception. Some HBAs have four 1K buffers or two 2K buffers, although some high-end HBAs have 128K and 256K of memory for buffer credits. Note that this memory ideally needs to be dual ported; that is, while some part of memory is receiving data from the Fibre Channel SAN, other parts of memory may be transferring data into the host PCI bus.

HBAs also play a role in ensuring high availability and failover solutions that provide multiple I/O paths to the same storage unit. This is described in Chapter 9.

4.7.1.1 Windows and HBAs

In Windows NT and Windows 2000, Fibre Channel adapters are treated as SCSI devices, and the drivers are written as SCSI miniports. As described in Chapter 2, the problem is that the SCSIPort driver is a little outdated and does not cater to features supported by newer SCSI devices, let alone Fibre Channel devices. Hence, Windows Server 2003 introduces the new Storport driver model that is meant to replace the SCSIPort driver model, especially for SCSI-3 and FC devices. Note that FC storage disks appear to Windows as if they were directly attached, thanks in part to the abstraction provided by the SCSIPort and Storport drivers.

4.7.1.2 Dual Pathing

Sometimes high performance and high availability are needed, even at a higher cost. In these cases a server is connected to dual-ported storage disks via multiple HBAs and multiple independent FC SANs. The idea is to eliminate any single point of failure. In addition, while everything is healthy, the multiple paths can be used to balance the load and improve performance. More details, including how vendors and Microsoft have built multipath solutions for Windows servers, are provided in Chapter 9.

4.7.2 Fibre Channel Cable Types

The two major types of cables used are optical and copper. Their major advantages and disadvantages are as follows:

- Copper cabling is cheaper than optical cabling.
- Optical cabling can support higher data rates than copper cabling.

- Copper cable can span a smaller distance, up to 30 meters, as compared to optical cable, which can span up to 2 kilometers for multimode cable and up to 10 kilometers for single-mode cable.
- Copper cable is more prone to electromagnetic interference and cross talk.
- Optical data typically needs to be converted to electrical connections for transmission through a switch backplane and then converted back to optical data for further transmission.

As alluded to here, there is only one type of copper cabling, but there are two different types of optical cabling: multimode and single-mode.

For short distances, a multimode cable is used, which typically has a 50- or 62.5-micron core. (A micron, or micrometer, is one millionth of a meter.) The light wave used has a wavelength of 780 nanometers, which is not supported on single-mode cables. For longer distances, a single-mode cable is used, which typically has a 9-micron core. The light wave used has a wavelength of 1,300 nanometers, and that does work with single-mode cable as well.

Because this book is about storage and networking, even though this chapter is about Fibre Channel, it must be stated that all these cables can also be used for other forms of networks, such as Gigabit Ethernet.

4.7.3 Connectors

Because Fibre Channel supports multiple cable types (and transmission technology), devices such as HBAs, interconnect devices, and storage devices are manufactured with a socket that will accept a connector to provide connectivity to the transmission media. This is done in the interest of keeping costs down. Given that there are different types of transmission media and technology, it is logical that there are different connectors:[3]

- **Gigabit interface converters (GBICs)**, which provide serial or parallel data transfer translation. GBICs offer hot-plug functionality; that is, one can pull out a GBIC and plug in a GBIC without affecting the other ports. GBICs have a 20-bit parallel interface.

---

3. Multiple physical standards exist, so the fact that there are only three basic types of technology (copper, single-mode cable, and multimode cable) does not mean that there are only three types of physical connectors. In addition, all of these connectors can and *are* used for other types of networks, such as Gigabit Ethernet.

- **Gigabit link modules** (**GLMs**), which provide functionality similar to that of GBICs but require the device to be powered down for installation. On the other hand, they are less costly than GBICs.
- **Media interface adapters**, which are used to allow conversion from copper to optical media and vice versa. Media interface adapters are typically used in HBAs, but they can also be used in switches and hubs.
- **Small form factor (SFF) adapters**, which allow more interfaces to be accommodated on a given card size.

4.7.4 Interconnect Devices

Interconnect devices provide the connectivity between various elements of the SAN building blocks. The functionality ranges from the low-cost low end of the Fibre Channel hub to the high cost, high performance, and high manageability provided by fabric switches. These devices are described in Sections 4.7.4.1 through 4.7.4.3.

4.7.4.1 Fibre Channel Arbitrated-Loop Hubs

FC-AL hubs provide a low-cost solution to connect multiple Fibre Channel nodes (storage, servers, computer systems, other hubs or switches) into a loop configuration. Typical hubs provide from 8 to 16 ports. A hub can support different transmission types—for example, copper or optical.

Fibre Channel hubs are passive devices; that is, any other device on the loop cannot detect the presence of a hub. Hubs provide simply two kinds of functionality:

1. A wiring backplane that can connect any port to any other port
2. The ability to bypass a port that has a faulty device

The biggest single problem with ports is that they allow only one Fibre Channel connection at a time. In Figure 4.7, if Port 1 wins an arbitration to establish a session to Port 8, none of the other ports can communicate for the duration of the session.

Hubs can be connected to Fibre Channel fabric switches (described in Section 4.7.4.3) without any upgrades. One can also cascade hubs simply by plugging in a cable between two hubs.

FC-AL represents a significant percentage of the total Fibre Channel deployment, but Fibre Channel fabric switches (FC-SWs) are gaining share as costs come down.

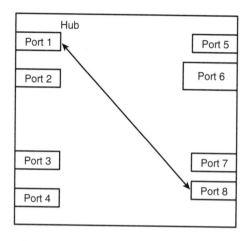

Figure 4.7 A Fibre Channel Hub

Gadzoox Networks, Emulex, and Brocade are some examples of companies that produce hubs.

4.7.4.2 Fibre Channel Arbitrated-Loop Switches

The biggest single advantage of FC-AL switches over hubs is that they allow multiple simultaneous connections, whereas hubs allow only a single connection at a time (see Figure 4.8).

Achieving this simultaneous transmission capability entails quite some work. Devices connected to the loop switch do not even realize this is happening. Loop switches play a role in data transmission and loop addressing. The next section provides more details. The following sections also discuss the roles of switches in a SAN and ways in which some vendors have added features to their offerings.

Loop Switches and Data Transmission

A server that wants to access a storage device will still send a Fibre Channel arbitration request to gain control of the loop. On a normal FC-AL loop with a hub, every device sees the arbitration packet before it is returned to the server HBA, indicating that the server has won arbitration. A loop switch will send a successful arbitration response immediately, without sending the arbitration to any other nodes. At that point the server HBA will send an Open primitive directed at a port that holds the storage device, and the loop switch will forward the Open primitive. Assuming that that particular port is not actively communicating with any

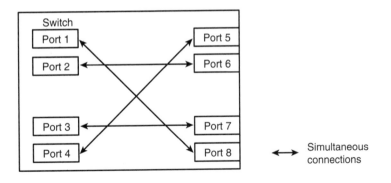

Figure 4.8 A Fibre Channel Switch

other port, all is fine. The problem arises when, say, the server HBA sends an Open primitive addressed to port 7 and port 7 happens to be busy already communicating with another port. To take care of this problem, the loop switch must provide for buffers to temporarily hold the frames directed at port 7. Some switch vendors provide 32 buffers per port for this purpose.

Loop Switches and FC-AL Addressing

FC-AL hubs play no role in device address assignment, other than forwarding the address primitive frames around the loop. The same is true for most switches as well. However, some devices insist on having a particular address. To manage this demand, some switch vendors allow the hub to control the order in which the ports are initialized, thereby allowing a particular port to initialize first, and the insistent device can be attached to that port.

Loop Switches and Loop Initialization

The FC-AL protocol requires loop reinitialization for the entry, removal, or reinitialization of a device. This loop reinitialization can cause disruption of existing communication between two other devices. Some switch vendors provide a capability to selectively screen and forward **loop initialization primitives** (**LIPs**). The idea is to minimize disruption, minimize loop reinitialization time, and allow existing communications to continue uninterrupted if possible. At the same time, one must ensure that no two devices ever end up having identical addresses.

If all devices were participating in a loop reinitialization, this would not happen, because the devices defend their addresses. However, if some devices are not participating in loop reinitialization, care needs to be taken that the address assigned to these devices is not also assigned to other devices that are participating in the loop reinitialization. Added logic in the loop switch ensures the uniqueness of the addresses. The idea is that when a storage device is added, the LIP should be sent to a server because the server communicates with storage devices, but the LIP need not be forwarded to a storage device if the storage device never directly communicates with another storage device.

Some storage devices do have the capability to communicate directly with other storage devices, and this is particularly useful for backup operations. See Chapter 5, which describes backup operations in more detail.

Loop Switches and Fabric

If all devices on the loop are fabric aware, things are relatively straightforward and the loop switch simply needs to pass the fabric-related frames through—for example, the Fabric Login frame. When the devices on a loop are not fabric aware and they need to communicate with devices that are connected to a fabric switch, the loop switch must do a considerable amount of work.

Some vendor loop switches cannot handle cascading. Some loop switches also need firmware upgrades before they can be connected to fabric switches. Some switches must be upgraded to full fabric capability before they can be connected to a fabric SAN.

Brocade, McDATA, Gadzoox Networks, Vixel, and QLogic are examples of companies that produce FC-AL switches.

4.7.4.3 Fibre Channel Fabric Switches

Fibre Channel fabric switches (FC-SWs) allow multiple, simultaneous any-to-any communications at very high speeds. Currently installed switches provide 1-Gbps transmission rates, and 2-Gbps switches are rapidly appearing. In general, fabric switches cost more per port as compared to hubs and FC-AL switches, but they also provide a lot more functionality.

Fabric switches are much more active as compared to hubs and FC-AL switches. For example, they provide the fabric services described here, they provide flow control via flow control primitives, and most importantly, some switches can emulate FC-AL behavior for backward compatibility.

Some fabric switches implement a feature called **cut-through routing**. Upon receipt of a frame header, the switch rapidly looks up the destination header in the frame and routes the frame to the destination port while it is still being received. The advantage is that the frame is delivered with lower latency, and one need not have a memory buffer to hold the frame, store it in the buffer, and then forward it. The disadvantage is that all frames are forwarded rapidly, including corrupted frames.

Fabric switches play an important role in Fibre Channel SAN security, as described in Chapter 7.

4.7.4.4 Comparing the Three Interconnect Devices

Table 4.5 summarizes the functionality and highlights the differences among the three interconnect devices.

Table 4.5 Fibre Channel Interconnect Devices

	Hub	FC-AL Switch	FC-SW Switch
Functionality	Single 100MB-per-second data transfer after negotiating permission to transfer.	Multiple 100MB-per-second data transfers after negotiating permission to transfer.	Multiple switched 1-Gbps to 2-Gbps data transfers, with no negotiation required; can emulate FC-AL when required.
Performance	Decreases as nodes increase.	Remains the same as nodes increase.	Remains the same as nodes increase.
Data visibility	All nodes see all data, whether or not data is intended for them.	Only receiving and transmitting nodes have data visibility.	Only receiving and transmitting nodes have data visibility.
Error recovery	Complex error recovery to reinitialize loop affects all nodes, including healthy nodes.	Error recovery affects only the faulty node	Error recovery affects only the faulty node.
Reconfiguration	When a node is added or removed, all nodes participate in loop re-initialization.	Only the new node and switch participate in reconfiguration.	Only the new node and switch participate in reconfiguration.

continued on page 128

Table 4.5 *(continued)*

	Hub	FC-AL Switch	FC-SW Switch
Data buffer	No data buffer in hub.	No data buffer in switch.	Extensive data buffers per port and per switch; allow transmission without checking if receiving node is ready.
Addressing	8-bit addressing, 127 nodes; with one node reserved for connection to switch.	16-bit addressing, up to 16 million nodes; supports subaddressing— that is, using fewer bits, such as the last five digits of a phone number for intra-company calls.	16-bit addressing, up to 16 million nodes.
Implementation complexity and cost	Low.	Medium.	High.
Manageability	Usually no manageability, sometimes available as add-on module for extra cost.	Good manageability.	Excellent manageability.
Advanced features	None.	Zoning.	Zoning and advanced security features; multipath failover if topology allows; trunking of links when allowed by some switches.

4.7.4.5 Bridges and Routers

For the purposes of this chapter in particular and this book in general, the terms *bridges* and *routers* do not refer to the traditional Ethernet bridges or IP routers. The bridges and routers here deal with Fibre Channel and not layer 2 or layer 3 network protocols.

Bridges are devices that provide for Fibre Channel and legacy protocols such as SCSI. Fibre Channel–to–SCSI bridges would help preserve existing investment in SCSI storage. Such a bridge provides both SCSI and Fibre Channel interfaces and translates between the two. Thus a new server equipped with a Fibre Channel HBA would be able to access existing SCSI storage via such a bridge.

Bridges provide an interface between a parallel SCSI bus and a Fibre Channel interface. Routers can do the same, but with multiple SCSI buses and one or more Fibre Channel interfaces. Storage routers, or intelligent bridges, routinely provide additional features, such as LUN masking and mapping (sometimes called *access controls*) and support for SCSI Extended Copy commands. As data movers, storage routers implement the Extended Copy commands for use by storage libraries, to move data from identified targets to the attached libraries. This is also referred to as *server-free backup*.

Crossroads Systems, Chaparral Network Storage, Advanced Digital Information Corporation (ADIC, via acquisition of Pathlight), and MTI are some examples of router and bridge device vendors.

4.8 Fibre Channel Management Concepts

The preceding sections have described the hardware elements that constitute SAN building blocks. A fair amount of software is involved in a SAN, particularly for management, data security, and SAN applications such as backup and restore. Sections 4.8.1 and 4.8.2 introduce some concepts essential to SAN management and data security. Indeed these concepts are the very heart of making SANs usable at all.

Now that single networks have multiple computers and multiple storage units, it is desirable to restrict views of particular computers (called *hosts* in Fibre Channel terms) to particular storage subsystems and particular units within those storage subsystems. This need is especially strong when a host is running Windows NT, because Windows insists on mounting any device that it discovers. UNIX systems on the other hand have a mount table and will mount only the devices explicitly mentioned in the mount table. Even with UNIX hosts, it is desirable to restrict access for security reasons and avoid possible data corruption. Access can be restricted by three different types of mapping or zoning functionality:

1. Basic functionality implemented within the host, perhaps within the software driver for the HBA
2. Functionality at the switch
3. Functionality at the storage subsystem level

4.8.1 Zoning

The term *zoning* is associated intimately with switches. Zoning allows certain ports on a switch to have connections with only certain other ports. In some instances, zoning may also be used to screen certain FC control frames from propagating; for example, when a new storage device enters a loop, the LIP may be optionally screened from other storage devices.

Functionally, zoning allows a particular computer to have a direct connection with a particular storage subsystem. The drawback is that the computer is given complete SAN resources for that connection and will typically underutilize those resources. In particular, zoning does not allow sharing of the bandwidth or the storage subsystem resources.

Think of zoning as being analogous to IP port configuration on a firewall router. Another way to think of zoning is as the equivalent of setting up virtual LANs (VLANs) within an existing LAN environment. In a VLAN, only certain devices can see each other, even though additional devices may be present on the same physical LAN. Similarly, zoning restricts elements on a SAN (especially initiators) to knowledge (of) and access (to) only certain storage units, even though additional servers and storage units may exist on the same physical SAN.

Figure 4.9 shows a simple view of zoning. The SAN has three servers and three storage units. The different shading indicates different zones.

LUNs can be shared via SAN file system sharing software. In this software, one or more servers act as metadata servers. Software is installed on the client computer (that wants to access a file on the SAN) and the metadata server. The metadata provides the client computer with the information that maps a logical offset in a file into a physical block number on a specified device. This knowledge allows the client computer then to directly access the file over the SAN without moving data through the server. If this is done cleverly enough, the regular file permissions on

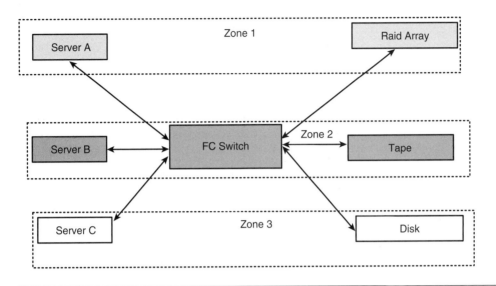

Figure 4.9 Zoning

the client computer will still apply and the administrator will not need to do anything different in terms of file-sharing permissions and security.

One may define multiple zones and also have a single node participate in multiple zones; that is, some zones may overlap with others. Zoning may be accomplished in multiple ways:

- **Zoning by port number**. The advantage here is flexibility. If a device at a port is replaced by another device, no reconfiguration is needed.
- **Zoning by World Wide Name**. We can accomplish zoning by specifying which WWNs are considered to be in the same zone. Some WWNs may be defined to be in multiple zones. The advantage here is security, but at the cost of flexibility. Reconfiguration changes may need a server reboot.
- **Soft zoning**. Soft zoning is accomplished by means of a name server (software) running within the switch. Soft zoning may be zoning by port number or by World Wide Name or a combination of both. The name server has a database that stores WWNs, port numbers, and zone IDs.
- **Hard zoning**. Hard zoning is accomplished by means of a routing table stored within the switch. Hard zoning is based on WWNs and does not take port numbers into consideration at all.

4.8.2 LUN Masking

Storage resources may be "partitioned" into multiple subunits called **logical unit numbers (LUNs)**. SCSI-2 supports up to 64 LUNs per target.

Functionally, LUN masking allows a particular computer to access a specific storage subunit on a specific storage system. More importantly, it is a way of ensuring that certain computers or servers do not have access to a particular LUN. LUN masking allows storage resources and, implicitly, network bandwidth to be shared, but the LUN itself is not shared. To allow true sharing of a single LUN by multiple computer systems, one needs an enhanced file system as described in Chapter 6. LUN masking is essential to guaranteeing data integrity in a SAN environment. Notice that LUN masking is an attempt to ensure only disk security and not necessarily file-level security. Additional software other than LUN masking is needed for the latter.

LUN masking does allow flexibility. LUNs can be easily reassigned to different computer systems. There are various ways of achieving LUN masking, each with its advantages and disadvantages. In general, the masking may be done

- In hardware at the HBA
- In hardware at the FC switch
- In hardware at the FC storage device
- In software at the host computer

These options are described in Sections 4.8.2.1 through 4.8.2.4.

4.8.2.1 LUN Masking in the HBA BIOS

In the HBA BIOS we accomplish LUN masking by masking away all LUNs that are not mapped in an HBA BIOS table. Thus the host (in which the HBA is installed) simply does not learn about the existence of the LUNs that it is not expected to see.

The drawback with this method is that it is voluntary and subject to the application of correct configurations. Any system that has an HBA that is incorrectly configured or does not implement this functionality can access LUNs that it is not supposed to access. Another problem with this approach is that dynamically managing and reconfiguring such a system can be problematic.

4.8.2.2 LUN Masking in Fibre Channel Switches

It is fairly easy for Fibre Channel switches to implement zoning. The incoming packet is either forwarded or not forwarded on the basis of the source and destination port addresses. LUN masking puts a little more overhead on Fibre Channel switches, requiring the switch to examine the first 64 bytes of each packet. This additional functionality is seen as a performance issue for most FC switches and therefore usually is not implemented.

4.8.2.3 LUN Masking in Fibre Channel Storage Controllers and Routers

This method of LUN masking is not voluntary for the attached hosts or subject to partial host participation. The LUN masking is implemented in the storage controller or router (firmware). Essentially the storage controller or router is configured to have a table of HBA WWNs mapped to the LUNs mapped within the controller that they are allowed to access. The big advantage here is that the configuration is independent of the configuration of intervening hubs or switches.

The drawback with this method is that the implementations are all vendor proprietary with no easy way for a single management console to reconfigure or even just query the settings, even though most vendors provide interfaces for managing the mappings.

Crossroads Systems, EMC, Dot Hill, and HP (with its StorageWorks offering) are some examples of vendors with such functionality. The vendors call this functionality by proprietary names; for example, Crossroads calls it *Access Controls*, and HP's StorageWorks calls it *Selective Storage Presentation*.

4.8.2.4 LUN Masking via Host Software

LUN masking is accomplished in host software, typically by means of code in a device driver. The code must be in kernel mode because the whole idea is to prevent the operating system from claiming ownership of a LUN, and the operating system would do that before a user mode application got a chance to run.

This masking can be accomplished either as part of the base operating system or outside the base operating system. In the absence of a solution from Microsoft, some vendors have added code to their HBA driver to provide LUN-masking functionality. Typically the driver issues a

Report LUNs command to each device on the bus, and before returning the list of LUNs to the Windows NT operating system, the driver culls LUNs from the list on the basis of some other data that it queries (such as registry information in Windows NT), thus "hiding" some LUNs from the Windows NT operating system.

The main problem with this method is that it is voluntary and hence subject to partial participation. This means that computers that do not have this custom HBA driver will not participate in the LUN masking. The solution also runs into problems with scaling for extremely large SANs because it is difficult to configure the many servers and their HBA drivers. The advantage is that this method makes it easy for LUNs to be shared by multiple servers.

Emulex, Dell, and JNI are some examples of vendors that offer such functionality.

4.8.2.5 LUN Masking and the Future of Windows NT

At press time, Microsoft is believed to be working on implementing LUN-masking capability in the port driver. However, this functionality is not present in Windows Server 2003. The advantage of having such functionality in the port driver is that the port driver is always loaded, so the window of opportunity for nonparticipation in the LUN masking is considerably reduced. The chances of having the wrong port driver loaded are considerably smaller than the chances of having both the wrong port driver and the wrong miniport driver loaded. Some preliminary indications are that any such implementation, were it indeed to happen, would allow an administrator to set the LUNs visible to a server. The administrator would be able to modify this list, including modifying this list in a nonpermanent way. In such cases a change could be made, but the change would no longer be applicable on the next reboot of the server.

4.9 Fibre Channel Interoperability

The phrase "let the buyer beware" summarizes the state of interoperability in the Fibre Channel world.

That said, one can say that most of the problems in interoperability for FC-AL configurations have been ironed out by work done by storage device, HBA, FC-AL switch, and router vendors. A lot of testing is done by device vendors, original equipment manufacturers, and solution provider vendors, but the basic situation is that although in theory interoperability is supposed to work, in practice a fair amount of time is spent testing and tweaking configurations to make them work. It is advisable to stick to configurations that have been tested by a solution provider or vendor.

The biggest problem is that adherence to standards is not necessarily guaranteed. In addition, adherence to standards does not guarantee interoperability either.

Solution providers such as IBM, HP, and EMC set up labs to test interoperability among various devices and then certify the solution. To a degree, various device vendors do so as well. One is well advised to stick to these certified solutions, thereby avoiding the problems that frequently arise when a device that is not part of this certified solution is added.

Although the overwhelming majority of FC SANs installed are operating at a speed of 1 Gbps, the first of the 2-Gbps SAN devices are now making a commercial appearance, bringing with them some new interoperability problems. The standards followed by vendors attempt to operate at 2 Gbps, but these devices revert to 1 Gbps when the devices with which they are attempting to communicate are capable of only 1 Gbps. Actually, an FC SAN is expected to operate at the speed of the slowest device within the SAN. Thus, if there is even a single 1-Gbps device in the SAN, the SAN will operate at 1 Gbps.

4.10 Practical Implications

Fibre Channel SANs provide the illusion that a storage device is directly connected to a server, even when it is really connected through a switch. Thus, as far as a Windows operating system is concerned, the Fibre Channel device is accessed via either the SCSIPort or the Storport driver model described in Chapter 2. Hence the implications of direct-attached storage also apply here.

The new Storport driver model provides a lot of functionality, including optimizing I/O and driving throughput. However, system administrators and IT procurement officials should note that the Storport driver model is applicable to only the Windows Server 2003 platform. IT procurement officials who have settled on the Windows platform will want to investigate the plans of their storage device vendor to adopt the Storport model and meanwhile investigate the same vendor device support on the Windows 2000 platform, including details of how the vendor had implemented the driver. Specifically, it is important to determine whether the system throughput is adequate with the soon-to-be legacy SCSIPort model driver if that's what the vendor is using. Also find out if the vendor has developed its own solution that does not use the SCSIPort driver at all and whether that solution has been certified and is supported by all relevant parties. Finally, investigate if the vendor will provide a smooth migration path from the current Windows 2000 solution to a Storport-based solution on Windows Server 2003.

LUN masking is currently not natively supported by any released version of the Windows operating system. Windows Server 2003 is not expected to change that situation. Before purchasing any new hardware and software, determine the vendor architecture for implementing LUN masking and confirm that the architecture is a good Windows citizen.

4.11 Summary

Fibre Channel SANs constitute an important element of enterprise storage. FC may be deployed in a low-cost loop configuration or, as is increasingly popular, in a switched-fabric topology.

Windows Server 2003 supports Fibre Channel devices by using a vendor-provided Storport driver. The vendor may choose to provide a SCSI port minidriver instead, but in that case the advantages of the Storport driver (better performance and error handling, to name a couple) are not available to the user. Windows 2000 and prior versions support Fibre Channel devices by using a vendor-provided SCSIPort minidriver.

Even though Windows NT allows LUN masking and zoning to be implemented, no native support for LUN masking yet exists in Windows NT. LUN masking in Windows NT may be implemented in vendor-written drivers.

CHAPTER 5

Backup and Restore Technologies

Backup is the process whereby a coherent copy of data is made. Backup has become more important as the amount of data has exploded, not just in importance, but in volume as well. One study estimates that more data will be created in the next few years than has been created since the dawn of history! It is interesting to compare the growth in data storage with the more widely known and appreciated growth in electronic chip density. Recall that Moore's law implies that the amount of electronics on a given chip area doubles every 18 months. A lot of industry analysts believe that the growth in digital storage is actually handily beating Moore's law in the sense that the amount of data doubles in much less than 18 months.

Historically, tape has been used as a medium for backing up data. Initially tape was a much cheaper medium than disk. Subsequently it was argued that optical media would become the media of choice, but for various reasons this vision never came to fruition. Although the medium of choice (for backup) remains predominantly tape, regular disk drives are increasingly becoming the medium of choice for an initial backup and system mirror. This trend is due mainly to the falling prices of disk storage, which reduces the cost advantage of tape over disk storage. Another reason for the increasing use of disk-based backup is the higher speed, which ensures minimal downtime for server-based applications.

Note that both disk and tape as media for backup have their advantages and disadvantages, and both will continue to be used. Tape-based backup/restore offers a very high-density medium that can easily be transported for off-site archive or disaster recovery purposes. When an initial copy of data is made to disk, very often a secondary backup operation to traditional tape media is made from that disk-based copy.

This chapter explains the technical challenges that need to be solved in order to back up and restore data in a timely way. The chapter also explains the various ways in which backup/restore techniques can be classified. Also included are discussions of new developments in Windows Server 2003 for accomplishing snapshots (volume shadow copy service) and of the Network Data Management Protocol (NDMP) and how it fits into the Microsoft vision of storage management.

5.1 Reasons for Backup and Restore

Backup is performed for various reasons, and those reasons very often dictate the investment made in accomplishing the backup. The assurance of data availability is the primary reason for creating backups. The higher the data availability requirements, the more investment needs to be made. For example, one form of backup that runs continuously is disk mirroring, in which every data write operation is reflected to another disk to guarantee extremely high data availability.

Data archival also is used to meet legal and other needs in which the data does not have to be accessible immediately but can be produced on demand in a reasonable amount of time, measured in hours, days, or weeks.

Backups are sometimes used to transport data—for example, when one decides to create another data center at a distant geographical location. A similar motivation is to migrate the data to new hardware or, more rarely, a different server platform.

5.2 Backup Problems

Before diving into the various ways that backup and restore operations are accomplished, it is advisable to understand the problems that need to be solved to accomplish the desired objective. The prominent issues are these:

- An ever decreasing amount of time, called the *backup window*, in which the backup operation must be accomplished
- An ever increasing number of APIs that backup applications need to support

■ An inability to back up files that are open and actively being used by an application

Sections 5.2.1 through 5.2.3 consider each of these issues in more detail.

5.2.1 The Backup Window

Historically, server applications were run during regular business hours only. Backup operations were typically done in the wee hours of the night when the applications could be stopped without causing user distress. Once the applications were stopped, the server would typically be taken offline and the data backed up. There are two problems with this old approach:

1. The huge explosion of data has meant that the backup is hard to accomplish within the given amount of time. Difficult as it may be to believe, writing to tape is an expensive operation, especially in terms of time and man-hours consumed. The correct tape has to be located, mounted, and then positioned. Once positioned, tapes are much slower to write to than disk. Whereas most hard drive interfaces are able to transfer data at a sustained rate well over 80MB per second, the fastest tape drives available today see maximum transfer rates of under 30MB per second. Robotic silos can be used to manage the multiple-tape media units, but they are expensive, and of course they can only alleviate the time spent in locating and loading a tape, not make the tape read or write any faster.

2. The second problem is that more and more applications, as well as the data they access, control, create, or modify, are considered important if not mission-critical. This means that the amount of time when the server could be taken offline to accomplish the backup is shrinking.

5.2.2 Explosion of APIs

Customers are deploying more and more enterprise applications that can be stopped rarely, if ever, for backup. Recognizing this fact, each application vendor has resorted to providing APIs for backing up and restoring the application data files in a consistent manner that ensures that no data is lost. Although the creation of these APIs sounds great, a closer inspection shows that the problem is rapidly worsening as a result.

Figure 5.1 illustrates the problem of an ever increasing need to support more APIs in the backup/restore application. As this example shows, customers typically have multiple applications, and very often multiple versions of the same application. Each backup vendor now must write code to use the APIs provided by each enterprise application. Because many backup application vendors choose to separately license the agents that deal with a specific enterprise application, just keeping track of the software licenses and the costs can make any IT manager dizzy. Furthermore, even all this does not take into account the deployment of the infrastructure, personnel, and discipline to accomplish these backups.

5.2.3 Open Files Problem

Another problem with doing a backup is that it can take a considerable amount of time. If a tape device has a rated throughput of 10GB per minute, it will take 10 minutes to back up a 100GB disk. During these 10 minutes, applications will need access to the disk and will also be chang-

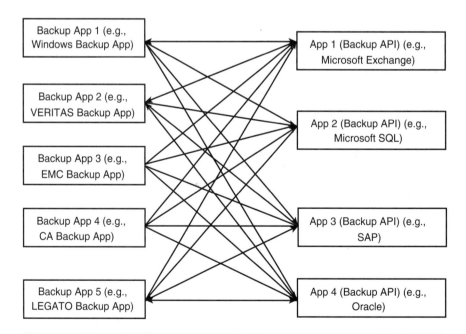

Figure 5.1 Backup API Explosion

ing data on the disk. To ensure that the backup is consistent, three approaches are possible:

1. To prohibit applications from accessing the disk while the backup is in progress. Blocking simultaneous user access to the application during backup was commonplace in the early days of PC computing, when 24x7 operations didn't take place. The backup was done in times of light load—for example, during night hours. Now this approach is not feasible, for a couple of reasons:
    - Operational requirements now often call for 24x7 application uptime, so there is no good time to do the backup.
    - The amount of data needing to be backed up has grown, so the operational hours have increased, and the backup window is often not long enough to accomplish the backup.
2. To back up the data while applications are accessing the disk, but skip all open files. The problem here is that typically, only important applications run while a backup executes, which implies that the important data will not be backed up!
3. To differentiate between I/O initiated by the backup application and other applications. Backup vendors came up with solutions that partially reverse-engineered operating system behavior. In particular, the solutions depend on the implementation being able to differentiate judiciously, a method that can break fairly easily. The implementations have generally used a varying degree of undocumented features or operating system behavior that is liable to change in new versions of the operating system. The solutions also depend on the availability of a sufficient amount of disk space. Another variation that applies to both techniques is whether the implementation works with one file at a time or is simultaneously applied to all files at once.

Three approaches have been tried to allow open files to be backed up yet have a consistent set of data on the backup media corresponding to the open files.

The first approach is to defer application writes to a secondary storage area, allowing the backup operation to back up all files. The approach must also be selective in operation; for example, it must allow the paging file writes to pass through but defer the writes to application data files or put them in a predefined secondary cache (often called a *side store*), ensuring that the data backed up is in a consistent state. I/O to or from the secondary storage area also needs to be treated specially depending on whether the backup/restore application or a different application is doing this I/O. Once the backup application is done, the data must be copied from the side store to the regular file area.

The second approach is to implement copy-on-write for the benefit of backup applications. When a backup application opens a file, other applications are still allowed to write to the file. To avoid a mix of old and new data in the backup application, the data being overwritten is copied to a side store. If regular applications request this data, the read is handled by the regular Windows file system drivers. When a backup application requests this data, the data is retrieved from the side store. St. Bernard Software is one example of a vendor that has implemented this approach to backing up open files.

Consider Figure 5.2 and notice the layering of drivers (a detailed explanation of Windows drivers, device objects, and so on is available in Chapter 1). The file system filter driver is layered over the NT file system (NTFS) driver, which itself is layered over the disk filter driver. The disk filter driver in turn, is layered over the disk class driver. There are other drivers below the disk class driver (as discussed in Chapter 1), but these are not relevant to the discussion here. When an application opens a file,

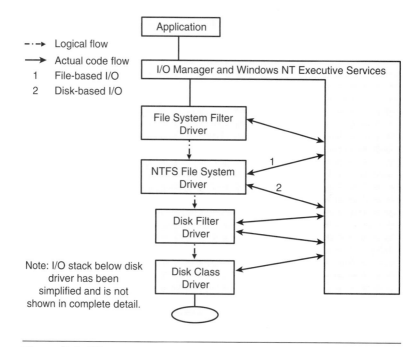

Figure 5.2 Windows NT Filter Drivers

NTFS (in response to application requests) issues a series of commands to read metadata (the location of the file in the disk) and then issues reads or writes to the logical blocks on which this particular file is stored.

The upper filter driver (above the file system driver) shown in Figure 5.2 is ideally placed to intercept file operations and divert the call, if that is what is desired to solve the problem of open files. Microsoft sells a product called the Windows Installable File System (IFS) Kit, which provides information needed to write such a filter driver. A backup vendor may choose to work at a lower level; for example, an image level would typically use a solution that involves writing a lower filter driver (above the disk class driver), as illustrated in Figure 5.2.

The I/O operations shown in Figure 5.2 operate at a file system level to begin with, as denoted by the path marked with the number 1 in the figure. The NTFS file system driver manages the mapping of file data to disk blocks; subsequently, the I/O operation is done at a disk block level, below the NTFS file system, as denoted by the path marked with the number 2. Microsoft conveniently ships the diskperf.sys filter driver as part of the Windows Driver Development Kit (DDK), which is exactly such a driver. Several backup vendors have started with this sample as their building block for a snapshot solution.

The third approach is to take a snapshot of the data and back up the snapshot while the applications unknowingly continue using the original volume. The snapshot may be created by means of a variety of hardware or software solutions. This is the approach Microsoft favors with Windows Server 2003.

5.3 Backup Classifications

Various types of backup schemes exist, and they can be categorized in different ways. In an actual data center, one typically uses multiple types of backups. In short, the categorization of backups should not be taken to be mutually exclusive. Backups can be classified on the basis of

- Architecture
- Functionality
- Network infrastructure

Sections 5.3.1 through 5.3.3 take a look at each of these types of classification.

5.3.1 Backup Classifications Based on Architecture

One way of classifying backups is based on the architecture. That is, backups are classified in terms of the objects they deal with and the amount of awareness the backup application has of these objects. The available types of architecture-based backups, described in Sections 5.3.1.1 through 5.3.1.3, are

- Image- or block-level backup
- File-level backup
- Application-level backup

5.3.1.1 Image- or Block-Level Backup

The backup application in this case deals with blocks of data. Typically, this kind of backup scheme needs all applications on the server to cease accessing the data that is being backed up. The application opens the disk to be backed up as a raw disk (ignoring the file locations) and literally does logical block-level read and write operations.

The advantages of this kind of backup are that the backup and restore operations are very fast, and it can be a good disaster recovery solution. One disadvantage is that applications and even the operating system cannot access the disk while the backup or restore is happening. Another disadvantage is that image-level backups of a sparsely populated volume can result in a lot of unused logical blocks being copied for the backup. Some backup applications provide the logic necessary to detect and skip unused logical blocks. These are called *sparse image backups*.

Finally, it is hard to retrieve just a particular file or a few files rather than restore all the data to a disk. To do so, the restore software must understand the file system metadata as it exists on the tape, retrieve this metadata, and from there, compute the location on the tape where the data for the particular file resides. Some vendors provide the ability to restore a particular file from an image-level backup, but these offerings are available on only certain operating system platforms and not others. Some restore applications do attempt to optimize restoring a file from an image-level backup. These applications write file metadata such as the file allocation table for FAT16 to the tape.

The version of NTFS included with Windows 2000 already keeps all metadata in files—for example, the bit map that represents logical block allocation. The restore application locates the required metadata. From this the software calculates the positions on tape of each of the required logical data blocks for the file being restored. The tape is then spooled in one direction, and all the relevant portions of the tape are read while the tape is moving in a single direction, thus providing the file data for restoration. The tape is not moved forward and backward at all, so not only is the restore time reduced, but the life of the tape is extended as well. Legato Celestra is one example of such a backup application.

Note that sometimes the choice of backup is limited. Consider the case in which a database uses a raw disk volume (without any kind of file system on that volume). In this case the only two choices are an image-level backup or an application-level backup (the latter is described in Section 5.3.1.3).

5.3.1.2 File-Level Backup

With this type of backup, the backup software makes use of the server operating system and file system to back up files. One advantage is that a particular file or set of files can be restored relatively easily. Another is that the operating system and applications can continue to access files while the backup is being performed.

There are several disadvantages as well. The backup can take longer, especially compared to an image-level backup. If a lot of small files are backed up, the overhead of the operating system and file and directory metadata access can be high. Also the problem of open files described earlier exists and needs to be solved.

Another disadvantage is related to security. This issue arises irrespective of whether the backup is made via a file-level backup or an image backup. The problem is that the restore is typically done through an administrator account or backup operator account rather than a user account. This is the only way to ensure that multiple files belonging to different users can be restored in a single restore operation. The key is that the file metadata, such as access control and file ownership information, must be properly set. Addressing the problem requires some API support from the operating system and file system involved (NTFS) to allow the information to be set properly on a restore operation. In addition, of course, the restore application must make proper use of the facility provided.

5.3.1.3 Application-Level Backup

In this case, backup and restore are done at the application level, typically an enterprise application level—for example, Microsoft SQL Server or Microsoft Exchange. The backup is accomplished via APIs provided by the application. Here the backup consists of a set of files and objects that together constitute a point-in-time view as determined by the application. The main problem is that the backup and restore operations are tightly associated with the application. If a new version of the application changes some APIs or functionality of an existing API, one must be careful to get a new version of the backup/restore application.

Applications either use a raw disk that has no file system associated with the volume/partition or simply have a huge file allocated on disk and then lay down their own metadata within this file. A good example of an application that takes this approach is Microsoft Exchange. Windows XP and Windows Server 2003 introduce an important feature in NTFS to facilitate restore operations for such files. The file can be restored via logical blocks, and then the end of the file is marked by a new Win32 API called SetFileValidData.

5.3.2 Backup Classifications Based on Functionality

Yet another way of classifying backup applications is based on the functionality that is achieved in the backup process. Note that a data center typically uses at least two and very often all types of the backups described in Sections 5.3.2.1 through 5.3.2.3: full, differential, and incremental.

5.3.2.1 Full Backup

In a **full backup**, the complete set of files or objects and associated metadata is copied to the backup media. The advantage of having a full backup is that only one media set is needed to recover everything in a disaster situation. The disadvantage is that the backup operation takes a long time because everything needs to be copied. Full backups are very often accomplished with the image- or block-level backup architecture.

5.3.2.2 Differential Backup

A **differential backup** archives *all changes since the last full backup*. Because differential backups can be either image block based or file based, this set of changes would represent either the set of changed disk blocks (for image-based backup) or the set of changed files (for file-based backup). The main advantage of differential backup is that the backup takes a lot less time than a full backup. On the other hand, the disadvantage is that recovering from a disaster takes longer. A disaster recovery operation involves running at least two restore operations, one corresponding to a full backup and one corresponding to a differential backup.

With low-end storage deployed, file-based differential backups are used when the applications by nature tend to create multiple small files and change or create just a few of them since the last full backup. In addition, when low-end storage is deployed, file-based differential backups are not typically used with database applications, because database applications, by their very nature, tend to make changes in small parts of a huge database file. Hence a file-based backup would still have to copy the whole file. A good example here is Microsoft Exchange, which tends to make changes in small parts of a huge database file.

With high-end storage deployed, image-based differential backup can be used in any situation, including with database applications. The reason for this flexibility is that the high-end storage units can track a lot of metadata and thus quickly identify which disk blocks have changed since the last full backup. Thus, only this small number of disk blocks needs be archived, and the large number of unchanged disk blocks that are present in the same database file can be ignored. Even though the backup with high-end storage is more efficient, APIs that start the backup at a consistent point and allow the I/O to resume after the backup has been accomplished are still needed. The efficiency of high-end storage simply minimizes the time during which all I/O must be frozen while the backup is being made.

5.3.2.3 Incremental Backup

An **incremental backup** archives *only the changes since the last full or incremental backup*. Again, the obvious advantage is that this backup takes less time because items not modified since the last full or incremental backup do not need to be copied to the backup media. The disadvantage is that a disaster recovery operation will take longer because restore operations must be done from multiple media sets, corresponding to the last full backup followed by the various incremental backups.

In the absence of high-end storage, file-based incremental backup is used only when a different set of files is typically created or modified. With high-end storage that can provide the required metadata tracking, block-based incremental backup may be used.

5.3.3 Backup Classifications Based on Network Infrastructure

One way of classifying a backup scenario is based on the network topology used, and how that topology lends itself to achieving the best method for backing up the attached hosts. The network infrastructure–based backup types—direct-attached backup, network-attached backup, LAN-free backup, and server-free backup—are described in detail in Sections 5.3.3.1 through 5.3.3.4.

5.3.3.1 Direct-Attached Backup

Direct-attached backup was the first form of backup used, simply because it emerged in the era when storage devices were typically attached directly to servers. Despite the advent of network storage, direct-attached backup remains a very popular topology for backing up Windows-based servers. Direct-attached backup is illustrated in Figure 5.3.

The advantage of direct-attached backup is that it is fairly simple. An application running on the server reads data from the appropriate disk volume and writes it to the tape device. The biggest problems with direct-attached backup are these:

- Tape devices are duplicated (one per server that needs backup), which is expensive. To put it differently, sharing the tape device between servers is difficult.
- The total cost of ownership is high because you need more administrators doing tape backups using multiple tape devices.
- Storing multiple tapes can be confusing.

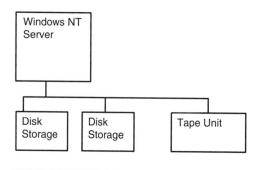

Figure 5.3 Direct-Attached Backup

■ Because the data on different servers is often duplicated, but slightly out of sync, the tape media reflects duplication of data with enough seemingly similar data to cause confusion.

■ Last, but not least, the server must be able to handle the load of the read/write operations that it performs to stream the data from disk to tape.

5.3.3.2 Network-Attached Backup

As Chapter 3 discussed, the era of direct-attached storage was followed by the client/server era with a lot of clients and servers sharing resources on a LAN. This LAN environment facilitated the possibility of having a server on the LAN with a tape backup device that could be shared by all the servers on the LAN.

Figure 5.4 shows a typical deployment scenario for network-attached backup. The left side of the diagram shows a couple of servers. These could be application or file-and-print servers, and there may be more than just a couple. The right side of Figure 5.4 shows a backup server with a tape unit attached. This tape device can be used for backing up multiple file-and-print or application servers. Thus, network-attached backup allows a tape device to be shared for backing up multiple servers, which can reduce costs.

The problems that network-attached backup introduced are these:

■ The backup operation consumes LAN bandwidth, often requiring careful segmentation of the LAN to put the backup traffic on a separate LAN segment.

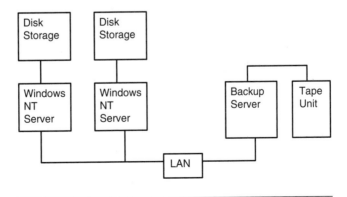

Figure 5.4 Network-Attached Backup

■ Host online hours (i.e., operating hours) increased; that is, the amount of time servers needed to be available for transactions and user access grew. In addition, the amount of data on the servers (that needed to be backed up) started increasing as well.

Increasingly, these problems led to the use of backup requirements as the sole basis for network design, determining the exact number of backup devices needed, and the selection and placement of backup devices.

5.3.3.3 LAN-Free Backup

The advent of storage area networks introduced new concepts for backup operations. The new functionality is based on the fact that a storage area network (SAN) can provide a high bandwidth between any two devices and also, depending on the topology, can offer multiple simultaneous bandwidth capability between multiple pairs of devices with very low latencies. In contrast, using Fibre Channel loop topology with many devices—that is, more than approximately 30—cannot offer multiple simultaneous high-bandwidth connections with low latencies, because the total bandwidth of the loop must be shared among all attached devices.

Figure 5.5 shows a typical SAN-based backup application. Note the FC bridge device in the figure. Most tape devices are still non-FC based (using parallel SCSI), so a bridge device is typically used. In this figure, the Windows NT servers have a presence on both the LAN as well as the SAN.

The backup topology in Figure 5.5 has the following advantages:

■ The tape device can be located farther from the server being backed up. Tape devices are typically SCSI devices, although FC tape devices are now more readily available. This means that they can be attached to only a single SCSI bus and are not shared easily among servers. The FC SAN, with its connectivity capability, neatly solves this problem. Note that one still needs a solution to ensure that the tape device is accessed properly and with appropriate permissions. Here are some possibilities:

   ■ One solution is to use zoning, allowing one server at a time to access the tape device. The problem with this solution is that zoning depends on good citizen behavior; that is, it cannot ensure compliance. Another problem with zoning is that it will not ensure proper utilization of a tape changer or multitape device.

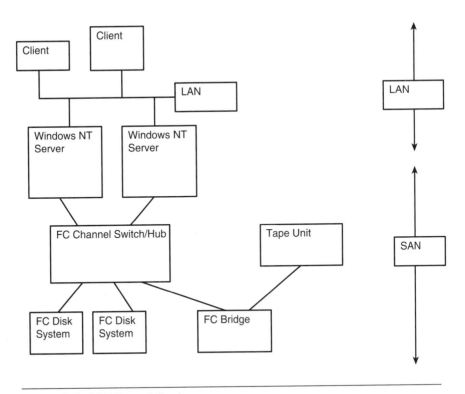

Figure 5.5 SAN-Based Backup

- Another solution is to use the SCSI Reserve and Release commands.
- Yet another solution is to have the tape device connected to a server, allowing for sharing of the tape pool by having special software on this server. Sharing of a tape pool is highly attractive because tape devices are fairly costly. IBM's Tivoli is one example of a vendor that provides solutions allowing the sharing of tape resources.
- The backup is now what is often referred to as a **LAN-free backup** because the backup data transfer load is placed on the SAN, lightening the load on the LAN. Thus, applications do not get bogged down with network bandwidth problems while a backup is happening.
- LAN-free backup provides more efficient use of resources by allowing tape drives to be shared.

- LAN-free backup and restore are more resilient to errors because backups can now be done to multiple devices if one device has problems. By the same token, restores can be done from multiple devices, allowing more flexibility in resource scheduling.
- Finally, the backup and restore operations typically complete a lot more quickly, simply because of the SAN's higher network speed.

5.3.3.4 Server-Free Backup

Server-free backup is also sometimes referred to as *serverless backup* or even *third-party copy*. Note that server-free backup is also usually LAN-free backup—LAN-free backup that also removes the responsibility of file movement from the host that owns the data. The idea is fairly simple, consisting of leveraging the Extended Copy SCSI commands.

Server-free backup began as an initiative placed before the Storage Networking Industry Association (SNIA) that evolved into the SCSI Extended Copy commands ratified by the International Committee for Information Technology Standards (INCITS) T10 Technical Committee (ANSI INCITS.351:2001, SCSI Primary Commands-2). Note that SCSI already supported a copy command, but the problem was that all SCSI devices required attachment to the same SCSI bus to use this command (the Copy command has since been made obsolete in the SCSI standards; see http://www.t10.org). The Extended Copy command adds features such that the data source and data destination may be on different SCSI buses and yet still be addressable because the syntax of the command allows for this.

In server-free backup, the backup server can remain relatively free to handle other work while the actual backup is accomplished by the data mover agent. The data is moved directly from the data source to the destination (backup media) (instead of being moved from the source to the backup server to the destination).

While appreciating the advantages of server-free backup, one should not forget that server-free restore is a very different issue. Server-free restore operations are still relatively rare; that is, backups made using server-free backup technology are very often restored via traditional restore technology that involves the use of a backup software server.

Server-free backup is illustrated in Figure 5.6. In the interest of simplicity, the figure shows the minimum number of elements needed to discuss server-free backup. In practice, however, SANs are much more complex. The figure shows a Windows server connected to an FC switch via an FC HBA. An FC-to-SCSI router is also present, to which

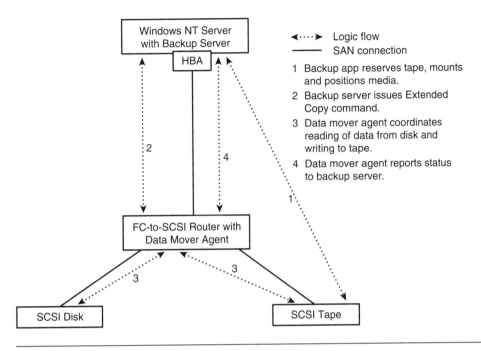

Figure 5.6 Server-Free Backup

are connected a SCSI tape subsystem and a disk device. The disk and tape devices need not be connected to the same router.

A backup server application on the Windows server discovers the data mover agent on the router, through Plug and Play. The backup application determines the details of the backup needs to be accomplished (disk device identifier, starting logical block, amount of data to be backed up, and so on). The backup server software first issues a series of commands to the tape device to reserve the tape device and ensure that the correct media is mounted and properly positioned. When that is done, the backup server software issues an Extended Copy command to the data mover, resident in the router, which then coordinates the movement of the required data. When the operation has been accomplished, the data mover agent reports the status back to the backup software on the Windows server.

Several different entities play a role in server-free backup architecture, including the data source, data destination, data mover agent, and backup server.

The **data source** is the device containing the data that needs to be backed up. Typically a whole volume or disk partition needs to be backed up. The data source needs to be directly addressable by the data mover agent (described shortly). This means that storage devices connected directly to a server (or cases in which the server and the storage device have exclusive visibility) cannot be data sources for server-free backup because they cannot be addressed directly from outside the server.

The **data destination** is typically a tape device where the data is to be written. The device may also be a disk if one is backing up to disk instead of tape. Tape devices are typically connected to a fabric port to avoid disruption of the tape data traffic upon error conditions in other parts of the SAN. For example, if the tape were connected to an FC arbitrated loop, an error in another device or, for that matter, the occurrence of a device joining or leaving the loop, would cause loop reinitialization, resulting in disruption to the tape data traffic.

A **data mover agent** typically is implemented in the firmware of a storage router because the data mover agent must be able to act on the SCSI Extended Copy command, which is sent to the router in an FC packet. Switches and hubs that examine only the FC frame header are not readily suited to house data mover agents, though this may change in the future.

The data mover agent is passive until it receives instructions from a backup server. Most tapes connected to SANs are SCSI devices, so a storage router (that converts between FC and SCSI) is typically required and provides a good location for housing the data mover agent. Fibre Channel tapes are now appearing on the scene, and some vendors, such as Exabyte, are including data mover agent firmware in the FC tape device itself. In addition, native FC tape libraries are usually built with embedded FC-to-SCSI routers, installed in the library, providing the ability for the library to have a data mover built in. Note that the data mover agent can also be implemented as software in a low-end workstation or even a server. Crossroads, Pathlight (now ADIC), and Chaparral are some examples of vendors that have shipped storage routers with data mover agents embedded in the firmware. A SAN can have multiple data mover agents from different vendors, and they can all coexist.

Of course, to be usable, a data mover agent needs to be locatable (via the SCSI Report LUNs command) and addressable (the WWN is used for addressing) from the backup server software. The data mover agent can also make two simultaneous backups—for example, one to a geographically remote mirror to provide a disaster recovery solution—but the two commands must be built by the server that issued the third-party copy command.

The backup server is responsible for all command and control operations. At the risk of being repetitious, it is worthwhile noting all the duties of the backup server. The backup server software first ensures availability of the tape device, using appropriate SCSI Reserve and Release commands as appropriate. The backup server software then ensures that the correct tape media is mounted and positioned. It is also responsible for identifying the exact address of the data source and the data's location in logical blocks, as well as the amount of data that needs to be backed up. Once the backup server has all this information, it sends an Extended Copy command to the data mover agent. The data mover agent then issues a series of Read commands to the data source device and writes the data to the data destination.

Computer Associates, CommVault, LEGATO, and VERITAS are some examples of vendors that ship a server-free backup software solution. Storage router vendors that ship server-free functionality routinely work with backup independent software vendors (ISVs) to coordinate support because many of the implementations use vendor-unique commands to supplement the basic SCSI Extended Copy commands.

Note that although server-free backup has been around for a while, there is very little support for server-free restore.

5.3.3.5 The Windows Server Family and Server-Free Backup

A lot of the trade press and vendor marketing literature claims that a particular server-free backup solution is Windows 2000 compatible. It is worthwhile examining this claim in more detail to understand what it means. The following discussion examines each of the four components that constitute the elements of a server-free backup solution: data source, data destination, backup software server, and data mover agent.

In most cases a data mover agent outside a Windows NT server will not be able to directly address data sources internal to the Windows NT server. The HBAs attached to servers usually work only as initiators, so they will not respond to the Report LUNs command. If the Windows NT server is using a storage device outside the server—say, a RAID array connected to an FC switch—it will be visible to the data mover agent. So rather than saying that storage used by a Windows NT server cannot constitute the data source for a server-free backup, one needs to state that storage internal to a Windows NT server cannot constitute the data source.

Having the data destination internal to the Windows server is also not possible, because the data destination also needs to be directly address-able from outside the Windows box (by the data mover agent).

Having the backup software run on the Windows server is certainly feasible. The HBA attached to the Windows server can issue a series of Report LUNs commands to each initial LUN (LUN 0) that it discovers. The backup software then enumerates the list of visible devices and LUNs, and checks which ones are capable of being third-party copy agents. The backup software would have to deal with some minor idio-syncrasies; for example, some products report extra LUNs that need to be used when Extended Copy commands are being issued. Many backup applications that use these devices go through an additional discovery process to verify the data mover's functionality.

The Windows NT SCSI pass-through (IOCTL) interface is capable of conveying the Extended Copy command to the data mover agent (from the Windows NT backup server). Windows NT does not have native support for data movers; Plug and Play can discover them, but drivers are required to log the data mover into the registry.

That leaves the last case—that is, whether a Windows NT server or workstation can be used to run the data mover agent software. One advantage is that such an agent would be able to address and access the storage devices visible to the Windows server. The backup server, how-ever, which might be outside the Windows NT box, would not be able to see these storage devices inside the Windows NT server. The data mover agent needs to be capable of acting as an initiator and target for SCSI commands. Because the HBA connected to the Windows NT server rarely acts as a target, the Extended Copy command may not get through to the data mover agent.

Note that in Windows NT, an application uses the SCSI pass-through interface (DeviceIoControl with an IoControlCode of IOCTL_SCSI_PASS_THROUGH or IOCTL_SCSI_PASS_THROUGH_DIRECT) to issue SCSI commands.

5.4 Windows 2000 Backup Utility

Windows 2000 ships with a backup program that is really a light version of the VERITAS Backup Exec program. The bundled backup utility in Windows 2000 is well integrated with other components of Windows 2000; for example, it integrates with the encrypting file system and also hierarchical storage management. The backup utility offers support for backing up and restoring the encrypting file system (EFS) included with Windows 2000. Chapter 6 provides information about the EFS. The bundled backup utility is also well integrated with the Removable Storage Manager (RSM, described in Chapter 7). RSM provides support for operations essential to backup such as

- Enumerating media loaded in tape libraries
- Loading and ejecting media in tape libraries
- Providing secure access and preventing data corruption in the mounted media
- Performing housekeeping functions for managing media and tape libraries—for example, cleaning a tape drive or media library

Full-fledged backup utilities offer features that the bundled backup utility in Windows 2000 does not offer. Included are features such as

- Backup agents for enterprise applications such as SQL and IIS
- Support for backing up open files
- Higher performance
- Centralized administration capabilities, including a centralized database that includes a directory and control software for all backup devices and backup catalog(s)
- Support for Extended Copy or third-party copy data movers

Note that the backup utility bundled with Windows Server 2003 has the capability to back up open files as well, because the backup is snapshot based.

5.5 Techniques to Create a Volume Snapshot

A **snapshot** is simply a consistent point-in-time copy of a volume. Consistency in this case is defined as the original application's ability to recognize the data; for example, a Microsoft Exchange server sees a data set as a valid Exchange store, and a Microsoft SQL server recognizes a data set as a valid SQL server database. The data set being referred to here is typically a logical volume.

Volume snapshots are becoming increasingly popular and are used for various different reasons, such as the following:

- To back up a clone of a volume created with snapshot technology while the original volume continues to be used by applications. This is what Microsoft has done with the Windows XP volume shadow copy service, in which a clone of the original volume (at a given point in time) is constructed (assuming that enough free disk space is available) and used to perform backup operations.
- To create a clone of live data for use in a data mining operation.
- To create a clone of live data for testing a newer version of the application in a "live" environment.
- To create a clone of live data as part of a disaster recovery operation.

So how is a volume snapshot created? There are several possible ways, all of them essentially duplication of write operations. The only real difference in the solutions is where the write operations are duplicated. There are four possible locations:

1. **In hardware**. The first obvious way to create a volume snapshot is to have the volume mirrored by hardware and then split the mirror. With low-end hardware and purely host-based (software-based) volumes, each write operation is split into two duplicate write operations—one targeted at the original volume and the other targeted at the mirror. This approach is fairly resource intensive because both of the write operations must be completed before the write response can be sent. Write error operations also need to be handled. The advantage is that although it is resource intensive to keep a mirrored volume, breaking the mirror and thereby creating a volume snapshot is extremely fast. The high speed and reliability of hardware mirroring comes with a cost, though: the expense of the duplicate disks needed for the mirror. With high-end storage units, there is an extensive amount of per-track metadata because instead of the writes themselves being split, after the mirror split the writes are tracked in the metadata. Further, high-end storage units do not delay the mirrored writes, because the writes are declared complete once they hit the storage unit's battery-backed cache.
2. **Above the file system**. The second way to create a volume snapshot in the Windows Server family is to write a file system filter driver that sits above the file system driver—for example,

NTFS or FAT—and duplicate each IRP (I/O request packet) sent to the file system driver. This process is rather complex and cannot easily take advantage of snapshot technology provided in hardware. Examples of products that implement such filters above NTFS include St. Bernard Open File Manager, Vinca (now LEGATO) Open File Manager, and Cheyenne Open File Agent. Note that these products do not necessarily implement snapshots.

3. **In the file system itself**. Moving down the driver stack chain, the third way to implement snapshots is in the file system itself. Network Appliance's WAFL (Write Anywhere File Layout) and the Linux SnapFS file systems are examples of products that implement such functionality. Obviously these are not products that run on Windows NT. Writing a file system is fairly complex, and writing snapshot technology inside a file system makes it even more complex. There is no such method available in the native file systems included with Windows NT.

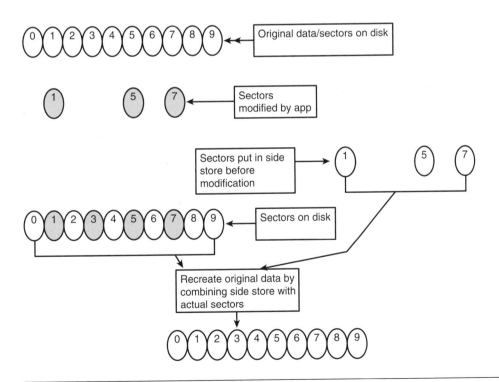

Figure 5.7 Copy-on-Write Snapshots

4. **Below the file system**. The fourth way of creating volume snapshots in Windows NT is to have a filter driver beneath the file system use copy-on-write technology. The idea is that logical blocks that are changed by an application are first copied to a side store, before the application writes are committed to those logical blocks. This is illustrated in Figure 5.7. This technique is also referred to as *differential snapshot* because only the difference is stored (rather than a complete mirror image/copy being made).

5.6 Windows XP and Windows Server 2003 Volume Shadow Copy Service

With Windows XP and Windows Server 2003, Microsoft has implemented the volume shadow copy service to provide a framework that allows a coordinated and consistent point-in-time copy of disk volumes. For legal reasons, Microsoft has chosen to refer to the functionality as a *volume shadow copy*, which is really no different from the more popularly known term, *snapshots*. Volume shadow copy service has been implemented via a filter driver (called volsnap.sys) beneath the file system.

Microsoft makes a volume shadow copy software development kit available on a nondisclosure basis. This SDK appears to be aimed at three broad categories:

1. ISVs who might wish to develop volume shadow copy writers, including Microsoft Exchange, SQL Server, Oracle, SAP, Sybase, and others.
2. ISVs developing backup and storage management applications. These vendors would develop requestors for the volume shadow copy service.
3. Independent hardware and software vendors (IHVs and ISVs) developing hardware and software for backup, fault tolerance, and data integrity. Examples include VERITAS, EMC, and their competitors in this area. These vendors would develop snapshot providers.

When an application does not have code to support the snapshot service, the application data will still be backed up in a state that will be consistent to the same degree as if the system had failed to shut down gracefully. When an application has code to support snapshot services, the application is expected to provide those services in a restore operation as well. This is logical because the application is now expected to furnish some data (such as what files need to be backed up, and a backup and restore methodology) when a backup is requested, and it is expected to interpret and act on this same data when presented with the data upon a restore operation.

The major advantage is that backup or restore, as it exists in Windows operating systems, is a tricky business that may not work reliably 100 percent of the time. The new snapshot service will facilitate total reliability while also enabling more complicated scenarios that until now were not possible in Windows.

The volume shadow copy architecture shipping with Windows XP and Windows Server 2003 consists of four types of modules, as shown in Figure 5.8:

1. Writers
2. Requestors
3. Volume shadow copy service
4. Providers

These modules are described in detail in Sections 5.6.1 through 5.6.4.

As far as the different modules that constitute the snapshot functionality are concerned, snapshot provider 2 has a kernel mode component,

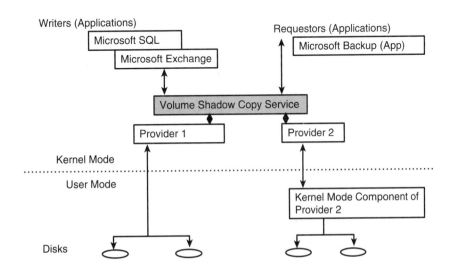

Figure 5.8 Volume Shadow Copy Architecture

and snapshot provider 1 does not. The snapshot provider service is shown in gray in Figure 5.8 to signify that Microsoft supplies this functionality and that vendors do not have to bother writing such a service. Microsoft also provides some of the other components shown, but their functionality is limited either in terms of working with a specific application or in terms of the range of features provided; hence vendors are expected and encouraged to write these components using the snapshot SDK.

Writers and providers need to implement a Component Object Model (COM) out-of-proc provider as described in the volume shadow copy SDK.[1] A provider is typically implemented as a finite state machine. The state machine transitions from one state to another upon receipt of an event that is generated by the shadow copy service. A provider will receive an event (generated by the shadow copy service), but exactly which event depends on the current state of the provider and whether an error has occurred. To state this differently, a provider has a preferred event that it expects to arrive, allowing it to transition to the next normally expected state. However, an error may occur and the provider may receive a different (from the expected) event, and the provider should be able to handle that as well.

The Microsoft shadow copy framework in Windows Server 2003 and Windows XP provides some core functionality needed for storage management, including the following:

- Defining the point in time at which the snapshot is triggered
- Providing synchronization services among applications, databases, operating systems, and file systems to flush cached data, suspend writers, create the snapshot, and provide notification to applications, databases, and operating system elements that they can resume normal mode of operation

---

1. For the benefit of readers unfamiliar with COM, suffice it to say that COM is an extremely important architecture in the Windows world that allows software to be constructed as a series of objects that interact with each other. These COM objects can be written in a variety of programming languages, such as C, C++, and Visual Basic, to name just a few. COM allows two interacting objects to be locally situated on the same machine or to be running on two separate machines altogether. Either these two interacting objects can both be running in the same process (if they are both on the same local machine), or they may be running in two separate processes. In the case of separate processes, COM provides mechanisms for interprocess communication. To summarize, an *out-of-proc* provider is simply a provider, implemented as a COM object, that runs in a separate process context.

- Providing a single API that can be used by backup/restore applications
- Providing a platform for managing the snapshot

The Microsoft shadow copy framework can handle a set of volumes for which a snapshot must be done as a single set. The only behavior supported is "all or none"; that is, if any one operation fails, all of them fail. The Microsoft shadow copy framework also issues a request (to the snapshot provider) to delete the snapshot when the requestor application is done with the snapshot. If the snapshot needs to be available later, the snapshot provider or requestor application must provide the necessary functionality. ISVs can build applications that can create, catalog, and manage multiple snapshots using the shadow copy architecture; however, such applications are not part of the Windows Server 2003 product available from Microsoft.

5.6.1 Writers

Snapshot **writers** are simply the applications that write data (applications simply reading data are not much of a problem). Examples of snapshot writers include Microsoft Exchange, Microsoft SQL Server 2000, SAP, and Oracle. Microsoft and third-party ISVs are both expected to develop snapshot writer–aware applications. Snapshot writers should be developed with the snapshot SDK. In particular, snapshot writers will receive two events from the snapshot service indicating that they should freeze all write activity, and a different thaw event indicating that write activity can now happen (hopefully signifying successful creation of the snapshot). There are other events that the writers can get from the snapshot service, and details can be obtained from the snapshot SDK. Because the applications can define the consistency of data they expect to achieve, they should be able to perform the quiesce operation fairly quickly.

Further, it is worthwhile understanding one big advantage of the volume shadow copy service architecture over traditional hardware-based snapshot mechanisms used with Windows 2000 and previous Windows versions. With these classic versions of creating a snapshot, the hardware-based mechanism had no means of determining the state of the application and of the operating system software and cache in particular. This meant that an appreciable percentage of the snapshots were inconsistent. Further, the only way of determining the health of the snapshot created required running an application data consistency checker, which could run for hours.

By comparison, the volume shadow copy–based architecture not only attempts to flush caches and hold writes, but it can also determine in a matter of a minute or so, whether the created snapshot is consistent or not. Once the thaw event has been signaled, the volume shadow copy service simply interrogates the writers as to whether they successfully managed to hold their write operations between the freeze and thaw events. If any of the writers failed, the snapshot is deemed to have failed.

Snapshot writers are also expected to provide data required for backup and restore—for example, what files need to be copied, what files need to be excluded, what collection of objects needs to be treated collectively as a single set. This data is stored by the snapshot service in a writer metadata document that is in XML format. Writers can also use this document to store data that is of interest to them. To restore data, the application simply hands the collection of data to the writer application to accomplish the restore operation.

Microsoft has announced that it will ship a SQL Server 2000 and Exchange writer, as well as writers for various other components of the Windows Server operating system. Microsoft is cooperating with ISVs to develop writers for other applications, including Active Directory.

5.6.2 Requestors

Requestors are typically backup applications that request the creation of a snapshot by making the appropriate API call to the volume shadow copy service provided by Microsoft. What's interesting here is the fact that the model remarkably simplifies some issues for the backup application writer. The backup application no longer has to solve the difficult issue of where the data to be backed up is, or what part of the data consists of application log files and what special treatment those files merit.

The appropriate writer (e.g., Microsoft SQL Server) is responsible for specifying the files and directories that should be included in the backup. Restore operations also become a lot simpler because the restore application again does not have to locate the data and figure out what files to pass to what API of the application (such as Exchange or SQL). The restore application simply hands the collection of data to the writer (application) and lets it accomplish the restore operation.

5.6.3 Volume Shadow Copy Service

The Windows NT **volume shadow copy service**, written by Microsoft, coordinates the activities for all the snapshot components. In particular, it provides the following:

- A single interface for backup applications or snapshot requestors to deal with, rather than multiple APIs from multiple applications.
- A single interface to produce, manipulate, and delete a crash-consistent volume snapshot or ghost volume.
- A single interface to allow different applications and snapshot providers to register and deregister as snapshot writers or snapshot providers.
- Synchronization and coordination among the various components to accomplish creation, deletion, or movement of snapshots, as well as backup and restore operations. The service prioritizes snapshot providers like this: Hardware providers have the highest priority, software providers are next, and the default Microsoft-provided snapshot provider has the lowest priority.

ISVs do not need to worry about writing a volume shadow copy service. Think of the snapshot service provided by Microsoft as being akin to a print spooler. You need only one print spooler. Some vendors (such as the provider vendors) simply need to write the equivalent of a printer driver. Other vendors need to write the equivalent of a printing application.

5.6.4 Providers

Snapshot **providers** are expected to be written by ISVs and IHVs to create, delete, and manipulate snapshots. As described earlier in this chapter, snapshot providers need to be written as a COM out-of-proc provider, via the snapshot SDK.

The provider may also have a kernel mode component—for example, a filter driver that is located between the file system and the Logical Disk Manager (LDM). This kernel mode functionality may also be optionally implemented in hardware instead. Note that even a hardware-based provider will still leverage the rest of the functionality provided by the framework—for example, definition of the point in time, I/O synchronization, and platform for building storage management applications, including backup, restore, and snapshot management applications.

One prime example of a snapshot provider is the volsnap.sys driver that ships with Windows XP and is also expected to ship with Windows Server 2003. This provider uses copy-on-write technology to create the necessary minimal data in a side store to be able to re-create the volume at a given point in time. The big assumption is that the required amount of free disk space is indeed available. This provider can handle NTFS, FAT32, and raw volumes on Windows Server 2003. However, this snapshot provider can provide only read-only snapshots and handle only one snapshot per volume. This limitation is in the provider itself and not the infrastructure. ISVs and IHVs can build richer functionality in their providers and writers if they so desire.

A complete description of all the events that are signaled to the snapshot provider via its COM provider is available in the snapshot SDK. A couple of important events are discussed here:

- **PreCommitSnapshot**. When the snapshot provider receives a PreCommitSnapshot event, it should start all I/O operations that take a long time—for example, synchronizing of the mirror.
- **CommitSnapshot**. When the provider receives a CommitSnapshot event, it should recognize that the snapshot service will time out the operation within 10 seconds. Hence the functionality here should be extremely fast. Further, until the snapshot is completed, Windows NT will wait to send any write operations to the volumes for which snapshots are being made. This means the provider should not do any I/O on this volume, and if it does, it should not expect the I/O to complete until the snapshot is either complete or is aborted.

Snapshot providers must provide certain mandatory functionality and may provide functionality that exceeds the mandatory functionality. The mandatory functionality is as follows:

- Providers are responsible for locating the storage needed to create the snapshot. The framework provided by Microsoft does not provide any such functionality.
- The provider must mount the snapshot in a different namespace and not have the snapshot mounted as a separate volume. An inspection of Windows XP shows that the Microsoft snapshot provider mounts the snapshot at \Device\HarddiskSnapshotX.

5.6.5 Windows NT I/O Subsystem Modifications

Though the modifications to the Windows NT I/O subsystem are not explicitly part of the snapshot environment, it is worthwhile noting that a fair amount of work was needed in the file systems, I/O stack, and file system filter drivers to accomplish a consistent and reliable point-in-time snapshot. In particular, Microsoft added two IOCTLs that all file systems and file system filter drivers need to implement:

1. **IOCTL_VOLSNAP_FLUSH_AND_HOLD_WRITES**, which should be both chained on and acted upon. The chaining is to allow drivers farther down the stack chain to also act on the IOCTL. The action consists of flushing and holding all file system metadata. Once all data has been flushed, no further writes should be issued until the outstanding IRPs issued to flush all data and metadata have completed.
2. **IOCTL_VOLSNAP_RELEASE_WRITES** also needs to be chained on and acted upon. This IOCTL indicates either successful completion of the snapshot or abandonment of the snapshot operation.

Some relevant portions of the Windows NT operating system have also been modified to trigger these IOCTLs at the appropriate time. Although Microsoft has already modified the file system and file system filter drivers that it ships to provide this functionality, ISV-shipped filter drivers need to do the same.

Section 5.8 describes an industry standard called Network Data Management Protocol (NDMP). But before that topic is discussed, it is worthwhile noting the relationship between volume shadow copy architecture in Windows XP/Windows Server 2003 and NDMP. The shadow copy architecture is a means of creating a clone of the data that needs to be backed up; NDMP can be used to move the data from the clone to tape or other backup media.

5.7 Windows-Powered NAS Devices and Snapshots

Microsoft offers a version of Windows NT that is sometimes referred to as "Embedded NT" and more often as the Server Appliance Kit, or SAK. This offering is based on Windows 2000, which does not have a volume shadow copy service. For the benefit of original equipment manufacturers that use the SAK to build NAS devices, Microsoft has licensed a snapshot solution and included it in the SAK. This snapshot product is the Persistent Storage Manager (PSM) from Columbia Data Products. This section provides a quick overview of PSM architecture and functionality.

PSM architecture is shown in Figure 5.9. PSM has a user mode component that facilitates snapshot management, including initiation and scheduling of snapshot creation. The snapshots are created via the services of the PSM filter driver that is layered over the disk class driver as shown in Figure 5.9.

PSM offers the ability to create multiple snapshots and manage them. Snapshots can be created according to a schedule, and older snapshots may be saved or written over. One can also "mount" the older snapshots and use them for backup or other purposes. Each snapshot has a date and timestamp associated with it.

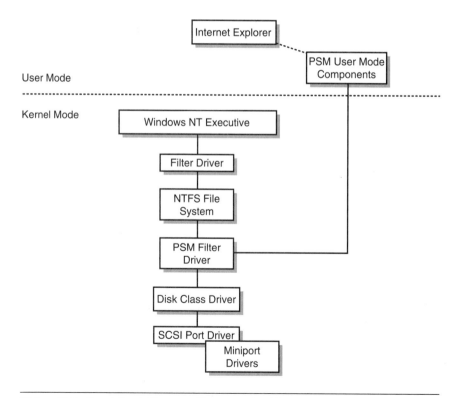

Figure 5.9 Persistent Storage Manager Architecture

5.8 Network Data Management Protocol

NDMP started as an effort primarily by Network Appliance and Intelliguard (now part of LEGATO) to provide some enhanced functionality in backup/restore applications, such as the following:

- A means to reduce and at least isolate operating system–dependent portions of backup/restore software by dividing up the functionality in a modular way
- A standardized means of communication between modules
- A means to separate the movement of data and commands onto separate channels or even networks
- Multivendor software integration

NDMP is now positioned as an open-standard protocol aimed at standardizing backup and restore operations in NAS environments. In the future, NDMP may evolve—for example, to also involve mapping of third-party copy to NDMP.

NDMP can be run in a wide variety of network environments—for example, Ethernet, Gigabit Ethernet, Fibre Channel—as long as the network transport protocol used is IP (Internet Protocol). The NDMP server and agents communicate using IP, and the NDMP server then issues the appropriate block-level SCSI commands.

NDMP is NAS centric and defines a way to back up and restore some data from a device, such as a NAS appliance, on which it is difficult to install a backup software agent. In the absence of NDMP, this data is backed up as a shared drive on the LAN that is accessed via network file protocols such as CIFS or NFS.

NDMP offers several advantages:

- Interfaces are implemented by vendors that have core competencies and can concentrate on their core competencies.
- The interfaces are standardized, offering Plug and Play possibilities for modules from different vendors.
- NDMP can cut down the LAN bandwidth requirements by offering data flow directly between primary and secondary storage without requiring data to flow to the backup software server and from there to the other device.
- NDMP can have the best of both worlds in that it can be controlled centrally via an NDMP control session, yet the data flow can still be local via NDMP data sessions.

5.8.1 NDMP Architecture

NDMP defines a standardized way to break up the backup and restore operations into multiple modules, with the idea that each vendor implements some of the modules. NDMP defines the following entities:

- A data mover agent
- NDMP services
- NDMP sessions

These are described in Sections 5.8.1.1 through 5.8.1.3.

5.8.1.1 Data Mover Agent

A **data mover agent** (**DMA**) is the primary backup application. It establishes NDMP sessions with NDMP service providers (described next) and orchestrates the sequence of steps required to establish a backup or restore operation. The data mover agent is also sometimes referred to as an **NDMP client**.

5.8.1.2 NDMP Services

NDMP defines services that may act as consumers or producers or allow one device to be both a consumer *and* a producer of data streams. NDMP v5 defines three kinds of services:

1. A **data service** that interfaces with the primary storage device (such as a NAS device). This service interacts with the volume or file system that is being either backed up or restored.
2. A **tape service** that interfaces with the secondary storage device, typically a tape device.
3. A **translator service** that performs transformations on data, including multiplexing multiple data streams into one data stream and vice versa.

5.8.1.3 NDMP Sessions

NDMP services interact with each other using NDMP interfaces. The result of this interaction is the establishment of an NDMP session that is termed a **control session** if the session is being used to achieve control for the backup or restore operation or **data session** if the session is being used to transfer actual file system or volume data (including metadata). There is exactly one control session between each NDMP service and the data mover agent. Control sessions are always TCP/IP based; data streams can be TCP/IP or SAN based. Even though the data streams can be SAN based, the requirement that the control session be TCP/IP based pretty much dictates the presence of a LAN. Data streams may be either between the DMA and an NDMP service or directly between two NDMP services.

The DMA and services can be distributed on two or more computers. Figure 5.10 shows NDMP in operation with just two computers. The NDMP DMA contacts the NDMP server and orchestrates the data movement between the primary and secondary storage devices. The data sessions are established between the NDMP server and the data source and data destination.

Figure 5.11 shows a conceptual implementation of NDMP on Windows NT. The NDMP DMA establishes two NDMP control sessions, one with each NDMP server. The data flows directly between the two NDMP servers and is not "dragged" from one NDMP server to the NDMP DMA and from there to the other NDMP server.

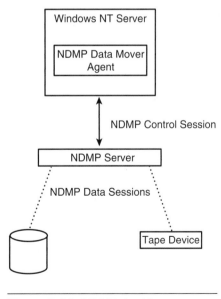

Figure 5.10 NDMP Architecture

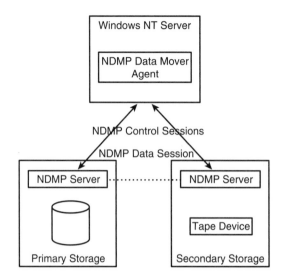

Figure 5.11 Conceptual Windows NT NDMP Implementation

5.9 Practical Implications

High-end storage, which can track metadata on a per-sector basis, allows backup/restore operations to be more efficient by allowing changes to be tracked very closely and having backup operations deal with just changed data.

To be certain that a snapshot is consistent from an application's point of view, it is essential to have the operating system (including file systems) and the application participate in the process of flushing the cache and temporarily suspending write operations while the snapshot is made. The volume shadow copy service shipping with Windows Server 2003 provides the needed operating system and file system support, as well as architecture for the needed application support. Microsoft Exchange and Microsoft SQL Server are two important applications that will take advantage of this architecture.

It remains to be seen how quickly other vendors adopt and support the volume shadow copy architecture.

5.10 Summary

Backup operations have evolved in terms of both user requirements and the technology used to accomplish backups. Usage requirements have dictated that backups be made more frequently, yet without disrupting application access to data. Backup operations evolved from stand-alone backups to backup operations happening across a LAN to backup operations happening in a SAN environment. One problem that backup applications need to solve is backing up open files being accessed by active programs while the backup is being done.

In addition, backup applications have had to deal with a multitude of APIs that are specific to an application version and specific to an operating system version. Yet another trend has been to create the initial backup from disk to disk, via a snapshot operation. Backup to tape is increasingly becoming a secondary backup operation, from the snapshot volume to tape.

The Windows volume shadow copy service provides an efficient way to create snapshots. The architecture provides for all important components, including major applications such as databases and messaging servers to participate in the snapshot creation. Microsoft provides only the infrastructure to create a snapshot. Software vendors may use this infrastructure to build an application that can create and manage multiple snapshots.

Once a snapshot has been created, a backup may be created from the snapshot. Standard protocols such as NDMP may be used to accomplish the backup operation.

CHAPTER 6

File Systems

A file system provides some essential functionality, including the following:

■ Maintaining data integrity while meeting user needs in terms of providing functionality to create, delete, read, and write files.

■ Providing high throughput and performance while showing resiliency to system and disk failures.

■ Providing support for a wide variety of devices, such as fixed disks and removable disks, and each of these with a wide range of size and performance.

■ Providing an abstraction for applications such that they need not bother about the physical characteristics of the underlying storage device or where exactly within that device the data of interest to the application for a given I/O resides. Applications simply treat a file as a series of linear bytes and seek within that series of bytes, doing read or write operations at will.

■ Providing an abstraction that allows an application to organize files into a hierarchy—for example, a directory containing other files and directories. In practice, the hierarchy is really an illusion maintained by the file system, since all data is just on the disk in random clusters.

■ Providing a security layer for data; for example, NTFS enforces the mandate that only authorized users are allowed access to appropriate resources such as files, directories, or volumes.

■ Providing support for concurrency—that is, allowing multiple users and multiple I/Os from each user—while also providing a serialization and locking mechanism that allows a particular user I/O operation to uniquely own a file or portion of a file. The file system must also recover from crashes of applications that may own file system resources such as a lock on a byte range of a file.

File systems do not reside in a vacuum; they reside on media of some sort. Although optical media such as CDs and DVDs have file systems as well, this book is about enterprise storage on Windows, and enterprise storage deals primarily with disks. Hence it is essential that one understand how Windows NT organizes disks. The first part of this chapter is dedicated to explaining how Windows NT organizes disks in terms of basic disks, dynamic disks, and their relationships to partitions and volumes.

After this discussion, the chapter moves on to describe significant details of the NTFS file system. This segment includes a description of important internal data structures, such as the master file table, as well as a description of features such as compression, the change log journal, link tracking, reparse points, and the encrypting file system.

The last part of the chapter is dedicated to describing SAN file systems, including advantages of a SAN file system and the technical issues in building one. Some vendor offerings in this area are also briefly examined.

6.1 Disks, Partitions, and Volumes

The term **disk** is used to refer to physical media such as IDE or SCSI drives, as well as to removable media disks such as USB drives and CD-ROM or DVD disks. A disk is logically thought to consist of multiple clusters that are specified in terms of the amount of data that a cluster can store—for example, 512 bytes, 1,024 bytes, 4,096 bytes. The term *disk* is always used to refer to a physical entity that one can touch and feel. In contrast, the terms *partition* and *volume*, explained in the next couple of paragraphs, represent logical concepts.

For administrative purposes, some disks (but not all)[1] may be divided into multiple logical divisions called **partitions**. Each partition has a capacity specified in the amount of data the partition can hold, and this value is an integral number of cluster units. For example, a disk with an 80GB capacity might be divided into two partitions—one dedicated to installation of the operating system and utilities, and the other dedicated to user data. Another popular reason for having a small separate partition on enterprise servers is to install some diagnostic programs on the partition.

A **volume** is a collection of one or more partitions. The combination may be for purposes of ensuring speed, capacity, data integrity, or a

---

1. Some examples of disks that are not divided (i.e., have only a single partition) are CD-ROM disks and DVD disks.

combination thereof. For example, two partitions may be concatenated to ensure a larger volume, or two partitions of equal size may be combined into a single mirrored volume in which the data is duplicated on each partition. These ideas are expounded further later in this chapter and in the description of RAID in Chapter 9. Note that there are some caveats as to how partitions may be combined; depending on the type of disk and the version of the Windows Server operating system. These caveats are also examined in more detail in this chapter.

To be concise, file systems reside on volumes. Volumes consist of one or more disk partitions. Disk partitions are logical divisions of a physical disk. Figure 6.1 shows this layering. The top layer is the file system layer, the next is the volume layer, and the bottom layer is the disk partition layer.

Figure 6.1 shows NTFS on volume V1, which itself is built by concatenation of the partitions D1-P1 and D2-P2. NTFS is also installed on volume V2, which is built by mirroring of partitions D1-P2 and D2-P1 (which must be identical in size). To indicate that volume V2 is constructed differently, the relationship between the volume and the constituent partitions is shown with dashed lines. FAT is installed on volume V3, which is built on just one partition, D3-P1. Disk D1 is divided into

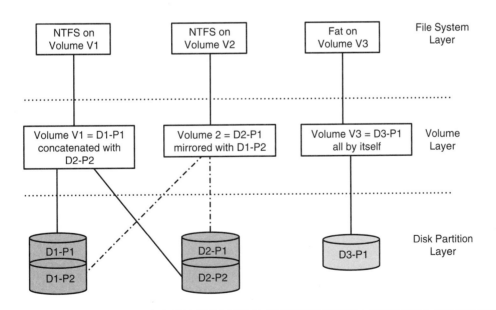

Figure 6.1 Disks, Partitions, and Volumes

two partitions: D1-P1 and D1-P2. Disk D2 is divided into two partitions: D2-P1 and D2-P2. Disk D3 is divided into just a single partition, D3-P1. Note that this figure is illustrative and does not represent all possible ways of building volumes.

With these concepts in mind, we can look more closely at details. In particular, the explanation of a partition as simply a collection of disk clusters left out some important details, such as how an operating system collects data on the number of partitions that exist on a particular disk and where a particular partition begins and ends. The answers to these questions are a little involved and are explained in Sections 6.1.1 (Basic Disks) and 6.1.2 (Dynamic Disks). In addition, as will be explained, whereas partitions on basic disks are called *hard partitions*, partitions on dynamic disks are called *soft partitions*. The terms are meant to reflect the fact that hard partitions are fixed in size (and cannot be extended or shrunk), whereas soft partitions may be shrunk or extended, even while they are actively being used.

One further caveat should be noted. This book refers to a hierarchy of disks being divided into partitions and partitions being combined into volumes. Beware, however, that a lot of literature uses the terms *volume* and *partition* interchangeably, especially when assuming that a volume consists of only a single partition. Further, a lot of literature also uses the terms *partition* and *disk* interchangeably. Throughout this discussion, keep in mind that there is a three-tier hierarchy here. Physical disks are subdivided into logical entities called *partitions*, and these logical entities can then be combined in some fashion into yet another logical entity, called a *volume*. File systems always use volumes.

6.1.1 Basic Disks

The idea of dividing disks has been around for a while. The term **basic disk** was coined in the Windows 2000 time frame to describe disks that have a legacy DOS-style mechanism of describing how a particular physical disk has been divided into logical partitions.

The first physical sector on any disk, regardless of whether it is a basic disk or a dynamic disk, is special. This sector contains a data structure called the *Master Boot Record* (*MBR*) that provides information about how the disk is organized and also plays a role in booting the system. The MBR is always the same in the PC world, no matter what the operating system. It can be up to 512 bytes in size and always consists of four elements:

1. A **boot program** that can be up to 442 bytes in size. This code is responsible for scanning the partition table (described below), locating the start sector for the active partition, loading the contents of this sector into memory, and transferring control to this code in memory.

2. A 4-byte unique number called the **disk signature**. The disk signature is always located at offset 0x01B8 (from the start of the sector) and is used as an index to the registry to store and retrieve information about the disk.

3. A **partition table** that can have up to four entries. The first entry is always at offset 0x01BE, and each entry is exactly 16 bytes long. One of the partitions described in this table is marked as the primary partition. This is the partition from which the system is booted. The first sector of each partition is referred to as the volume boot sector (VBS) and is similar in concept to the MBR. The difference is that there is only one MBR per physical disk, but there is one VBS per partition. Thus a single physical disk may have multiple volume boot sectors existing on it. Each VBS has information about the volume, such as the size, number of sectors, and label. The VBS also contains the actual boot code, which is loaded and executed by the boot code on the MBR.

4. An **end-of-MBR marker** that is always set to 0x55AA.

Notice that the MBR can accommodate only four partition entries, implying that the disk can be subdivided into a maximum of four partitions. To provide for more than four partitions, one of the four partitions may be designated in a special manner (called an *extended partition*), and that partition may itself have another partition table. This recursion of partition tables can theoretically continue without any limit.

Basic disks are supported as legacy devices on Windows 2000, Windows XP, and Windows Server 2003. Although this support is welcome, it is not without some caveats.

One caution is that Windows 2000, Windows XP, and Windows Server 2003 do not support the creation of fresh complex volumes from hard partitions existing on basic disks. *Complex volume* is a term used to refer to volumes that combine hard partitions from different basic disks. An example of a complex volume is a volume that concatenates two hard partitions existing on two different basic disks to create a single large volume. Such a volume was called a *spanned volume* in the Windows NT 4.0 time frame. On basic disks, existing spanned volumes can be supported in Windows 2000 and Windows Server 2003, but new ones may not be created.

Legacy complex volumes that were already created in the pre-Windows 2000 time frame may be imported and are indeed supported by Windows 2000, Windows XP, and Windows Server 2003.

Basic disks have some drawbacks. For one, they are highly sensitive to any corruption or failure of the first sector containing the MBR. Only a hardware RAID (redundant array of independent disks) solution will suffice. Software RAID cannot help for several reasons. (RAID is discussed in Chapter 9.) The MBR data is not duplicated by software RAID, and for a very good reason: When the system is booting and the MBR is accessed, the software RAID driver has not yet been loaded; hence it cannot help fix any data corruption in the MBR.

Another drawback is that configuration changes to basic disks need a system stop and restart.

6.1.2 Dynamic Disks

Windows 2000 introduced the concept of **dynamic disks**. Dynamic disks are designed to overcome the limitations of basic disks.

Dynamic disks can be reconfigured on the fly, even while applications (and file systems) are accessing the disk. The server does not need to be restarted for the new configuration to be visible. Volumes on a dynamic disk can be reconfigured without access to the volume having to be interrupted or the system having to be rebooted. Dynamic disks also are more fault tolerant than basic disks because essential disk configuration information is stored redundantly, both within a single physical disk and also replicated across other physical disks that are members of the same disk group.

As shown in Figure 6.2a, each dynamic disk maintains a 1MB database (the Logical Disk Manager, or LDM, database) at the end of the (physical) disk. In an effort to prevent data corruption (e.g., from a legacy utility or a foreign operating system), all dynamic disks still have the MBR, just as basic disks do. For dynamic disks that do not have operating system files on them, the MBR is constructed to show that a single partition encompasses the entire disk.

Recall that Windows NT has the concept of a boot partition and a system partition.[2] The boot partition is where the operating system files, such

---

2. This terminology is confusing for more than one reason. The first issue is that file systems exist on volumes; hence the correct terminology should be boot *volume* and not boot

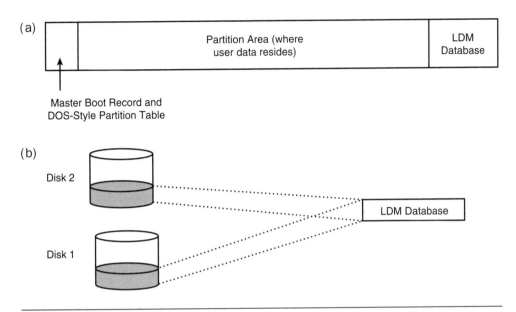

Figure 6.2 (a) Dynamic Disk Layout; (b) LDM Database Mirrored within Disk Group

as all the files in the WinNT directory, are stored. The system partition is the one where the boot code exists. Because the Windows NT booting code does not understand dynamic volumes at all, the MBR is sometimes (when the disk has the system partition on it) constructed to show a partition so that the necessary boot code may be located and executed.

Dynamic disks are organized in groups; however, the Logical Disk Manager (LDM) can support only one disk group. We construct a name for the default (and only) disk group supported by the LDM by appending the string "dg0" to the end of the computer name. As Figure 6.2b shows, this database contains information about *all* dynamic disks within the group and is replicated across all physical disks within the group, providing an element of redundancy and data protection. Figure 6.2b shows just two disks within the disk group, but there may be more. The database contains not just disk organization information, but also mount details for volumes—that is, the drive letter or directory to which the volumes on that disk are mounted.

---

partition. The second thing to remember is that the boot code is on the "system" and the operating system files are on the boot volume. The terms appear to be opposite of what one would expect. The justification is that the names should be used in the "to" sense and not "from"—that is, boot *to* this volume and not boot *from* this volume.

In essence, dynamic disks keep all information pertaining to a disk on the disk itself, and for this reason they are sometimes referred to as *self-describing disks*. In contrast, the mount information (drive letter) for basic disks is kept in the system registry.

Although dynamic disks are the favored format for the Windows NT family of operating systems, note that, as always, there are two sides to every coin. Disadvantages of dynamic disks include the following:

- They have a format that renders the disk unreadable to operating systems other than Windows 2000 or later versions when directly read by the operating system, as in a direct-attached disk or a disk attached to a fabric switch accessed by a server. Other operating systems can still access the disk by using a Windows 2000 server and connecting to a share created by the Windows 2000 server.

- Dynamic disks are not supported on laptops or removable storage such as Iomega Jazz and removable 1394/USB hard drives.

- The Microsoft Cluster Server does not support the use of dynamic disks on the cluster-shared SCSI bus, unless the VERITAS Volume Manager is also deployed. On a purely speculative note, the reasons appear to be both technical and legal in nature. Recall that only the VERITAS Volume Manager supports multiple disk groups. Clusters are often used in an active-active mode. Considering the simplest case of a cluster, a two-node cluster, one would typically divide the disk resources into two groups and assign one group to each node. When any one node failed, the disk group belonging to that node would fail over to the other node. This means that one would need two disk groups, and hence the natively shipping Logical Disk Manager, which can handle only one disk group, would not be able to handle the situation.

- The only way to convert a dynamic disk back to a basic disk is to back up all the data to another medium, reformat the disk, and restore the data.

- Support for dynamic disks is still a work in progress. In particular, because essential components such as the boot-time code do not understand dynamic disks, some elements of old-style hard partitions are still retained in the Windows operating system. Also dynamic disks are not fully supported during setup.

Windows 2000 and Windows Server 2003 support basic disks, as well as conversion from basic disks to dynamic disks. However, the conversion has some caveats, and in general it is best to back up all data to a secondary medium, delete all data and partitions from a disk, convert the "empty" disk to a dynamic disk, reorganize the disk, and restore the data. If one simply converts a basic disk to a dynamic disk, not all of the benefits of a dynamic disk may be available; for example, one may not be able to dynamically resize the (soft) partitions on a dynamic disk, if it is a dynamic disk upgraded from a basic disk rather than a freshly created dynamic disk.

6.2 Volumes and Volume Managers

As explained earlier in this chapter, volumes are an abstraction built on top of disk partitions. The disk partitions themselves may be soft partitions (existing on dynamic disks) or hard partitions (built on top of basic disks). Volumes are implemented in the Windows Server family by a device driver generically referred to as a **volume manager**. Volume managers and how they fit into the Windows storage stack were discussed in Chapter 1. This section concentrates on describing the functionality of volumes in the post-Windows 2000 world and relates that functionality to the three specific volume managers that are available for the Windows operating system in the post-Windows 2000 world:

- The **FtDisk Manager** that ships natively with Windows 2000 and Windows Server 2003. In Windows NT 4.0, the FtDisk driver was only optionally loaded because it dealt only with enhanced volume functionality such as fault tolerance. In Windows 2000, FtDisk is always loaded because it handles all volumes on basic disks.
- The **Logical Disk Manager** (**LDM**) that ships natively with Windows 2000 and Windows Server 2003.
- The **VERITAS Logical Volume Manager** (**LVM**) that is available from VERITAS as a commercial product and functionally is a superset of the Logical Disk Manager.

All of the volume managers listed here provide functionality that can be summarized as follows:

- Storage virtualization wherein a file system does not need to know which physical disk the file system is residing on. The volume manager also can concatenate multiple partitions from multiple disks into a single larger volume.

- Data protection by storing data redundantly (using some form of RAID; RAID is described in Chapter 9) or storing the data with a checksum.
- Performance by storing data in a way that it can be retrieved efficiently.

Table 6.1 summarizes the capabilities of the three major volume managers available for Windows 2000 and Windows Server 2003 products.

LDM and LVM are referred to as if they were a single entity, but each one is implemented as four different drivers, each with a varying amount of functionality. The idea is to reduce code size and complexity for normal runtime situations. In reality, LDM and LVM are implemented as four different drivers:

1. **DMConfig** is a driver that can read and update the LDM database. When any configuration changes are made, DMConfig reflects the change in a memory copy of the database. The corresponding driver for LVM is called *VxConfig*.

2. **DMIO** (dmio.sys) is the equivalent of FtDisk and implements the volume manager functionality for normal data read and write operations to the partitions. DMIO also creates the volume device objects. DMIO size is reduced because it does not have code to read or write the LDM database or interpret the LDM on disk format. The corresponding driver for LVM is called *VxIO*.

3 and 4. **DMBoot** (dmboot.sys) can only read the LDM database. DMBoot is loaded if a fourth driver, **DMLoad** (dmload.sys), determines that there are one or more dynamic disks present. Both of these are boot time–only drivers. The corresponding drivers for LVM are called *VxBoot* and *VxLoad*.

When a basic disk is converted to a dynamic disk, the old entities are transformed into new entities, as detailed in Table 6.2.

Windows 2000 introduced remarkable changes in the way volumes are managed. For example, Windows 2000 not only removes the limitation of 26 volumes, but also allows volumes to appear and disappear dynamically without requiring a system reboot. To implement these volume management changes, two new system components—the Partition Manager and the Mount Manager—were introduced. Sections 6.2.1 through 6.2.4 describe these two components, as well as the new volume management functionality.

Table 6.1 Volume Manager Capabilities

Feature	FtDisk Manager	Microsoft Logical Disk Manager (LDM)	VERITAS Logical Volume Manager (LVM)
Simple volumes (all partitions on single physical disk)	Yes	Yes	Yes
Spanned volumes (partitions that exist across multiple physical disks combined)	No	Yes	Yes
RAID 0 (striping)	Yes	Yes	Yes
RAID 1 (mirroring)	Yes	Yes	Yes
RAID 10	No	No	Yes
Maximum number of partitions that can be combined into a volume	32	32	256
Online volume creation	No	Yes	Yes
Online growth of simple and spanned volumes	No	Yes	Yes
Online growth of RAID volumes	No	No	Yes
Mirroring support	No	No	Yes, for up to 32-way mirroring
Clustering support	No	No	Yes
Multiple disk group support	No	No	Yes

Table 6.2 Windows NT 4.0 and Windows 2000 Volume Terminology

Old Entity in Windows NT 4.0	Equivalent New Entity in Windows 2000
System partition	Simple volume
Boot partition	Simple volume
Volume set	Spanned volume (a volume built out of up to 32 partitions that can exist on one or more physical disks)
Striped set	Striped volume (a RAID 0 volume built out of up to 32 partitions)[a]
Mirror set	Mirror volume (a RAID 1 volume built out of up to 32 partitions)[a]
Stripe set with parity	RAID 5[a]

[a] See Chapter 9 for a description of RAID, including RAID 0, RAID 1, and RAID 5.

6.2.1 Partition Manager

The **Partition Manager** is a driver newly introduced in Windows 2000 and also present in Windows XP and Windows Server 2003. The Partition Manager is an upper filter driver (filter drivers are described in Chapter 1) that registers with the Windows NT Plug and Play (PnP) subsystem requesting notifications for new device objects created by the disk class driver.

The Partition Manager communicates with the volume managers in general using a private interface, and it forwards notifications of device creation to the volume managers. When a volume manager finds that it has all disk partitions that collectively constitute a volume, it creates a device object representing the volume. The Partition Manager also notifies PnP of partition or device object destruction (e.g., when deleting a partition). The Partition Manager communicates with the volume managers to inform them about partitions that dynamically come and go. The functioning of the Partition Manager is further explored in Sections 6.2.3 and 6.2.4.

6.2.2 Mount Manager

The **Mount Manager** is a driver newly introduced in Windows 2000 and also present in Windows XP and Windows Server 2003. The Windows NT Mount Manager (mountggr.sys) offers functionality to provide storage management for volumes. This storage management functionality consists of

- Mounting volumes
- Dismounting volumes
- Keeping track of volume mount points and drive letters in a database file called :$MountMgrRemoteDatabase, which is present in the root directory of every NTFS volume
- Creating and destroying namespaces (and their associations) that make volumes visible to user mode applications

Not surprisingly, the Mount Manager depends on Plug and Play to be notified of events that signal volume arrival and removal. For volume mount operations, the Mount Manager consults the appropriate volume manager using the private interface. If the volume is on a basic disk, the volume manager will be FtDisk, which will consult the registry it maintains to suggest a drive letter. If the volume is on a dynamic disk, the volume manager will be LDM, which will consult the mount point information maintained in the LDM database on the dynamic disk.

The Mount Manager maintains a database of (unique) volume IDs that it has encountered before, as well as the path or drive letter on which the volume was previously mounted. When the Mount Manager is notified of the arrival of a volume and the volume manager fails to suggest a mount point, the Mount Manager consults this database and attempts to use the same drive letter or path that was used the last time the volume was mounted. If there is no entry for this volume in the Mount Manager database, or if the suggested mount point is already in use, the Mount Manager assigns the drive a new mount point. Upon device removal, the Mount Manager is also responsible for dismounting the volume. However, the entry is not deleted in the database.

The Mount Manager is responsible for assigning drive letters, as needed, for volumes on basic disks (but only for basic disks that arrive after the system has been started). The Mount Manager assigns drive letters, starting from the drive letter C:, in a prioritized fashion. Legacy fault-tolerant volume sets[3] have the highest priority, followed by a primary partition on a fixed disk, followed by removable disks (e.g., Jazz, USB), followed by CD-ROM disks. Once all of these have been taken

---

3. A drive letter assigned to a fault-tolerant volume set is stored on the volume set. When the fault-tolerant volume set is migrated, the drive letter is noted.

care of, floppy disk volumes are assigned a drive letter starting with the drive letter A:. CD-ROM drive volumes are assigned a drive letter starting with the drive letter D:.

The Mount Manager stores the assigned drive letter in the registry, ensuring that it is "sticky" in the sense that if the system configuration is changed, each partition is assigned the same drive letter it previously had. The Mount Manager does not enforce drive letter protection for partitions that are offline. Thus if a partition is assigned a drive letter and is then taken offline, the same drive letter may be reassigned to a different partition that comes online for the first time.[4]

Mount Manager operations can be controlled from the command-line utility mountvol.exe. With Windows Server 2003, Mount Manager functionality has been updated so that an application may optionally refuse to mount volumes that have never been seen on a particular system before. This is a somewhat lame attempt to provide functionality equivalent to the UNIX mount table. The idea is to prevent accidental volume corruption when a volume is exposed to a Windows system by mistake.

6.2.3 Device Tree for Volumes on Basic Disks

Once we understand the abstraction and functionality provided by volumes, it is interesting to see how volumes are handled in the storage device I/O stack. This section presents details of the storage I/O stack for a volume on a basic disk, and Section 6.2.4 presents details of the storage I/O stack for a volume on a dynamic disk.

Chapter 1 discussed the device tree for a simple volume on basic disks where the volume is built on top of only a single (hard) partition. Note that FtDisk supports legacy volumes built out of multiple partitions. In reality, the code to support volumes built out of multiple partitions is in FtDisk. Starting with Windows 2000, the tools to build a nonsimple volume on basic disks have been withdrawn.

Consider Figure 6.3. Starting from the bottom right-hand corner, the PnP subsystem and PCI bus drivers cooperate to create the PDO (physical device object) and FDO (functional device object) for the PCI bus. Next the PCI bus driver enumerates devices on the PCI bus and creates a PDO for the SCSI adapter. The SCSIPort driver creates the FDO for

---

4. For the gory details, see Microsoft Knowledge Base article number 234048, titled "How Windows 2000 Assigns, Reserves, and Stores Drive Letters."

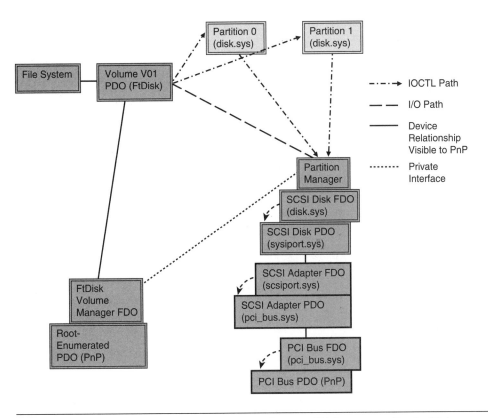

Figure 6.3 Device Object Tree for a Legacy Spanned Volume on a Basic Disk

the SCSI adapter. Next the SCSIPort driver creates a PDO for the one disk present in the system, and the disk class driver creates an FDO for that disk.

The Partition Manager watches the IRPs go by and ensures that it is in the I/O path for IRP completion. When the Partition Manager sees a IRP_MN_QUERY_DEVICE_RELATIONSHIPS request being completed, it quietly removes all details of relevant (disk) devices discovered. In this case, that would be the device objects for the two partitions, Partition 0 and Partition 1, that were created by the disk.sys disk class driver. Hence the two device objects, Partition 0 and Partition 1, are never discovered by the PnP subsystem at all. That's why the device objects for Partition 0 and Partition 1 are shaded differently from the other device objects in Figure 6.3.

The Partition Manager passes details of the device objects it discovers (and "steals") to registered volume managers. When volume managers initialize, they register with the I/O subsystem. The Partition Manager calls each volume manager in turn, passing them information about the disk device objects it trapped in the IRP_MN_QUERY_DEVICE_ RELATIONSHIPS request. The volume managers inspect the disk device objects "stolen" by the Partition Manager and either claim or reject ownership. The FtDisk manager claims ownership of all volumes not claimed by other volume managers.

In the example shown in Figure 6.3, the FtDisk driver claims ownership of these device objects. The FtDisk manager then inspects the volume configuration and determines that the volume has two underlying partitions, and it claims ownership of both the partitions. At this point the FtDisk driver creates a device object to represent the volume (called *Volume V01* in Figure 6.3). The file system can then be mounted on this volume.

What is noteworthy here is that there are actually two separate device stacks. One stack represents the logical entity, the volume; the other stack encompasses the physical devices in the system, such as the PCI bus, the SCSI adapter, and the disk drive. The volume manager acts as a bridge between the two stacks.

In Figure 6.3, the FtDisk driver sends all IRPs that it understands directly to the disk class driver. Of course, the FtDisk driver also transforms volume-relative offsets to disk-relative offsets before it does so. In addition, IOCTLs that the FtDisk driver does not understand are sent to either Partition 0 or Partition 1 as appropriate.

6.2.4 Device Tree for Volumes on Dynamic Disks

It is worthwhile examining the device tree for volumes on dynamic disks because there are some subtle differences from volumes on basic disks. Figure 6.4 shows the device tree for volumes on dynamic disks.

In the interest of keeping things simple and understandable, the volume considered here is a truly soft volume, existing on the dynamic disk. The dynamic disk does not have any operating system boot or system partitions. Thus the dynamic disk has a Master Boot Record (MBR) showing the whole disk to be a single partition. Of course, the LDM database exists on the last 1MB of space on the dynamic disk.

Figure 6.4 shows the two separate device trees that should by now be familiar: a physical device tree on the right and a logical device tree on the left, with the Logical Disk Manager spanning the gap between the two. Starting from the bottom right-hand corner of Figure 6.4, we have the PDO/FDO pair representing the PCI bus. Moving up from there, we

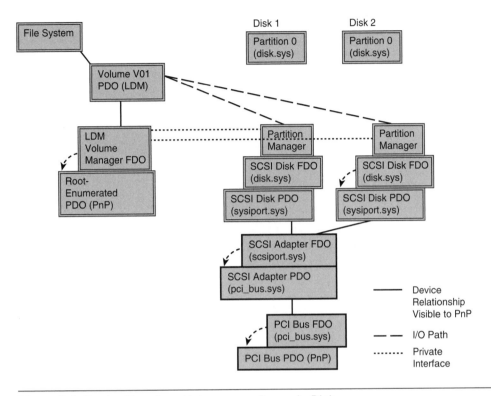

Figure 6.4 Device Tree for a Volume on a Dynamic Disk

have the PDO/FDO pair for the SCSI adapter. In this example, two dynamic disks are present. The next layer up shows the PDO/FDO pair for the two physical disks present in the system. The Partition Manager is layered over the two disk FDOs created by the disk class driver.

The Partition Manager registers a completion routine for all IRPs that it sees. In the completion routine, it pays special attention to the IRP_MN_QUERY_DEVICE_RELATIONSHIPS IRP and in particular watches for disk device objects being reported. The disk class driver, acting as a bus driver, creates a device object to represent the one partition representing each dynamic disk. The Partition Manager forwards information about these disk device objects to the registered volume managers in the system. In this example, the only volume manager shown is the LDM, which is loaded as a root-enumerated logical driver. In this case the LDM will claim responsibility for the disk device objects. Assume that the volume in question is constructed by concatenation of the two disks, to create a single large volume. The LDM inspects the volume configuration, and when it is satisfied that it has ownership of all underlying partition objects, it creates a device object representing the volume, called *Volume V01* in this example.

The LDM directs I/O from the volume object to either disk, as appropriate. Note that the two partition objects—Partition 0 for Disk 1 and Partition 0 for Disk 2—are never reported to PnP and hence are shown with no connections to other objects.

6.3 Device Namespace

The device namespace has evolved over the years with different versions of the Windows NT operating system. To allow backward compatibility, the new namespace is joined with the old namespace via symbolic links. In addition, kernel mode drivers create a namespace in kernel mode, using the services of the Object Manager. User mode applications see a different namespace, and the two are logically mapped to each other via symbolic links. Staying on top of the namespace issues is not an easy task. This section takes a humble stab at enumerating most of the storage-related important device names created.

The disk class driver creates device objects to represent each physical disk. These objects are named in the format "\device\harddiskX," where X is a number starting from value zero and increases by one for each new hard disk found on the system.

The disk class driver also creates a device object for each primary partition that it finds. The disk class driver uses the I/O Manager API IoReadPartitionTable to identify all primary partitions on a disk. These primary partitions are named in the format "\device\harddiskX\partitionY," where X represents the physical disk number and Y represents the primary partition number on that physical disk. The I/O Manager creates a symbolic link in the format "\??\PhysicalDriveX," where X is a number starting from zero that maps to "\device\harddiskX\partitionY".

The LDM volume manager creates an object for each volume that it is responsible for. This device object has a name with the format "\Device\HarddiskDmVolumes\PhysicalDmVolumes\BlockVolumeX," where X is an identifier that the volume manager assigns to the volume. This kernel mode device is mapped to a Win32 device created by the Mount Manager with the format "\??\Volume[GUID]," where *GUID* is a globally unique identifier. The LDM volume manager also creates a symbolic link in the format "\Device\HarddiskDmVolumes\ComputerName Dg0\VolumeY" for each volume and maps it to the corresponding device in the PhysicalVolumes directory. *ComputerName* is replaced with the actual computer name, and *Y* is replaced with a volume identifier.

To allow raw access to a volume, the LDM volume manager also creates an object for each volume it is responsible for. This device object has a name in the format "\Device\HarddiskDmVolumes\PhysicalDm Volumes\RawVolumeX".

Note that this section is not an exhaustive list of all the possible device names and their formats. It is simply meant to indicate the complexity involved. Avid readers are encouraged to run the Windows GUI disk and volume management tools and study the GUI output.

6.4 Nonprimary File Systems

Windows NT provides support for several different file systems, for various purposes. The primary, full-featured file system is NTFS. Microsoft has clearly indicated that the legacy FAT file system is primarily in maintenance mode, with no new significant feature development planned at all. Besides NTFS and FAT (described in the following sections of this chapter), the other file systems supported include

- An ISO 9660–compliant CD-ROM file system (CDFS) for I/O on CD-ROM disks.
- Universal Disk Format (UDF), defined by the Optical Storage Technology Association (OSTA). Support for UDF was introduced with Windows 2000. UDF will be the successor to CDFS, which also supports DVD. Windows 2000 initially shipped with only read-only support, but read and write support shipped in Windows XP.

Note that often a single Windows system may be running multiple file systems. To elaborate, a single Windows system typically has multiple volumes, and not all of the volumes need to be operating with the same file system.

6.4.1 FAT File System

Windows 2000 supports an updated version of the FAT (file allocation table) file system, with the following highlights:

- There are two versions of the FAT file system: FAT16, which uses 16-bit pointers, and FAT32, which uses 32-bit pointers.
- FAT16 supports partitions up to 4GB in size, using 64K clusters. FAT32 can support partitions up to 32GB in size, using 16K clusters.
- The root directory can contain only 512 entries.
- Compression and security are not supported.

6.5 NTFS

The NT file system was designed to be the file system of choice for Windows NT. Since its introduction, several feature enhancements have been made, but the underlying robust design has remained the same. FAT and HPFS (High-Performance File System), the existing file systems from Microsoft when NTFS was designed, were inadequate to meet NT needs. In particular,

- FAT does not offer the needed amount of file or object security.
- FAT does not have the features needed to handle the extremely large disks available today. (Recall that FAT originally was designed to handle 1MB disks.)
- Neither FAT nor HPFS offers transactional features needed to offer reliability and recovery from a system crash.

NTFS offers various features, summarized here and explored in detail later in this chapter:

- NTFS transactional features log all file system metadata changes to a log file that allows recovery in the case of a system crash.
- All data, including file system metadata, is stored in files.
- NTFS and Win32 APIs use 64-bit pointers for file data structures.
- NTFS supports file names that can be up to 255 characters long. NTFS also supports the Unicode character set for internationalization.

- The data structures support fast directory traversal and navigation.
- The file system supports compression and sparse files.
- Starting with Windows 2000, an encrypting file system is also supported.
- The file system supports fault tolerance features—for example, bad disk cluster or sector remapping.
- NTFS removes the 8.3 file name limit that MS-DOS introduced. NTFS supports case-sensitive, long file names, as well as the Unicode standard, and provides POSIX file name compatibility by supporting trailing dots and trailing spaces. However, sometimes problems arise when names that are not 8.3 compliant are used. The primary reason for the problems is that some of the tools and utilities used may not support long file names that are not 8.3 compliant. Individual file names in NTFS can be up to 255 characters long, and full pathnames are limited to 32,767 characters.
- NTFS uses 64-bit file pointers and can theoretically support a file size of 2^{64} bytes.

NTFS supports multiple data streams per file. The stream can be opened with the Win32 API CreateFile function, and a stream name in the format ":StreamName" can be appended to the end of the file name—for example, File1:Stream25. These streams allow reading, writing, or locking independently of other streams that may be open. The Windows NT Macintosh server uses this feature to support Mac clients where files have two "forks": a data fork and a resource fork.

Note that although NTFS supports multiple streams, many tools and applets do not. Thus a file with a size of 1,024 bytes in the regular unnamed stream and 1MB of data in a named stream is reported to be of size 1,024 bytes by the "dir" command (which does not support multiple streams). When a file with multiple streams copies from NTFS to FAT, for instance, only the default unnamed stream data will copy. The data in the other streams is lost.

Table 6.3 summarizes the differences between the FAT and NTFS file systems.

Table 6.3 Comparison of Windows NT File Systems

Comment	FAT16	FAT32	NTFS
Maximum length of file name	8.3	255	255
Maximum file size	2GB	4GB	Maximum theoretical 16 exabytes
Maximum size of volume	2GB	2 terabytes	2 terabytes
Compatible with floppy	Yes	Yes	No
Multiple drives in a single volume	No	No	Yes
File- and directory-level security	No	No	Yes
File- and directory-level access auditing	No	No	Yes
Fault-tolerant features (multiple copies of critical data, journaling of metadata)	No	No	Yes
Encryption and compression of files	No	No	Yes

6.5.1 NTFS System Files

NTFS organizes everything on disk as a series of files, including not just the user files, but also the files containing metadata that pertains to data internal to the file system itself. This section describes the files that NTFS uses for its internal organization process.

The **master file table** file ($Mft) is always the first file in an NTFS volume. The MFT contains multiple records and has at least one entry for every file or directory on the volume, including an entry for the MFT itself. Each entry in the MFT can be from 1,024K to 4,096K in size, depending on the size of the volume on which the file system resides. Files that have many attributes or are extremely fragmented may require more than one record. The MFT is stored at the beginning of the volume.

System performance is significantly better when the MFT records are stored in contiguous disk clusters—that is, when the MFT is not fragmented and occupies a contiguous area on the disk. To facilitate this, NTFS reserves an area called the *MFT zone* at the start of the volume or partition and attempts not to use this area for anything but MFT records. The first files or directories are stored after the MFT zone.

About 12 percent of the volume is reserved for the MFT zone. Starting with Windows NT 4.0 SP4, a new registry key was introduced to control the size of the MFT zone. This registry key can take a value between 1 and 4, indicating the size range for the MFT zone, from minimum (1) to maximum (4). The disk defragmenter indicates the current size of the MFT zone.

The first 24 entries in the MFT table are reserved for Microsoft use. Some of the entries have been reassigned between different releases of the operating system, particularly with the release of Windows 2000. Table 6.4 summarizes the various NTFS system files, also referred to as *metadata files*.

Table 6.4 NTFS System Files

File[a]	Record Number	Description
$Mft	0	Master file table
$MftMirr	1	Master file table mirror containing copy of first 16 files in the MFT
$LogFile	2	Log file (for crash recovery and file system consistency)
$Volume	3	Volume description, including volume serial number, date and time of creation, and volume dirty flag
$AttrDef	4	Attribute definition
. (dot)	5	Root directory
$Bitmap	6	Cluster allocation bitmap
$Boot	7	Boot record of drive
$BadClus	8	Bad cluster list
$Quota	9	Defined as user quota file in NT4, but never used
$Secure	9	Redefined as security descriptors in Windows 2000 and now actually used
$UpCase	10	Uppercase table
$Extend	11	Directory that contains $ObjId, $Quota, and $UsnJrnl files; used from Windows 2000 on
—	12–23	Reserved for future use

[a]By convention, the dollar sign ($) in front of a file name indicates that this is a metadata file.

The $MftMirr file mirrors the first 16 MFT entries and is simply a way to ensure that the volume is usable even if the sectors on which the MFT resides become corrupted for some reason. The $MftMirr file is stored in the middle of a volume. Larger volumes may have more than one MFT mirror.

The log file ($LogFile) is used to recover from system crashes and unexpected conditions. NTFS is a transactional, or journaling, file system: It logs all file system metadata changes to the log file before attempting to make the changes. The log files contain redo and undo information used to recover from a system crash and maintain file system consistency.

Note that the metadata stored in the transactional log file is only sufficient to ensure file system integrity—for example, to ensure that disk clusters are correctly marked as being free or belonging to a particular file and constituting a particular portion of the file data. The content of these data clusters, the actual user data, is not tracked in the transaction log. Once the transaction has been committed and the metadata is changed, a completion record entry is added to the log file.

All log file operations are accomplished by means of the NTFS log file service, which is really a set of routines in the NTFS file system driver. NTFS uses a circular buffer for the log file. The beginning area of this buffer contains a pointer to a location within the buffer where the recovery process should begin. This pointer is stored twice (redundantly) in the log file to ensure recoverability in case of corruption in one area of the log file.

The $Volume file contains the name of the volume, date, and time-stamp, indicating when the volume was created, information about the NTFS version on the volume, and a dirty bit that is used to decide whether the system was properly shut down or not. This is also the bit that is checked when a system is booted, to determine whether or not the infamous CHKDSK utility should be run.

The $AttrDef file lists all the attributes that are supported on that particular volume. For each attribute, various information, such as attribute name, attribute type, attribute minimum length, and attribute maximum length, is stored.

The root directory is another important directory. All file and directory lookup operations that are not cached from prior lookups must begin by searching this directory.

The $Bitmap file has a bit representing every disk cluster on the volume. The bit indicates whether the corresponding cluster on the disk is free or in use.

The $Boot file is a placeholder to protect the boot code that must always be at a fixed location toward the beginning of the volume. When a volume is formatted to have NTFS on it, the formatting utility ensures that the $Boot file is shown to be owning the disk clusters where the boot code resides, thus protecting the boot code.

The $BadClus file has an entry for every bad cluster on the disk. The file is dynamically updated; that is, for any new bad cluster dynamically discovered, a new entry is added to this file.

The $Secure file was introduced with Windows 2000. NTFS enforces security on each file and directory. Prior to Windows 2000, the security information was stored in each file or directory MFT entry. Because a lot of files and directories have similar access information, the security information was duplicated a lot. For example, if a user has particular access rights—for example, read and execute rights to 100 files that constitute a particular application (Microsoft Office might be a good example)—all those files will have the same security information. Starting with Windows 2000, the security information is stored only once in the $Secure file, and all the files simply refer to this security information.

The $UpCase file is a table used to convert file names and pathnames from lowercase to uppercase, and to map file names to uppercase for applications that treat file names and pathnames as case sensitive.

The $Extend directory was introduced with Windows 2000 and contains files used to implement some NTFS features that are optional. The files within the $Extend directory are as follows:

- The **$ObjId** file stores file and directory object identifiers. These object identifiers are used to track files and directories when they are migrated. For more details, see Section 6.5.15.
- The **$Quota** file is used to store quota limit information on volumes that have quotas enabled. Quota tracking is a feature described in more detail in Section 6.5.9.
- The **$UsnJrnl** file holds information related to changes made to files and directories. This is explained in more detail in Section 6.5.13.
- The **$Reparse** file holds information about all the files and directories that have a reparse point tag associated with them. Reparse points are a mechanism used to implement symbolic links and are explained in Section 6.5.22.

6.5.2 NTFS Logical Cluster Numbers and Virtual Cluster Numbers

NTFS works with an integral number of disk sectors as the basic minimum allocation unit. This unit is called a **cluster**. The cluster size for a volume is defined when the volume is formatted. Different volumes can have different cluster sizes. For the benefit of readers who are familiar with UNIX, the Windows term *cluster* is similar to the UNIX term *file system block size*. The file system decides the size of the disk cluster, taking into consideration the size of the disk and the type of file system being used. The range can be from 1K to as much as 64K. The cluster size is decided when the volume is formatted, on the basis of either the "format" command-line utility or the disk management GUI. Obviously the higher size can be wasteful; for example, to store a file of size 1K, one would still allocate one cluster of size 64K.

NTFS uses some important parameters that relate to clusters. The first one is the **logical cluster number** (**LCN**). NTFS divides the whole disk into clusters and assigns each cluster a number starting from zero. Thus the first cluster is Cluster 0, the next one is Cluster 1, the next is Cluster 2, and so on. This number, which uniquely identifies the position of the cluster within the volume, is the LCN. The second important parameter is the **virtual cluster number** (**VCN**). The VCN identifies the logical position of the cluster within a particular file. Thus an LCN of 25 indicates the twenty-sixth (start counting from zero, not one) cluster in a volume, and a VCN of 25 indicates the twenty-sixth cluster in a particular file.

To summarize, the VCN allows calculation of the position of the attribute—for example, file data offset within a file. The LCN allows calculation of the offset relative to the volume or partition for that particular data block.

6.5.3 NTFS MFT Record Structure

As discussed earlier, every file and directory on an NTFS volume has an entry in the master file table. This entry is also referred to as an MFT record. Each MFT entry is a fixed size, which is decided at disk formatting time and is typically from 1,024 bytes to 4,096 bytes. With Windows NT 3.51, the MFT entry size was set at 4K. With Windows NT 4.0, Microsoft changed this to a minimum of 1K or the cluster size, whichever is larger, after analysis showed that the MFT entries were wasting disk space.

The MFT record contains a standard header, followed by a series of attributes that are stored in the following form:

- Attribute header
- Attribute name
- Attribute data

Examples of attributes include file name, file security ACLs, and the file data. Table 6.5 summarizes the various attributes that an NTFS file or directory may have.

Table 6.5 NTFS Attributes

Attribute	Attribute Type Value	Description
$STANDARD_INFORMATION	0x10	File standard information
$ATTRIBUTE_LIST	0x20	Used to indicate nonresident attributes
$FILENAME	0x30	File name stored as a possible multivalued attribute because files can have multiple names (NTFS name, DOS name, and hard links)
$VOLUME_VERSION	0x40	Defined but unused in Windows NT 4.0; deleted in Windows 2000
$OBJECT_ID	0x40	64-byte value used from Windows 2000 on for link tracking; does not apply to prior Windows NT versions; see Section 6.5.15
$SECURITY_DESCRIPTOR	0x50	Security descriptor (file ACL); see Section 6.5.6
$VOLUME_NAME	0x60	Volume name; present only in the $Volume file
$VOLUME_INFORMATION	0x70	Volume information; present only in the $Volume file
$DATA	0x80	File user data stored as possible multivalued attribute because NTFS files can have multiple data streams

continued on page 202

Table 6.5 *(continued)*

Attribute	Attribute Type Value	Description
$INDEX_ROOT	0x90	Used in large directories
$INDEX_ALLOCATION	0xA0	Used in large directories
$BITMAP	0xB0	Used in directories only
$SYMBOLIC_LINK	0xC0	Defined but unused in Windows NT 4.0
$REPARSE_POINT	0xC0	Presence indicates file has reparse point metadata; see Section 6.5.22
$EA	0xE0	OS/2 extended attributes
$EA_INFORMATION	0xD0	OS/2 extended attributes information
$PROPERTY_SET	0xF0	Property set; defined but unused in Windows NT 4.0
$LOGGED_UTILITY_STREAM	0x100	Used by the encrypting file system; see Section 6.5.20

If the attribute data is small, it may be stored directly in the MFT record and is referred to as *resident attributes*. Alternatively, when the data is too large to be contained within the MFT, the MFT contains information about the clusters where the data is stored. Such data is termed *nonresident attributes*. There is nothing special about the file data, and it is just another attribute. Any attribute stored can be resident or nonresident.

Consider Figure 6.5, which shows some file data being stored in a nonresident fashion. The data structure involved, a **run list**, has three elements:

1. A **virtual cluster number** (**VCN**), which indicates the position of a cluster relative to a file. For example, a VCN of 0 indicates that the cluster in question is the first cluster of a file attribute.

2. A **logical cluster number** (**LCN**), which indicates the position of the cluster relative to the volume or partition. For example, an LCN of 25 indicates that the cluster in question is the twenty-sixth cluster on the volume or partition.
3. The **number of clusters** in a particular "run"—that is, the number of contiguous clusters allocated to the file attributes.

If the run list for a file does not fit into a single MFT entry, it is stored in additional MFT entries.

NTFS also supports multiple data streams. The default data stream is opened when one uses the CreateFile API and specifies just the file name using either a relative path or an absolute path. One can open a different data stream by specifying a file name followed by a colon and a data stream name—for example, \directory1\File1:DataStream2. NTFS stores this as just another attribute in the MFT and stores the data associated with this second data stream as just another attribute.

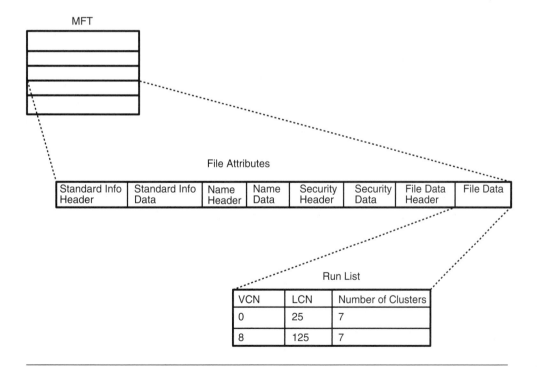

Figure 6.5 MFT Record Structure

6.5.4 NTFS Directories

NTFS directories are simply files that happen to contain directory information. NTFS stores directories in a way that facilitates quick browsing. When the data needed for a directory does not fit into the MFT, NTFS allocates a cluster and a run structure, similar to data or other attributes. All directory entries are stored as B+ trees.

A **B+ tree** is a data structure that maintains an ordered set of data and allows efficient operations to find, delete, insert, and browse data. A B+ tree consists of "node" records containing the keys, along with pointers that link the nodes of the B+ tree together. The advantage of using such a structure is that a B+ tree tends to widen rather than increase in depth, ensuring that performance does not degrade too much even when a directory has a large number of entries.

The entries within a directory are stored in sorted order. Each entry stores the file name, a pointer to the file MFT record, and the file date/timestamp stored redundantly in the directory entry (this information is already stored in the file MFT record) so as to facilitate a quick response time when somebody lists the contents of a directory. B+ trees are very efficient in terms of the number of comparisons required to find any given directory entry.

6.5.5 NTFS Recovery Log

NTFS has been designed to be a high-performance, reliable file system that can recover from system failures. To achieve this goal, NTFS logs all file system metadata changes to $LogFile before attempting to make the changes. The log files contain redo and undo information used to recover from a system crash and maintain file system consistency. Note that the metadata stored in the transactional log file is only sufficient to ensure file system integrity; for example, it ensures that disk clusters are correctly marked as being free or that they belong to a particular file and constitute a particular portion of the file data. The content of these data clusters—that is, the user data—is not tracked in the transaction log. Once the transaction has been committed and the metadata has been changed, a completion record entry goes into the log file.

All log file operations are accomplished by means of the NTFS log file service, which is really a set of routines in the NTFS file system driver. NTFS uses a circular buffer for the log file. The beginning area of this buffer contains a pointer to a location within the buffer where the recovery process should begin. This pointer is stored twice (redundantly) in the log file to ensure recoverability in case of corruption in one area of the log file. The actual recovery operation is done in multiple phases.

With Windows NT 4.0, the log file was cleared with every successful reboot. With Windows 2000, the entries in the log file can survive multiple reboots.

6.5.6 NTFS Security

NTFS security is derived from the Windows NT security and object model. Each file and directory has a security descriptor associated with it. The security descriptor consists of the following:

- A security token identifying the owner of the file.
- A series of access control lists (ACLs) that explicitly or implicitly allow access to the file for the users described within those ACLs.
- An optional series of ACLs that explicitly or implicitly disallow access to the file, for certain users; if a user exists on both the allowed and disallowed lists, no access is granted.

With Windows NT 4.0, the security descriptor was stored in the file's MFT record. Because many files and directories have similar access information, the security information was duplicated a lot. For example, if a user had particular access rights, such as read and execute rights to 100 files that constitute a particular application (Microsoft Office is a good example), all those files would have the same security information. Starting with Windows 2000, the security information is stored only once in the $Secure file, and all the other files simply have a reference to this security information.

6.5.7 NTFS Sparse Files

NTFS supports a feature called **sparse files** that allows a file to store only nonzero data. When a file is representing a data structure such as a sparse matrix, this feature is especially useful. This feature can be enabled and disabled administratively for a whole volume, a directory (and the files and directories contained within that directory), or just an individual file. This administrative setting can be overridden by a program when it is creating a file or directory. When an existing volume or directory is marked as *sparse*, no action is taken on files already existing in it. The setting applies only to new files or directories created within that volume or directory.

Sparse files and compressed files are two completely different and independent implementations, both an effort to reduce disk resource consumption. A file may be compressed and not sparse, and vice versa. Compression is explained in Section 6.5.8.

The term *sparse files* refers to files that have some data, then no data for a large byte range thereafter, then a small amount of data, and again a huge gap between that data and the next. For these empty ranges of a sparse file, NTFS does not allocate any disk clusters. Recall that a VCN defines a cluster position relative to its position in a file, and an LCN defines a cluster position relative to its offset on the volume. For sparse files, NTFS allocates the file-relative VCN, but it allocates no clusters on the volume. Thus the volume-relative LCN for some VCNs is simply unallocated. NTFS zero-fills data in the specified buffer corresponding to these gaps if an application tries to read. When an application writes data in these sparse ranges, NTFS will allocate the required disk clusters as needed.

Consider Figure 6.6. Recall that a virtual cluster number (VCN) indicates a cluster position relative to a particular file, whereas the logical cluster number (LCN) indicates the position of a cluster relative to a volume.

Figure 6.6 shows two run lists—one when a file is stored via a nonsparse technique, and the other for the same file, but stored with the sparse technique. The run list with the nonsparse technique shows three entries in the run list; the first entry starts with a VCN value of zero (indicating the start of the file), which is is stored on logical cluster 125. Four clusters accompany this information, indicating that four clusters are stored contiguously. The next entry in the run list indicates that the next portion of the file—VCN 4 (fifth cluster in the file)—starts at LCN 251 and is eight clusters long. This cluster is shown shaded in Figure 6.6 and is different from the other clusters in that there is no data in the file corresponding to this range. The last entry in this run list shows that the next cluster in the file is stored at LCN 1251.

The second run list shows the first entry to be identical. The file still has four clusters allocated starting from LCN 125. The next entry in the run list shows the last seven clusters of the file; VCN 12 (eleventh cluster in the file) starts at LCN 1251. There is no entry in the run list for the intervening portion of the file that has no data.

When data is requested from a file, NTFS accesses the file MFT record, locates the corresponding VCN in the file, looks up the corresponding LCN and translates that LCN into a volume-relative offset. If needed, the relevant part of the volume is read, via the services of the

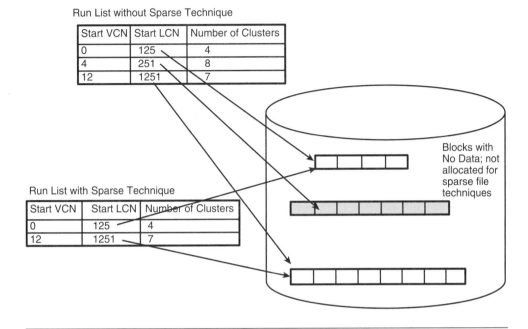

Figure 6.6 NTFS Sparse File Cluster Allocation

disk class driver and volume manager. If the LCN is not allocated, NTFS simply returns zeros in the data buffer. If an application writes to a portion of the file where no LCN is allocated, NTFS simply allocates clusters in that area and adds them to the run list. The data is then copied from specified buffers and written to those clusters.

With the falling prices of disk storage, the savings in disk space using sparse files is not so significant. What is more significant is that access to sparse files can be more efficient because a lot of disk I/O is avoided (to retrieve data that is just a stream of zeros).

Applications set file attributes to be sparse using the FSTCL_SET_ SPARSE function code to the DeviceIoControl API. Applications can query as to whether a file is sparse or not using the GetFileAttributes API.

6.5.8 NTFS Compressed Files

NTFS also supports compression on files stored in a volume with a cluster size of 4K or less. Data is compressed and uncompressed on the fly in manner that is transparent to the user when an application issues a read or write API call. Compression can be enabled and disabled administratively for a whole volume, a directory (and the files and directories contained within that directory), or just an individual file. Again, programs can override this setting when creating a file or directory. When an existing volume or directory is marked as compressed, no action is taken on files already existing in that volume or directory. The setting applies only to new files or directories created within that directory.

Compressed files are stored in runs of 16 clusters. NTFS takes the first 16 clusters of a file and attempts to compress them. If the result of the compression is 15 or fewer clusters, the file is compressed; otherwise NTFS abandons the attempt to compress.

While reading a file, NTFS needs to detect whether that file is compressed. One way of doing that is to check the final LCN in a run. A value of zero in the final LCN indicates that the run is compressed. Recall that the assignment of LCN number zero is for storing the boot sector; hence, it can never be part of a normal file (run). For a compressed file, when an application seeks to a random location, NTFS may have to decompress an entire run of clusters.

Figure 6.7 shows two run lists for the same file. With the first run list, at the top left of the diagram, no compression is applied. The file is stored in three runs of clusters, each 16 clusters long. The first 16 clusters start at LCN 125, the next 16 at LCN 251, and the last 16 at LCN 1251. The file occupies 48 clusters on the volume. With the second run list, at the bottom left in Figure 6.7, compression is applied. The file now occupies only 12 clusters, in three runs. The first 4 clusters start at LCN 125, the next 4 at LCN 251, and the last 4 at LCN 1251.

By looking at the next VCN and the number of clusters, NTFS can determine whether or not the run is compressed. Compressed data is decompressed into a temporary buffer and stored in the cache. The data is copied into an application buffer as needed.

Compression costs CPU time and delay in I/O, with a resulting drop in performance. With the rapidly decreasing prices of storage drives, it is not always an obvious advantage to use compression; hence, in Windows 2000, compression is turned off by default. Some Knowledge Base articles issued by Microsoft recommend not using compression, especially for applications that do a large amount of I/O.

Applications can set a file to be compressed using the FSTCL_SET_COMPRESSION function code to the DeviceIoControl API. Applications can use the GetFileAttributes ATP to inquire as to whether or not a file is compressed.

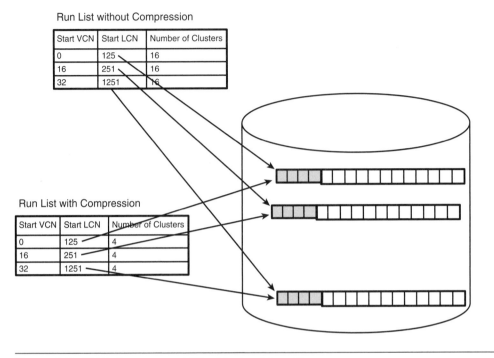

Figure 6.7 NTFS Compressed File Cluster Allocation

6.5.9 NTFS User Disk Space Quotas

With Windows 2000, Microsoft introduced features whereby NTFS supports tracking, the issuance of alerts, and limits on disk resource usage on a per-user basis. These are features of NTFS, and not of the Windows 2000 operating system itself. Hence they are not available on other file systems, such as FAT or UDF. The highlights of the quota implementation are as follows:

■ Quotas are implemented and tracked on a per-volume and per-user basis. All data associated with quotas is kept within the NTFS file system on the volume in the $Quota file that resides in the $Extend directory. Different users may be assigned different quota limits. System administrators are not subject to quotas. Further, default quota limits may be defined that will apply to a new user when the user first starts using disk resources.

- System administrators have tools for quota management by which the quotas on a volume can be set to one of three states:
  1. Disabled. In this state NTFS retains the information, taking no action. If quotas on the volume are reenabled, then this retained quota information is instantly available for use.
  2. Enabled for tracking purposes only.
  3. Enabled for tracking and limiting disk resource usage—that is, limiting the amount of disk space used.
- When a user exceeds the warning limit on disk quota, NTFS creates an entry in the Windows NT event log file. Only one such entry per user is written within an hour, though the user may repeatedly exceed the warning quota.
- Quota calculations report the length of a file as if the compressed clusters were uncompressed and as if the sparse clusters that were not allocated appeared allocated. The size calculation takes into account the size of the disk cluster allocated to the file. Thus a file that is only 5,000 bytes long may be reported as using 8,192 bytes toward disk resource usage if the file is using two disk clusters, each of size 4,096 bytes. The apparent thought behind such a design is to handle cases in which a user has files on a compressed volume and then attempts to copy those files to another volume that is uncompressed and gets errors about quotas being exceeded. With the design as described, quotas may be compared across volumes irrespective of the compression state.
- Quota settings are administered by the Microsoft-supplied GUI management tools. Dragging and dropping quota information from one volume to another, in order to have the same quota settings applied on both volumes, allows for easy administration of these settings. Further, exporting quota settings into various formats, including CSV (comma-separated values) and Unicode text, provides additional setting administration. These settings can then be imported into a tool of the users' choice—for example, Excel—and manipulated there.

6.5.10 NTFS Native Property Sets

Windows 2000 introduces support for native property sets that consists simply of user-defined metadata that can be associated with a file. This metadata can also be indexed with the Index Server that now ships with the Windows 2000 server. For example, metadata can be used to track the name of a document's author or its intended audience. Users can then search for a document by these user-defined tags or metadata. NTFS treats files as a collection of attribute value pairs. The user-defined properties are simply stored as additional optional attributes on a file.

6.5.11 File Ownership by User

Windows 2000 assigns a security identifier (SID) to each user, group, and computer that has an account on the domain or system. All internal security checking is accomplished via the SID. NTFS in Windows 2000 can scan the MFT table and identify all files owned by a particular user on the basis of the SID for the user. One use of such functionality is to allow administrators to clean up files after a user ID has been deleted.

6.5.12 Improved Access Control List Checking

NTFS in Windows NT 4.0 kept access control lists (ACLs) on a per-file and per-directory basis. If a user had 50 files, the identical ACLs were stored 50 times, once in each file. NTFS in Windows 2000 stores ACLs in a directory and indexes them as well. Therefore, for the scenario just described, the ACL would be stored just once, and each of the 50 files would have a "pointer" that would help identify the ACL. The result would be a reduction in storage requirements. In addition, the internal implementation for ACL checking is now more efficient.

This change facilitates bulk ACL checking used by the Indexing Service. When a user performs a search, the Indexing Service prepares a list of files; and before returning the list to the user, the Indexing Service performs ACL checking and eliminates all files that the user cannot access. Thus a user will see only the files that the user can access.

The new mechanism allows other scenarios as well—for example, determining what a given user can and cannot do with a given set of files.

6.5.13 Change Log Journal, USN Journal, and Change Log File

Starting with Windows 2000, NTFS offers application developers a reliable way to track changes to files and directories using a mechanism called the **update sequence number** (**USN**). This optional NTFS service is designed for developers of storage management applications that handle things such as content indexing, file replication, and Hierarchical Storage Management. For any change made to a file or directory, a log record is written to a file. Every record is given a unique number; this is the update sequence number. The reasons for which a record is created include the following:

- Creating or deleting a file
- Creating or deleting a directory
- Modifying, deleting, or adding data to a file data stream (any data stream, named or unnamed)
- Modifying (including adding or deleting) attributes of a file or directory

These change records are stored in the $Extend or $UsnJrnl log file. This file can survive multiple reboots and is stored as a sparse file. To keep the log file from growing too big, older records are deleted in 4K chunks, implying that an application may not be able to access all the changes that have occurred. However, the APIs provided allow an application to determine that some log records are unavailable, and the application can take appropriate action, which can include a complete scan of the volume. To maximize performance, the USN value actually represents the offset within the file of the respective log record. When no information has been lost, an application queries all the log records one by one and identifies the files and directories that have changed.

Not only is the list of files and directories that have changed available, but the cause of change is also identified. On the basis of cause, there are three types of changes:

1. Changes made by applications.
2. Changes made by storage management applications (such as Hierarchical Storage Management) and replication applications.
3. Changes made by applications that build auxiliary data on the basis of the primary data in a file. A good example is an imaging application that builds a thumbnail picture.

The idea behind identifying the cause of the change is to allow applications to make intelligent choices and ignore certain changes as they deem appropriate.

Applications can start the change-logging service using the FSTCL_CREATE_USN_JOURNAL function to the DeviceIoControl API. Applications read USN records using the FSCTL_QUERY_USN_JOURNAL function code.

6.5.14 NTFS Stream Renaming

Windows NT NTFS has always shipped with support for multiple data streams per file. One example of an application that uses multiple data streams is the Windows NT Macintosh server. Streams can be created via the CreateFile API and deleted via the DeleteFile API. Note that when a file containing a non-default-named data stream is copied from an NTFS volume to a FAT volume (which does not support named streams), the named stream data is lost.

Until Windows 2000, there was no way to rename a data stream once it was created. One could create a new file with a new named data stream and then copy the contents of the old file to the new one, including the contents of the old data stream to the new (named) data stream, but this approach is rather inefficient. NTFS shipping with Windows 2000 introduced an API to allow an application to rename an existing named data stream.

6.5.15 Object IDs and Link Tracking

Windows 2000 implements link tracking. Links can be shortcuts for files or OLE (Object Linking and Embedding) objects such as Excel or PowerPoint documents embedded within a file. An application can track a link even when the source object behind the link moves in some way, such as

- Moving a document representing the link source within the same volume on a Windows NT server
- Moving a document representing the link source between volumes on the same Windows NT server
- Moving a document representing the link source from one Windows NT server to another Windows NT server within the same domain
- Moving a complete volume containing the link source from one Windows NT server to another Windows NT server within the same domain
- Renaming a Windows NT server with a mounted volume that contains the link source
- Renaming a network share on a Windows NT server that contains the source of the link
- Renaming the document representing the link source
- Any combination of the above

All of this functionality is based on a requirement that both the source and destination files reside on a volume that is a version of the Windows 2000 or higher NTFS file system.

Each file in Windows 2000 (and higher Windows NT versions) can have an optional unique object identifier (the 16-byte $OBJECT_ID structure described in the Section 6.5.3). To track a file, an application refers to that file by its unique object identifier. When the file reference fails (e.g., when the file has been moved) a user mode link-tracking service is called (by the operating system) for assistance. The user mode service attempts by trial and error to locate the file, using its object ID for all the scenarios just described.

To enable programmatic use of object IDs and link tracking, the following APIs are available:

- Applications create an ID for a file or directory using the FSCTL_CREATE_OR_GET_OBJECT_ID file system control function code.
- Applications delete an object ID using the FSCTL_DELETE_OBJECT_ID file system control function code.
- Applications query an object ID using the FSCTL_CREATE_OR_GET_OBJECT_ID file system control function code.

6.5.16 CHKDSK Improvements

Windows 2000 NTFS reduces the number of situations in which CHKDSK needs to run, while significantly reducing the amount of time taken to run CHKDSK. The phrase "your mileage will vary" comes to mind in view of the fact that the exact amount of improvement depends on the size of the volume and the nature of the corruption. For volumes with millions of files, however, an improvement that reduces the amount of time needed to run CHKDSK by a factor of ten is quite possible.

6.5.17 File System Content Indexing

Windows 2000 Server ships with the Indexing Service fully integrated with the operating system and tools:

- Access to indexing functionality through the **Find files or folders** dialog in Explorer, allows a method for using the service.
- The Indexing Service can index file contents and file attributes, including user-defined attributes, as well.

- The Indexing Service can also index offline content managed by Remote Storage Services.
- On NTFS volumes, the Indexing Service uses the change log journal to determine which files have changed since the last index run.
- The Indexing Service uses the bulk ACL-checking feature and will return files only in response to a user search for which the user has permissions. Files that are not allowed access by that user don't appear in the search results.
- The Indexing Service can also work on FAT volumes, but it will work less efficiently on FAT volumes as compared to NTFS volumes because it cannot use NTFS-specific features such as the change log journal.

6.5.18 Read-Only NTFS

Starting with Windows XP, NTFS can now handle read-only volumes. The underlying volume itself is marked read-only. NTFS still checks the log file, and if the log file indicates that some log transactions need to be redone, the volume mount request will fail. Read-only volumes have some important applications, including mounting multiple versions of a single volume that have been created with a snapshot technique.

6.5.19 NTFS Fragmentation and Defragmentation

In fragmentation, a file is stored as a series of clusters that are not contiguous. A 64K file would occupy 16 clusters, each 4K. If these clusters were all contiguous, there would be only one entry in the MFT for mapping the file LCN to a VCN. However, if the disk were fragmented to the point where the file were stored as 16 noncontiguous clusters, each separate from one another, the MFT would have 16 entries, each one with a mapping between a VCN/LCN pair. Fragmentation is bad because it causes performance degradation. Positioning the disk head once and reading 16 clusters is much more efficient than positioning the disk head 16 times and reading one cluster each time.

Fragmentation can occur for various reasons. To start with, a newly created NTFS file system is well laid out on the volume and would have

- The MFT at the beginning of the volume
- Free space for the MFT to grow
- System and user files
- Additional free space

Fragmentation can occur because of the file system behavior or the application behavior, and typically it is due to a combination of both. Examples include

- Installations of a Windows NT service pack that involve allocating new files and deleting old files. On a perfectly defragmented disk,[5] the allocation of new files starts from the beginning of free space for files. When the old files are deleted, small holes are left behind.
- Other application activity—for example, Word or Excel saving a file as a temporary file, deleting the old file, and renaming the temporary file to be the file that was just deleted.
- Application behavior that could lead to the allocation of file space that is not really used by the application. A good example is an OLE document that contains a mix of Microsoft Office files—such as a Word document that also contains an embedded PowerPoint slide or two and an Excel spreadsheet. When one of these is changed, the new version is saved at the end of the file, and the old version is marked deleted but stays embedded within the file. Microsoft shipped a reparse point filter driver to support a feature called Native Structured Storage to cater to this situation and the Microsoft Office documents are actually be stored in different files, yet appear to be a single file to the Microsoft Office application. Although this feature was present in one of the Windows 2000 beta releases, it was withdrawn in the final release of Windows 2000.[6]
- Directory fragmentation is another problem caused by the fact that some directories—for example, an application directory that contains application executable files—rarely grow or shrink, whereas other directories, such as the My Documents and Temp directories, see a lot of files added and deleted. If the MFT for such a directory is allocated early in system installation, the directory will have multiple MFT records, all of them potentially noncontiguous with respect to each other.

---

5. Literature talks about *disk defragmentation*, and the same terminology is used here as well. However, this is really volume defragmentation and not disk defragmentation.

6. This is a concrete example of the caution throughout this book that at least parts of the book are forward-looking in nature and could be erroneous. This is also a concrete example of the reason that Microsoft strives to explain that the only way of determining features in a release is to examine the release once it has occurred.

Windows NT 4.0 introduced support for a set of defragmentation APIs. These APIs allowed defragmentation applications to query file allocation data and manipulate it. The APIs worked on both FAT as well as NTFS and allowed for writing of a defragmentation application without any knowledge of the on-disk structure. There is also an API to read an MFT record, but that obviously assumes knowledge of the MFT structure and its on-disk form. This API documentation is found on third-party Web sites, but not authored by Microsoft, perhaps to allow for changes to the format and structure in the future.

With Windows 2000, Windows XP, and Windows Server 2003, Microsoft has successively enhanced this support in various ways. Some of the highlights for Windows XP and Windows Server 2003 include

- Support for defragmentation of the MFT. The first 16 entries of the MFT, however, cannot move. This is not an issue because these are not typically fragmented. The sole possible exception here is the root directory.
- Support for defragmentation of disks with cluster sizes greater than 4K.
- Use of the MFT zone for temporarily defragmenting files. When the disk is full and the user or an administrator attempts to defragment an operation, temporary disk space is needed. Prior to this enhancement, the defragmentation operation would fail if free space were not available outside the MFT zone, even if there were plenty of free space in the MFT zone.
- Defragmentation of the default data stream, as well as of its reparse point data and attribute lists. Reparse points and attribute lists can be opened and manipulated just as if they were named data streams.
- Defragmentation of the area between the logical end of a file and the actual physical end of a file as indicated by allocated clusters. Applications such as backup/restore applications preallocate clusters to a file and then set the valid length of file using the Win32 SetFileValidData API. Windows 2000 can defragment only the valid data of a file and not the area between the logical end of the file and the end of the clusters allocated and assigned to the file.
- Prevention of the defragmentation of open files, which applications do by opening the file and issuing a newly defined FSCTL code (FSCTL_MARK_HANDLE, with option MARK_HANDLE_ PROTECT_CLUSTERS).

- Defragmentation of encrypted files without their being read (i.e., decrypted). This closes a security hole where the files may be decrypted into system cache and be available for users with malicious intentions.

6.5.20 Encrypting File System

Windows 2000 ships with an encrypting file system (EFS) that shuts down a major security hole. NTFS enforces security, provided that an application accesses disk resources using NTFS. A malicious user that managed to access a server and reboot using a different operating system or one that managed to steal a hard disk could open the disk in "raw mode" without using any file system and read the data off the hard disk. To guard against this possibility, Windows 2000 provides the encrypting file system, which ensures that all of its data is encrypted before the data is written to the disk. EFS can be enabled on a per-directory or per-file basis. In contrast, earlier solutions for the Windows 9X platform worked on a per-partition basis.

EFS uses both symmetric and asymmetric cryptography. The architecture allows different encryption algorithms to be plugged in as well. The data can be decrypted via the same key because the Data Encryption Standard (DES) is a symmetric cipher.

In Figure 6.8, the data is encrypted via a randomly generated 128-bit key with a variant of the DES encryption algorithm. Step 1 shows the file data encryption using a randomly generated key. Step 2 shows how this randomly generated key is encrypted with the file user's public key and stored in the Data Decryption field attribute of the file. This field is used for decryption purposes, as will be shown later in this section. Finally, the randomly generated encryption key is encrypted again, via the public key of a different entity, called a *recovery agent*. This entity could be simply the system administrator or another designated user. This generation of the Data Recovery field is shown as step 3 in Figure 6.8. The Data Recovery field provides a secondary means of retrieving the file data, should the user not be available or should a disgruntled user attempt to render the data irretrievable.

When the file is read, the Data Decryption field is read and decrypted with the user's private key (Step 1 in Figure 6.9) to retrieve the 128-bit key needed for decrypting the file data. The data is then decrypted with this 128-bit key (step 2). Figure 6.9 also shows an optional step (step 3), recovering the 128-bit encryption/decryption key by decrypting the Data Recovery field (instead of the Data Decryption field).

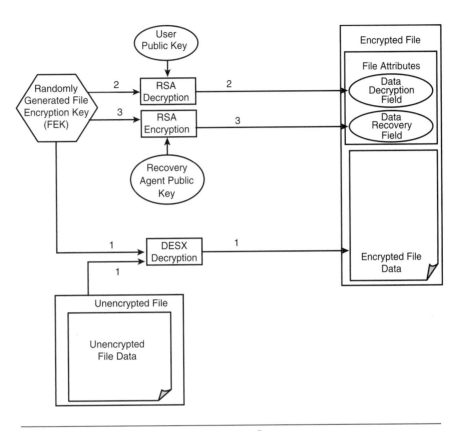

Figure 6.8 EFS File Encryption Overview[7]

Figure 6.10 shows the architecture for EFS implementation. The EFS driver is a file system filter driver that layers itself over NTFS. (EFS does not work on other file systems, including FAT.) The driver implements runtime callouts, called the FSRTL (for File System Run-Time Library), that handle file operations such as read, write, and open on encrypted files. The FSRTL interacts with NTFS to read or write the encryption-related metadata such as the Data Decryption field or Data Recovery field.

The EFS service implements functionality to accomplish the encryption/decryption and generation of encryption keys using the

---

7. RSA is a de facto standard for asymmetric key cryptography, and DESX is a de facto standard for symmetric key cryptography. More details are available at http://www. rsasecurity.com/rsalabs/faq/3-1-1.html.

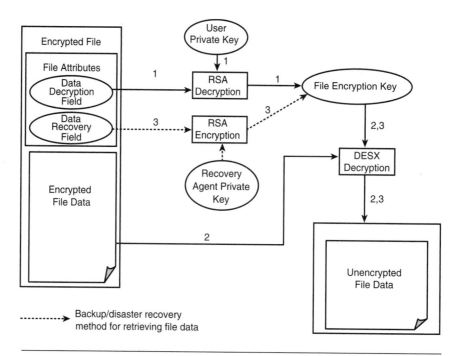

Figure 6.9 EFS File Decryption Overview

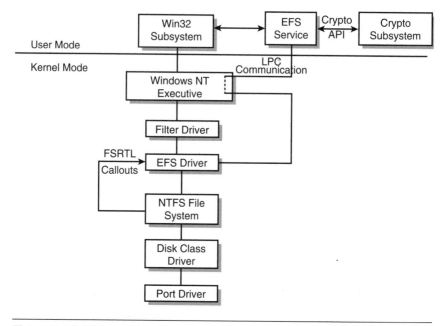

Figure 6.10 EFS Architecture

Crypto API infrastructure that is part of Windows NT. The EFS service communicates with the EFS driver using local procedure call (LPC), a facility made available by the operating system.

Windows 2000 does not support the use of an encrypted file by multiple users, but Windows Server 2003 is expected to do so. However, this functionality can be achieved by encryption of the symmetric key multiple times via the public key for multiple users.

To allow programmatic access to encrypted files, the APIs Encrypt-File and DecryptFile are provided.

6.5.21 NTFS Hard Links

NTFS supports two kinds of links: soft links and hard links. Note that as of Windows Server 2003, hard links are supported only on files, whereas soft links are supported only on directories. Soft links are implemented with an architecture called *reparse points*, which is described in Section 6.5.22. Hard links are described in this section.

Hard links allow a single file to have multiple path names. Application of hard links is valid only on files and not on directories. Hard links are used, for example, in header files that need to be included in multiple build projects and thus need to have any changes reflected in all build projects. The alternative to hard links is to have multiple copies of the file. Hard links are implemented through a single MFT record for the file that simply stores multiple name attributes. The Win32 API called CreateHardLink creates hard links and takes as input parameters a pathname to an existing file and a pathname to a nonexistent file.

Hard links have been implemented in NTFS since Windows NT 3.X days and were a requirement for the POSIX subsystem. What has changed recently is simply the exposure of the API to create and delete hard links. Files are deleted after deletion of the last name for the file. To put this differently, if a file has hard links that are designated link1.doc and link2.doc, deleting link1.doc will still leave link2.doc in existence.

6.5.22 Reparse Points

Reparse points represent a significant new architectural feature in NTFS and the Windows NT I/O subsystem. Reparse points provide the foundation for implementing features such as

- Volume mount points
- Directory junction points

- Single Instance Storage
- Remote storage (Hierarchical Storage Management, or HSM)

This section is dedicated to examining reparse point architecture in detail. Sections 6.5.22.1 through 6.5.22.4 provide descriptions of the applications of reparse point listed above.

Note that this section describes reparse points as being integral with NTFS. Although it is true that the FAT file system does not support reparse points, it is conceivable that an independent software vendor (ISV) or Microsoft could write another file system, different from NTFS, that also supported reparse points. Such a task would not be trivial by any means, but three components are crucial to implement:

1. The file system—for example, NTFS
2. The I/O subsystem and the Win32 API set
3. The tools and utilities

Microsoft has obviously done the necessary work in all three areas; hence it is conceivable for a new file system to support reparse points as well.

A **reparse point** is an object on an NTFS directory or file. A reparse point can be created, manipulated, and deleted by an application via the Win32 API set in general and CreateFile, ReadFile, and WriteFile in particular. Recall that the Win32 API set allows an application to create and manipulate user-defined attributes on a file or directory. Think of reparse points as simply user-defined attributes that are handled in a special manner. This includes ensuring uniqueness about some portions of the attribute object and handling in the I/O subsystem. An ISV would typically write the following:

- Some user mode utilities to create, manage, and destroy reparse points
- A file system filter driver that implements the reparse point–related functionality

Each reparse point consists of

- A unique 32-bit tag that is assigned by Microsoft. ISVs can request that such a unique tag be assigned to them. Figure 6.11 shows the structure of the reparse tag, which has of a well-defined substructure:
  - A bit (M) indicating whether or not a tag is for a Microsoft device driver.

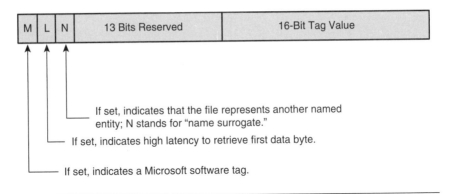

Figure 6.11 Reparse Point Tag

- A bit (L) indicating whether the driver will incur a high latency to retrieve the first data byte. An example here is the HSM solution, in which retrieving data from offline media will incur a high latency.
- A bit (N) indicating whether the file or directory is an alias or redirection for another file or directory.
- Some reserved bits.
- The actual 16-bit tag value.
- A data blob that is up to 16K in size. NTFS will make this data blob available to the vendor-written device driver as part of the I/O subsystem operation that handles reparse points.

To understand the sequence of operations and how reparse points are implemented, consider Figure 6.12. To keep the discussion simple, assume that the user has the required privileges for the requested operation. Also note that in the interest of keeping things simple and relevant, Figure 6.12 shows only one file system filter driver.

The sequence of steps in creating reparse point functionality includes the following, as illustrated in Figure 6.12:

Step 1: Using the Win32 subsystem, an application makes a file open a request.

Step 2: After some verification, the Win32 subsystem directs the request to the NT Executive subsystem.

Step 3: The Windows NT I/O Manager builds an I/O request packet (IRP) with an open request (IRP_MJ_OPEN). Normally this request would go to the NTFS driver. Because filter drivers

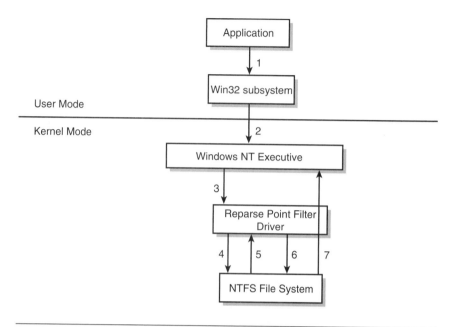

Figure 6.12 Reparse Point Architecture

are involved—in particular, a reparse point filter driver—the I/O Manager sends the request to the filter driver, giving it a chance to preprocess the IRP before the NTFS driver gets a chance to process it.

Step 4: The reparse point filter driver specifies a completion routine in its part of the IRP and sends the IRP on to the NTFS driver.

Step 5: The IRP reaches the file system. The file system looks at the IRP_MJ_OPEN request packet, locates the file or directory of interest, and notes the reparse point tag associated with it. NTFS puts the reparse point tag and data into the IRP and then fails the IRP with a special error code.

Step 6: The I/O subsystem now calls each filter driver (one at a time) that has registered a completion routine for the IRP. Each driver completion routine looks at the error, and if the error indicates a special reparse point error code, the driver completion routine inspects the reparse point tag in the IRP. If the driver does not recognize the tag as its own, it invokes the I/O Manager to call the next driver's I/O completion routine. Assume that one of the drivers recognizes the reparse point tag as its own. The driver can then use the data within the reparse point to resubmit the IRP with some changes based on the data in the reparse point; for example, the pathname is changed before the IRP is resubmitted.

Step 7: NTFS completes the resubmitted IRP operation. A typical example might be that the pathname was changed and the open request succeeds. The I/O Manager completes the open request; each file system filter driver may then be invoked at its completion routine again. The driver notices that the open request succeeded and takes appropriate action. Finally, the IRP is completed, and the application gets back a handle to the file.

If no filter driver recognizes the reparse point tag, the file or directory open request fails.

Some applications may need to be aware of reparse point functionality; other applications may not care and never even realize that a reparse point exists at all. A Microsoft Office application simply opening a Word, PowerPoint, or Excel document may not care at all about reparse point functionality that redirects the open request to a different volume. However, some applications that walk a tree recursively may need to be aware of the possibility of having paths that create a loop.

Applications can suppress the reparse point functionality by appropriate options (FILE_OPEN_REPARSE_POINT) in the CreateFile, DeleteFile, and RemoveDirAPI requests. The GetVolumeInformation API returns the flag FILE_SUPPORTS_REPARSE_POINTS. The GetFileAttributes, FindFirstFile, and FindNextFile APIs return the flag FILE_ATTRIBUTE_REPARSE_POINT to indicate the presence of a reparse point. Reparse points are created via the FSCTL_SET_REPARSE_POINT function code with the DeviceIoControl API.

Windows 2000 allows an application to enumerate all the reparse points and/or mount points on a volume. To facilitate this process, NTFS also stores all reparse point data (including mount points) in the file $Extend\$Reparse. All reparse points on an NTFS volume are indexed within a file called $Index that lives in the \$Extend directory. An application can thus quickly enumerate all reparse points that exist on a volume.

6.5.22.1 Volume Mount Points

Windows NT 4.0 required that a drive letter be used to mount volumes or partitions. This constraint limited a system to having 26 volumes or partitions at the most. Windows 2000 allows mounting a volume without using a drive letter. The only limitations are as follows:

- A volume may be mounted only on a local directory; that is, a volume cannot be mounted on a network share.
- A volume may be mounted only on an empty directory.
- This empty directory must be on an NTFS volume (only NTFS supports reparse points).

Applications accessing the directory that hosts the mount point do not notice anything special about the directory unless the application explicitly requests such information.

APIs that allow the addition and modification of volume mount points are now included in the Windows SDK. Examples of these APIs include

- **GetVolumeInformation**, which may be used to retrieve volume information, including an indication of whether or not the volume supports mount points
- **FindFirstVolumeMountPoint** and **FindNextVolumeMountPoint**, which are used to find the volume mount points
- **FindVolumeMountPointClose**, which frees up resources consumed by FindFirstVolumeMountPoint and FindNextVolumeMountPoint
- **GetVolumeNameForMountPoint**, which returns the corresponding volume name to which a volume mount point resolves

6.5.22.2 Directory Junction Points

Directory junction points are closely related to volume mount points. The difference is that whereas volume mount points resolve a directory to a new volume, directory junction points resolve a directory to a new directory that exists on the same local volume where the directory junction point itself resides. Directory junction points may be created by use of the linkd.exe tool or junction.exe tool that ship with the Windows 2000 Resource Kit and Windows 2000 companion tool, respectively.

6.5.22.3 Single Instance Storage

Windows 2000 ships with Single Instance Storage (SIS) for Remote Installation Services (RIS). RIS provides functionality to efficiently create boot images and application images on a network share and allow clients to use these images. Very often enterprise customers create multiple images—for example, one for the Engineering department, a different image for the Accounting department, yet a different image for the Human Resources department, and so on. Many files are common across all images.

Using symbolic links to share a single file across multiple installations runs the risk that a change being made for one installation will be visible to all the installations. Consider a .ini file that is shared across all three departments mentioned here. If the Engineering department makes a change to this .ini file, the install images for the other two departments also pick up this change. SIS is a way to have a single file copy where possible, yet automatically break that single copy into multiple different versions when needed.

Windows customers typically have multiple images for different clients. For example, Engineering workstations are configured slightly differently from PCs used in the Accounting department, and so on. As a result, many duplicate files on these various images are created. SIS provides a way to store these files just once.

The whole SIS architecture is geared toward accomplishing the following functionality:

- Detecting files that are identical and stored multiple times.
- Copying in a special store the files that are stored multiple times. This functionality is similar to Hierarchical Storage Management, except that the file is always stored in a special SIS store on the disk.
- Implementing SIS links for these files. SIS links are simply stub files in the original location with a SIS reparse point that points toward the copy of the file in the SIS store.

As Figure 6.13 illustrates, SIS implementation architecure has the following components:

- A SIS store
- A SIS filter driver
- SIS APIs
- A SIS groveler

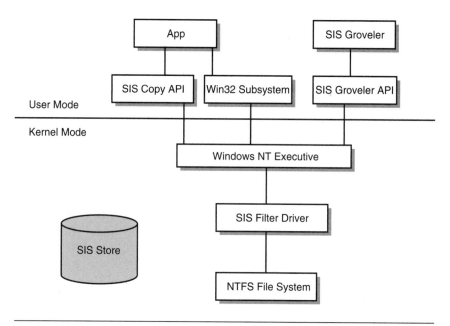

Figure 6.13 Single Instance Storage Architecture

SIS implements a protected store that contains all files identified as SIS candidates. The advantage with such a scheme is the avoidance of problems associated with operations on common files such as delete, move, and rename. The disadvantage is that the cost to be paid includes the overhead of a file copy operation. The files in the common store contain a back-pointer to the files they represent.

The SIS file system filter driver implements reparse point functionality that provides a link between a file and its copy in the SIS common store. The SIS driver implements two important IOCTL functions.

The first is SIS_COPYFILE, which copies a file into the SIS common store and turns the source file into a link file; this link file is actually created as a sparse file with no data blocks and only the MFT table entry. The file contains a SIS reparse point tag whose data contains a link to the actual file in the SIS common store that has the data for the file. These IOCTL functions are called by any application as long as the application has read permissions for the source and write permissions for the destination. The copy happens if the source file is not already a SIS file. If the source file is already a SIS file, a back-pointer is added to that source file linking it with the file in the common store. One reason for copying files is that applications can open a file by its file identifier (ID). When a file is moved or renamed, its file ID remains the same. Thus if the file were renamed, applications would be opening the file in the SIS store, rather than the link file. The drawback is the performance penalty incurred while large files are copied from one disk location to another.

The second important IOCTL function implemented by the SIS driver is SIS_MERGE_FILES, which merges two files. The IOCTL function is protected and called by the user mode component of SIS— namely, the SIS Groveler, which is explained later in this section.

Beyond the specific IOCTL functions, the SIS driver is responsible for implementing SIS links (which are similar to symbolic links) that allow an application to refer to a file, but the driver implements functionality to provide the file data from the file in the SIS common store.

The SIS Groveler is responsible for scanning all files on the volume and detecting duplicate files. The Groveler uses the SIS driver functionality to move the duplicate files that it detects into the SIS common store. The Groveler uses the NTFS change log journal to detect changed files. Once a full disk scan has completed, the change log allows the Groveler to be efficient and limits its scanning to only those files that have changed.

SIS does not manage all volumes. When the SIS service starts, it scans all NTFS volumes to locate volumes that have a SIS Common Store folder and attaches itself only to volumes that have this folder. This is the folder containing the SIS common store, and it is created at the time of SIS installation.

When an application opens a file, it may really be opening just a SIS link file, and the actual data content of the file may be coming from the common file in the SIS store. Consider an example in which a .ini file is shared by, say, three departments: Engineering, Human Resources, and Accounting. There would be a single copy of the .ini file in the SIS common store and three link files, one corresponding to each department. Assume that the Engineering department decides to change a value in the .ini file. SIS ensures that the two other departments—Accounting and Human Resources—are not forced to also accept the change.

SIS ensures this departmental independence by doing a copy-on-close when the application writing to what it thinks is the Engineering department .ini file closes the file after doing the appropriate edits. The reason for copy-on-close rather than copy-on-write is that statistics show that an extremely high percentage of write operations in the relevant situations end up changing the whole file, rather than just limited portions of the file. Thus, copy-on-write would needlessly copy data from the existing file and then overwrite that freshly copied data. When the whole file is not freshly written, unchanged portions of the file are extracted from the existing SIS common store and added to the freshly written parts of the file.

The SIS implementation provides APIs for backup applications in order to ensure that all the different SIS links do not end up as full-fledged files on the backup media. The idea is to ensure that only one copy of the SIS common store file data ends up on the backup media and that the appropriate link files and a copy of the SIS common store data files are restored as relevant.

6.5.22.4 Hierarchical Storage Management

Hierarchical Storage Management (HSM) is described in Chapter 7 in more detail. For now, suffice it to say that such applications can be built on top of the reparse point mechanism described in Section 6.5.22.3. Indeed, Microsoft's implementation of HSM is one such example. HSM migrates files from disk to other media and leaves behind stub files with a reparse point. When applications open this file, the reparse point mechanism can be invoked to seamlessly retrieve data from other media, as appropriate.

6.6 SAN File Systems

Storage area networks allow administrators to have a pool of storage resources that coexist with a group of servers and have individual storage resources assigned to a particular server. SANs still require that at any given moment, only a particular server may be accessing a particular storage resource. SANs just facilitate the easy reassignment of a storage resource from one server to another. To understand this better, consider Figure 6.14.

Figure 6.14 shows a typical three-tiered SAN deployment. At the top are clients accessing servers using a LAN. The servers are connected to a Fibre Channel switch. In addition, several storage disks are connected to the Fibre Channel switch. The storage disks can be considered to be a pool of storage disks, consisting of Disks D1 through D4. Figure 6.14 shows Server 1 and Disks D1 and D3 shaded to indicate that Server 1 is exclusively accessing Disks D1 and D3. Server 2 is exclusively accessing Disks D2 and D4.

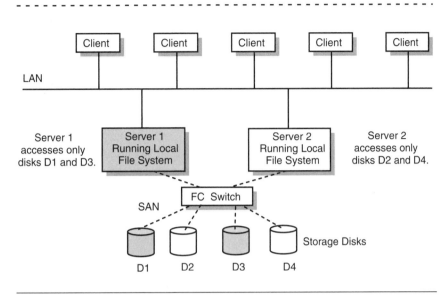

Figure 6.14 SAN Usage Scenario with a Local File System

The SAN simply facilitates relatively easy movement of a disk from one server to another. SANs do not facilitate true simultaneous sharing of the storage devices. SANs simply make some storage resources appear to be direct-attached storage resources, as far as upper layers of software such as file systems (and above) are concerned. This is true whether the SAN is Fibre Channel based or IP storage based.[8]

To allow a storage resource such as a volume to be truly simultaneously shared and accessed by different servers, one needs an enhanced file system, often referred to as a *SAN file system*. SAN file systems allow for multiple servers to access the same storage device simultaneously while still providing for some files or parts of files to have exclusive access by only a particular server process for some duration of time. Astute readers might argue that even network-attached storage allows for files to be simultaneously shared, and they would be correct. The difference is that network-attached storage has a single server (the NAS server) acting as a gatekeeper, and all file operations (e.g., open, close, read, write, lock) are issued to that server.

---

8. IP storage is discussed in detail in Chapter 8.

The NAS server can easily become a bottleneck. Network file systems such as CIFS and NFS (described in Chapter 3) provide file system sharing at the file level for clients accessing servers using a network protocol such as TCP/IP. SAN file systems provide for sharing of storage devices at the block level for clients accessing the storage device using a block mode protocol such as SCSI. With SAN file systems, each server is running what it thinks is a file system running on a local disk. In reality, however, multiple such servers are operating under this illusion, and the SAN file system operating on each server correctly maintains file system state on the volume that is being simultaneously operated on by multiple servers.

A diagram might help explain this. Figure 6.15 shows two scenarios. The left-hand side of the figure shows a network-attached storage disk being accessed by multiple servers via a network file system, and the right-hand side of the figure shows multiple servers accessing a single disk via a SAN file system. In the first case, each server uses its network file system (such as SMB or NFS) to send requests to the server on the NAS device. The NAS device thus constitutes a potential single point of failure, as well as a potential bottleneck. When a SAN file system is deployed, there is no such potential bottleneck or failure point. The storage

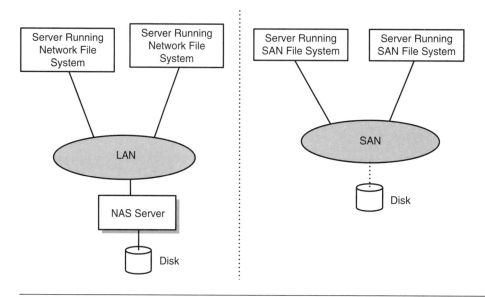

Figure 6.15 SAN and NAS File System Usage Scenario

disk can be accessed in a load-sharing fashion via both Servers 1 and 2. If one of the servers fails, the disk data can still be accessed via the other disk. Of course, the cost here is the added complexity and cost of the SAN file system.

6.6.1 Advantages of SAN File Systems

The advantages of SAN file systems include the following:

- SAN file systems provide a highly available solution. Multiple servers can access each volume, so the servers are not a single point of failure. In addition, it is relatively cheap to ensure that a volume is fault tolerant (i.e., the appropriate RAID solution is deployed), whereas a fault-tolerant cluster is more expensive to procure, and a lot more expensive in terms of operational costs.
- The solution provides high throughput because a server I/O bus typically is the bottleneck for I/O requests. With multiple servers accessing the same volume, the I/O-binding constraints wane. All disks appear to be locally attached disks. Data copy operations are minimal in a local-attached disk solution compared to a NAS solution. For example, for a read issued by a client, data is typically copied from server buffers to TCP/IP buffers and, at the client end, from TCP/IP buffers to the application buffers.
- Storage consolidation allows the user to avoid unnecessary duplication and synchronization of data, which occur when a server is not capable of meeting required performance criteria because of heavy load and the server needs its own private storage unit with identical volumes, since two servers may not simultaneously access a single storage disk without a SAN file system.
- Demands on management overhead of data storage are reduced, leading to lower total cost of ownership. One needs to manage only one instance of a file system rather than multiple instances.
- SAN file systems provide for an extremely scalable solution in which one can easily add servers, storage, or more SAN devices (such as switches) as needs change.
- Applications can choose the type of storage most appropriate to their needs—for example, RAID 0, RAID 1, RAID 5.
- The solution is truly scalable, resembling the computing equivalent of the LEGO brick. For more computing, we simply drop in another server and configure it to access the existing shared disk.

6.6.2 Technical Challenges of SAN File Systems

One of the engineering feats in implementing SAN file systems is striking the right balance between concurrent access and serialization. Concurrent access to files and disks is required to have a highly scalable system that allows multiple processes to access the same set of files simultaneously. Synchronization is required to ensure that the integrity of user data and file system metadata is maintained, even while multiple processes or users are simultaneously accessing files.

Note that this challenge of concurrent access and serialization exists even on non-SAN file systems such as NTFS. The difference is that the mechanisms needed to ensure the proper serialization are much simpler and are provided by the operating systems; for example, the synchronization mechanisms provided by the Windows operating system, such as spinlocks and semaphores, are perfectly adequate for non-SAN file systems such as NTFS.

A complete description of the technology behind creating SAN file systems is beyond the scope of this book. Suffice it to say that the issues involved include the following:

- A synchronization mechanism, also often referred to as a *distributed lock manager*, is needed that can operate across multiple machines and tolerate network latency and reliability issues.
- Problems arise from some machines crashing while they hold resources such as file locks.
- Problems arise when the configuration is deliberately or inadvertently changed. For example, a network (TCP/IP or SAN) experiences some topology changes that render some of the machines inaccessible.
- Deadlock detection capability is necessary. Deadlock occurs when one client holds some resources that a second client is waiting for, while the second client simultaneously holds resources that the first client is waiting for.
- Software-based RAID either cannot be used at all or needs a fair degree of complexity. With software-based RAID, two levels of mapping are involved. First the file system maps file-relative I/O to volume- or partition-relative I/O. Next the software RAID component (Logical Disk Manager in Windows 2000) maps the volume-relative block I/O to a physical disk-relative block I/O. Further, to prevent data corruption, implementations using two

levels of SAN locking are needed. The first is at the file system level to ensure that there is serialization between different windows systems attempting to write overlapping data to the same file. Further, because the software RAID component will attempt to update the parity data for this file, the different software RAID components (Logical Disk Manager or equivalent) running on different Windows systems must also implement a mutual SAN locking mechanism.

■ Differences exist between the operating system and the file systems that the various clients are running. This is a complex problem by itself, and an area in which vendors, including NAS vendors, have expended considerable effort with a good degree of success. There are really several issues here, including the following:

   ■ Providing for some mapping between the different ways in which user and group accounts and permissions are tracked on different operating systems.

   ■ Providing for semantic differences between file open and locking in operating systems and file systems.

   ■ Providing for differences between file naming conventions. Different file systems have different ideas about maximum file name lengths, file name case sensitivity, and valid characters within a file name.

   ■ Different operating systems support different timestamps. Whereas Windows NT supports three timestamps per file, UNIX file systems typically support only two timestamps. Even when the number of timestamps is identical, the units may be different.

   ■ The file systems on the heterogeneous systems can also have different sizes; for example, some are 32-bit file systems, and others are 64-bit file systems. All structures need appropriate mapping. In terms of implementation details, we have to map data structures back and forth, keeping in mind that they may need to be padded to 4-bit, 8-bit, 16-bit, 32-bit, or 64-bit boundaries.

At an extremely high level, SAN file systems may be designed in two ways:

■ A truly symmetric approach, in which every node on the SAN is a peer and the synchronization mechanism is truly distributed across all of the nodes. To date, a symmetric file system is not yet commercially available for the Windows platform.

■ An asymmetric approach, in which one particular node acts as a metadata server and a central synchronization point. This metadata server is responsible for managing all file system metadata (e.g., disk cluster allocation). The other servers implementing the SAN file system obtain metadata from this server—for example, disk cluster allocation information, as well as disk target ID, LUN ID, and so on—and then do the actual user data I/O directly over a SAN. Several vendors, including ADIC and EMC (to name just a couple), ship a commercially available product for the Windows NT platform based on the asymmetric approach.

The asymmetric approach to a SAN file system is illustrated in Figure 6.16:

Step 1:   A client connects to a server and requests some data from a file using a protocol such as CIFS (explained in Chapter 3).

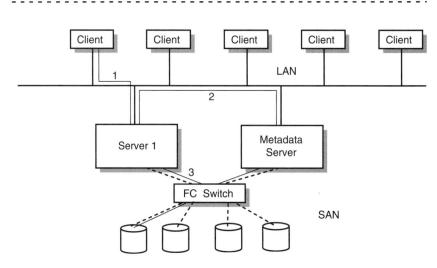

1 Client makes request to Server 1 over LAN.

2 Server 1 requests file metadata from metadata server; request succeeds, and Server 1 receives file disk/block info over LAN.

3 Server 1 requests file data directly from storage unit over SAN.

Figure 6.16 SAN File System with Metadata Server

Step 2:   The server contacts a metadata server and obtains information about the storage device on which the file resides, including particulars of the disk block on which the file resides.

Step 3:   At this stage the server can accomplish all I/O directly, using the data it received from the metadata server.

6.6.3 Commercially Available SAN Systems

Some vendors have implemented SAN file systems for the Windows NT platform using the asymmetric approach. Examples include EMC, with its Celerra HighRoad product line; Tivoli, with its SANergy product; and ADIC, with its StorNext product (formerly known as CentraVision). All of these products use a Windows server for implementing the metadata server and support access to the metadata server by secondary Windows servers. Some of these products support a standby metadata server; some do not. In addition, some of these products support other servers (such as Netware, UNIX, or Solaris) accessing the metadata server, and some do not.

It is interesting to explore the details of how such functionality is implemented and the details of the execution, with respect to the Windows NT I/O stack.

Figure 6.17 shows the Windows NT network I/O stack, as well as the local storage (Storport and SCSI) I/O stack. The SAN file system filter driver (shaded in the figure) layers itself over the network file system in general and the CIFS redirector in particular. The filter driver intercepts file open, close, create, and delete requests and lets them flow along the regular network file system stack. The interception is simply to register a completion routine. For all files successfully opened, the filter driver then optionally obtains information about the exact disk track, sector, and blocks where the file data resides.

This is done for all large files. Some implementations choose not to do this for small files, the underlying thought being that the overhead of obtaining disk track or sector information for small files is comparable to the actual read or write operation on those few sectors. Thereafter, all file operations such as read or write operations (that do not involve manipulation of file system metadata) are handled directly by block-level I/O between the server and the storage disk.

The drawback of having a centralized metadata server is that this server can become a bottleneck, as well as a single point of failure. Some vendors provide capability in their products to have a standby metadata

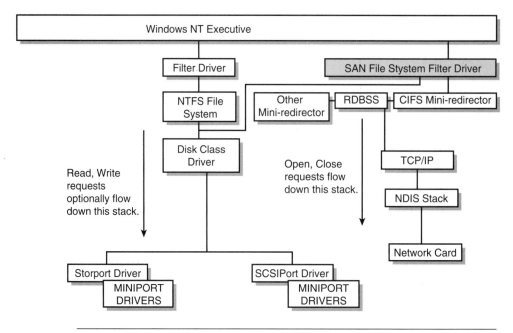

Figure 6.17 Windows NT SAN File System I/O Stack

server take over in case of failure of the primary metadata server. On the other hand, the metadata server is the only server that caches metadata, so clusterwide I/O to read and write metadata is avoided.

6.7 Practical Implications

Windows 2000 introduced support for dynamic disks. It is worthwhile watching how Microsoft improves support for dynamic disks—for example, during system setup and for OEM factory installation procedures.

The reparse point architecture should be of considerable interest to ISVs. IT officials should cross-check whether vendor software such as HSM software is making use of this architecture or not.

It is notable that other than Microsoft, no vendor has found it worthwhile to develop and sell a file system for the Windows NT platform. At least not yet.

6.8 Summary

Windows NT releases have shown a steady progression of new storage-related features. Windows 2000 introduced dynamic disks that allow file system volumes to be managed online without application access to the volume being interrupted.

NTFS is a rich file system that added more features with Windows 2000. NTFS volumes can now be encrypted, thus preventing unauthorized access even when the disk volume is accessed via a different file system. Another notable feature is the change log journal that allows storage applications such as a replication agent or a Hierarchical Storage Management application to quickly and efficiently identify all files and directories that have been changed. NTFS in Windows 2000 also implements reparse points, a feature that forms the basis for implementing Hierarchical Storage Management, symbolic links, volume mount points, and Single Instance Storage.

SAN file systems offer several advantages in a SAN environment. Some vendors have implemented a SAN file system in the Windows NT environment using a centralized metadata server approach.

CHAPTER 7

Storage Management

Efficient and cost-effective storage management is an increasingly important requirement for solving various problems that the modern-day industry faces. These problems include the following:

- The ever increasing amount of storage deployed is forcing an increase in storage administration personnel, even as the amount of storage administered by individual administrators is on the rise. The significant cost reduction for disk storage (especially lower-end disks) has also contributed to the ever increasing rise in deployment of storage.
- The storage subsystem requirements have become more onerous in terms of tolerating less and less downtime.
- The operating environment has moved from a single storage vendor deploying a high-end solution in a large corporation environment to a multitude of operating system and storage solution vendors deployed in smaller corporate environments. The problems are compounded by a need to control costs and the large number of vendor-proprietary management solutions from the various storage vendors.

As emphasized in the introduction, this is not a how-to book. So rather than explaining the various GUI tools that can be used for storage management (e.g., disk administration), this chapter describes the architecture and technologies that can be (and are) used for storage management.

This chapter starts with an introduction to the DMTF-defined and SNIA-adopted management model called the Common Information Model (CIM). The introduction to CIM is followed by a description of Windows Management Instrumentation (WMI), which is Microsoft's implementation of CIM. Following an overview of storage virtualization, the Microsoft vision for storage virtualization—including its disk and fabric virtualization services—is described. Next the chapter describes the SNIA and Microsoft HBA API approaches. That discussion, in turn, is followed by a description of Microsoft's Hierarchical Storage Management architecture as it first appeared in Windows 2000. Finally, the chapter ends (as it began) with a storage management standard from the Storage Networking Industry Association originally code-named Bluefin, now formally known as the Storage Management Initiative (SMI).

7.1 The Common Information Model and WBEM

Simple Network Management Protocol (SNMP) is a stable technology for management that has its advantages and disadvantages. SNMP has provided a reliable means for monitoring and raising events, but it has not been good at is modeling relationships and providing a proactive means of storage management.

In recognition of the need for a new systems management paradigm, Web-Based Enterprise Management (WBEM) was started as an industry initiative in 1996 and became an industry standard body initiative under the auspices of the Distributed Management Task Force (DMTF, formerly the Desktop Management Task Force). WBEM defines a model called the Common Information Model (CIM) that can also integrate existing standards such as SNMP and DMI (Desktop Management Interface).

WBEM defines a comprehensive Common Information Model that covers not just storage, but also networks and systems, as well as modeling the internal and external relationships between elements—for example, the relationship between one storage device and another or that between a storage device and a system. CIM defines a series of schemas for defining management information and relationships between entities. The following list represents an illustrative (and not necessarily comprehensive) inventory of CIM schemas that are defined by the DMTF:

- CIM core
- CIM application
- CIM network
- CIM network QoS (quality of service)
- CIM user
- CIM storage

The important point is that the DMTF defines CIM as a model and not an implementation. In an effort to make CIM more attractive and provide cross-platform compatibility in a heterogeneous environment, the DMTF has also defined a way in which heterogeneous systems can exchange management information using HTTP as a transport and XML documents to contain the management information.

CIM is still evolving, and no doubt it will only grow in importance, especially given the recent CIM demonstrations by several vendors at the Storage Networking World conference in March 2002. The main problem that CIM has now is that management application vendors, as well as hardware vendors, are learning by trial and error. Hardware vendors do not have clear guidance as to what particular instrumentation needs to be developed, and management application vendors do not have clear direction as to what classes and instrumentation they can expect to have that will always be available or only sometimes available (depending on the vendors). No doubt, time will smooth out this issue.

7.2 Windows Management Instrumentation

As stated earlier, CIM is the DMTF-defined and SNIA-adopted Common Information Model. WMI is the Microsoft implementation of CIM. In other words, WMI is "CIM for Windows."

WMI has been implemented in both kernel mode and user mode. Windows NT 4.0 SP6 shipped with only the user mode WMI. Windows 2000, Windows XP, and Windows Server 2003 have WMI implemented in both kernel mode and user mode.

WMI has a three-tiered architecture as shown in Figure 7.1. The three layers are

1. WMI application layer
2. WMI service provider layer
3. WMI provider layer

At the top is the WMI application layer. WMI applications are typically systems management applications. Independent software vendors (ISVs) write management applications using the interface provided by the WMI service or using the scripting interface provided on top of the WMI service. Multiple WMI applications can coexist on the same machine.

The WMI service layer is the next layer and consists of a single entity, the WMI service. The WMI service is a Windows NT service provided by

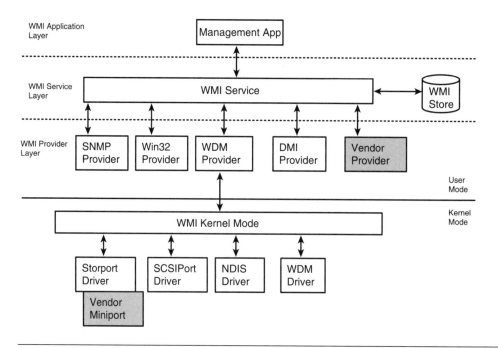

Figure 7.1 WMI Architecture

Microsoft as part of the Windows NT operating system. The WMI service instantiates a schema based on CIM. Sometimes the WMI service is also referred to as a CIM Object Manager, or CIMOM. The WMI service provides a single interface for management applications to use, no matter what the source of the information is or which management applications use the provided services. In other words, the WMI service multiplexes and demultiplexes requests between applications and the various providers. The WMI service also implements the WMI scripting interface that allows access to WMI managed objects from any scripting language supported by the Windows Scripting Host (e.g., Visual Basic, JScript, VBScript).

The last tier in the hierarchy is the WMI provider layer. There are various WMI providers, some written by Microsoft and some written by other vendors. WMI providers are created via the WMI SDK that is part of the Platform SDK and consist of simple user model dynamic link libraries (DLLs). Microsoft has written numerous WMI providers itself. OEMs, IHVs, and ISVs can also write a provider to differentiate their products. For example, an OEM could write a WMI provider for its server enclosure that could instrument the various component temperatures and fans and possibly even raise an alert when the server's chassis opens.

Microsoft has written various WMI providers that instrument Windows user mode applications and services. One special case is the Windows Driver Model (WDM) provider that enables data and events from kernel mode drivers to be made available to user mode management applications. The kernel mode code and drivers are instrumented via WMI code, but the driver writers themselves do not need to write WMI providers.

WMI extensions to WDM provide a means of publishing information and raising events from kernel mode drivers. WMI may be implemented in any driver that receives I/O request packets (IRPs). WMI may also be implemented in SCSI miniport, Storport miniport, and NDIS miniport drivers. In each of these cases, the port driver shipped by Microsoft performs the necessary translation between IRPs and the miniport interface. Microsoft has implemented WMI in various class and port drivers. Vendors may also differentiate their products by including WMI features in their hardware's device driver. WMI is implemented in drivers by means of just the Windows Driver Development Kit. WMI defines new functionality via IRP_MJ_SYSTEMCONTROL. It also allows the control of device settings.

WMI provides a rich set of functionality for management applications. For example, a management application can register with WMI for notification in the following circumstances:

- When a particular managed object changes in a prescribed manner; for example, the temperature exceeds a certain value.
- When a new instance of a managed object is created.
- When an existing instance of a managed object is destroyed.
- When a complex condition is satisfied (for example, condition 1 and condition 2, but not condition 3, are met). Note that different providers may instrument the monitoring of conditions. Further, the query to indicate the complex set of conditions is built with a language called WMI Query Language (WQL) with syntax extremely close to that of SQL. WQL allows managed objects to be queried but not modified.
- When a given managed object can be extended by the writing of a provider.

Another important aspect is that WMI provides a standardized way for hardware and software vendors to differentiate their products. A vendor can write a WMI-enabled driver or a WMI provider that addresses an interesting aspect of its device. Management applications can dynamically discover and deal with the new management objects that the vendor provides, through WMI code in either the vendor-written driver or the vendor-written WMI provider.

Microsoft uses WMI extensively for storage and application management. Microsoft Exchange 2000 and SQL Server 2000 are managed via the WMI providers that each of them have written. Disk management and iSCSI management are some other examples that rely on WMI code.

7.3 Storage Virtualization

Storage virtualization is very often positioned as a new technology that is a wonderful solution for all problems. In reality, the term *storage virtualization* represents a slew of technologies, some of which are new, and some of which have actually been around for quite some time.

Simply put, **storage virtualization** offers the ability to specify functional and application characteristics of the desired storage requirements without paying any attention to the details of the underlying hardware (e.g., type, vendor, location). As a simple illustration, consider the following example: An administrator specifies the need for an 80GB volume to back up data, but unfortunately all the hardware underlying the backup application has a maximum disk size of 40GB. To solve this dilemma, a volume manager might virtualize two separate physical disk drives into a single larger volume. With the growing attention to total cost of ownership (TCO) and the exploding amounts of storage, storage virtualization offers the hope of providing manageability, ease of use, better utilization of storage resources, and a reduction of the storage TCO.

Storage virtualization can be implemented in various ways, each offering different functionality and advantages. Indeed, there are several ways of classifying storage virtualization. One way is to specify the physical location; another is to specify the functional layer at which the virtualization lives. The following sections examine the various ways of classifying storage virtualization.

7.3.1 Virtualization in the (Host) Server

Virtualization has existed in the host server for quite some time, although it usually goes by a different name. Good examples include the Logical Volume Manager (LVM) and Hierarchical Storage Management (HSM).

A volume manager (such as the Windows 2000 Logical Disk Manager, or LDM) can provide virtualization in several ways:

- By turning inexpensive unreliable disks into reliable disks using RAID software
- By providing larger volumes through virtualization of smaller disks into larger volumes

The Logical Disk Manager is described in Chapter 6.

Hierarchical Storage Management provides a way for applications to access files transparently without regard to whether the file is residing on a hard disk or on removable media such as tape. The HSM that is shipped by Microsoft is described in Section 7.8.

Virtualization in the host server represents a mature and stable technology. However, there is the perception that it contributes to islands of storage where certain storage effectively is dedicated to certain servers. This perception is especially true, given the lack of popularity and availability of clustered file systems and volume managers with cluster support that allows multiple servers to truly share and simultaneously access the same storage devices, file systems, or volumes.

7.3.2 Virtualization in the Storage Hardware

Virtualization in the storage hardware has also been around for quite some time. A good example is RAID implementation in the storage subsystem. One advantage is that the implementation is efficient because it is hardware based. Another advantage is that this implementation is robust and secure because of the close proximity of the data repository. Consider a data storage device that is managed by virtualization in the host (server). A malicious user may circumvent the software virtualization in the host or deliberately bring a host online without the required virtualization present in the host and then access the data repository.

The disastrous effects of this scenario can be prevented with a storage unit that implements its own virtualization. Another advantage is that the solution works for a multitude of servers, irrespective of the actual operating system used on the server. The drawback is that the data virtualization is managed in a proprietary way by the hardware vendor, which can cause interoperability issues.

7.3.3 Virtualization in the Storage Network

Instead of doing virtualization at the two end nodes (the host server or the storage hardware subsystem), the virtualization is done in the storage network, either in the switches or routers or via special hardware deployed just for the purposes of virtualization and storage management.

7.3.4 In-Band Virtualization

In **in-band virtualization**, the virtualization occurs in the active data path. The host software does some I/O, and a device that sits in the data path between the host server and the storage hardware handles the I/O.

The advantage is that the solution works for a range of activities, including file-oriented and block-oriented access of storage. The appliance can provide a single point of management.

The disadvantage is that the in-band virtualization appliance device can become a single point of failure and a performance choke point. We can alleviate these problems by having multiple such appliances, adding more memory to the appliance, using higher-performance components, or building caching into the appliance. However, these tactics add cost and create a more complicated solution that requires clustering of the management devices.

7.3.5 Out-of-Band Virtualization

With **out-of-band virtualization**, the data path along which the storage management information flows exists apart from the control path. One can compare out-of-band virtualization with asymmetric clustered file systems, in which a metadata server controls the file system metadata access. The virtualization server typically communicates with virtualization clients, which are lightweight software running on the host server or devices in the storage network such as fabric switches or HBAs.

The advantage is that the data access can be much faster because the data does not have to go through an additional device. Another advantage is that one can have a single point of control.

The disadvantage is that one ends up with a different problem involving managing multiple out-of-band virtualization devices. Multiple virtualization devices are typically needed for several reasons, including

- To provide redundancy
- To provide the needed performance

■ To conform to what the fabric topology dictates (e.g., multiple SAN islands that are physically disjointed from each other would each require a virtualization device)

Disk virtualization refers to software and firmware that has been shipping as part of disks for years. The functionality maps bad sectors to good ones transparently to the operating system. The functionality also hides the intricacies such as number of spindles, heads, and so on from the operating system.

Block virtualization also refers to technology that has been present for quite some time. Good examples on the Windows NT platform are the Logical Disk Manager and the FtDisk driver that provides RAID functionality and the ability to present a single large volume to an application that may be larger than any individual physical disk's capacity.

File virtualization refers to functionality that abstracts the location and characteristics of files and directories. A good example is Hierarchical Storage Management, or HSM.

File system virtualization refers to functionality that abstracts multiple file systems into one perceived file system. A good example of such functionality on Windows NT is the distributed file system (Dfs) described in Chapter 3.

Tape virtualization refers to functionality that abstracts tape media and tape drives. In the absence of tape virtualization, a host server typically has a dedicated tape unit, its own tape libraries, and its own tape media. Tape virtualization typically simulates tape devices and tape media, caching the I/O happening to the simulated tape onto disk instead. The cached I/O streams at a convenient time to a real tape device. The advantage is that the I/O completes faster, and the need for numerous tape devices is minimized.

7.4 Microsoft Storage Virtualization Vision

With Windows Server 2003 and the storage-related features that will ship beyond Windows Server 2003, Microsoft is clearly working diligently toward a vision of steadily enhancing the Windows NT platform with more storage-related features. Virtualization at the volume level (FtDisk and Logical Disk Manager) and file system level (Hierarchical Storage Management and distributed file system) has been available on the

Windows NT platform for quite some time now. Microsoft is working toward building better infrastructure into the Windows NT platform for storage management. Among other things, this infrastructure will allow an administrator to easily accomplish routine tasks in a highly automated manner.

As an example, consider an administrator that wants to do a backup. This administrator does the following:

1. Sets up a volume (some disk or RAID management may be required)
2. Ensures that the volume is visible to a snapshot engine (rezoning may be needed)
3. Performs a snapshot
4. Moves the snapshot volume to be visible to a backup server
5. Performs the backup
6. Frees the volume and moves it back into the free storage pool

The goal is to allow administrators effective control of each of the steps above, either programmatically, via a command-line interface, or via a management GUI application. At each step, the desired functionality is specified in a functional manner rather than a physical manner. For example, the volume allocation step should be stated like this: "create a volume, make it 50GB, RAID 5, and so on"—and not like this: "make E: 50GB." To achieve this vision, Microsoft is shipping the disk virtualization service with Windows Server 2003 and the fabric virtualization service at a later date.

7.4.1 Disk Virtualization Service

The disk virtualization service provides functionality to manage block storage that is itself virtualized. The disk virtualization service can provide this functionality irrespective of where the virtualization occurs (e.g., host, RAID hardware). In particular, the disk virtualization service provides functionalities such as these:

- Creation of LUNs by characteristics
- Creation of file systems
- Management of paths

As shown in Figure 7.2, the virtual disk service has a three-tiered model, consisting of applications, the disk virtualization service, and several

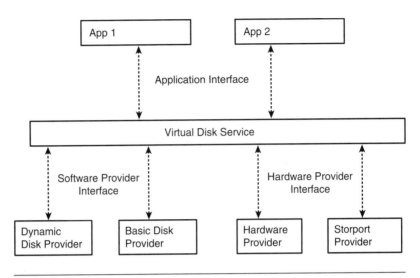

Figure 7.2 Virtual Disk Service

providers, some developed by Microsoft and some developed by third parties.

Software providers are responsible for managing volumes; providers are implemented as COM servers. Software providers implement functionality as specified in the virtual disk service SDK, which is available from Microsoft on an NDA (nondisclosure agreement) basis. The functionality includes creating COM objects that represent the volume, disk, and provider itself, as well as other objects. A software provider also exports status and health information about the objects it manages, and it sends out notifications. The virtual disk service receives all notifications; it then filters the notifications and sends them on to applications that have registered for the appropriate alerts. The virtual disk service coordinates with file systems as needed—for example, while extending or shrinking a volume.

Hardware providers are responsible for managing LUNs. Just like software providers, hardware providers are implemented as COM servers and implement functionality as specified in the virtual disk service SDK available under NDA. Hardware providers implement functionality related to LUNs, drives, LUN masking, and so on and send notification events.

Microsoft will ship three providers, and RAID hardware vendors are expected to write hardware providers for their particular offerings. The three providers that Microsoft will ship are

1. A Storport provider that caters to host-based RAID hardware (this is local direct-attached hardware and not SAN hardware)
2. A provider that manages basic disks (which are described in Chapter 6)
3. A provider that manages dynamic disks (also described in Chapter 6)

It appears that the virtual disk service will be extremely useful to a slew of storage management applications, including utilities for managing disks, backup, mirroring, and snapshot applications. It also remains to be seen how Microsoft itself builds management applications and utilities using the virtual disk service. Note that historically, Microsoft has put some useful tools or utilities in the resource kit rather than the operating system offering itself. An excellent example is the linkd.exe utility for creating links. Thus the reader should also check out the Windows Server 2003 Resource Kit to see if it has any storage management tools.

The virtual disk service is expected to run on multiple Windows NT servers. The software providers will run only on servers where the appropriate volumes are mounted. A management application that uses the virtual disk service can run remotely or on the same machine. The virtual disk service will run in OEM installation environments (called WinPE or Windows NT Lite). In WinPE, a machine boots with a minimal Windows NT configuration and installs Windows NT in a custom configuration on that machine or runs some tests. In such situations, a minimal configuration might be the virtual disk service and the basic disk provider.

7.4.2 Fabric Virtualization Service

The fabric virtualization service plays a key role in offering a capability to automate storage management. In particular, the fabric virtualization service provides programmatic and management applet (GUI or command line) access for managing storage interconnects.

Note that the fabric virtualization service is not part of Windows Server 2003. In reality, it may or may not ship at all. Few details beyond this presentation have been available on a nonconfidential basis. It is also interesting to note that many industry vendors, including at least one prominent switch vendor, have declared their intent to adopt the DMTF or SNIA Common Information Model. Taken to its logical conclusion,

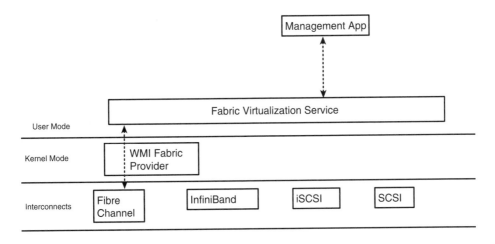

Figure 7.3 Fabric Virtualization Service

this would mean that the vendor APIs for switch management would have secondary importance to the methods and objects exposed via the Common Information Model. How this evolves and how the fabric virtualization service architecture fits into this evolution is something only time (and perhaps a later edition of this book) will tell.

Figure 7.3 is a highly speculative attempt to define the fabric virtualization service architecture. The fabric virtualization service will present an API for the benefit of management applications and get information about the fabric from a WMI provider.

7.5 HBA API

In a storage area network, HBAs provide extremely important functionality and provide a means of physical connectivity between a server and other elements of the storage network, including storage devices, switches, and other hosts. As storage networks grow in complexity, the need for automatic discovery and management of devices becomes increasingly important.

The Storage Networking Industry Association (SNIA) defined a C library API to allow storage management applications to manage Fibre Channel HBAs. The management applications using the API can implement a single interface, no matter what the HBA model or vendor is, as long as the vendor supports the SNIA-defined HBA API. The APIs defined include support for querying and setting HBA configuration management, as well as measuring HBA performance statistics. In particular, the HBA API can provide the following:

- HBA attributes such as model, vendor name, and World Wide Name (WWN, a unique 64-bit number assigned by the vendor and registered with the IEEE; the IEEE assigns a range of numbers to each vendor).
- Port attributes such as port ID (a 24-bit number that is unique for each node), type of port, current port state, and maximum frame size that the port can support.
- Port Fibre Channel protocol attributes such as SCSI bus number or SCSI target ID.
- Port statistics such as frames received, frames transmitted, time since last occurrence of statistics reset, and errors encountered (nature and number of occurrences).
- FC-3 (Fibre Channel functional level 3) management information such as WWN or port ID; the noteworthy point here is that the API allows a storage management application to query Fibre Channel services such as name servers. The API also allows querying and setting of node information such as WWN and port ID.

Although Microsoft and SNIA members both support the HBA API, the approaches differ a little. The SNIA approach, illustrated in Figure 7.4, requires three components:

1. A generic HBA API DLL owned and maintained by SNIA. This DLL exposes a standard interface for the benefit of management applications; at the bottom layer, the DLL interfaces with several vendor-written DLLs.
2. An HBA vendor-written DLL that plugs into the generic HBA API DLL. This vendor-written DLL reveals management information and interacts with the vendor-written driver using proprietary IOCTLs.
3. A vendor-written device driver for the HBA.

Although this standardization effort has its merits, Microsoft sees some problems with this approach:

- There is no clear way to manage the distribution and versioning of the proposed dynamic link libraries. This is one more example of a

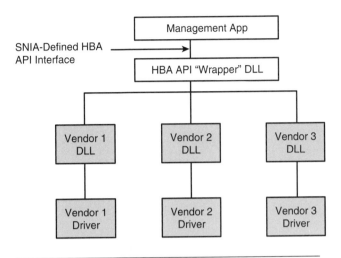

Figure 7.4 The SNIA HBA API

potential DLL problem in which various applications will install versions of the libraries and potentially overwrite libraries that other applications have installed.

■ The HBA vendor must not only write the device driver and private IOCTL interface to the driver, but must also write the vendor-specific DLL library, as well as potentially modify the wrapper HBA library to handle vendor-specific interfaces to the vendor DLL.

■ It will be extremely hard to test and certify vendor drivers that implement private IOCTLs; for example, how does one verify that the driver code will not result in a buffer overrun situation when bad parameters are passed on the IOCTL call?

■ The architecture appears to be extensible at first sight, but upon closer inspection, one realizes that the HBA vendors will be forever chasing the management application vendors to add code that deals with vendor-specific enhancements.

■ The solution does not allow communication and management in kernel modes. The SNIA approach dictates that a management application must wait until the Windows NT user mode subsystem is fully operational. For management purposes such as LUN masking, however, it is desirable that a kernel mode driver be able to take some action while the system is booting and even before the user mode subsystem has been started.

Microsoft advocates a slightly different approach, illustrated in Figure 7.5, which consists of the following components:

- A generic HBA API DLL owned and maintained by Microsoft. This DLL exposes a SNIA-defined standard interface at the upper edge for the benefit of management applications. At the bottom edge, the DLL interfaces with Windows Management Instrumentation (WMI), the Microsoft implementation of the Common Information Model (CIM), which, as stated earlier, is an object-oriented systems management model adopted by both SNIA and the DMTF. This DLL also does the required translation back and forth between the SNIA HBA API and WMI.
- A vendor-written device driver for the HBA; this driver implements WMI and makes the management and configuration interface available in the WMI repository. Because WMI is a two-way interface, the driver also implements WMI IRP functionality that allows a management application to set configuration parameters for the driver. Note that the vendor is required to write a driver anyway; the additional burden being imposed here is to implement WMI code in that driver.

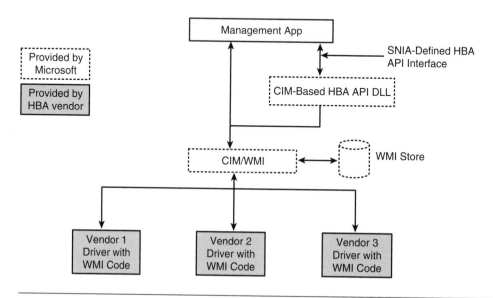

Figure 7.5 The Microsoft HBA API

The advantages with the Microsoft approach are as follows:

- All interfaces presented are standardized, whereas in the SNIA approach, the interface between the generic HBA API DLL and the vendor-written DLL is proprietary for each vendor. The Microsoft approach is consistent with the SNIA adoption of the DMTF Common Information Model.
- The approach also allows for extensibility, since a vendor can easily extend an existing WMI class or define a new one and populate management information into that class. Again, this just emphasizes the extensibility of the SNIA-adopted CIM model.
- The biggest advantage is that management applications can use either the SNIA HBA API or the SNIA CIM model. If applications use the SNIA HBA API, they still work unaltered, thanks to the WMI code in the driver and the Microsoft dynamic link library that maps WMI information to the SNIA HBA interface.
- The architecture allows a kernel mode component to interrogate the vendor-written driver and take some management action.
- The management applications do not (and should not) care about how the underlying code obtains the necessary information. As long as the management applications use the SNIA HBA API (and this is what Microsoft recommends), the underlying code may obtain the necessary information using the SNIA-advocated DLLs or the Microsoft-advocated WMI. In both approaches management applications still write to a single interface.

Note that the WMI interfaces needed to code the HBA driver shipped with Windows 2000. Therefore, if one had the Microsoft dynamic link library mapping WMI information to the SNIA, along with the SNIA HBA dynamic link library, the solution would work on Windows 2000 as well. The problem is that the Microsoft dynamic link library is indeed available with Windows Server 2003, but it remains to be seen whether Microsoft offers a version of this library for the Windows platform as well.

7.6 Management Command-Line Utilities

Windows 2000 introduced a trend to have both GUI and command-line tools for systems management. Windows Server 2003 continues that theme with command-line tools available for managing the following:

- File system features, including defragmentation
- Volume shadow copy service
- Volumes, disks, and partitions
- Remote Storage Services (RSS)

Windows Server 2003 also accelerates the trend introduced in Windows 2000 to provide performance and management information using WMI. Modifications to more parts of the operating system, to provide management information using the WMI architecture—including Storport, volume shadow copy service, and the distributed file system, to provide some examples—are now included in the base code.

7.7 SAN Security

SAN security is still evolving. As of now, SAN security consists of guarding physical access and ensuring that two different entities have two physically separate SANs deployed. As will be discussed later in this section, switch vendors, for instance, have developed some solutions, and the Storage Networking Industry Association (SNIA) Security Working Group actively advocates solutions and educating the industry.

The SNIA Security Working Group is active in

- Defining the problems and threats
- Developing and evangelizing about best practices
- Developing educational materials for the industry

The working group has identified some areas that need attention, in order to ensure SAN security. Here are the highlights:

- Solutions developed for SAN security need to secure both data access and storage management activities.

- Data confidentiality needs certainty on an end-to-end basis—not just between the two communicating end nodes, but also between the two communicating applications.

Fibre Channel switches, especially high-end Fibre Channel switches, play an increasingly important role in SAN management and SAN security. Switches play a role in fabric management, port enabling and disabling, and zone management. Switch vendors such as Brocade and McDATA have added features in their switches to enhance SAN security, including the following:

- The ability to associate a device with a particular port on the switch; for example, an HBA connected to a server connects to only a particular switch port. The association uses the World Wide Name of the device, in this case, the HBA WWN. Any attempt at access from a port that fails the match fails. In this example the server will not function on a different port, and a new malicious server cannot connect to the fabric using a random port.
- The requirement of authorization for switches to join the fabric. Authorization is enforced by several techniques. If no new switches can join a fabric without explicit administrator intervention, the fabric ports will allow operation on F, G, or E ports only. (See Chapter 4 for a review of the different Fibre Channel port types.) The basic idea is to restrict the ability of the port to autodetect the type of device at the other end and configure itself accordingly. Another way is to require new switches joining a fabric to provide security information such as a digital certificate and password.
- Secure configuration changes made to the SAN by well-known security techniques; for example, all configuration changes require a digital certificate, user identity, and password.
- Restriction of ways to allow changes; for example, only certain designated switches can make fabric changes, resulting in a rejection of all changes initiated by other switches.
- Zoning (explained in Chapter 4), which is another way to ensure SAN security.

7.8 Hierarchical Storage Management

Hierarchical Storage Management (HSM) is sometimes confused with backup products and backup auxiliary products that help keep track of a file's archival position on a tape, or even its archival condition. Although both HSM and backup do deal with moving files and data between a primary medium (typically disk) and a secondary medium (typically tape or optical media), there is a big difference. The difference is the degree of transparency that backup and HSM provide. With HSM, the file appears to be present still. In some cases the file may have special attributes to indicate that the access time may be higher. With backup products, the application does not see a previously backed-up and deleted file.

Another way to look at HSM is to compare it to virtual memory. **Virtual memory** is an imaginary area of memory—that is, memory that a computer system believes it has but is not physically present in the machine. Operating systems create virtual memory by swapping out regions of memory (precious and fast online resources) that are not actively in use to hard disk (relatively inexpensive and slower media), and then allocating the freed memory to another process. When a different process tries to access the memory swapped out to disk, that process halts temporarily while the required memory contents are restored from disk, allowing the process to continue running. HSM does the same thing, except that the precious resource with HSM is online disk storage, and the relatively inexpensive resources are tape or other media, such as optical media.

Some HSM products integrate backup with the HSM products. To strike a balance between HSM functionality and to avoid disruption of regular data center activities, HSM products typically establish some benchmarks. When the free disk space reaches a particular benchmark, the HSM product kicks in, even during regular hours, to migrate some files to offline media and free up disk space.

7.8.1 Remote Storage Services

Windows 2000 Server includes a Remote Storage Services (RSS) module that provides Hierarchical Storage Management functionality. RSS keeps track of free space and files accessed on volumes, called **managed volumes**. A storage administrator establishes criteria about the minimum free disk space required, how long a file needs to be unused before it is a candidate for migration to offline storage, and so on.

RSS has an engine that periodically checks the amount of free disk space, scans files for premigration, and when the disk space falls below a minimum, truncates the premigrated files. (A complete description of premigration is included later in this section.) The unused files are migrated to an offline medium—for example, tape—depending on various criteria, explained in detail later in this section. The reparse point data is set for this file, including information necessary for migration of the file.

File migration selects the appropriate files on the basis of policies set by the administrator. These policies deal with

- The amount of free disk space desired to be maintained
- The last date and time the file was accessed
- The size of the file
- Some administrator-defined inclusion or exclusion rules as to what files or directories may be migrated

RSS integrates into the rest of the Windows 2000 platform as follows:

- The Explorer GUI shows a special icon for files that have been migrated to removable media.
- The command-line window, when listing files that have been migrated to removable media, shows the size of the file within parentheses.
- The Windows NT backup application coordinates with RSS; Windows NT backup opens the file using option FILE_OPEN_ NO_RECALL in the CreateFile API. This ensures that the backup application can read the file data to back up the file, yet not cause the file to be migrated back to disk because of the file's backup status.
- RSS jobs are submitted via the Windows NT job scheduler, and they can be administered like any other ordinary jobs.
- The Windows 2000 Indexing Service can recognize the fact that a file has not changed, other than the file being migrated between disk storage and remote storage.
- Network timeouts are automatically extended when a file on remote storage is accessed, allowing a chance for the file to be migrated.

RSS deals with files that can be in one of three states:

1. A **normal file**, wherein the file is resident on disk.
2. A **premigrated file**, wherein the file's unnamed data stream is

copied to offline media, yet it is also left untouched on the disk. A premigrated file also has a reparse point on the file.

3. A **migrated file**, wherein the file's unnamed data stream is copied to offline media and deleted from the disk; the file is marked with the sparse attribute, and the FILE_ATTRIBUTE_ OFFLINE attribute is set. The reparse point is set on the file with a special tag, IO_REPARSE_TAG_HSM.

Figure 7.6 shows the RSS architecture. Remote Storage Services consists of multiple user mode and kernel mode components, described in the following paragraphs.

When accessing a migrated file, the RSS filter driver catches the IRP and queues it up. The RSS filter driver communicates with the RSS file system agent, requesting that the file data be restored from the removable media. The RSS file system agent, in turn, invokes the services of the RSS engine. The RSS engine retrieves the data and streams it to the RSS filter driver, which restores the file data piece by piece as it receives the pieces of data. If any I/O is pending for the data thus retrieved, that I/O is completed. The data retrieved so far is used to satisfy any I/O that may be

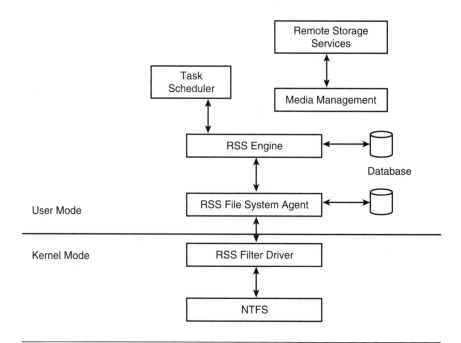

Figure 7.6 RSS Architecture

pending, waiting for the appropriate data. The file status (including reparse point data) is updated to move the file back into a premigrated stage from its current condition of being marked as migrated.

When a migrated file is accessed via the FILE_OPEN_NO_RECALL option in the CreateFile API, the IRPs that are read are satisfied in a similar manner, with the difference being that the file is not migrated from tape to disk. The data is restored off the tape and is fed to the application without being written to the disk. Note that Windows 2000 can handle only one file recall (migrating the file from remote storage back to tape) at a time.[1] This is true even when multiple Remote Storage drives are available and the files accessed are on two separate paths on two separate media in two separate drives.

The RSS engine acts as a Removable Storage Management (RSM) client, using RSM to manage the media. The RSS engine uses a database to store details about the media it uses.

The RSS file system agent is responsible for periodically scanning managed NTFS volumes and preparing a list of files that need to be migrated. This list is prepared on the basis of the criteria decided by the administrator. The file system agent communicates the list of files to be migrated to the RSS engine. Once the files have been premigrated by the RSS engine, the RSS file system agent adds the file to its database of files that are in the premigrated state.

When the free space falls below a benchmark set by the administrator, an automatic task initiated by the RSS file system agent runs. The file system agent deletes the data stream of files that have been premigrated (moves the file from premigrated state to fully migrated state) after verifying that the files have not changed since they were premigrated. This verification is accomplished via the USN journal mechanism described in Chapter 6.

Remote Storage Services do not install by default. RSS comes with a GUI management tool that allows the management GUI to run remotely on a Windows machine. The GUI has several components:

- A **Windows Explorer component** that allows users to view information such as date and timestamp of when the file was premigrated or file data location on remote storage; users can force

---

1. Windows Server 2003 is expected to have the same limitation as well. Given that the code implementing Hierarchical Storage Management has been licensed by Microsoft from a company that is now part of Sun Microsystems, one can expect some interesting developments in the successor to the Windows Server 2003 product.

premigration of a user-selected file, provided that they have proper access to that file.

- A **disk management component** that shows volume information such as free or busy space, amount of storage used by premigrated files, amount of storage used by file placeholders, and so on.
- A **user interface** that allows an administrator to cancel a file recall (migration from remote storage to disk) operation.
- A **management interface** to establish the high and low benchmarks, free disk space, criteria that establish selection of files for migration, and so on.

RSS has several limitations, including the following:

- RSS shipping with Windows 2000 does not have clustering support. One can speculate that a future version of Windows NT may include RSS clustering support.
- The Windows 2000 product supports 4-millimeter tape, 8-millimeter tape, and digital linear tape (DLT) as secondary media. Future versions of Windows NT may include support for other media types, such as optical media.
- RSS will provide migration only for the unnamed data stream, and it does not handle named data streams at all.
- RSS uses reparse points that are new to the NTFS version that ships with Windows 2000. Hence, RSS cannot support older versions of NTFS volumes.
- RSS can manage only fixed volumes. It cannot work with volumes on removable media—for example, DVD or a Jazz drive.
- RSS should be installed only after the managed volume has been compressed (if that is desired).
- RSS should be installed after the Indexing Service is installed, if the Indexing Service is desired.
- RSS currently maintains a database on the system volume. This means that a volume managed by RSS is not completely self-referencing, and thus the volume cannot easily be moved from one server to another
- RSS cannot migrate hidden, system, encrypted, or sparse files, or any files with extended attributes, to or from remote storage.

7.8.2 Windows 2000 Removable Storage Management

Windows 2000 Removable Storage Management (RSM) is a subsystem that provides some important functionalities, including

- Support for tape devices, tape robots, and jukeboxes
- Management of removable media such as tapes and CDs
- Provisions for sharing of the tape devices, robots, and jukeboxes between different applications, such as backup and Hierarchical Storage Management

Windows 2000 provides a set of components that jointly facilitate storage management and development of applications dealing with re-movable storage media. These components consist of

- Removable storage administrative module
- Removable Storage Manager (API)
- Removable storage database

Removable Storage Services is a tool used to accomplish a variety of tasks, including backup. Thus it is not a replacement for backup, but a tool used to accomplish and manage backup and restore operations.

To understand these components, it is best to understand the overall architecture of the Removable Storage Management, as described in the next section.

7.8.2.1 Windows 2000 RSM Architecture

Figure 7.7 shows the overall architecture of the Windows 2000 RSM sub-system. The RSM Service plays a significant role in the RSM subsystem. The RSM Service acts as the repository of the RSM API implementation. It receives requests from applications and places them in a queue, han-dling the requests as the desired resources become available. When the service starts, it also performs some inventory and initialization of the various libraries, identifying stand-alone drives and associating drives with changers.

Vendors developing changer and other RSS-type hardware should write a minichanger driver. The changer class driver implements a lot of the functionality common across devices and takes care of creating device objects to represent the device. However, the minichanger driver

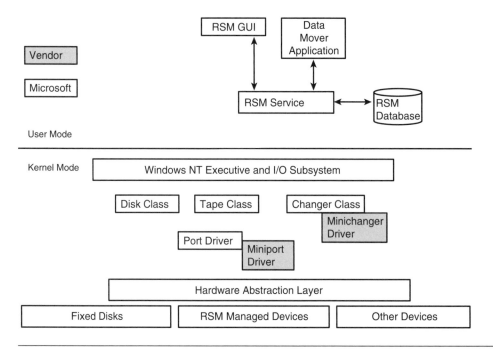

Figure 7.7 RSM Architecture

does have to deal with some knowledge of Windows NT drivers, including IRPs. Nevertheless, the range of functionality that the minichanger driver must supply is limited, compared to regular Windows NT drivers.

Note that RSM is involved in managing and setting up a device that houses removable media, as well as the media itself. After establishing device ownership, and mounting and positioning the appropriate media, RSM is no longer in the data path, meaning that it adds no I/O overhead at all.

7.8.2.2 Windows 2000 RSM APIs

The Windows 2000 Platform SDK describes how to build an application using the RSM APIs and provides details about them. The biggest contribution of these APIs is the simplicity they bring to building storage management applications.

Figure 7.8 shows the situation before the RSM API existed. Each application was complex because it had to deal with individual devices and device types. Further, every time a new device or device type was introduced, every application would require modification.

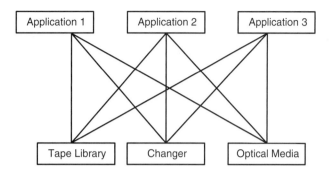

Figure 7.8 Application Development before
RSM APIs

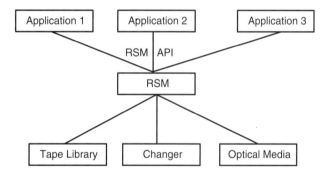

Figure 7.9 Application Development Simplified by
RSM APIs

Figure 7.9 shows the simplification provided by RSM APIs in developing the application. Obviously RSM provides extensibility in addition to simplification. When RSM adds support for a new type of device, the application can now deal with a new device with little or no modification at all. The list of devices supported by RSM is continually changing; the latest list is available at the Microsoft hardware compatibility list Web site (http://www.microsoft.com/hwdq/hcl).

RSM APIs can be divided into several categories, on the basis of the functionality they provide. This functionality includes the following:

- Drive cleaning–related APIs such as reserve cleaner, inject cleaner, eject cleaner, and (run) cleaner
- Device state change detection APIs on stand-alone drives
- Database-related APIs for backing up and restoring the RSM

database, as well as registering and deregistering for database notifications

- Library control functions for injecting, moving, and ejecting media (within a library), as well as enabling and disabling drive and changer resources
- Mounting, dismounting, and managing media pools
- Other APIs necessary to build a robust storage management application, such as APIs to query status, cancel outstanding operations, or deal with RSM objects

7.8.2.3 RSM Database

The RSM database stores information vital to the RSM subsystem. Examples of the kind of information stored here include

- Media inventory
- Media pool details, including pool configurations and contents of pools
- Library configurations

The database does *not* contain catalog information of which files are on which media. That type of functionality is up to the storage application.

Users can back up the database by manually copying the files. These files are normally stored under the %SystemRoot%\System32\ntmsdata folder. Obviously the RSM Service must stop before the files will allow copying.

The database also allows backup via an RSM API. In this case the service must still run, but it is advisable that the service not be actively in use by other programs.

7.8.2.4 Media Pools

Media pools provide for ease of use, including administrative use. A media pool is simply a collection of media such as tapes or CDs that share a common property. There are two kinds of media pools: application pools and system pools.

System pools are used by the operating system for its purposes. There are three kinds of system media pools:

1. **A free pool** contains media that any application can claim for its use and return to the free pool when it is finished with them.

2. An **import pool** contains media that are recognizable but never before encountered. A good example might be a medium that was written to use a known backup software program on a different computer system and has been mounted for the first time on this computer system.

3. An **unrecognized pool** contains media recognized to be non-blank, but Removable Storage Services is unable to determine the nature of the data on the media. An example may be media created on a different operating system or a backup software signature that is unknown. The intent is to allow the administrator to recognize the situation and save the media from being overwritten.

Application pools are created by storage management applications via the RSM APIs. Examples of applications that do this include Windows backup and Windows Remote Storage (HSM).

7.8.2.5 RSM Administration User Interface

The Removable Storage Management administration user interface first shipped with Windows 2000. It is simply a Microsoft Management Console (MMC) snap-in, which allows the storage or system administrator to view and configure objects. Various objects—such as media pools, work queues, and physical properties of storage devices—represent these object types.

7.9 The Future of SNIA Storage Management: The Storage Management Initiative

Recently the Storage Networking Industry Association has developed a standards specification called the Storage Management Initiative (SMI), which at its inception was code-named Bluefin. This specification provides for storage management of logical and physical resources in a SAN using a vendor-independent API. The areas of storage management covered by SMI include device discovery and operations management, which includes configuration management, alerting, performance, and security management. SMI was first publicly demonstrated in the spring of 2002, and it is supported by several industry vendors.

SMI is designed around existing industry standards:

- The SMI design is based on the SNIA-defined Common Information Model. SMI specifies the use of HTTP for a transport protocol and XML to describe the contents of the messages transported via HTTP. To ensure privacy and data integrity, SMI specifies the use of Transport Layer Security (TLS). Defined in RFC 2246, TLS is a protocol that ensures privacy and data integrity for data communications between two applications. TLS is based on the well-known Secure Sockets Layer protocol.
- To ensure security, SMI specifies the use of HTTP Digest Access Authentication. Defined in RFC 2617, HTTP Digest Access Authentication is basically an extension of HTTP to allow a client to send its identity and password information in an encrypted manner rather than in plain text.
- SMI specifies the use of Service Location Protocol (SLP) for storage resource discovery. Defined in RFC 3224, SLP defines a way to discover network services in a vendor-extensible manner.
- SMI encompasses lock management, which allows multiple applications, possibly from different vendors, to use lock management services to share storage resources.

7.10 Practical Implications

It is worthwhile watching how support for Windows Management Instrumentation is evolving from a recommended to a required status in Microsoft development kits and Microsoft logo requirements. This progression is consistent with past Microsoft practices in which features evolve from recommended to required status as the technology matures.[2]

It is also worthwhile watching how vendors develop support for storage management standards and how well the products based on these standards interoperate.

The volume shadow copy service and virtual disk service represent possible significant opportunities for vendors to develop storage management applications that integrate very well with the Windows NT platform.

---

2. Yours truly will be watching closely because in a past life at Microsoft, I was the WMI program manager.

7.11 Summary

Storage management is a problem that is increasing in importance as the amount of storage hardware deployed grows. Several vendors have provided solutions, but most of them are proprietary in nature. The Storage Networking Industry Association is making an effort to standardize storage management using the Common Information Model. Microsoft has also adopted a trend to have storage management available from either a GUI application or a command-line utility. The intent is to enable storage management via scripting.

Microsoft is building infrastructure into Windows NT for storage management. The virtual disk service will provide a standardized way for management applications to discover and manage storage resources. The virtual disk service also allows storage hardware vendors to provide information about their devices to these management applications in a standardized way. Similarly, the fabric virtualization service (for which very few details are yet available) will allow fabric management in a standardized way.

Windows 2000 also includes a comprehensive infrastructure for Hierarchical Storage Management that is fully integrated with the other pieces of the operating system and includes applications such as the Explorer GUI, command-line window, backup application, and job scheduler.

CHAPTER 8

IP Storage and InfiniBand

This chapter introduces two emerging new technologies: IP storage and storage over InfiniBand.

IP storage is a collection of technologies providing access to enterprise storage using an Internet Protocol (IP) network. The technologies popularly lumped into the term *IP storage* include (but are not limited to) iSCSI, FCIP, and iFCP, each of which is described briefly in this chapter.

InfiniBand is not a storage protocol per se; it is a high-speed, low-latency, generic network fabric. Some InfiniBand working groups are exploring using it to connect to storage, but the real focus of InfiniBand is on high-performance clusters of servers. With the advent of 3GIO, InfiniBand has lost some of its prominence as a replacement for the PCI bus.

This chapter provides a simple overview of IP storage and Infini-Band, in the interests of people who are unfamiliar with the technologies. The goal is to present the bare minimum required to understand the Microsoft implementation. Persons wishing to learn these technologies in detail may refer to the sources listed at the end of this book. After the introduction, some details about Microsoft's intended implementation of these technologies are presented. Given that Microsoft has yet to release the described software, the reader is cautioned that what is presented here is merely a best guess. No firm commercial product plans or deployment plans should be made on the basis of this chapter alone.

IP storage and InfiniBand are qualified as emerging technologies in the sense that they still have relatively minuscule commercial adoption. Of course, some of them have been in development for quite some time now.

8.1 IP Storage

IP storage refers to a group of technologies that provide block-level access between storage devices or servers using the IP family of protocols as a transport mechanism. The astute reader would argue, and rightly so, that data access over IP networks has been in use for quite some time—for example, in applications accessing data from a server using the CIFS or NFS protocol. The difference is that the applications are file oriented and the translation from file-level I/O to block-level I/O happens at the NAS device or server, after the request has made its way across a network. With IP SANs, the requests and responses traveling across a network consist of block-level I/O and not file-level I/O.

Figure 8.1 shows the basic outlines of direct-attached storage (DAS), network-attached storage (NAS), storage area networks (SANs), and IP SANs. Observe the following:

- With DAS, no network is involved.
- With NAS, the IP network is between the file system and the storage device. Of course, one can have a non-IP network for NAS as well, but IP is the most prevalent. The I/O flowing across the network is file-level I/O. There are always exceptions to the rule, and an example here is a NAS device such as EMC's Celerra High-Road that is connected to both a LAN and a SAN. This scenario is described in more detail in Chapter 6 (Section 6.6).
- With storage area networks, the network is between the file system and the storage device; however, the I/O is block-level I/O and not file-level I/O. Classic SANs almost always use Fibre Channel for the network.
- With IP storage, the network is again between the file system and the storage device, except in this case the network is a classic IP network.

8.1.1 Why IP Storage?

IP storage grew out of the realization that it is probably not necessary to have two kinds of networks. These two networks are the IP and Ethernet networks connecting clients and servers (the so-called *front-end network*), and storage networks are termed the *back-end networks* between servers and storage.

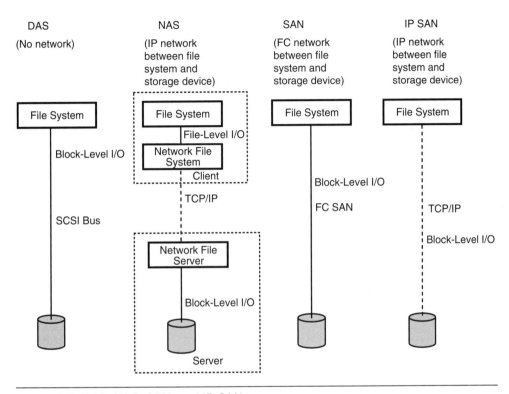

Figure 8.1 DAS, NAS, SAN, and IP SAN

IP storage is likely to make rapid progress for several reasons:

- IP is an established, well-understood technology that has solved many of the problems involved in running IP-over-Ethernet, ATM, and so on.
- IP routing is an established technology that provides multiple paths between servers and storage devices in the face of a dynamically changing network.
- In some sense, the problem of storage management is the equivalent of the well-known problem of managing IP-based networks.
- IP provides for geographical separation between servers and storage units.
- IP networks are used to build the largest-scale networks in the world, including the Internet, and have addressed many of the scalability and congestion issues.

Proponents of IP storage argue that IP has won and it is time to move on from "IP-over-everything" (Ethernet, Token Ring, ATM, Gigabit Ethernet, and so on) to "Everything-over-IP" (including SCSI command data blocks, or CDBs—more simply, SCSI-commands/results-over-IP, and so on).

Chapter 4 explained that there are two worlds: the worlds of I/O channels and networks. Channels such as SCSI typically operate over smaller distances, are dedicated to a limited set of purposes, and typically are implemented with a lot of the functionality built into hardware. Networks, on the other hand, can operate over larger distances, are more general-purpose in nature, and comparatively get more of their functionality from software. Whereas Fibre Channel represents an effort to combine the best of both worlds from a channel-centric view, IP storage represents an attempt to combine the best of both worlds from a network-centric point of view.

The new term *storage wide area network (SWAN)* refers to the deployment and use of IP storage technologies over IP-based wide area networks.

The following sections describe the various IP storage technologies and, where relevant, provide details of Microsoft implementation of those technologies.

8.1.2 iSCSI

iSCSI (short for "Internet SCSI") is a protocol that specifies a means of establishing one or more TCP/IP connections between two devices to be used for exchanging SCSI commands, responses, and status information over those established TCP connections. To put it differently, iSCSI is an end-to-end encapsulation protocol that encapsulates SCSI command, response, and status information.

Figure 8.2 shows how IP, TCP, iSCSI, and SCSI are related in terms of encapsulation. The iSCSI packet is the data or payload for the TCP/IP stack, and it carries the SCSI command and data as *its* data and payload. The iSCSI header provides information about how to extract and interpret the SCSI commands within the payload. The TCP header is

Figure 8.2 iSCSI Protocol Encapsulation

responsible for guaranteed, sequential delivery of packets, and the TCP packet itself is the data and payload of an IP packet. The IP header facilitates routing.

Of the three major IP storage protocols—iSCSI, FCIP (Fibre Channel over IP), and iFCP (Internet Fibre Channel Protocol)—iSCSI is the only one that has no relationship to Fibre Channel other than as a complete replacement for Fibre Channel. In lacking any mention of Fibre Channel, Figure 8.2 shows that iSCSI evolved with no Fibre Channel support in mind.

iSCSI is layered on top of the existing layers of TCP/IP, IP, and lower-level hardware protocols that support TCP/IP (such as Ethernet and Gigabit Ethernet).

As Figure 8.3 shows, SCSI is an application protocol. iSCSI provides services to the SCSI application protocol and avails itself of the services of TCP/IP for reliable transmission, routing, and so on.

All iSCSI devices (targets as well as initiators) have two different names:

1. An **iSCSI address**, which consists of an IP address, a TCP port, and an iSCSI name in the format "<domain name>:<port number>:<iSCSI name>".
2. An **iSCSI name** in a human-readable format—for example, "FullyQualifiedName.DiskVendor.DiskModel.Number".

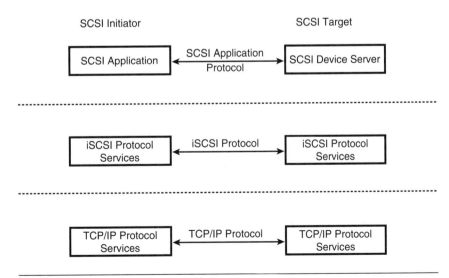

Figure 8.3 iSCSI Protocol Layers

The naming authority iSNS (Internet Storage Name Service) is common to iSCSI, iFCP, and FCP (Fibre Channel Protocol). iFCP and FCP are described in Section 8.1.5. In addition to using iSNS as a naming service, iSCSI has an accompanying specification that deals with defining a MIB (Management Information Base) for SNMP-based management of iSCSI devices. iSCSI also defines a process to implement remote booting.

iSCSI establishes sessions between initiator and target. These are iSCSI sessions, and a single iSCSI session may use one or more TCP sessions. When the session is established, the two sides (initiator and target) negotiate options such as security, buffer size, and whether or not unsolicited data can be sent. An iSCSI session may end normally with a logout or terminate because of an error. Regardless of how many TCP sessions are used, the iSCSI protocol guarantees that the SCSI commands and responses are delivered in order. Note that TCP guarantees sequential delivery for a particular TCP session but does not provide any semantics to synchronize traffic over two different TCP sessions. Hence it is up to the iSCSI protocol to implement synchronization among the multiple different TCP sessions when needed. Some iSCSI requirements here include the following:

- Different SCSI commands *may* flow over different TCP sessions.
- All data and parameters corresponding to a particular SCSI command must flow over the same TCP session as the one on which the command originated.
- iSCSI defines the concept of an initiator tag. All responses will have the corresponding initiator tag sent in the original command. An initiator must ensure that initiator tags are unique and not reused, until all outstanding responses to that tag are received back at the initiator. The tags must be unique per initiator (Windows NT is a multitasking system, and the initiator may be acting on behalf of multiple processes and applications).
- iSCSI defines the concept of command numbering to ensure sequential delivery of commands across multiple TCP sessions.
- iSCSI also defines an end-to-end CRC (cyclic redundancy check) mechanism because layer 2 CRC checking (e.g., Gigabit Ethernet) or layer 3 (TCP/IP checksums) may be unreliable, especially when one considers that there may be interposing IP devices (e.g., network address translators, routers)—hence the need for a guaranteed end-to-end error detection mechanism. This is consistent with the fact that storage providers are historically more sensitive to data integrity checking.

iSCSI also has its disadvantages. It introduces issues such as security, congestion control, and quality of service. However, these issues are mostly related to issues with operating a TCP/IP network, which are well-understood issues.

8.1.3 Windows NT iSCSI Implementation

Microsoft has indicated that it is actively implementing iSCSI support in Windows NT. There is no exact release period, especially since the iSCSI specification itself is not yet finalized. The fact that the initial iSCSI draft specification was finalized in the summer of 2002 should help firm up iSCSI support from Microsoft. Current indications are that Microsoft will have native iSCSI support in the post-Windows Server 2003 time frame, but this is something only time will tell, and the reader is cautioned not to make any plans on the basis of this estimate. iSCSI support certainly is not natively part of Windows Server 2003.

Figure 8.4 shows the architecture for the Windows NT iSCSI implementation.

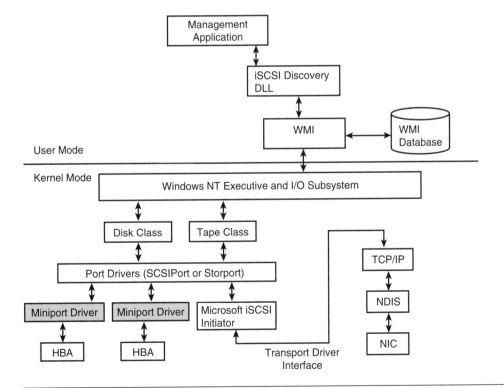

Figure 8.4 iSCSI Architecture

The iSCSI initiator is implemented as a miniport driver for either a SCSIPort miniport or a Storport miniport.

The iSCSI discovery dynamic link library (DLL) tracks all changes dynamically and acts as a single repository for all LUNs discovered through any mechanism, including iSNS client or port notification. The discovery DLL provides an API for management applications to discover new LUNs and, if appropriate, a means for the management application to direct the discovery DLL to log in to the new LUN.

Highlights of Microsoft iSCSI plans include the following:

- The focus is on implementing iSCSI on the Windows Server 2003 platform, but supporting it on the Windows 2000 platform is also being considered. Only a final announcement at the time when the software is actually made available will provide any certainty.
- The focus is on implementing iSCSI on the Windows Server 2003 platform. However, Microsoft will also provide iSCSI code for the Windows 2000 and Windows XP platforms. This code is expected to be available within months of the Windows Server 2003 release.
- Microsoft will provide code for an iSNS server and client.
- Microsoft emphasizes the use of IPsec as a data protection and security mechanism.
- The idea is to focus on iSCSI initiator implementation, and there are no current plans to implement iSCSI target on the Windows NT platform.
- All communication between discovery DLL and iSCSI initiator is through Windows Management Instrumentation (WMI). The discovery DLL might turn into a service, or it might not.
- A core feature is the separation of target discovery from target access. A management application initiates access via the discovery DLL, which in turn contacts the miniport driver (via WMI). The miniport driver reports a BusChangeDetected event (described in the Windows NT DDK), causing a device enumeration. From this point on, device enumeration is no different; for example, a Report LUNs command will be sent to the newly discovered device.
- The use of IPsec (IP security) for security considerations is strongly advised.
- The use of WMI for management and reporting purposes is encouraged. It is expected that some WMI classes will be required to

be implemented and others may be recommended. Exact details are available only privately through an agreement with Microsoft.[1]

Even though a lot of the information provided in this chapter is speculative, it is provided because the widespread adoption of iSCSI can be accomplished only with native operating system support. This means that the reader needs to be aware of OS vendor plans in this area. However, the reader is also cautioned about the speculative nature of the information.

8.1.4 FCIP

Fiber Channel over IP provides a means of preserving existing investment in equipment and of connecting geographically distributed SANs using a TCP/IP-based tunneling protocol. The IETF FCIP specification covers the following areas:

- Encapsulation of Fibre Channel frames being transported via TCP/IP, including the encapsulation required to create a virtual Fibre Channel link connecting Fibre Channel devices and fabric.
- Specification of the TCP/IP environment, including security, congestion control, and error recovery. FCIP requires both Fibre Channel and TCP to play a role in error handling and recovery.

Figure 8.5 shows the details of FCIP encapsulation.

The SCSI data forms the payload. The SCSI data is encapsulated within Fibre Channel Protocol (FCP), which itself is encapsulated within FCIP. TCP thinks of FCIP as its own payload. In the encapsulation, IP is unaware of the Fibre Channel nature of the data, and the Fibre Channel part, in turn, is completely unaware of the presence of IP.

Encapsulation protocols typically have implementation overheads as the data goes through a series of layers, with some protocol processing being executed at each layer. FCIP is no exception to the rule of having some implementation overheads. To the IP network in Figure 8.6, the

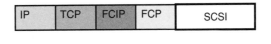

Figure 8.5 FCIP Encapsulation

---

1. To correspond with the relevant folks at Microsoft, send e-mail to iscsi@microsoft.com.

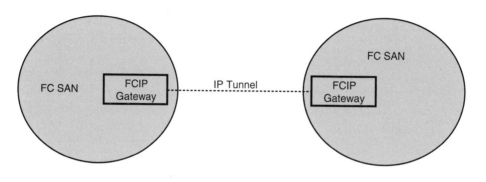

Figure 8.6 FCIP Connecting Two SANs

FCIP gateways appear to be IP devices; to the Fibre Channel networks, however, the FCIP gateways appear to be Fibre Channel devices. Only the two FCIP gateways communicating with each other are aware of the Fibre Channel encapsulation.

Figure 8.6 shows how FCIP is typically used to connect two distinct and separate SAN islands. With FCIP, the storage network remains Fibre Channel–centric, and all addressing, routing, and other operational aspects of the storage network remain unaltered—that is, just as in a Fibre Channel network. FCIP depends on TCP/IP for routing and management, including congestion control. FCIP depends on both TCP/IP and FCP to detect and correct data corruption. FCIP also relies on both TCP/IP and Fibre Channel to ensure data loss recovery. FCIP maps Fibre Channel addresses to IP addresses. FCIP provides connectivity between E ports. (Chapter 4 describes different types of Fibre Channel ports.)

Typical FCIP applications could include the following:

- Remote backup and restore
- Remote backup to ensure a geographical disaster recovery solution
- At sufficiently high bandwidth between the two FCIP gateways (a distinct possibility with the overaccumulation of geographical cable), synchronous mirroring and geographical data sharing, as well as shared or pooled storage

FCIP requires no changes to the Fibre Channel Network. Figure 8.7 shows the FCIP and iFCP protocol stacks. (iFCP is described in Section 8.1.5.) Note that the Fibre Channel functional layers, including FC-4 and the lower Fibre Channel layers, remain unaltered in a FCIP

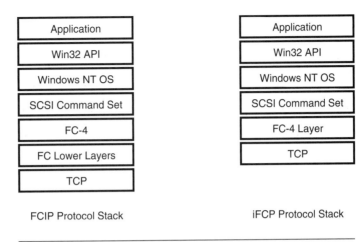

Figure 8.7 Comparison of FCIP and iFCP Protocol Stacks

environment. Compared to the typical hierarchy of file system, volume management, class, and port layers in Chapter 1, the SCSI command layer exists in this model up to the port layer. Thus the FC-4 and lower layers in Figure 8.7 would be implemented in hardware below the Windows NT port driver layer. The one caveat is that normally one would expect hardware to simply provide much of the functionality beneath the port driver. In this case there is also a TCP/IP stack that is very often implemented in software.

FCIP has some advantages compared to IP-over-Ethernet. Whereas Ethernet packets typically carry approximately 1,500 bytes of data, FCIP frames carry approximately 2,000 bytes. When one considers that Ethernet frames, with Gigabit Ethernet, support jumbo frames that hold typically 8K or more, this advantage is mitigated.

The problem with FCIP is still that customers have two networks to maintain. FCIP is expected to be used more as a way to do channel extension or remote mirroring to an existing device, than as a "new" storage protocol being deployed natively at the host level.

8.1.5 iFCP

Internet Fibre Channel Protocol is a gateway-to-gateway protocol that allows two Fibre Channel networks to connect to each other via a TCP/IP transmission network. Essentially, the Fibre Channel fabric components are replaced by the TCP/IP switching and routing elements. Whereas FCIP aims at providing SAN-to-SAN connectivity, iFCP targets more at providing connectivity for individual Fibre Channel devices into an IP network.

iFCP is a gateway-to-gateway protocol that uses two gateway devices to enable the rest of the devices in the Fibre Channel SAN to remain unmodified while allowing connectivity. Figure 8.8 shows a typical iFCP deployment.

Two iFCP gateways are deployed as edge devices in an IP network. Fibre Channel–enabled nodes such as disks, tapes, and servers may be connected to the gateways. As Figure 8.8 shows, the two gateways establish an IP tunnel that carries device-to-device session traffic. Thus, iFCP works on a device-to-device basis, whereas FCIP works more like an Ethernet bridge that forwards everything from one island to another.

iFCP supports Fibre Channel Protocol (FCP), which is the standard for transporting SCSI commands and responses on a serial link. As shown in Figure 8.7, the iFCP protocol stack replaces the FC-2 layer (the transport layer of Fibre Channel described in Chapter 4) with a TCP transport layer, but leaves the FC-4 layer untouched. iFCP messaging and routing services terminate at the gateway. Thus, even though device-to-device connectivity exists, the two Fibre Channel SANs remain physically apart.

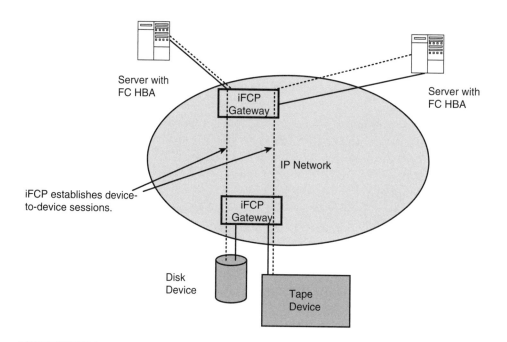

Figure 8.8 iFCP Deployment

Think of this scenario as somewhat equivalent to broadcast frames that do not propagate through a router. iFCP provides connectivity only between Fibre Channel F ports. (See Chapter 4 for a description of the various Fibre Channel port types and their functionality.) iFCP creates multiple TCP/IP sessions, and these sessions are from one Fibre Channel device to another.

Comparing the FCIP and iFCP protocol stacks in Figure 8.7, one notices that FCIP implements all layers of the Fibre Channel protocol, whereas iFCP implements only layer 4. One can thus conclude that FCIP is more Fibre Channel–centric.

iFCP uses TCP/IP to ensure reliable data transmission. This means that the underlying IP network itself need not be reliable. The iFCP specification allows for high latencies in networks, and this helps it operate in low-latency unreliable networks where the network appears to be a high-latency reliable network, thanks to the efforts of TCP in providing a reliable sequential transport mechanism. Because iFCP uses multiple TCP/IP connections, it is more robust and less prone to congestion than when a single TCP/IP connection is used for all storage device connectivity.

iFCP gateway devices provide a means for storage devices to register with an iSNS name server (see the next section).

8.1.6 Internet Storage Name Service

The **Internet Storage Name Service** (**iSNS**) provides registration and discovery services for storage devices. Because iSNS is a lightweight protocol, it can easily be implemented in servers as well as storage devices. iSNS provides a single model that can apply to both SCSI and Fibre Channel devices, thus facilitating the mapping between IP storage and Fibre Channel devices. Fibre Channel–based devices register with iSNS through means provided by an iFCP gateway. iSCSI devices register directly with the iSNS service. Initiators locate the iSNS server in one of two ways:

1. Through statically configured information
2. Through the Service Location Protocol (SLP)

iSNS also provides zoning functionality through the concept of discovery domains, which allow an administrator to specify groups of devices. When a member of the group queries the iSNS server, the returned results are limited to members of the same group. In addition, iSNS provides notification services—for example, when a new target device comes online.

iSNS servers play an important role in storage security. One way of enforcing security is through discovery domains. In other words, iSNS servers can store and enforce access control policy (that is, which initiators are allowed to access which devices). In addition, iSNS servers play a role in providing a mechanism for a device to register its public key certificate with the iSNS server, and the server can then provide this information to other devices that query it.

Microsoft appears to be a proponent of the iSNS protocol. It has not yet publicly indicated whether it will ship an iSNS server, an iSNS client, or both.

8.1.7 TCP Offload Solutions

With the advent of IP storage, it has become even more imperative to have an efficient TCP/IP implementation. Testing shows that significant CPU resources can be consumed by TCP/IP processing overheads. Even the TCP/IP checksum calculations by themselves can be a significant drain on CPU resources. In addition, the data is copied multiple times, and this overhead can add up when one considers the vast number of data copies that are made.

For example, TCP must provide sequential delivery (not provided by IP), so it must temporarily store packets that arrive out of sequence. This means that data is copied into a temporary buffer and then later copied into the user buffer. The hardware requirements for supporting even something as simple as receiving packets out of order can be onerous. A 1-Gbps (gigabits per second) WAN link can require 16MB of memory to store and reassemble nonsequential packets. A 10-Gbps WAN link can require as much as 125MB of memory. The point is that the number of situations in which buffer copies are needed must be reduced, either through more efficient software or through enhanced hardware, or a combination of the two.

TCP offload solutions developed recently make an effort to move some of the overhead to a hardware network interface adapter. With the increasing importance of TCP/IP performance, given the advent of IP storage, these efforts have only accelerated. The proposed solutions include the following:

- Offload the entire TCP/IP stack to hardware. Although this is the best approach in terms of performance, it is also the most ambitious and has some tough issues to solve—for example, coordination between different TCP stacks running on different NICs (network interface cards) on the same Windows NT server.

■ Offload the TCP data movement and checksum generation, but not the connection control.
■ Offload "normal" processing, but handle the exceptions in software.
■ Offload some IPsec and even some iSCSI processing into the hardware.

Windows 2000 introduced NDIS (Network Driver Interface Specification) version 5.0, which includes support for TCP/IP offload. Specifically, Windows 2000 introduced support for the following functions:

■ Offloading the TCP/IP checksum calculation to hardware for both sending (generating checksum) and receiving (verifying checksum).
■ Offloading TCP segmentation wherein data that is larger than the maximum transmission unit can be passed in and the hardware will accomplish the required segmentation into multiple packets.
■ Offloading IPsec implementation. IPsec is a standard (applicable to both IPv4 and IPv6) that ensures data integrity and authentication on a per-packet basis. IPsec can be operated in two modes: a transport mode that ensures data integrity and authentication between two end user applications, or a tunnel mode that ensures security in data exchange between two routers. Both can be offloaded.
■ Fast packet forwarding, wherein Windows 2000 routing code can directly forward a packet from one network port to another without having the packet ever enter host memory.

8.2 InfiniBand

InfiniBand is a new standard (and architecture) that defines a switched-fabric interconnect between a host and storage or network peripheral devices. The InfiniBand Trade Association (IBTA) drives the InfiniBand specification. The IBTA is an association that came into existence through the merger of two competing specifications: Future I/O led by Intel, and Next Generation I/O led by IBM, HP, and Compaq.

InfiniBand supports several changes, one of which is the replacement of an I/O bus (such as PCI) with a switched-fabric network. A switched serial fabric has several advantages over an I/O bus, the most notable being that a fabric can support more devices over vastly greater distances using a significantly lower number of electrical pins. Not only that, but a fabric can support simultaneous multiple data transfers and also provide fault tolerance. Before diving into the details of InfiniBand architecture, it is worthwhile to recollect the limitations of the PCI (Peripheral Component Interconnect) bus.

Although PCI has its merits—most notably that it replaced a slew of competing standards (ISA, EISA, MCA) with one standard that provided additional functionality—the fact is that PCI seems to have limitations, especially given the rapid advances made in CPU, memory, and peripheral technology. PCI limitations can be briefly summarized as follows:

- Although PCI was fast when it was newly introduced, it no longer meets the bandwidth requirements—the CPU memory front-side bus now has speeds of up to 1,066 Mbps—and Gigabit Ethernet NICs and high-end storage devices (SCSI 3) can be choked by PCI bus speed.
- PCI has problems with manageability in general and failure detection in particular. A single bad PCI card can bring the whole system down, yet it is hard to determine which particular card is faulty.
- There are physical limitations in terms of how long the bus can be, how fast the bus can be, and the number of buses allowed. At the fastest bus rate, one may be able to connect only a single peripheral (device).

Note that although InfiniBand was initially also positioned as a PCI replacement, the advent of 3GIO has reduced the importance of InfiniBand as a PCI replacement.

8.2.1 InfiniBand Advantages

InfiniBand offers numerous advantages, including

- Reduction in cabling complexity because InfiniBand can replace three cables—Ethernet, storage, and an interprocess communication cable—with a single interconnect. The result can be considerable simplification in silicon on the blade, backplane wiring density, and complexity. Further, the blades connect to a couple of edge connectors, and only a couple of high-bandwidth interconnects come out of the rack.

- Built-in fault detection, which makes it easy to quickly identify a failed component.
- Reduced memory bandwidth consumption because of fewer memory-to-memory copy operations.
- Reduced number of context switches, including user and kernel mode switches.
- Reduced protocol overhead—for example, TCP/IP checksum calculations.
- Provision for high availability with the alternative routes in a fabric environment and redundant components such as routers and switches. The redundant paths also cater to multipath and load-balancing solutions. Further, InfiniBand components allow hot plug, and they unplug easily.
- InfiniBand can facilitate having a blade boot from an external device without any loss of efficiency, thus reducing blade silicon even more.

8.2.2 InfiniBand Architecture

The InfiniBand architecture specifies a point-to-point logical connection topology made over a switched fabric. The switched fabric itself has the following primary components:

- Host channel adapters
- Target channel adapters
- InfiniBand switches
- Physical media

Figure 8.9 shows the InfiniBand I/O bus and the relationship of the various components to each other. The following text discusses some of the components depicted in this figure.

A **host channel adapter** (**HCA**) is a device that acts as a connection point between a host CPU and the InfiniBand fabric. Host channel adapters are closely associated with servers and tend to be located close to them. An HCA has built-in intelligence that will minimize interrupts and operating system involvement and can accomplish transfers directly into memory. Each HCA has a unique IPv6-based identifier associated with it.

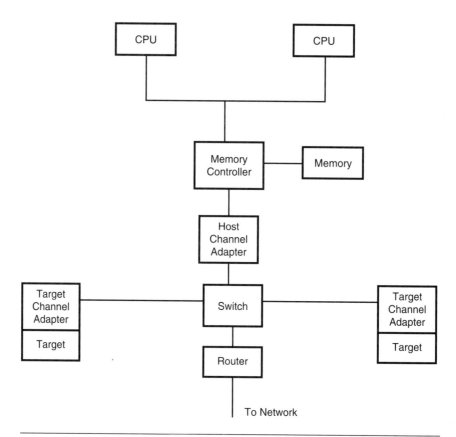

Figure 8.9 InfiniBand I/O Bus

A **target channel adapter** (**TCA**) is the equivalent of an HCA, but for a peripheral device instead of for a host CPU. Target channel adapters are associated with storage peripherals and tend to be located close to them. Just like an HCA, each TCA has a unique IPv6-based identifier associated with it.

An InfiniBand switch provides a means to connect multiple TCAs to a single HCA. Switches also provide functionality for routing among multiple logical divisions of the fabric (called *subnets*). Whereas InfiniBand switches provide connectivity *within* a subnet, InfiniBand routers provide connectivity *between* subnets. Routers typically are implemented such that they are a superset of switch functionality.

InfiniBand allows for the use of off-the-shelf copper or optic cables. The links can be up to 17 meters for copper wire and 100 meters for optical cables. InfiniBand specifies a connection consisting of varying number of links that each operate at 2.5 Gbps. The supported combinations run from 1X (1 wire), to 4X (4 wires) for a 10 Gbps connection, to 12X (12 wires), up to 30 Gbps.

The physical entities that collectively constitute the InfiniBand architecture have just been described, but the InfiniBand architecture also specifies some logical concepts and entities, in addition to the physical components.

8.2.2.1 InfiniBand Link and Network Layers

At the link layer, each InfiniBand link is subdivided into a maximum of 16 lanes and a minimum of 2 lanes. One of the lanes is always dedicated to fabric management. Lanes receive QoS (quality of service) priorities, and a management lane (virtual lane 15; lanes 0 to 14 are data lanes) has the highest priority and QoS.

Note that whereas a link is a physical entity, a lane is a logical entity. A lane allows two endpoints to communicate with each other. Two communicating endpoints can support a different number of virtual lanes, and InfiniBand defines an algorithm to handle this situation. The communicating endpoints are called a **queue pair**. The queue pairs have send and receive buffers associated with them. Each virtual lane (VL) has its own credit-based flow control. The management packets provide for device enumeration, subnet management, and fault tolerance.

InfiniBand supports collision-free[2] simultaneous data transfer operations. To ensure reliable data transmission, InfiniBand uses end-to-end flow control and not one, but two, CRC checks. It accomplishes flow control by having the receiving node set aside multiple buffers for data reception and communicate the number to the sender. This number represents the number of data buffers that the sender can send without receiving acknowledgments. Two CRC values are calculated and included in the data transmission, regenerated by the receiver, and then compared with the received value. A 32-bit CRC is created for end-to-end communication. Meanwhile, data may also pass through intermediate nodes. A 16-bit value exists between the intermediate and end node or between two intermediate nodes.

---

2. Although InfiniBand does not have Ethernet-like collisions and random transmission delays to avoid these collisions, it does have flow control mechanisms and may delay data transmission when required. To an application, the effect is the same, a noticeable delay in data transmission and reception, and a poor throughput of data.

InfiniBand defines the basic unit of communication to be a *message*. A message may be sent or received via an RDMA operation, a send or receive operation, or a multicast operation. RDMA (remote direct memory access) is direct exchange of a message from one node memory to another without operating system interrupts and services being required. InfiniBand defines six communication modes for data transfer:

1. Reliable connection, wherein hardware is responsible for generating and checking packet sequence numbers to ensure a reliable connection; the hardware also detects duplicate and lost packets and ensures error recovery.
2. Unreliable connection.
3. Reliable datagram.
4. Unreliable datagram.
5. Multicast connection (implementation is optional).
6. Packet transfer (implementation is optional).

An InfiniBand message can consist of one or more packets. Packets can be up to 4,096 bytes long but may be smaller. Packets allow interleaving on a VL. Routing executes at a packet level. Packets that route between subnets have a global routing header that facilitates this routing.

InfiniBand architecture also defines a network layer that provides for routing between different subnets. Subnets allow traffic to be localized to just the subnet; for example, broadcasts and multicast packets stay inside the subnet. Subnets provide functionality similar to that of VLANs (virtual LANs) and can enforce security. Subnets use a 16-bit identifier for each device. This identifier is unique per subnet. Each packet routed contains an IPv6 address for source and destination nodes.

8.2.3 Microsoft and InfiniBand

Microsoft initially indicated that at an unspecified time in the future, the Windows Server family would natively support InfiniBand. Subsequently, in the third quarter of 2002, Microsoft and some other industry leaders indicated that they were rethinking their plans for InfiniBand support. Microsoft has indicated that it is now refocusing resources away from InfiniBand and on other areas, including IP storage via Gigabit Ethernet. Accordingly, this chapter may seem a little incomplete to some readers, given that there is no Microsoft implementation of InfiniBand to describe.

8.3 Practical Implications

The IT administrators and procurement officials should note that Microsoft intends to have native support for iSCSI in the post-Windows Server 2003 time frame. Hence, any iSCSI solutions they procure before then will need to be designed wholly by the vendor, and how these solutions interact with the native Windows iSCSI support, once it is indeed available, is something only time will tell.

Vendors interested in developing an iSCSI solution for the Windows platform are in for an interesting time. There is still some confusion here, and very often opportunities await where there is confusion. Vendors should contact Microsoft at iscsi@microsoft.com to participate in the iSCSI development process that is still evolving. Current indications from Microsoft are that when it designs an iSCSI solution, it will natively support iSCSI for both the Windows 2000 and Windows Server 2003 platforms. Given that some vendor solutions will require the vendor to develop a miniport driver, these vendors should keep in mind that the Storport driver model (described in Chapter 2) is not available for Windows Server 2003. Hence they need to decide whether to develop their miniport driver to accommodate the lower common denominator of the SCSIPort driver, which runs on both, or to accommodate both SCSIPort and Storport.

It is highly likely that IP storage will mature rapidly, once there is widespread native operating system support. Some Linux versions already support iSCSI, and hence, in this sense, Windows is playing catch-up. The new opportunities created by wider adoption of IP storage are likely to attract a lot of attention, and consume a lot of resources.

8.4 Summary

IP storage, a group of technologies for accessing storage devices over IP-based networks is growing in importance, as standards are defined and vendors start shipping products. Microsoft has indicated Windows NT native support for at least iSCSI, one of the core constituents of IP storage.

With the increased use of IP storage, it becomes even more imperative to have an implementation of the TCP/IP stack (and related protocols) that is as efficient as possible. One way to have a more efficient implementation is to have some of the protocol processing in hardware.

With NDIS 5.1, Microsoft has indicated native Windows NT support for TCP offload network cards.

InfiniBand is a new standard that defines a switched-fabric interconnect that may be used to provide connectivity between host CPU and storage peripherals. Although some of the industry is continuing InfiniBand development, Microsoft has decided to refrain from shipping native InfiniBand support in the Windows NT operating system.

CHAPTER 9

High Availability

The increasing amount of data storage is accompanied by a growing need not only to protect the data, but also to make it highly available round the clock. This means that we must protect data from corruption, while simultaneously avoiding high performance penalties. RAID (redundant array of independent disks) is one way to achieve this balance of high availability and high performance. The first part of this chapter provides an overview of RAID.

To ensure high availability and quick disaster recovery, data is stored in multiple locations and continuously updated to reflect changes. This is the idea behind the mirroring and replication schemes developed in general and for the Windows Server family of operating systems in particular.

There can be no single point of failure in the path from the server to the data storage device. This is the basic idea behind the multipath solutions. Multipath solutions developed for the Windows Server family of operating systems are described in Section 9.3.

9.1 RAID

RAID stands for "redundant array of independent disks" (originally the term *inexpensive* was used instead of *independent*). RAID was invented at the University of California in what is now famously termed "The Berkeley Paper" in 1988. It is a common offering from many vendors. In 1993, the RAID Advisory Group formed the RAID Conformance Program whereby vendors would ensure that their hardware passed the conformance test in return for certification by the RAID Advisory Board, including permission to use the official RAID logo on their devices. The different versions of RAID provide different levels of performance and data protection, and the implementations used differ for those particular needs.

An idea that is common to almost all the RAID implementations is the notion of **striping**. Striping consists of defining a basic unit of I/O (which is typically in a range between 512 bytes and 4MB or 8MB)[1] and then defining how these I/O units are physically placed on different disks to provide a logical block for higher-level clusters and so on. Thus the first unit could be on disk 1, the second unit on disk 2, and so on.

RAID can be implemented in hardware or in software, in the following ways:

- In host (server) software
- In an HBA connected to the host (server)
- In the storage device

In some cases a single corporation uses a combination of these varieties of RAID. For example, the corporation may have RAID implemented in the host, as well as, say, inside storage devices.

Windows NT Logical Disk Manager is one example of software that implements RAID functionality in software. **Host-based RAID**, also referred to as *software RAID*, has the following advantages:

- Hardware costs are lower because the storage units can be relatively dumb.
- It has interoperability in terms of being able to use dumb disks from multiple vendors
- When implemented in a volume manager–like solution, virtualization services are provided that overcome hardware limitations; for example, multiple smaller disks can be combined so that they look like a single large disk.
- The configuration is more flexible. For example, software-based RAID can apply mirroring across two independent RAID systems, consolidate LUNs into a single larger logical LUN, or divide a single large physical LUN into multiple smaller logical storage volumes.

Software-based RAID also has some shortcomings, which include the following:

- The parity calculations and other calculations that are needed take a fair amount of CPU time. Some Microsoft applications discourage the use of software RAID as being too CPU expensive.

---

1. There are exceptions. For example, a supercomputer at Thinking Machines used 16-byte stripes in its RAID 3 storage subsystem.

- For each write operation, two write operations flow across the I/O bus—one for data and one for parity.
- With software-based RAID, two levels of indirection can add a fair amount of complexity and overhead:
    1. The file system abstracts file-based I/O to volume-relative block I/O.
    2. The volume manager (software RAID implementer) adds another level of indirection, translating volume-relative blocks to physical disk-relative blocks. In the case of a distributed file system, this also means that two levels of locks must be obtained, either physically or virtually (e.g., a file opened in exclusive mode may be treated as if virtually locked).

There are several different types of RAID implementations. These are discussed in Sections 9.1.1 through 9.1.7.

9.1.1 RAID 0

RAID 0 consists of simply striping data across multiple disk drives. Thus, RAID 0 can provide some performance advantages, but it does not provide redundancy or data protection.

As Figure 9.1 shows, data is written in turn to different disks when

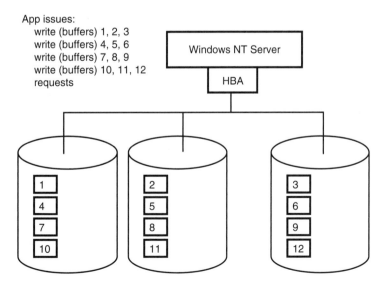

Figure 9.1 RAID 0

RAID 0 is deployed. The application in this figure issues multiple write requests. For the sake of simplicity, assume that the application always issues write requests with a fixed-size buffer and that this buffer size exactly matches the stripe size—that is, the amount of data that the RAID configuration deals with as an integral unit. Figure 9.1 shows that the data is sprayed onto multiple disks in a round-robin fashion (each number inside a box represents a different write request).

RAID 0 is extremely efficient in terms of delivering I/O performance because disk read and write operations to the independent disks can happen in parallel. However, the biggest problem with RAID 0 is that it is not fault tolerant. Thus, if any single disk drive in a RAID 0 configuration fails, one is faced with a total loss of data, which explains the saying "lose one, lose all."

Further, striping can increase performance, but when used excessively or in the wrong situations, it can actually decrease performance. Transaction-oriented applications typically do I/O in small blocks of 1K or less. Streaming media applications tend to do I/O in much larger blocks. Nevertheless, storage devices tend to achieve their highest throughput when the I/O block size is much larger, typically about 512K. If one were to apply an eight-way stripe in this situation, the I/O block size per disk would be reduced to just 64K, and that would likely reduce the throughput in this case.

9.1.2 RAID 1

RAID 1 is essentially a solution in which write operations mirror onto primary and secondary drives. Figure 9.2 shows a RAID 1 configuration. The application issues a request to write a buffer denoted as *buffer-1*. The data in buffer-1 is written to two separate physical disks. Similarly, the application issues another request to write buffer-2. This data is also written to not one but two separate physical disks.

Under ideal conditions, the primary and secondary drives would be identical. This means that read operations will perform very efficiently if they are split across the primary drive and the secondary drive. RAID 1 delivers the best data read performance, bar none, of all the various RAID configurations. The disadvantage is that RAID 1 requires a lot of storage space—twice the space required by other RAID implementations. The reduction in disk prices somewhat mitigates this drawback. The big advantage with RAID 1 is that the data is instantaneously available from the secondary drive if the primary drive fails. RAID 1 is the only choice if the disk array can involve only two disks.

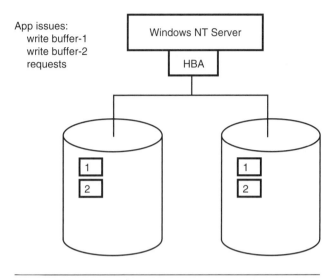

App issues:
  write buffer-1
  write buffer-2
  requests

Figure 9.2 RAID 1

9.1.3 RAID 2

RAID 2 is no longer used. **RAID 2** computes ECC (error correction code) information across stripes, but modern disk drives already store and compute ECC information across disk stripes.

9.1.4 RAID 3

RAID 3 is also referred to as *striping with dedicated parity*. In this RAID implementation, the parity is always stored in a particular dedicated disk while the data is spread across multiple drives.

Figure 9.3 shows a RAID 3 configuration. The application issues a single write request that consists of data in buffers 1, 2, and 3. This data ends up on different disks. RAID 3 also computes a parity (P1) that encompasses all three buffers, and this parity is written to yet another disk that is different from the disk where data buffers 1, 2, and 3 are written. Similarly, data buffers 4, 5, and 6 are written to different disks, and the parity corresponding to these buffers is called P2; the buffers 7, 8, and 9 are also written to different disks, and the parity corresponding to these buffers is called P3; and so on. Note that all the parity buffers are written to the same disk.

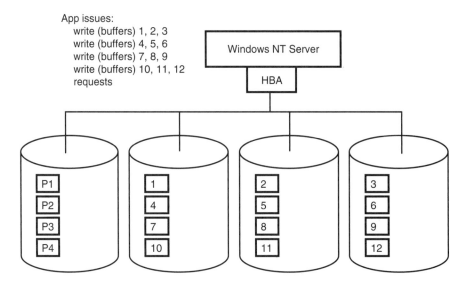

Figure 9.3 RAID 3

RAID 3 typically requires that a single read or write operation will involve all drives in the array. If a drive fails, a new drive is inserted into the array and the data on the lost drive is recovered from the data on the other drives and the parity information. Although RAID 3 has limited support in the PC world (e.g., Adaptec controllers do not support it), it has been used in the ultra-high-performance world of supercomputers.

9.1.5 RAID 4

RAID 4 is similar to RAID 3, except the disk drive stripe used is relatively large. Read operations overlap between different drives; however, write operations do not occur in parallel. RAID 4 has limited support from vendors; for example, Adaptec controllers do not support it.

9.1.6 RAID 5

RAID 5, also referred to as *striping with distributed parity,* is the most successful of RAID data-striping implementations. The only technical difference between RAID 3 and RAID 5 is that whereas RAID 3 stores the parity on a dedicated drive, RAID 5 distributes the parity across all participating drives.

Figure 9.4 shows a RAID 5 configuration. The application issues a single write request that consists of data in buffers 1, 2, and 3. This data ends up on different disks. RAID 5 also computes a parity that encompasses all three buffers, and this parity (P1) is written to yet another disk that is different from the disk where data buffers 1, 2, and 3 are written. Similarly, data buffers 4, 5, and 6 are written to different disks, and the parity corresponding to these buffers is called P2; buffers 7, 8, and 9 are also written to different disks, and the parity corresponding to these buffers is called P3; and so on. Note that unlike RAID 3, the parity is also sprayed across different disks and not confined to a single disk.

RAID 5 offers a good balance between performance and data protection. With RAID 5, read operations can be handled in parallel by multiple disks. Write operations typically involve at least two disks—one for data and one for parity. RAID 5 is the most commonly used scheme in practice. RAID 5 requires the use of at least three drives. It also requires some effort to rebuild when a drive goes bad and needs to be replaced.

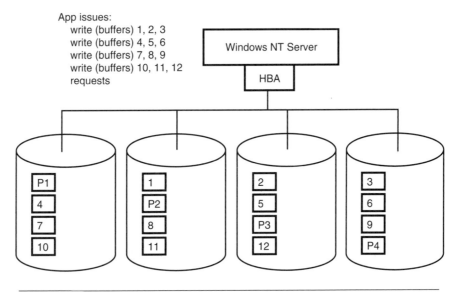

Figure 9.4 RAID 5

9.1.7 Dual-Level RAID

Dual-level RAID is also sometimes referred to as *hybrid RAID*. Dual-level RAID schemes combine the basic RAID implementations in different ways, attempting to preserve and build on the advantages, while minimizing the drawbacks. We will look briefly at RAID 10, RAID 30, and RAID 50.

As shown in Figure 9.5, **RAID 10** combines RAID 0 and RAID 1 features. Data is written in stripes to two different disks, while each of these disks is mirrored. This is also called *striping of mirrored arrays*. RAID 10 requires a minimum of four disks, but it can tolerate the failure of two disks without data availability being affected. RAID 10 is fairly popular because it provides redundancy and high performance but is also simple to implement.

RAID 30 combines RAID 0 and RAID 3 features (see Figure 9.6). With RAID 30, data stripes across different disks (RAID 0) and a dedicated parity disk. This is also referred to as *striping of dedicated parity arrays*. RAID 30 requires a minimum of six disks to implement and can tolerate the loss of two disks, one per array. RAID 30 is typically used

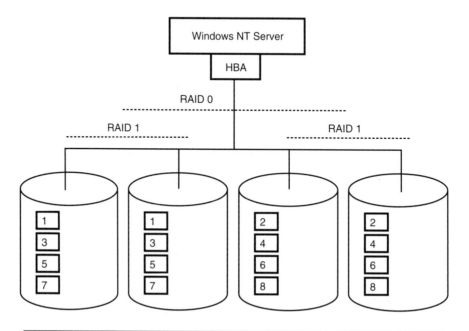

Figure 9.5 RAID 10

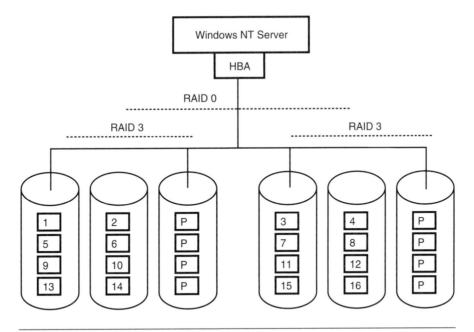

Figure 9.6 RAID 30

when the data consists of large files that are accessed sequentially—for example, in video streaming.

As shown in Figure 9.7, **RAID 50** combines RAID 0 and RAID 5 features. With RAID 50, data stripes across different disks as in RAID 0, and parity is written to all the disks involved in a round-robin fashion, as in RAID 5. This is referred to as *striping of nondedicated or distributed parity arrays*. RAID 50 needs a minimum of six disks and can tolerate failure of up to two disks, one per array. Unlike RAID 30, RAID 50 is geared toward data files that are relatively small.

Some RAID controllers have the capability to act as multiple SCSI identifiers; that is, a single RAID controller can use multiple SCSI identifiers. The RAID controller also supports the concept of multiple LUNs per SCSI device, or *multi-LUN support*.

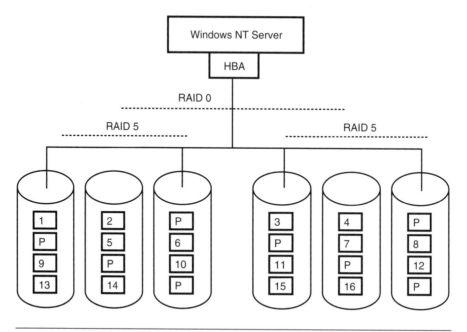

Figure 9.7 RAID 50

9.2 Windows NT and RAID Implementation

One obvious way to have RAID with Windows NT is for RAID to be implemented in hardware, such as in the HBA or the storage device controller.

Several drivers in the Windows Server family implement (host-based) RAID, including the fault-tolerant FtDisk driver, the Logical Disk

Table 9.1 RAID Capabilities of Several Windows Volume Managers

RAID Level	FtDisk	Windows 2000 Logical Disk Manager	VERITAS Logical Volume Manager
RAID 0	Yes	Yes	Yes
RAID 1	Yes	Yes	Yes
RAID 5	Yes	Yes	Yes
RAID 10	No	No	Yes

Manager (LDM) driver that ships with Windows 2000, and the VERI-TAS Logical Volume Manager (LVM) product available for Windows 2000 from VERITAS. All of these drivers were discussed in Chapter 1 and also in Chapter 6. The RAID support provided by these pieces of software is summarized in Table 9.1.

9.3 High Availability Using Redundancy

One way of ensuring high availability is literally to have two of everything. One can have a clustered server instead of a single server to ensure availability in case of a server failure.

Figure 9.8 shows a server with multiple HBAs. Each HBA is connected to a switch, and each switch has dual paths to the dual-ported storage device. The single point of failure in Figure 9.8 is the server. As pointed out earlier, clusters support the removal of this single point of failure. However, this section will consider a single server and explore the

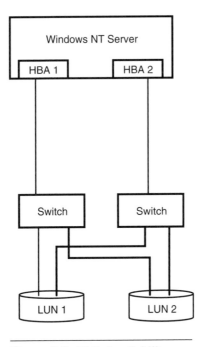

Figure 9.8 High-Availability Configuration

architecture in more detail. The focus is on the dual HBA within a single server, and once understood, the same architecture can exist on other servers within the cluster as well. Simply having two HBAs in a Windows NT server is not enough. One also needs special software; Sections 9.3.1 and 9.3.2 explore details of that needed software.

9.3.1 Microsoft Multipath Support in Windows 2000 and Windows Server 2003

Microsoft has announced native support for a multipath failover and load balancing solution for its Windows 2000 and Windows Server 2003 products. Microsoft provides a generic solution that the OEM or IHV needs to tune to take advantage of specific hardware features. The vendor needs to obtain a development kit that is available under a nondisclosure agreement. The end user can obtain a complete solution only from the vendor and not directly from Microsoft.

Before getting into the details of the solution, it is worthwhile examining the situation to convince oneself that a problem indeed exists. Consider Figure 9.8 again, which shows a Windows NT server with two dual-ported HBAs. The HBAs all connect to dual-ported disks. To keep matters simple, assume that each storage disk is formatted as a single volume. The idea is that there are multiple I/O paths between the server and the disk storage units to provide fault tolerance. For the configuration shown in Figure 9.8, consider the device object hierarchy that the Windows storage driver stack will create.

Figure 9.9 shows the device object tree for the system configuration shown in Figure 9.8. Again, as explained in Chapter 1, note the pairs of physical device objects (PDOs) and functional device objects (FDOs) that cooperate to enable particular device functionality. Recall that PDOs, among other things, represent information required to use the device. For storage devices, that information would include the SCSI bus identifier, target identifier, and LUN. Recall that FDOs, among other things, represent information needed to access the device. For storage devices, a good example would be details of the disk organization.

Starting from the bottom of Figure 9.9, the PnP system finds the PCI bus, creates a PDO for the PCI bus, and loads the PCI bus driver. The PCI bus driver creates an FDO for the bus and attaches it to the PDO. Next, devices on the PCI bus are enumerated. As a result, the two HBAs are located. The PCI bus driver creates the two PDOs, one for each adapter. The PnP system locates the driver for these adapters and loads either the SCSIPort or the Storport driver, along with the vendor-written

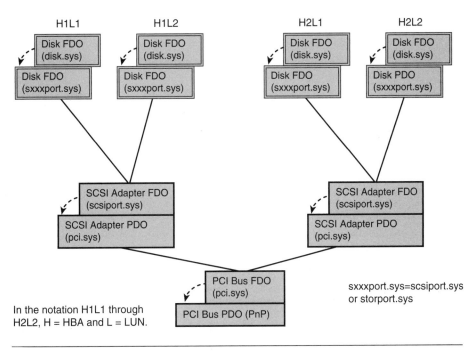

Figure 9.9 Device Object Tree without Multipath

miniport. Either Storport or SCSIPort creates an FDO for each adapter and attaches it to the respective PDO.

Next the SCSIPort or Storport driver behaves like a bus driver and enumerates devices on the SCSI bus. Because there are two (disk) devices on the bus, two (disk) devices are reported. In addition, because there are two SCSI adapters and enumeration is done on both of them, both will report two devices each. Thus, SCSIPort or Storport, as the case may be, sees four disk devices. The PDOs for these four disk devices are created, the disk class driver is loaded, and the disk class driver creates four FDOs and attaches each one to its respective PDO. Without a multipath I/O solution, the partitions on the disk FDOs would be enumerated, and either the FtDisk or the Logical Disk Manager (volume manager) would be loaded to handle the volumes that exist on those partitions. (For simplicity, assume that each disk has only one partition and that each partition constitutes an independent volume.)

Higher-level software entities will see four storage volumes, where in reality only two exist. Assuming that these two volumes are formatted for NTFS, the file system will assume there are four volumes, and NTFS will attempt to run on all four. Obviously the NTFS running on the volume residing on disk H1L1 and the NTFS running on volume H2L1 in Figure 9.9 would not be synchronized. So they would certainly overwrite each other's data—for example, the data in the log file—and the result would be volume corruption.

To ensure proper operation, several vendors have implemented a solution that not only prevents this problem, but also provides a rich set of additional functionality, such as failover, failback, and load balancing. **Failover** refers to functionality that will automatically move I/O from a failed I/O path to a different I/O path. **Failback** refers to functionality in which a failed I/O path is repaired, enabling the system to go back to using this repaired path. **Load balancing** refers to the distribution of I/O across all available I/O paths using a particular algorithm. The algorithm could be to distribute I/O in a round-robin fasion, or on the basis of the outstanding I/O on each path, or simply across all I/O paths, or in some other way. The Microsoft solution is described next, followed by a description of what some other vendors have now in terms of a shipping product.

Microsoft designed the multipath architecture with several goals in mind, including but not limited to the following:

- Coexisting with all other existing drivers and architecture, including Plug and Play (PnP) and power management. Indeed, the goal is not simply to coexist, but really to use the existing infrastructure—for example, have device notifications flow using the existing PnP mechanism.
- Providing dynamic discovery of devices and paths without requiring any special static configurations.
- Providing a solution that allows for coexistence of multiple multipath solutions from different vendors, something that at this time is extremely difficult, if not altogether impossible.
- Providing a generic solution, but one that leaves room for OEMs, IHVs, and ISVs to add value such as load balancing or failback. The sample device-specific module (DSM) provided by Microsoft does offer some load balancing features, but this load balancing is most efficient when used in a static way; for example, all I/O to LUN 1 uses path 1, and all I/O to LUN 2 uses path 2.
- Providing a solution that allows up to 32 paths per LUN and works for both Fibre Channel and SCSI.

Figure 9.10 shows the Windows NT device tree in detail, with a multipath solution deployed, for the same configuration shown in Figure 9.9.

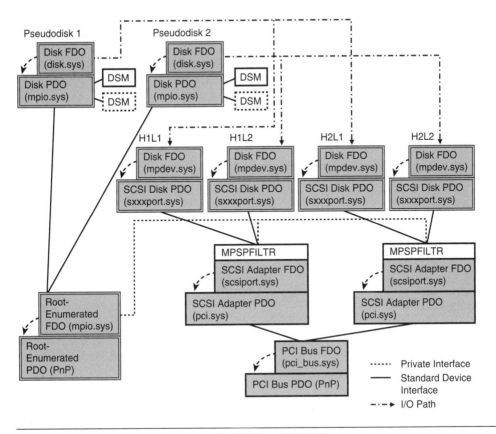

Figure 9.10 Device Object Tree with Multipath Solution

The device driver tree shown also includes the various filter drivers and related device objects for the Microsoft multipath architecture.

The solution consists of four different pieces:

1. An upper filter driver called **MPSPFLTR** that is supplied by Microsoft.
2. A class driver called **MPDEV** supplied by Microsoft.
3. A pseudo bus driver called **MPIO** that is supplied by Microsoft.
4. A **DSM** that needs to be supplied by the vendor that is building and selling the solution. The vendor licenses an MPIO development kit from Microsoft that contains the first three drivers already mentioned and provides all needed information (including header files and sample code) to build a DSM.

The first thing to note about Figure 9.10 is that there are actually two distinct device stacks: a logical device stack on the left of the figure and a physical device stack on the right of the figure. The MPIO software bridges the two.

The second thing to note is the similarity with respect to device trees for volumes on basic or dynamic disks (discussed in Chapter 6). This similarity should not be surprising, given that volumes are logical entities that may encompass multiple LUNs or part of an individual LUN, and that the MPIO infrastructure is trying to map LUNs that are visible using multiple paths to one logical LUN. The functionality of the Partition Manager while handling partitions is fairly similar to the functionality of the MPSPFLTR driver. Both pay particular attention to IRP_MN_QUERY_DEVICE_RELATIONSHIPS IRPs and forward details of the objects reported to their respective partners—the volume manager in one case and the pseudo bus multipath driver MPIO in the other case. Both the Partition Manager and the MPSPFLTR driver own responsibility for keeping their counterparts (volume manager and MPIO pseudo bus driver, respectively) informed about PnP and power events.

In comparing Figures 9.9 and 9.10, notice that the MPSPFLTR driver is an upper filter driver on the adapter FDO. Another difference is the PDO/FDO pair created for the MPIO pseudo bus driver by PnP and the MPIO driver itself. Notice the private communication channel between the MPSPFLTR driver and the MPIO pseudo bus driver. Further, on the top left-hand side of Figure 9.10, note the two PDOs for the pseudo disks created by the MPIO bus driver. This ensures that the MPIO bus driver gets a chance to handle the I/O, and it, in turn, can invoke the help of the DSM as needed.

Attached to each PDO created by the MPIO are two DSM objects. One is in active use; the other is shown in a different box simply to emphasize that MPIO allows DSMs from different vendors to coexist. Switching to the right-hand side of Figure 9.10, note the four disk PDOs that are created by the port driver (either SCSIPort or Storport) as usual. However, the disk PDOs attached to these PDOs are created by the MPDEV class driver and not by the disk class driver.

Mpdev.sys is a disk class replacement driver with some twists. The MPDEV class driver can handle only SCSI requests and not IRP functionality. In other words, MPDEV understands only a limited set of IRP functionality, the most important one of which is IRP_MJ_SCSI. MPDEV does not implement the classic IRP functionality, such as read and write IRPs (IRP_MJ_READ and IRP_MJ_WRITE). This means that user mode applications cannot access the physical device stack directly because user mode applications can only send down IOCTL requests. Of course, kernel mode drivers can send MPDEV SCSI command data blocks (CDBs), and indeed this is exactly what the disk class driver does.

Thus, MPDEV can handle requests from the MPIO stack (shown with the dot-dash line in Figure 9.10) because those requests come from the disk class driver (layered over the PDO created by MPIO) that translates the IRP requests (such as read and write) into SCSI CDBs. Further, Microsoft has created a tight security ACL for the device objects owned by the MPDEV class driver.

9.3.1.1 Device-Specific Module

The device-specific module (DSM) is designed to provide some important functions, including the following:

- Handling device-specific initialization.
- Providing functionality to decide whether two LUNs accessed using two different paths are really the same LUN simply accessed in different ways. Microsoft expects to use a built-in identifier from storage and not a software-written signature on the media to allow the DSM to identify these LUNs. The generic DSM module provided by Microsoft accomplishes this using the serial number page (80h) or device identification page (83h) defined by the SCSI command set. Vendors are not limited to the use of just these two mechanisms.
- Handling certain special SCSI commands, mostly related to device control and querying device capability, such as Read_Capacity, Reserve, Release, and Start_Stop_Unit, and deciding if the command will go down all paths or just a specific one.
- Making routing decisions on I/O requests.
- Handling errors.
- Handling PnP- and power-related requests with the assistance of the library routines provided by Microsoft in the pseudo bus multipath driver.
- Handling management-related requests that are delivered to a driver in the form of Windows Management Instrumentation (WMI; see Chapter 7) IRPs. The pseudo bus multipath driver will invoke the appropriate routines within the DSM. The pseudo bus multipath driver is able to locate these routines and invoke them.

The DSM is implemented with the MPIO kit, which can be licensed from Microsoft. The DSM is implemented as a legacy driver that exports an interface for the benefit of the pseudo bus driver MPIO.

9.3.1.2 Pseudo Bus Multipath Driver

The pseudo bus multipath driver is loaded natively as part of the Windows NT operating system once the appropriate vendor package has been installed.

Upon initialization, the pseudo bus multipath driver interacts with the MPSPFLTR filter driver that is layered over the SCSIPort FDO (see Figure 9.10) to create a pseudodevice for each logical device that has multiple paths for accessing the device. For each such pseudodevice, on a per-DSM basis, the pseudo bus multipath driver offers the DSM a chance to claim or reject ownership of the device.

For all I/O requests, the pseudo bus multipath driver consults the DSM via a specified routine. The DSM has access to each IRP and can post a completion routine for the IRP if it so desires. For device control requests such as Reserve and Release, the DSM may direct the I/O to happen on all paths to the device. For regular I/O requests such as read or write, the DSM may direct I/O on any one path, depending on whether it is doing dynamic or static load balancing. On an I/O request completing with error, the pseudo bus multipath driver invokes the DSM at a specified entry point and the DSM may redirect the I/O to another path in an effort to perform failover.

9.3.2 Existing Multipath Solutions

Several vendors offer a multipath solution that implements at the very least a failover solution, and some of them also offer failback, as well as load balancing.

These solutions do work. Now that they have been deployed for a while, however, two drawbacks have emerged:

1. The configuration can be cumbersome and somewhat confusing because the solution is not fully integrated with PnP, so dynamic discovery is not ensured.
2. The solution precludes interoperability with a solution from another vendor. This means that if a particular Windows server has a solution deployed from one vendor, the same Windows server cannot also have a solution from any other vendor deployed on it.

9.3.2.1 EMC PowerPath

EMC has implemented a failover and load balancing solution for Windows NT for quite a while. Figure 9.11 shows the architecture that EMC has implemented.

Unlike other architectures, EMC's architecture has a filter driver between the volume manager and SCSIPort or RAID port class drivers. For each logical volume that exists, the solution enumerates N logical volumes, where N is the number of independent ways in which the volume is accessed.

For each device with N different paths to access the device, Windows NT will see N logical devices. If I/O happened simultaneously down all these paths, data corruption might occur. Hence, PowerPath sets $N - 1$ of these devices to be in a disabled state in which no I/O or IOCTL activity can happen. The GUI administration utility shows one active device and $N - 1$ grayed-out devices corresponding to the disabled devices. The

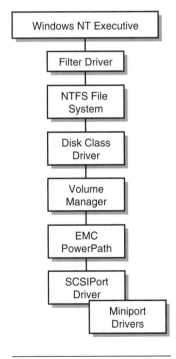

Figure 9.11 EMC
PowerPath
Architecture

administrator needs to do a fair amount of configuration, especially if security is desired in terms of limiting which HBAs can access which devices. The EMC Symmetrix product allows an administrator to implement this security by specifying the World Wide Name of the HBA that can access a particular LUN within the EMC Symmetrix box.

The administrator may specify a policy for accomplishing load balancing. The possible policies are described as follows:

- The I/O requests are sprinkled to each path in turn, in round-robin fashion.
- The next I/O is sent to the path that has the least number of pending requests.
- The next I/O is sent to the path that has the least number of blocks pending.
- An EMC Symmetrix optimization mode is used in which the next I/O is sent to the path that is estimated to have the least completion time.

9.3.2.2 HP (Compaq) SecurePath

HP (Compaq) offers a multipath failover and load balancing solution for Windows NT called SecurePath. The Compaq solution is slightly different between Windows NT 4.0 and Windows 2000.

Figure 9.12 shows the HP (Compaq) SecurePath architecture for Windows 2000. The solution consists of a block storage filter driver that is above the port (SCSIPort or Storport) class driver and below the disk class driver. A user mode service and user mode applications constitute the other pieces of the puzzle, and these play a role in administration and notification.

On Windows NT 4.0, HP (Compaq) SecurePath requires the use of an HP-written disk class driver called *HSZDisk* (see Figure 9.13). The solution also involves a filter driver.

On Windows 2000, the failover and load balancing functionality is provided within a filter driver that HP calls *Raidisk*. On Windows 2000, the class driver provided by Microsoft is not replaced by any other driver. The Raidisk driver performs

- Failover
- Load balancing (for nonclustered environments)

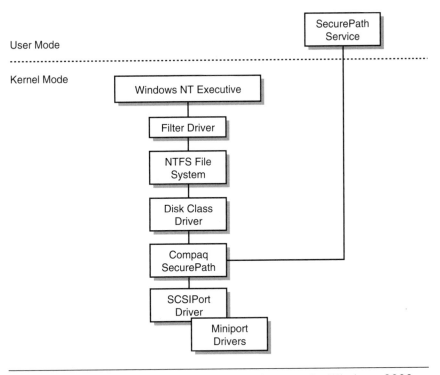

Figure 9.12 HP (Compaq) SecurePath Architecture for Windows 2000

- Failback when the fault is corrected
- Path verification to the storage volumes

A user mode SecurePath Windows NT service provides administration capabilities and interacts with the SecurePath filter driver via private IOCTL control codes.

9.3.2.2 HP AutoPath

HP AutoPath offers dynamic load balancing and autofailover capabilities for Windows NT. As shown in Figure 9.14, HP implements AutoPath using a filter driver between the disk class driver and the port driver.

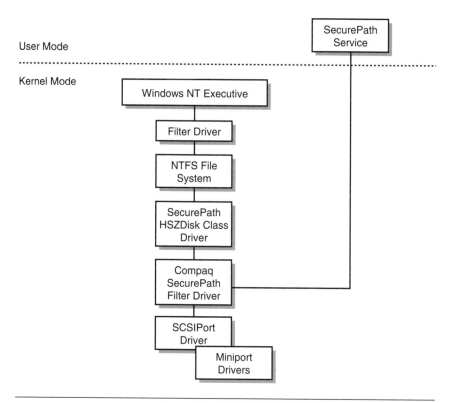

Figure 9.13 HP (Compaq) SecurePath Architecture for Windows NT 4.0

HP AutoPath load balancing performs according to a policy that the administrator sets. The choices of policy are:

- Round-robin, in which I/O is sprinkled across the various different paths
- No load balancing, in which all I/O to a particular storage device is statically sent down a path that the administrator can select
- Shortest queue on the basis of outstanding requests, in which the I/O is sent to the path with the minimum number of outstanding requests
- Shortest queue on the basis of outstanding bytes awaiting I/O
- Shortest queue on the basis of service time, in which all outstanding requests queued to a path are summed up and the I/O is sent to the queue with the smallest total

User Mode

Kernel Mode

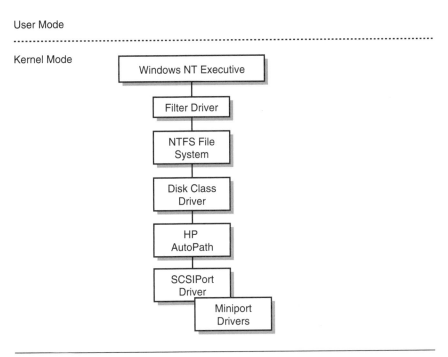

Figure 9.14 HP AutoPath Architecture

9.4 Local and Remote Mirroring

Mirroring was mentioned in Section 9.1 but not examined in detail. **Mirroring** is simply making a duplicate copy of the data available to ensure that another copy of the data is available in case the primary data store becomes unavailable for some reason.

Some popular reasons for mirroring or replication include the following:

- To provide a disaster recovery solution
- To provide load distribution or content distribution
- To provide high availability
- To use a secondary volume for data warehousing, backup, or testing with live data

Mirroring is local or remote. Local mirroring can happen at various levels:

- **Application level in the host server**. The application issues two identical write requests to two different disks, as illustrated in Figure 9.15.
- **Host-based RAID level**. The application issues a single write request. Host-based RAID implemented in the form of a volume manager driver turns the single write request into two identical write operations, as illustrated in Figure 9.16.
- **HBA level**. The application issues a single write request, which is turned into two identical write requests by the HBA in the host server, as illustrated in Figure 9.17.
- **Storage controller level**. This type of mirroring is done within the storage subsystem, as illustrated in Figure 9.18.

All of these solutions apply only to local mirroring. The problem is that local mirroring is not exciting. The solutions described remain local simply because of limitations on buses; for example, SCSI devices can be only tens of feet away. One could put in a Fibre Channel SAN and have the storage unit farther away, of course. Alternatively, one could put

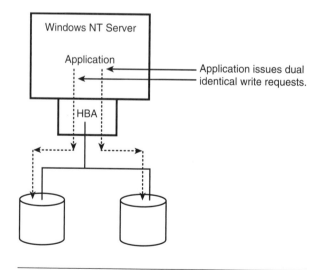

Figure 9.15 Mirroring at the Application Level

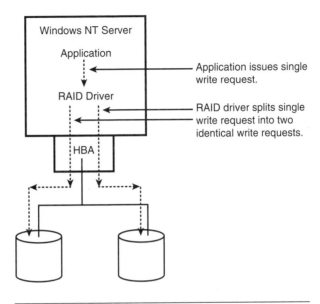

Figure 9.16 Mirroring at the Host-Based RAID Level

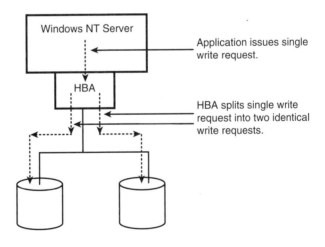

Figure 9.17 Mirroring at the HBA Level

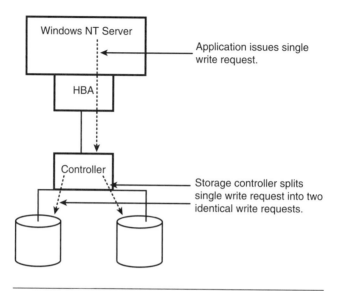

Figure 9.18 Mirroring at the Storage Subsystem Level

intelligence behind the replication at both ends (that is, both a source and a destination for replication), as illustrated in Figure 9.19.

Having intelligence at both ends of replication nodes allows for some interesting possibilities, including:

- Performing the replication in a synchronous or asynchronous manner
- Performing the replication in a bidirectional fashion, thus allowing the server at each end to actively perform a service while simultaneously acting as a standby for the other server
- Performing intelligent error recovery and check pointing

Replication can be done at the disk block level (in other words, below the file system) or by means of a file system filter driver that can replicate files and directories.

Replication can be synchronous or asynchronous. With **synchronous replication**, a write operation is applied to both nodes (source and secondary, where the mirroring is being done), and a confirmation is received from both that the write was completed successfully before the

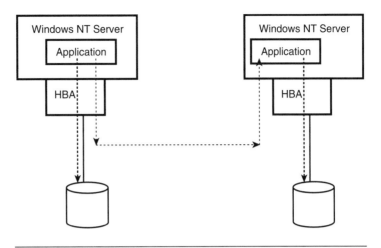

Figure 9.19 Remote Mirroring with Intelligence at
Both Ends

application gets an acknowledgment that the write completed successfully. Thus, application performance is adversely affected. With **asynchronous replication**, the write request to the remote end is queued,
the write request to the local node is issued while control returns to the
application, and the write operations are executed asynchronously.

Synchronous replication favors data synchronization at the cost of
poorer application performance. Asynchronous replication favors application performance at the cost of the two mirrored disks being temporarily out of sync while the data is "in flight." Once the data arrives and is
applied to the remote disk, the two mirrored disks will once again be
identical. Both synchronous and asynchronous replication solutions preserve the order of write operations to the storage device.

Several solutions have been developed by ISVs to enable high availability in a Windows NT environment using a replication solution and are
already available. Note that some products will switch dynamically
between synchronous and asynchronous I/O. The solution starts out handling all replication in a synchronous fashion, but if a glitch arises on the
remote end, the volume is marked as nonsynchronized or unhealthy, and
the system will switch to an asynchronous replication model.

Sections 9.4.1 through 9.4.3 examine some commercially available
products. Note that the choice of products examined does not represent

any recommendations, implicit or otherwise. Nor does the fact that a product is not described here reflect any opinion about that product. The choices were made with two characteristics in mind:

1. Information about these products was available relatively easily.
2. The sum of the products reviewed covers the various different ways in which a solution with the desired functionality might exist.

9.4.1 VERITAS Volume Replicator and VERITAS Storage Replicator

VERITAS is another ISV that specializes in storage, storage management, and disaster recovery solutions for a host of platforms, including Windows NT platform.

VERITAS Volume Replicator provides replication of volumes and deals with disk block data. VERITAS Volume Replicator leverages the fact that it already has a filter driver between the file system and the disk class driver—that is, the VERITAS Volume Manager. A new filter driver hooks into the Volume Manager driver and forwards write requests to the remote volume.

VERITAS Storage Replicator replicates file data rather than disk block data. As Figure 9.20 shows, a file system filter driver overlays itself above the file system. The VERITAS Storage Replicator also preserves the order of the data written. A Windows NT system can be both the primary and the secondary system; that is, it can act as both source (which generates replication data) and target (which receives replication data from another system running VERITAS Storage Replicator). When making configuration changes, services may need to stop and be restarted for the VERITAS Storage Replicator to function as desired. This is not the case with VERITAS Volume Replicator, which requires no reboot. Figure 9.20 shows the architecture for the VERITAS Volume Replicator and VERITAS Storage Replicator products.

Both the Volume Replicator and the Storage Replicator products use the Transport Driver Interface (TDI) library interface to send and receive data. The VERITAS Storage Replicator product is a file system filter driver that layers itself over a file system. The VERITAS Volume Replicator product is a disk filter driver (rather than a file system filter driver). Figure 9.20 attempts to emphasize the fact that the TDI is a linked library rather than a stand-alone driver.

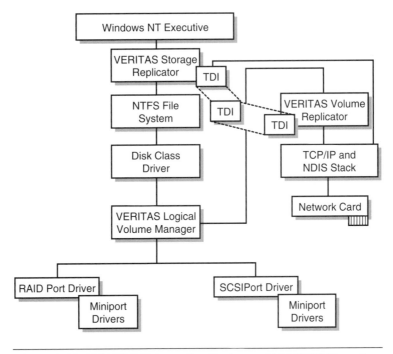

Figure 9.20 VERITAS Volume Replicator and VERITAS Storage Replicator

9.4.2 LEGATO RepliStor

RepliStor is an asynchronous file- and directory-level replication solution from LEGATO (through its acquisition of Octopus) that attempts to make copies of files (and keep them synchronized) to ensure performance and high availability. RepliStor can also replicate registry keys.

While specifying files, directories, or shares, RepliStor also allows specification of a list of files or directories excluded from the replication. RepliStor can also synchronize open files as long as the files synchronized are specified before they are opened by any application. RepliStor can also replicate Windows NT 4.0 Dfs shares, but not Windows 2000 Dfs shares. The Windows 2000 version of RepliStor has Active Directory integration, which allows users to store configuration data in Active Directory. Once a file has replicated, RepliStor replicates only the delta when a file is changed.

RepliStor can be optionally configured to use a dedicated NIC (network interface card) in an effort to isolate the RepliStor network traffic.

Further, this network traffic is encrypted to protect the data during transmission. Each network packet allows for digital signature as well.

RepliStor can replicate information on a one-to-one or one-to-many basis. The target of the replication may be another Windows NT server (which could be running on different hardware) or a cluster member. The source of the replication can also be a cluster member server. RepliStor achieves replication in an asynchronous manner; that is, the writes to the remote site queue up, while local writes happen without confirmation from the remote site.

RepliStor complements the other LEGATO offerings, such as Co-StandbyServer, which cannot mirror system disks (the drive from which Windows NT is booted). Because RepliStor is a file- and directory-based replication engine, it can replicate system disks as well.

RepliStor offers a configurable timer that causes the source system to ping the secondary system. If the ping fails, the secondary system first sends an ICMP (Internet Control Message Protocol) ping to ensure that the primary has really failed.

When a switchover does occur, RepliStor allows several configurable actions, including the following:

- The services will be started on the secondary system as part of the failover.
- The IP address and subnet mask values are forwarded to the secondary system.
- The commands execute on the secondary system as part of the failover; these commands can include batch files.

9.4.3 LEGATO Co-StandbyServer

LEGATO Co-StandbyServer is a clustering solution for Windows NT. Each server in the cluster can be active, and changes made by each server to disk replicate bidirectionally. If any of the clustered servers fail, Co-StandbyServer can fail over IP addresses, shares, server names, and other resources to the remaining healthy server.

As Figure 9.21 shows, LEGATO Co-StandbyServer offers bidirectional synchronous block-level replication capabilities between two Windows NT servers that can be up to 10 kilometers (approximately 6.25 miles) apart. Note that both ends can act as source and sink for each other. Thus, Figure 9.21 shows that whereas one disk is replicated from left to right, the other disk is replicated from right to left.

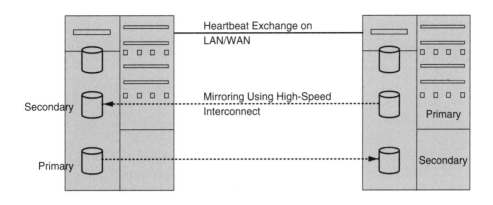

Figure 9.21 LEGATO Co-StandbyServer

The two servers between which the block-level mirroring happens need not be identical; the only requirement is that both servers be running Windows NT and have hardware that is on the Windows NT hardware compatibility list. The mirroring function cannot exist on the system boot drive.

LEGATO Co-StandbyServer has some problems when it is used with Windows 2000 LDM striping configurations. Co-StandbyServer offers two different pieces of functionality:

1. **Mirroring**, where writes on one server are duplicated to the other.
2. **Shared storage mode**, where if one server storage fails, data from the shared storage is made available to that server so that it can continue working.

The advantages of the LEGATO Co-StandbyServer include the following:

- No special hardware is required, and the primary and secondary servers may be running on different hardware; for example, one can be a multiprocessor system while the other is a single processor system.
- Co-StandbyServer includes support for multiple kinds of Windows 2000 servers, including domain controllers, member servers, and others.

- Co-StandbyServer includes supporting scripts to implement failover for popular Windows NT applications, such as IIS, SQL, or Exchange.

9.5 Practical Implications

RAID presents an attractive solution for ensuring performance and high availability. Several RAID schemes have been designed to meet a variety of needs. For the Windows NT platform, software RAID solutions are available. In particular, Windows 2000 and Windows Server 2003 ship with the Logical Disk Manager driver that implements software RAID solutions. Software RAID solutions can consume a measurable amount of CPU cycles because each I/O needs to be translated twice. The first translation is performed within the file system from a file-relative offset to a volume-relative offset. The next I/O is performed within a software RAID solution (assuming it is deployed for the I/O of interest), where the I/O is translated from a volume-relative offset to a disk-relative offset.

Microsoft has made available to vendors an MPIO development kit for building a high-availability and high-performance multipath I/O solution. Customers need to get the solution from vendors and not directly from Microsoft. The MPIO kit allows for compliant solutions from multiple vendors to coexist on the same Windows server. This is unlike the solutions previously available from vendors, in which the vendor solutions did not interoperate. It appears that there will be downward pricing pressure in this area of the market. Furthermore, solutions built on the Microsoft MPIO kit will not require customers to lock in to only one vendor, because different vendor solutions can now coexist. Storage solution procurement officials should bear this in mind when talking to their vendors. It is also worth watching whether Microsoft introduces some kind of logo scheme for such solutions and how rigorous the testing requirements are to achieve that logo.

Several vendors have also designed software mirroring and replication schemes. While considering such software, procurement officials should also keep in mind the new volume shadow copy architecture described in Chapter 5, which could be a better alternative for their needs.

This segment of the market also bears watching with the advent of IP storage because it is very likely that some vendors will build similar solutions using iSCSI.

9.6 Summary

Several RAID schemes have been defined that differ in cost, performance, and availability. Windows NT 4.0 implemented software RAID in the FtDisk driver. Windows 2000 implements software RAID via the Logical Disk Manager driver that ships with the operating system.

The Microsoft multipath architecture offers a standardized architecture for the Windows 2000 and Windows Server 2003 platforms to implement a storage solution with high availability and high performance. The architecture allows for load balancing as well as I/O path failover. This solution is available from Microsoft in the form of a development kit that vendors can license and add value to. End users can obtain the solution only from vendors.

Several vendors have implemented mirroring and replication schemes for the Windows NT platform.

Storage Features by Windows Product Release Cycles

The previous chapters explained the Windows architecture behind the particular storage feature of interest within that particular chapter. This chapter is dedicated to storage professionals who fancy their knowledge to be complete with respect to storage technology, but are looking for details of storage features that have appeared or will appear with particular releases of the Windows Server operating system.

More importantly, this chapter also contains some forward-looking statements that may or may not turn out to be true. I want to emphasize that the chapter assumes that features discussed by Microsoft *will* ship. Indeed, there is no guarantee that they will ship, let alone when and whether the functionality and architecture will be as described in this book.[1] The reader should take all of this into account before making any decisions.

This chapter attempts to describe storage features by Windows cycle, but the Microsoft release process can sometimes make the discussion confusing. Very often, key features are developed for a particular release of Windows NT but are also made available for prior version(s) of Windows NT. In such cases, the feature is still reported as shipping with the newer version of Windows NT.

---

1. Microsoft makes it clear that product features will be decided on the basis of multiple factors and that no particular feature can be guaranteed to ship in a forthcoming release. Microsoft states that the only certain way of ascertaining which features exist in a particular release is to study that product after it has been released.

10.1 Windows NT 4.0

Windows NT 4.0 was positioned primarily as a file-and-print server and as an application platform, albeit one that happened to have some features conducive to SANs. This is apparent in light of the vast advances in storage features that Windows 2000 made over Windows NT 4.0.

The significant features of Windows NT 4.0 as they relate to storage are described in Sections 10.1.1 through 10.1.4.

10.1.1 Improved Storage Unit Accessibility

Windows NT 4.0 Service Pack 5 introduced support for a feature called *Large LUNs*, whereby Windows NT 4.0 supported up to 255 LUNs per SCSI target. Prior to this service pack, Windows NT supported only eight LUNS per target device.

10.1.2 CIFS, NFS, NetWare, and Macintosh Client Support

Windows NT 4.0 served as a good network-attached storage device because it could readily act as a file-and-print server to a wide variety of clients, including Windows clients running the SMB or CIFS network file-sharing protocol, various UNIX clients running the NFS protocol, NetWare clients, and Macintosh clients.

10.1.3 Defragmentation APIs

Windows NT 4.0 introduced defragmentation APIs that allowed independent software vendors (ISVs) to write defragmentation applications. As a result, ISVs could write applications that stood a better chance of working well and continuing to work well with future Windows NT versions and service packs. These APIs were designed in close consultation with ISVs to meet their needs.

10.1.4 Distributed File System

Dfs allows IT administrators to have a naming hierarchy that reflects the corporate organizational structure and do away with requiring users to track server names and file locations. Dfs also supports a heterogeneous operating environment in which servers running other operating systems besides Windows can also participate. In other words, Dfs provides a way to organize and manage network shares, much as a file system provides a way to organize and manage files.

A Windows client communicates with a Dfs server using CIFS, but once the client has obtained a referral to the actual server where a file is stored, it can connect to that server using another protocol, such as NFS or NCP (Network Control Protocol). This means that a single Windows NT server acting as a Dfs server can extend the benefits of Dfs to heterogeneous servers as well. Dfs uses File Replication Service functionality. The mappings between the physical location of a file and its logical path as accessed by a client are stored in the registry.

The advantages of using Dfs are

- Ease of administration, because server shares can be moved around without user access being affected. Users access a resource that administrators can remap to point to a different server or server share.
- Ease of use, because users are provided with an abstraction that does not require them to track physical storage associated with files.

10.2 Windows 2000

The most remarkable advance of Windows 2000 was to make the Windows NT platform highly conducive to being used in a SAN or NAS environment. This release also established Windows as a player in the NAS environment. Sections 10.2.1 through 10.2.13 review the storage-related advances made in Windows 2000.

10.2.1 Improved Storage Unit Accessibility

Windows 2000 dramatically enhances storage unit accessibility by

- Vastly reducing the scenarios in which a system reboot is required to change storage unit configurations—for example, add, remove, grow, or shrink volumes
- Vastly increasing the number of storage units that the operating system can handle

Windows NT 4.0 requires that a system be rebooted before it can access a new physical storage device (called a *target* in storage terminology).

Windows 2000 PnP improvements support the dynamic addition and removal of storage targets. The bus driver reports an event called BusChangeDetected, and the operating system responds with action that may involve rescanning for all devices attached to the bus. The improvement is that the operating system and associated drivers support access to new devices without requiring a reboot, and the operating system also does not require the storage bus (e.g., SCSI, Fibre Channel) to be reset—an operation that consumes a fair amount of time. A new target may be added or a logical unit number (LUN) on an existing target may be dynamically made visible, and neither operation requires a bus reset.

Note that Windows NT (including Windows 2000) still will claim ownership of all LUNs that it sees. Microsoft has indicated that it is working on a feature that will allow an administrator to specify which LUNs should be accessed by Windows NT (and which ones should not). This feature would allow for LUNs to be visible to Windows NT (the operating system, and not Windows NT applications), yet Windows NT would not use them and in the process possibly destroy existing data on those LUNs.

Windows 2000 supports vastly improved storage connectivity by being able to address up to 128 targets (SCSI identifiers) and up to 255 LUNs per target. By comparison Windows NT 4.0 supported only 8 targets and 8 LUNs per target, and Windows NT 4.0 Service Pack 5 supported 255 targets and 8 LUNs per target.

10.2.2 New Volume and Disk Management

Windows 2000 introduced a new concept called **dynamic disks**. The term *dynamic disk* is a logical concept that is applied to the physical disk. Physical disks remain basic disks with a partition table, just as they used to be in Windows NT 4.0, until they are explicitly converted to dynamic disks. To put it differently, dynamic disks are physical disks with a different partition table format that allows the partitions on the disks to shrink and grow dynamically. This new partition table is stored in a redundant fashion, to ensure that it is always available, even when some disk clusters are corrupted. Complete details are available in Chapter 6.

Dynamic disks can be recognized only by Windows 2000 and higher versions of Windows NT. Dynamic disks still retain the old-style partition table as well, to ensure that data does not become corrupted when the disk is accidentally referenced either by a Windows NT 4.0 system or in a heterogeneous operating environment in which the other operating system understands only the old-style partition table. However, the partition table simply contains a single entry that shows the whole disk as being in use. This old-style partition table does not reflect the true logical organization of the disk.

Two new kernel mode components have been added. The Mount Manager handles mount operations for basic and dynamic disks, including assigning drive letters. The Partition Manager handles PnP operations, as well as power management and WMI operations on disk partitions. The two combine to provide functionality that allows two volume managers to coexist in the system. One is the old FtDisk driver, which in some senses is indeed a volume manager. The other one is either the default Logical Disk Manager (LDM) shipped with Windows 2000 or the Logical Volume Manager (LVM) upgrade product sold by VERITAS.

Together with improvements in PnP, the new disk management features ensure that

- Volumes may be dynamically shrunk and grown without the operating system having to be shut down and the system rebooted. While a volume is being grown, an application can continue to access and use it.
- Volumes may be mounted and unmounted on the fly. Of course, an unmounted volume is no longer available for use, but the system does not need to be rebooted after a volume has been gracefully removed or a new volume has been added.
- Volumes may be converted from using one RAID class to using another RAID class without a system reboot. RAID 0, RAID 1, and RAID 5 volumes can be configured, broken, and rebuilt on the fly, all without requiring a reboot.
- Legacy volumes, including volumes that use a form of RAID supported by the legacy FtDisk volume manager, are still supported.
- Dynamic disks are self-describing; that is, all metadata needed to figure out the layout of a disk is stored on the disk itself. Windows NT 4.0 stored part of this metadata in the registry instead. This means that dynamic disks may be freely transported between Windows 2000 systems and be readily available for use without any further reconfiguration needed.
- The new disk management features make a GUI and command-line tool available for disk management.
- New APIs have been added to enable volume management applications. Examples include APIs to enumerate all volumes (Find-FirstVolume to enumerate the first volume, FindNextVolume to

enumerate the next, and FindVolumeClose to end the search and free up resources associated with the search). GetVolumeInformation returns information about the volume, including whether the volume supports reparse points (described in Section 10.2.10).

10.2.3 Dfs Improvements

Dfs was introduced in Windows NT 4.0. Dfs allows an administrator to manage shares efficiently on a network, and it allows users to work with share names or directories that reflect their work environment. Users do not need to correlate the physical network and server share environments with their work environment. For example, users in a company could access \\MyCompany\Accounts for all files and directories related to the Accounting department and not have to worry about the real physical server name or its shares.

Dfs has been substantially improved in Windows 2000. The improvements include the following:

- **Better availability and fault tolerance**. Windows 2000 introduces Dfs support for clustering and also removes the single point of failure in terms of the single Dfs root server by allowing for multiple servers to host the Dfs root directory. This is done by providing Dfs and Active Directory integration in the form of storing the Dfs topology data in Active Directory. Furthermore, changes to the Dfs topology can be made and are immediately effective without the Dfs service having to be stopped and restarted. Dfs can now also work with the Windows 2000 File Replication Service to replicate changes in the Dfs replicas.
- **Better administration**. Dfs is now administered via a graphical Microsoft Management Console (MMC) tool. Dfs also supports more configurable parameters—for example, the amount of time a Dfs entry can be cached. Dfs in Windows 2000 is integrated with Active Directory, so the administrator has one less domain to worry about.
- **Performance optimizations**. Windows 2000 clients select a Dfs replica that is on the same site rather than selecting a replica randomly that may be on a remote site. When multiple replicas are on a local site, the Windows 2000 client selects a replica randomly. Windows NT 4.0 clients do a lot more processing to use Dfs than Windows 2000 clients do. The older Dfs clients are really

Dfs unaware and simply try to resolve a path, assuming that the path contains a valid server name. Only after the attempt to connect to a nonexistent server fails does the client use the services of the dfs.sys driver to resolve the path. Windows 2000 clients instead assume a Dfs-aware path and first use the dfs.sys driver to attempt to resolve the pathname.

■ **Load balancing**. Because multiple servers may store the same set of files, a client can access any of them, and different clients may access the same file on different servers.

10.2.4 Offline Folders and Client-Side Caching

Windows 2000 allows an administrator to mark shares on a server as containing cachable files. The files within that share (e.g., data and program executable files or dynamic link libraries) are then downloaded to the client and stored locally. This download happens when the user first opens the file. Files that are not opened are not downloaded. The files are synchronized in the background or when the user logs on or off. When synchronization results in a conflict (because the locally made changes now conflict with changes that were meanwhile made on the server folder), the conflict is resolved with the assistance of the user. The main advantages are these:

■ Performance gains because reading a local disk is much faster than reading a file over the network
■ Improved availability because the user can keep working on the client even when the server is offline
■ Improved availability when the user is undocked from the network and traveling

Offline folders can be administratively set to have the following options:

■ Manual caching for documents, where an administrator explicitly marks the document files that users may cache
■ Automatic caching for documents, where all document files opened by a user are automatically cached
■ Automatic caching for program files, where all program files (e.g., .exe and .dll files) are automatically cached

10.2.5 File Replication Service

Windows 2000 introduces a full two-way File Replication Service (FRS) that uses the NTFS change log journal to detect changed files and directories. The File Replication Service is used extensively by Active Directory for its internal needs. It is also used extensively in conjunction with Dfs to make multiple copies of files and the Dfs metadata available on multiple servers, thus allowing for load balancing and fault-tolerant features.

10.2.6 File System Content Indexing

Windows 2000 server ships with the Indexing Service fully integrated with the operating system and tools. For example,

- Indexing Service functionality can be accessed simply via the **Find files or folders** dialog in Explorer.
- The Indexing Service can index file contents and file attributes, including user defined attributes, as well.
- The Indexing Service can also index offline content managed by Remote Storage Services.
- On NTFS volumes, the Indexing Service uses the change log journal to determine which files have changed since the last index run.
- The Indexing Service uses the bulk ACL-checking feature and will return files only in response to a user search to which the user has permissions. Files that a user is not allowed to access are eliminated from the search results.
- The Indexing Service can also work on FAT volumes, but it will work less efficiently on FAT volumes than it does on NTFS volumes because it cannot use NTFS-specific features such as the change log journal.

10.2.7 Setup Improvements

Windows 2000 setup can create a native NTFS volume. Earlier, the process involved setting up a FAT partition and then converting the FAT partition to an NTFS volume. Note the almost interchangeable use of the terms *partition* and *volume*. As explained in Chapter 6, partitions and volumes refer to the same concept but have slightly different behavior. For one, whereas a volume can be dynamically resized, a partition cannot.

10.2.8 File System Improvements

Windows 2000 makes some improvements in the area of file systems. Although the majority of the enhancements are in NTFS, Windows 2000 also includes major improvements in optical media file systems, as well as the venerable FAT file system. However, the expectation is that the FAT file system code is in maintenance mode at Microsoft, and no significant enhancements in the FAT file system should be expected. NTFS improvements are so significant that they rate their own individual section (10.2.9).

10.2.8.1 FAT File System Improvements

Windows 2000 supports FAT32—the first time that FAT32 has been supported on the Windows NT platform. FAT32 was of course supported on the Windows 9X platform. FAT32 can support volumes up to 2 terabytes (TB) in size and a maximum file size of 4GB. For performance reasons, the utilities to create a FAT volume limit a FAT volume size to 32GB, but this limitation is a function of the utility and not of the underlying file system itself. FAT32 uses a smaller disk cluster and hence is more efficient in using disk space.

10.2.8.2 Optical Media File Systems

Windows NT 4.0 supported CDFS (CD-ROM File System), and this support is continued in Windows 2000. Windows 2000 adds the Universal Disk Format (UDF) file system defined by the Optical Storage Technology Association (OSTA) to the list of file systems supported on the Windows NT platform.

10.2.9 NTFS Improvements

NTFS in Windows 2000 has been enhanced in numerous ways. The enhancements require a change in the NTFS-on-disk structure. When a Windows 2000 system mounts a legacy NTFS partition for the first time (*legacy* as in "one created with a prior version of Windows NT"), the partition is silently converted. The conversion is fairly efficient, and the time taken for conversion is independent of the underlying partition size. Windows NT 4.0 SP4 and higher has been provided with an upgraded version of NTFS that can recognize the new NTFS partition.

Implementing these features required a change in the on-disk structure for NTFS. For existing volumes, the on-disk structure is changed when the volume is first mounted on a Windows 2000 system. For the system volume, this is done when the system is upgraded from Windows NT 4.0 to Windows 2000.

Microsoft has also invested in considerable enterprise-level testing of Windows 2000 in general and NTFS in particular. Some examples include the following:

- The maximum tested file size was $2^{44} - 64K$, which is approximately 16TB. By contrast, the theoretical maximum file size is $2^{64} - 1$ bytes, which is approximately 17 exabytes (EB).
- The maximum number of files tested per volume was approximately 34 million. By contrast, the theoretical maximum limit is $2^{32} - 1$, which is approximately 4 billion.

10.2.9.1 Native Property Sets

Windows 2000 introduces support for native property sets that is simply user-defined metadata that can be associated with a file. This metadata can also be indexed with the Index Server that now ships with Windows 2000 Server. An example is defining a document author or intended document audience. Users can then search for a document by these user-defined tags or metadata. NTFS treats files as a collection of attribute/value pairs. The user-defined properties are simply stored as additional optional attributes on a file.

10.2.9.2 File Scan by Owner

Windows NT tracks user accounts by a unique security identifier (SID). NTFS in Windows 2000 can scan a volume and identify all files owned by a particular SID. This process facilitates administration; for example, when an intern leaves, the files owned by the intern can be quickly identified and cleaned up.

10.2.9.3 Improved Access Control List Checking

NTFS in Windows NT 4.0 kept access control lists (ACLs) on a per-file and per-directory basis. If a user had 50 files, the probably identical ACLs would be stored 50 times, once in each file. NTFS in Windows 2000 stores ACLs in a directory and indexes them as well. So for the scenario just described, the ACL would be stored just once, and each of the 50 files would have a "pointer" that would help identify the ACL.

This change facilitates bulk ACL checking, which is used by the Indexing Service. When a user performs a search, the Indexing Service prepares a list of files, and before returning the list to the user, it performs ACL checking and eliminates all files to which the user does not have access. Thus a user will see only the files that it can access.

Bulk ACL checking can be used in other scenarios as well. For example, it can be used to determine what a given user is allowed to do with a given set of files.

10.2.9.4 Journal Log File

NTFS tracks changes to the file system for two purposes: (1) to be able to recover in case of a disaster by first logging undo and redo information and (2) to offer application developers access to information that indicates which files or directories were changed and the nature of the change. Only the changes are tracked here, and the information tracked in the journal log file is insufficient to implement an undo operation. The journal file survives across reboot operations. If the file becomes full or is deleted, applications can detect the fact that some change information has been lost and behave accordingly—for example, rescan all the directories and files of interest. This facility is extremely useful to a broad range of applications, such as replication and backup.

10.2.9.5 NTFS Stream Renaming

The Windows NT NTFS has always shipped with support for multiple data streams per file. One example of an application that uses multiple data streams is the Windows NT Macintosh server. Until Windows 2000, there was no way to rename a data stream, once it was created. One could create a new file with a new named data stream and then copy the contents of the old file to the new one, but this approach is rather inefficient. The version of NTFS that ships with Windows 2000 now provides an API to allow an application to rename an existing named data stream.

10.2.9.6 Object IDs and Link Tracking

Windows 2000 implements link tracking. Links can be shortcuts for files or OLE objects such as an Excel or PowerPoint document embedded within a file such as a Word file. An application can track a link even when the source object behind the link moves in various ways, including the following:

- A document representing the link source is moved within the same volume on a Windows NT server.
- A document representing the link source is moved between volumes on the same Windows NT server.
- A document representing the link source is moved from one Windows NT server to another Windows NT server within the same domain.
- A complete volume containing the link source is moved from one Windows NT server to another Windows NT server within the same domain.
- A Windows NT server with a mounted volume that contains the link source is renamed.
- A network share on a Windows NT server that contains the source of the link is renamed.
- The document representing the link source is renamed.
- Any combination of the above.

Basically each file in Windows 2000 (and higher Windows NT versions) can have an optional unique object identifier. To track a file, an application refers to the file by its unique object identifier. When the file reference fails, a user mode link-tracking service is called for assistance (by Windows NT). The user mode service attempts to locate the file, using its object identifier in a trial-and-error fashion for all the scenarios just described.

10.2.9.7 NTFS Sparse Files

Windows NT 3.51 implemented file system compression. The implication was that a file with a lot of zeros as data would be compressed. However, compression and decompression does take time, and the compressed data still occupies some clusters on the disk. Consider a file that is logically 1GB long but contains only 4K of data at the very beginning and 4K of data at the very end. With Windows 2000, a file such as is, if marked as a sparse file, will occupy just 8K on the disk (assuming an appropriate disk cluster size).

NTFS organizes its internal data structures to recognize the fact that there are "missing data blocks," and when an application issues a read request for data within this region, NTFS zero-fills the application buffer.

The application never realizes that there is anything special about the file when it does read or write operations on the file. Sparse files have a user-controlled attribute that can be set to indicate that the file is sparse. Applications that are not aware that the file is sparse will function normally, but the system will run a little less efficiently because some time will be spent returning zeros for data that is in unallocated blocks of the file. Applications that are aware of the sparse-file attribute can bypass this behavior.

File and directory enumeration APIs (e.g., FindFirst, FindNext) return the flag FILE_ATTRIBUTE_SPARSE_FILE. The Win32 APIs BackupRead, BackupWrite, CopyFile, and MoveFile have been updated to be sparse file aware (for example, CopyFile will preserve a file as a sparse file and does not do read or write operations that would turn the file into a nonsparse file).

10.2.9.8 Disk Quotas

Disk quota tracking and management features are implemented in NTFS that ships with Windows 2000. Disk quotas are tracked on a per-user and per-volume basis. An administrator can

- Turn the feature off
- Use the feature simply to track usage
- Use the feature to track usage and also enforce policies that limit the amount of disk storage a given user can consume

Disk quotas are tracked by the user security identifier (SID), a unique identifier assigned to every user that logs on to a Windows NT machine (the user can be another computer or a system account that is also just a user with a different set of privileges than a human user has), and each file or directory contains the SID of the owner. Disk quotas are set on a per-volume basis and the administrative tools allow the policy to be replicated to other volumes.

Recall that Windows 2000 can also return a list of files on a per-user basis. This functionality is simply a subset of quota tracking, because quota tracking computes the total size of the storage used by the list of files returned by a per-user search.

10.2.9.9 CHKDSK Improvements

Windows 2000 NTFS reduces the number of situations in which CHKDSK needs to run, and it significantly reduces the amount of time taken to run CHKDSK. The phrase "your mileage may vary" comes to mind in view of the fact that the exact amount of improvement depends on the size of the volume and the nature of the corruption, if any. For volumes with millions of files, however, an improvement that reduces the amount of time needed to run CHKDSK by a factor of 10 is quite possible.

10.2.9.10 Defragmentation

Windows 2000 ships with a defragmentation applet that is really a light version of DiskKeeper from Executive Software, an ISV. Like Windows NT 4.0, Windows 2000 supports defragmentation APIs. The built-in defragmentation applet has some limitations that full-fledged defragmentation applications typically do not have. For example,

- It cannot defragment the NTFS MFT (master file table) or the system paging file.
- It cannot defragment directories.
- It does not have Microsoft Cluster Server support.

10.2.10 Reparse Points

Reparse points represent a significant new architectural feature in NTFS and the Windows NT I/O subsystem. Note that reparse point implementation requires changes in the I/O subsystem and also the NTFS file system. It is conceivable that somebody can implement reparse points in a file system other than NTFS. In addition, reparse points provide the basis of some very important functionality. Thus, reparse points rate their own subsection, rather than being buried as an NTFS feature improvement.

Reparse points provide the foundation for implementing the following features:

- Symbolic links
- Directory junction points
- Volume mount points
- Single-instance storage
- Remote storage (Hierarchical Storage Management)

We will look at these features in more detail in Sections 10.2.10.1 through 10.2.10.4.

A **reparse point** is an object on an NTFS directory or file. A reparse point can be created, manipulated, and deleted by an application using the Win32 API set in general, and CreateFile, ReadFile, and WriteFile in particular. Recall that the Win32 API set allows an application to create and manipulate user-defined attributes on a file or directory. Think of reparse points as simply user-defined attributes that are handled in a special manner. This includes ensuring uniqueness about some portions of the attribute object and handling in the I/O subsystem. An ISV would typically write the following:

- Some user mode utilities to create, manage, and destroy reparse points
- A file system filter driver that implements the reparse point–related functionality

Each reparse point consists of a tag and a data blob. The tag is a unique 32-bit tag that is assigned by Microsoft. ISVs can request that such a unique tag be assigned to them. Figure 10.1 shows the structure of the reparse tag, including the following elements:

- A bit (M) indicating whether a tag is for a Microsoft device driver or not.
- A bit (L) indicating whether the driver will incur a high latency to retrieve the first data byte. An example here is the HSM solution, in which retrieving data from offline media will incur a high latency.

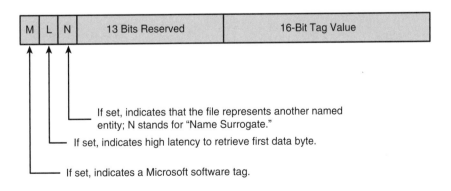

Figure 10.1 Reparse Point Tag Structure

■ A bit (N) indicating whether the file or directory is an alias or redirection for another file or directory.
■ Some reserved bits.
■ The actual 16-bit tag value.

The data blob portion of the reparse point is up to 16K in size. NTFS will make this data blob available to the vendor-written device driver as part of the I/O subsystem operation handling reparse points.

To understand the sequence of operations and how reparse points are implemented, consider Figure 10.2. For simplicity, this discussion assumes that the user has the required privileges for the requested operation. In addition, Figure 10.2 shows only one file system filter driver, in the interest of keeping things simple and relevant.

The sequence of steps in creating reparse point functionality includes the following, as illustrated in Figure 10.2:

Step 1: Using the Win32 subsystem, an application makes a file open request.

Step 2: After some verification, the Win32 subsystem directs the request to the NT Executive subsystem.

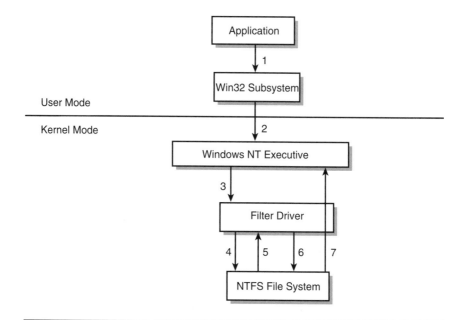

Figure 10.2 Reparse Point Operation

Step 3: The Windows NT I/O Manager builds an IRP (IRP_MJ_OPEN) and sends it to the NTFS file system. The IRP is intercepted by the reparse point file system driver.

Step 4: The filter driver intercepts the IRP, specifies a completion routine that should be called when the IRP completes, and using the services of the I/O Manager, sends the IRP to the NTFS file system driver.

Step 5: The IRP reaches the file system. The file system looks at the IRP_MJ_OPEN request packet, locates the file or directory of interest, and notes the reparse point tag associated with it. NTFS puts the reparse point tag and data into the IRP and then fails the IRP with a special error code.

Step 6: The I/O subsystem now calls each filter driver (one at a time) that has registered a completion routine for the IRP. Each driver completion routine looks at the error and the reparse point tag in the IRP. If the driver does not recognize the tag as its own, it invokes the I/O Manager to call the next driver's I/O completion routine. Assume that one of the drivers recognizes the reparse point tag as its own. The driver can then use the data within the reparse point to resubmit the IRP with some changes based on the data in the reparse point; for example, the pathname may be changed before the IRP is resubmitted.

Step 7: NTFS completes the resubmitted IRP operation. A typical example might be that the pathname was changed and the open request succeeds. The I/O Manager completes the open request; each file system filter driver may then be invoked at its completion routine again. The driver notices that the open request succeeded and takes appropriate action. Finally, the IRP is completed, and the application gets back a handle to the file.

If no filter driver recognizes the reparse point tag, the file or directory open request fails.

Whereas some applications may need to be aware of reparse point functionality, other applications may not care and never even realize that a reparse point exists at all. For example, a Microsoft Office application simply opening a Word, PowerPoint, or Excel document may not care at all about reparse point functionality that redirects the open request to a different volume. However, some applications that walk a tree recursively may need to be aware of the possibility of having paths that create a loop. Applications can suppress the reparse point functionality by appropriate options (FILE_OPEN_REPARSE_POINT) in the CreateFile,

DeleteFile, and RemoveDirAPI requests. This is how the reparse point data can be created, modified, or deleted. The GetVolumeInformation API returns the flag FILE_SUPPORTS_REPARSE_POINTS. FindFirstFile and FindNextFile APIs return the flag FILE_ATTRIBUTE_REPARSE_POINT to indicate the presence of a reparse point.

All reparse points on an NTFS volume are indexed within a file called $Index that lives in the \$Extend directory. An application can thus quickly enumerate all reparse points that exist on a volume.

Note that this section describes reparse points as being integral to NTFS. Although it is true that the FAT file system does not support reparse points, an ISV or Microsoft could conceivably write another file system, different from NTFS, that also supported reparse points. Such a task would not be trivial, but note that reparse points need to be implemented in three areas:

1. The file system—for example, NTFS
2. The I/O subsystem and the Win32 API set
3. The tools and utilities

Microsoft has obviously done the necessary work in all three areas, and hence it is conceivable for a new file system to support reparse points as well.

Sections 10.2.10.1 through 10.2.10.4 describe applications of the reparse point mechanism.

10.2.10.1 Volume Mount Points

Windows NT 4.0 required that a drive letter be used to mount volumes or partitions. This constraint limited a system to having 26 volumes or partitions at the most. Windows 2000 allows mounting a volume without using a drive letter. The only limitations are as follows:

- A volume may be mounted only on a local directory; that is, a volume cannot be mounted on a network share.
- A volume may be mounted only on an empty directory.
- This empty directory must be on an NTFS volume (only NTFS supports reparse points).

Applications accessing the directory that hosts the mount point do not notice anything special about the directory unless the application explicitly requests such information.

APIs have been added and modified to provide application support for volume mount points. GetVolumeInformation indicates via a flag whether the volume supports mount points. FindFirstVolumeMountPoint and FindNextVolumeMountPoint are used to find the volume mount points. FindVolumeMountPointClose is used to free up resources consumed by FindFirstVolumeMountPoint and FindNextVolumeMount- Point. GetVolumeNameForMountPoint returns the volume name to which a volume mount point resolves.

10.2.10.2 *Directory Junction Points*

Directory junction points are closely related to volume mount points. The difference is that whereas volume mount points resolve a directory to a new volume, directory junction points resolve a directory to a new directory that exists on the same local volume where the directory junction point itself resides. Directory junction points may be created by use of the linkd.exe tool that ships with the Windows 2000 Resource Kit.

10.2.10.3 *Single Instance Storage*

Single Instance Storage is a feature that can significantly reduce storage space requirements by detecting duplicate files and replacing the duplicate instances with a special link. Single Instance Storage is used with the Remote Installation Service (RIS), which allows Windows NT systems to boot from a network share.

With RIS, administrators typically create multiple images—for example, an image for the Accounting department, an image for the Engineering department, and so on. In each image, a lot of the same files are duplicated again and again. However, a simple link file will not serve the purpose here. If the administrator later decides that one image should be slightly different and changes a particular file, all other images with links that point to that file will also be affected. Enter SIS.

SIS replaces duplicate files via a sparse file with no allocated region and a reparse point on this sparse file. The reparse point has enough information to locate the backup file, which is the one file left in its original state. (If there are four files that are duplicates, one file is left as the backup file, and the other three are turned into sparse files with reparse points.) The size of the sparse file will still show the original size of the file. When an application opens a SIS sparse file, the filter driver intercepts the file open IRP request, opens the file backing the SIS file, and passes a handle to this other file back to the calling application. Thereafter, the application does its I/O on the backup file.

10.2.10.4 Remote Storage (Hierarchical Storage Management)

Remote Storage is a storage management service that provides functionality to move files transparently between online media (e.g., disk) and offline media (e.g., tape). When a file is moved to offline media, a stub file is left behind on the disk. The stub file uses NTFS reparse points to mark the file as special in some way and to indicate where exactly on offline storage the file data can be located. Remote Storage is also often referred to as Hierarchical Storage Management (HSM) because the service deals with two distinct tiers of storage.

The administrator can set some policies, such as the amount of disk space that should be kept free and the types of files that should be dealt with by Remote Storage Services. RSS periodically runs and checks if the disk space use is in compliance with the policies set by the administrator. RSS periodically checks the last-accessed timestamp on files and locates files that have not been accessed for a while (typically 30 days). These files are then periodically copied to offline storage, but the file is still left on disk and marked as premigrated by an NTFS reparse point being set on the file. When the disk space falls below a set value, RSS deletes the file data from the disk and modifies the reparse point data to indicate that the file has now been moved from a premigrated state to a fully migrated state.

Remote Storage Services cannot deal with hidden, system, encrypted, or sparse files, or with files that have extended attributes. Remote Storage is well integrated with the rest of the operating system components. For example,

- Remote Storage Services interacts with the Indexing Service.
- Remote Storage Services uses the Windows 2000 job scheduler to schedule its backup jobs.
- Windows backup can recognize files that have been migrated to offline media and refrain from restoring those files simply for the purpose of backing them up.
- Remote Storage Services is also integrated with NTFS security; for example, RSS will recall a file from offline media only if a user is permitted access to the file.

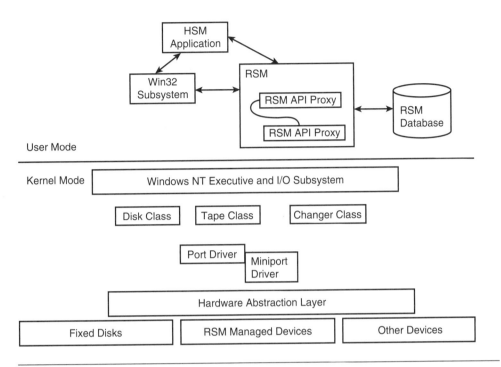

Figure 10.3 HSM and RSM Architecture

- The Explorer GUI is also Remote Storage aware. Files that have been migrated from disk to offline media are shown with a special icon.
- The NFTS change log journal is also Remote Storage aware, and a flag indicates when a file moves between online and offline media. An application can use this flag to determine that the underlying file has not changed in any manner.

Figure 10.3 shows the Remote Storage (HSM) and Removable Storage Management (RSM) architecture. The HSM application uses the RSM API (described in Section 10.2.11). RSM itself is a user mode subsystem that has its own private database to keep track of the media and devices that it is managing.

10.2.11 Removable Storage Management

Removable Storage allows an application to manage all enterprise removable media, irrespective of whether the media is online or offline. Whereas the online media could be in a variety of devices, including changer, tape jukebox, or robotic library, the offline media are typically sitting on a shelf.

Figure 10.4 illustrates the architecture and advantage of using RSM. The application deals with a single interface provided by RSM. RSM itself deals with the intricacies of new devices and devices that come and go.

RSM uses a concept of **media pools** to organize and manage media. A media pool represents a collection of media. Media pools are broadly categorized into two types: systems and applications. The **system pool** holds media for system-related purposes, as well as unrecognized and unassigned media. The system pool is further categorized as follows:

- The **free pool** holds media that is currently not in use and is freely available for assignment.
- The **import pool** holds newly added media that are recognized. Media in the import pool are later manipulated by applications and moved into the application pool (if the application deems the media to be of use) or to the free pool if the application determines that the media is no longer of any interest.
- The **unrecognized pool** holds newly added media that has not been recognized. As with the import pool, an application may later move media into the application pool or the free pool.

Application pools hold media created by applications such as backup or Remote Storage.

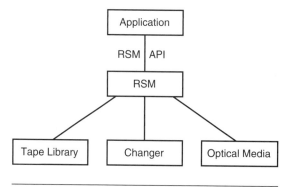

Figure 10.4 Removable Storage Management

10.2.12 Encrypting File System

Windows 2000 introduces the encrypting file system (EFS), which is really a service that is layered on top of NTFS. The service provides a mechanism to encrypt data before it is written to the disk by NTFS and decrypt data after it is read by NTFS but before it is passed back to the application that requested the data. EFS also provides a mechanism to manage the keys needed for the encryption, as well as recovery keys to allow an authorized entity other than the file owner to retrieve the data.

The data is encrypted by a symmetric cipher (in particular, a variation of DES), and the randomly generated key for this symmetric encryption is written to the file after it has been encrypted by an asymmetric cipher and the user's public key. To ensure that the file can be retrieved (e.g., when a disgruntled employee is fired and refuses to cooperate), the randomly generated symmetric cipher key is also encrypted with an authorized entity's public key and written to the file.

Encrypted files cannot be compressed; that is, either a file can be compressed or it can be encrypted, but not both. EFS ensures that the data remains encrypted even when somebody manages to access the disk directly without going through NTFS and its security mechanism that would disallow the access. EFS can be enabled on a per-file or per-directory basis.

More details about EFS are available in Chapter 6.

10.2.13 System File Protection

One of the problems plaguing Windows has been the fact that operating system files get corrupted or replaced. Application vendors often replace system files with either their own files or newer versions. This practice can lead to system management problems at best, and reliability problems at worst. Starting with Windows 2000, Microsoft introduced a feature called System File Protection.

This feature protects certain system files using a background mechanism. A list of monitored system files is stored in a cache folder. A copy of the relevant files is also cached in the folder. If the file is not available, it is loaded from the media (Windows CD). The background process computes a file signature for the actual files and compares them to the signature within the cache. If the signatures do not match, the file is silently updated from the cached copy. The service pack and hot-fix installation utilities have the necessary code to update both the cache and the non-cache copy of the file.

10.3 Windows Server 2003

Windows Server 2003 continues the trend of each successive Windows NT release building on the strengths of the previous release and adding more storage-related features of its own. To appreciate the amount of work put in by Microsoft, consider Figure 10.5.

The unshaded boxes in Figure 10.5 represent storage features that are expected to ship with Windows Server 2003 and have already been described in this chapter. The shaded boxes show components shipping after Windows Server 2003. The release vehicle for these components is undecided. Judging by the past practices adopted by Microsoft, the possibilities include the following:

- Ship in the next major release cycle of Windows NT (currently code-named Windows Longhorn).
- Ship via Windows Resource Kit or a service pack.
- Ship via release to the Web—for example, download from the Microsoft Web site.
- Ship via ISVs and IHVs; for example, Microsoft makes the software available to partners who bundle it with their offerings.

10.3.1 Storport Driver Model

As explained in Chapter 1, the Windows NT operating system provides for a layer of device drivers to achieve efficient and scalable I/O operations.

For a complete description of the Windows storage I/O stack and all the layers, please refer to Chapter 1. For now, suffice it to say that one of these layers is the port driver layer. The port driver is responsible for receiving I/O requests from upper layers, preparing a SCSI command data block (CDB), and passing the request to the device. Port drivers are responsible for maintaining information that allows communication with the device. While preparing CDBs and interpreting the command results, port drivers use the services of a miniport driver that is expected to be written by the device vendor.

Prior to Windows Server 2003, Microsoft provided a SCSIPort driver and expected vendors to write SCSIPort miniport drivers that handled their SCSI and Fibre Channel devices. A particular Windows installation may have multiple miniport drivers corresponding to devices from multiple vendors. The SCSIPort driver routes the request to the appropriate vendor-written SCSI miniport driver.

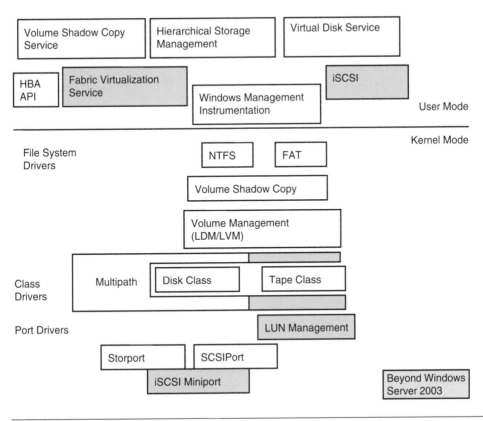

Figure 10.5 Windows Storage Feature for Windows Server 2003 and Beyond

There are several problems with this situation:

- The model assumes that Fibre Channel devices have capabilities similar to SCSI devices, which is just not true! Further, the model assumes that newer SCSI-3 devices are similar to older SCSI devices, which again is patently untrue.
- In the interest of simplifying the task of writing a miniport driver, the SCSIPort driver follows a single threading model without any support for full duplex communication. This may prevent the system from attaining the desired and achievable I/O throughput.
- The port driver has some information that it does not pass to the miniport, instead requiring the miniport to collect this information laboriously via multiple calls. In particular, this is true for scatter/gather lists.

- Out of sheer frustration, Fibre Channel device vendors resorted to either writing a monolithic driver that encompassed the functionality of the port and miniport drivers or replacing the port driver with their own port driver. Because this process required that the functionality of the port driver be reverse-engineered, the attempts, at best, have worked with some varying degrees of success. Of course, things become rather interesting when a different vendor comes along and tries to make its miniport run with a port driver written by another vendor.

With Windows Server 2003, Microsoft has introduced a new driver model with a Storport driver. HBA vendors are now expected to write miniports that link with the Storport driver rather than the SCSIPort driver. To keep this effort to a minimum, Microsoft has kept the Storport model backward compatible with the SCSIPort model. So vendors who want to put in minimal work may easily reap some (but not all) of the advantages of the new model. To take complete advantage of the new model, these vendors will have to do some more work beyond a simple recompile and relink.

The new architecture has the following major advantages:

- Storport enables higher performance by allowing full duplex I/O. The drawback is that the miniport driver now needs to worry about serializing execution, where appropriate. Thus the higher performance is achieved at the cost of higher complexity.
- Storport optimizes the interface between the port and miniport drivers. For example, the new interface allows a miniport to collect scatter/gather I/O information with a single callback rather than using multiple callbacks in a loop. *Scatter/gather list* is a generic term applied to a situation in which I/O is initiated into multiple separate (and disjointed) buffers simultaneously.
- Storport improves the interface to meet requirements of high-end storage vendors, particularly Fibre Channel and RAID vendors. For example, the old SCSIPort model allowed for very little in terms of queue management. Newer devices need sophisticated management. The Storport model allows for 254 outstanding requests per logical unit per adapter. The maximum number of outstanding queues per adapter is limited simply by the number of logical units per adapter, as illustrated in Figure 10.6.
- Storport allows for a tiered hierarchy of resets to recover from error conditions. Whereas the older model did a highly disruptive (bus)

reset, resets in this architecture are done in a minimally disruptive fashion (LUN, then target, and then if all else fails, bus reset).

■ The new model allows for an enhanced interface dedicated to manageability.

■ The new model provides an interface that removes the requirement to create a "ghost device." The SCSIPort model does not allow an application to query capabilities if no unit is mounted. So vendors created a ghost device, simply to be able to make certain queries. The Storport model removes the requirement to create a ghost device by supporting query capabilities even when no miniport unit is yet mounted or attached.

■ All of this is provided in as minimally disruptive a fashion as possible because Storport is literally backward compatible with SCSI-Port. Vendors can choose to recompile and relink their existing code to work with Storport (instead of SCSIPort) with very little effort. They will benefit from the new model but will not reap all the advantages if they adopt this minimal-effort path. Legacy SCSI devices can continue to run with the existing SCSIPort driver.

For further details, see Chapter 2.

10.3.2 Volume Shadow Copy Service

Windows Server 2003 introduces the volume shadow copy service and related infrastructure. Volume shadows are also popularly referred to as *snapshots*. The different terminology is intended to respect intellectual property rights. The volume shadow copy architecture is shown in Figure 10.6. The architecture consists of four types of components, three of which typically have multiple entities present. The four components are

1. Volume shadow copy service
2. Shadow copy writers
3. Shadow copy requestors
4. Snapshot providers

This service enables the creation of consistent, point-in-time copies of data to be created and managed. The highlights of the service include the following:

■ The **volume shadow copy service** is written by Microsoft and provides APIs for backup applications to request the creation of

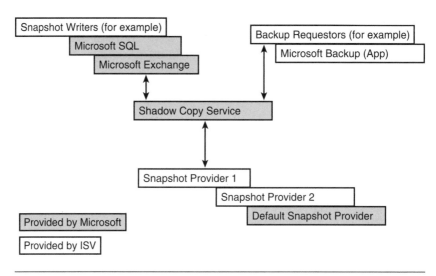

Figure 10.6 Volume Shadow Copy Service

snapshots. This service provides the coordination necessary to ensure that all I/O operations are properly held, caches have been flushed, and both system I/O and application I/O are frozen to allow a point-in-time copy to be accomplished.

- **Shadow copy writers** are basically applications such as SQL or Microsoft Exchange with some volume shadow copy service code integration. It is desirable for all applications, including databases and enterprise resource planning applications, to have a shadow copy writer provider for integration with the shadow copy service. Microsoft is expected to make available Active Directory, SQL Server, and Microsoft Exchange providers.
- **Shadow copy requestors** are backup applications or applications that cause a volume copy to be created—for example, create a copy of data for testing with beta software. Some of these will be written by Microsoft, and some are expected to be written by other ISVs. The backup application that ships natively with Windows Server 2003 is also a shadow copy requestor.
- **Snapshot providers** are the entities that actually create the snapshot or volume copy. Microsoft provides a default software provider that creates a volume copy using a copy-on-write technique. Storage unit vendors are expected to write more providers. The architecture allows for a variety of schemes to be used for creation of the snapshot, including breaking a mirror in hardware.

Note that the infrastructure provided by Microsoft allows for the creation of only a single snapshot. However, the infrastructure does cater to an ISV's requirements for creating snapshots one at a time, for organizing and managing multiple snapshots, and for allowing for read-only mounting of any given snapshot.

More details about the volume shadow copy service are available in Chapter 5. The volume shadow copy service SDK is available from Microsoft on a nondisclosure basis only.

10.3.3 Virtual Disk Service

The virtual disk service (VDS) is a management interface that ships with Windows Server 2003 and is meant to provide an abstraction for disk virtualization, no matter where the virtualization is accomplished.

Before describing some architectural details of the virtual disk service, it is worthwhile to step back and consider the motive behind this service. The grand vision is to allow a storage administrator to programmatically, through a batch file and through a management GUI, specify functionality such as the following:

- Obtain a storage volume, make it RAID 5, and make it at least 10GB in size
- Obtain a storage volume, make it 10GB in size, and make it a simple volume with no RAID features

The idea is that storage administrators routinely allocate storage for making a snapshot and backing up the snapshot, and later release the snapshot storage volume back into the free pool. VDS provides a way to accomplish such tasks, irrespective of where the virtualization is done and works for all kinds of different storage hardware, as well as all kinds of storage interconnects.

Figure 10.7 shows the architecture of the virtual disk service. The shaded boxes represent components written by Microsoft that ship with the server operating system. IHVs are expected to write hardware providers. VDS provides an abstraction so that management applications can be written via a single interface, no matter what the characteristics of the underlying storage hardware happen to be. VDS also allows for a management application to remain unmodified, yet useful, even when new storage hardware ships after the management application has shipped. Storage hardware vendors can innovate and be assured that their new hardware will be discovered and managed, thanks to the integration with VDS.

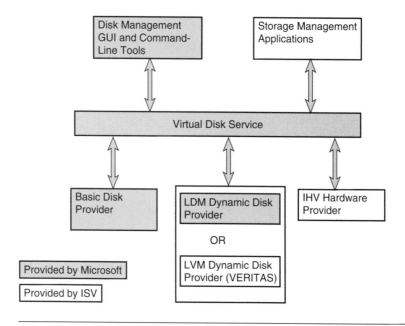

Figure 10.7 Virtual Disk Service

Microsoft will ship two VDS providers that cater to basic disks and dynamic disks. (For a description of basic disks and dynamic disks, see Chapter 6.)

Storage hardware vendors are expected to write VDS providers. Each VDS provider is simply a COM server invoked by the VDS service. Hardware providers are expected to make available the following kinds of functionality:

- LUN discovery
- LUN creation, destruction, and other LUN management
- COM objects for LUNs, the storage controller, the drive, and even the provider itself
- Remote access so that a management application can run on a workstation and communicate with the VDS service running on a server

The interfaces to write a provider are currently (as of this writing) available from Microsoft on a nondisclosure agreement basis. See Chapter 7 for more details about the virtual disk service.

10.3.4 Multipath I/O

Multipath I/O is a high-availability solution for the Windows NT server family that Microsoft is introducing with Windows Server 2003 and also making available for Windows 2000 Service Pack 2 and higher. Microsoft provides a multipath development kit to OEMs, IHVs, and ISVs that they use to develop and distribute their solution to end users. The highlights of the solution are as follows:

- It works on both Windows 2000 and Windows Server 2003.
- It is a fairly complicated architecture that involves three device drivers written by Microsoft and a minidriver written by the vendor.
- It provides for failover, failback, and load balancing. It also allows for up to 32 alternate paths to the storage unit.
- It is based on PnP notifications and needs no static predefined configuration definitions.
- It is compatible with Microsoft Cluster Server.

The vendor-written minidriver (called a *device-specific module,* or *DSM*) is responsible for

- Identifying multiple paths to the same storage unit
- Assigning an initial path (using load balancing or a preferred path or other algorithm)
- Upon an I/O error, deciding if the nature of the error dictates a permanent error or whether the I/O operation is worth retrying
- Deciding if the error requires a failover operation and which alternate path should be used
- Detecting conditions that warrant a failback operation
- Performing device-specific initialization
- Handling select commands such as Reserve and Release, and deciding if the commands should be sent down all I/O paths or just certain select paths

Multipath I/O is described in more detail in Chapter 9.

10.3.5 Improved Manageability

Windows 2000 introduced a trend to have both GUI and command-line tools for systems management. Windows Server 2003 continues that theme with command-line tools available to do the following:

- Manage file system features, including defragmentation
- Manage volume shadow copy service
- Manage volumes
- Manage Remote Storage Services (RSS)

Windows Server 2003 also accelerates the trend introduced in Windows 2000 to provide performance and management information using WMI. More parts of the operating system have been modified to provide management information using the WMI architecture. Storport, volume shadow copy service, and Dfs, are some examples.

10.3.6 SAN-Aware Volume Management

Readers familiar with UNIX will readily understand that Windows has no equivalent to the UNIX mount table. Thus, Windows attempts to mount any volume it happens to see. If the file system on a volume is not recognized, the raw file system claims ownership of the volume. Before a Windows server joined a SAN, then, the administrator had to carefully use LUN masking, zoning, and other management techniques to ensure that the Windows server would be able to see only a limited amount of storage (that belonged to it). Windows Server 2003 changes this situation.

Microsoft has changed the Mount Manager driver (described in Chapter 6) to be more SAN friendly. Specifically, the Mount Manager can be configured to mount only volumes that it has previously seen and to ignore any new volumes it sees. The easiest way of managing the configuration settings is to use the mountvol command-line utility.

10.3.7 SAN Application Enabling

Windows Server 2003 introduces several features that enable ISVs to write powerful storage management applications for a SAN environment. These include the following:

- Volumes can now be mounted in a read-only state.
- Applications can now use a new API that, when used in conjunction

with the volume shadow copy service, allows an application to perform a read from a specified volume shadow (popularly also referred to as a *snapshot*). ISVs thus are able to create versatile applications that can deal with N-way mirrors and can check data integrity.

- A new API allows an application to set the valid length of a file. ISVs can thus write a distributed file system, as well as backup and restore applications, to perform streaming block-level copies to disk and then set the valid length of the file.
- Administrators can now manage volumes yet have lower-level security privileges.
- New APIs have been added to allow file system filter driver writers better stream management functionality. File system filter driver writers can also benefit from better heap management and device object management routines, as well as new security management routines. New volume management APIs are present as well.

10.3.8 NTFS Improvements

Windows Server 2003 has made some significant improvements in NTFS, including the following:

- It provides 10 to 15 percent improvement in NTFS performance.
- The defragmentation APIs and the limitations on what they can accomplish have also improved remarkably.
- NTFS can now mount volumes in a read-only state.
- Default ACLs on NTFS volumes have been strengthened to improve security.

10.3.9 Defragmentation Improvements

Windows Server 2003 builds on the defragmentation APIs supported by the Windows I/O subsystem in general and NTFS in particular. The defragmentation improvements include the following:

- The NTFS master file table (MFT) can now be defragmented. Entries in the MFT can be moved around, even when the file represented by an entry in the MFT is opened by an application.
- Encrypted files can be defragmented without the file having to be opened and read, so security and performance are improved.

- Noncompressed files are now defragmented at the disk cluster boundary rather than at the memory page boundary.
- NTFS can defragment files even when the disk cluster size is greater than 4K.
- NTFS can defragment not just the unnamed data stream, but also reparse points and file attributes.

10.3.10 EFS Improvements

The encrypting file system (EFS) was first introduced in Windows 2000. Windows Server 2003 adds refinements to the EFS to improve security. Specifically, the additional functionality provided includes the following:

- The encrypting file system now allows multiple users to access an encrypted file. Recall that EFS encrypts a file using a symmetric key algorithm (the same key is used to encrypt or decrypt), and the symmetric key itself is encrypted via an asymmetric key algorithm. Specifically, the symmetric key is encrypted with a user's public key and stored in the same file. Windows Server 2003 simply allows the symmetric key to be encrypted and stored multiple times, using a different user's public key.
- EFS now supports full revocation list checking for a user's certificate, thus allowing a user that is no longer authorized to access a file that he or she may have been able to access in the past.
- EFS now supports more encryption algorithms by providing support for the Microsoft cryptographic service provider.
- End-to-end encryption over WebDAV can now be done. The Windows 2000 version decrypted files before transferring content over the network using WebDAV. The content transmitted over WebDAV is now encrypted and decrypted locally at the client.
- The offline files can now be stored in an encrypted form. Windows 2000 EFS support did not include encrypting the offline file cache.
- EFS encrypted files can now be stored in a Web folder.

10.3.11 Remote Storage Services

The Hierarchical Storage Management (HSM) provided by Remote Storage Services in Windows 2000 supported only tape as the secondary media. (RSM in Windows 2000 supported other media such as optical drives, changers, and jukeboxes, but the HSM solution did not.) Windows

Server 2003 provides HSM support for other secondary media besides tape.

10.3.12 Boot Improvements

Windows XP and Windows Server 2003 have been invested with optimizations to minimize the boot time for a system. The loader (ntldr) uses a single I/O operation per file while reading the required files off the disk. The operating system also overlaps disk I/O with device initializations, and it delays the initialization of system processes and services that are not essential for a boot.

10.3.13 CHKDSK Improvements

Windows 2000 improved availability by significantly reducing the number of situations in which CHKDSK needed to be run fully, as well as the amount of time taken by CHKDSK when it did need to run. Windows Server 2003 continues this trend. Here is some quantitative data that may or may not hold true in the final shipping product: A test case with 3 million files completed CHKDSK on Windows Server 2003 in approximately one-twelfth the time that the same test case took on Windows 2000.

10.3.14 Caching Behavior Improvements

Windows XP I/O benchmarks reported a much lower throughput with SCSI disks as compared to the performance benchmarked with Windows 2000. And therein lies an interesting tale.

Operating system and storage disk vendors have provided caching features, in an attempt to boost performance and throughput. Windows NT has a Cache Manager that provides caching features for all file systems. Some storage disks also provide a high-speed cache memory within the storage subsystem. Although caching can improve performance, the tradeoff is that when data is written to a cache instead of to the storage media, there is a potential loss of data if the data is never transferred from the cache to the disk media. To allow an application writer to control caching behavior, Windows NT provides the following facilities:

- An application can specify the FILE_FLAG_WRITE_THROUGH parameter in the CreateFile API to indicate that a device may not complete a write request until the data is committed to media.

The Windows NT drivers are expected to communicate this behavior to the storage device using the SCSI Force Unit Access (FUA) flag. The FUA flag is specified by the SCSI standards and can be used to disable caching within a storage device on a per-I/O basis.

- An application can specify the FILE_FLAG_NO_BUFFERING parameter in the CreateFile API to indicate that no caching should be performed in the file system layer.

- An application can use the FlushFileBuffers API to force all data for an open file handle to be flushed from the system cache, and it also sends a command to the disk to flush its cache. Note that contrary to its name, this API affects all data stored in the device cache.

The problem is that the Windows platform has been mishandling application requests to refrain from caching, and Windows Server 2003 is the first Windows platform that correctly handles write-through requests. This meant that performance benchmarks were artificially high on the Windows NT 4.0 and Windows 2000 platforms. In addition, some operating systems competing with Windows NT have a similar bug. Microsoft recommends that administrators use the configuration utility supplied by the storage vendor to disable the storage drive cache. However, the matter has some other complications, such as the following:

- Windows XP fixed the bug for basic disks, but not for dynamic disks. Thus it appeared for a while that Microsoft heavily favored dynamic disks. The concept of basic and dynamic disks, which pertains to how information about the logical partitioning of the disk is written on the disk, is explained in Chapter 6.

- Microsoft literature has been incorrectly requiring application writers that favor higher performance to also use the FILE_FLAG_WRITE_THROUGH parameter in the CreateFile API. Microsoft has indicated that it will be fixing all applications, tools, and utilities it owns to remove the FILE_FLAG_WRITE_THROUGH parameter when the emphasis is on performance. Microsoft has also indicated that it will make available an application compatibility layer to take care of applications that have not yet been modified to remove the FILE_FLAG_WRITE_THROUGH parameter when the emphasis is on performance.

10.3.15 Automated System Recovery

Windows Server 2003 improves system reliability by providing a mechanism to perform a disaster recovery operation. In particular, a server can be recovered from a disk failure via a one-step restore process that will restore all operating system information and system state. Automated System Recovery is based on use of the volume shadow copy service, and it requires the presence and use of a floppy drive.

10.3.16 Dfs Improvements

Dfs was first introduced in Windows NT 4.0 and enhanced in Windows 2000. Windows Server 2003 provides some more enhancements to Dfs, including the following:

- Dfs now supports multiple roots. This means that an enterprise can enjoy the advantages of consolidating views into a namespace, yet also have multiple namespaces for security and administrative purposes. This is extremely useful for corporations that have multiple divisions—for example, a corporation that provides consumer products and also homeland security products. Another case where this would be useful is when a corporation acquires another corporation and wishes to administer the two separately.
- File replication has been improved.
- Load balancing has been improved.
- Users can select servers closest to their location, improving performance.

10.3.17 WebDAV Redirector

Windows 2000 servers and clients provided a wide range of connectivity, offering support for CIFS, NFS, NetWare, and Macintosh client or server connectivity. Windows Server 2003 adds a WebDAV client. *WebDAV* stands for "Web Distributed Authoring and Versioning," an Internet standard protocol that allows file transfer using HTTP as the transport protocol. Just as a person downloading an Excel file from a server is unaware that the CIFS protocol is being used, users are not aware that a file may be retrieved from a server via WebDAV.

10.3.18 Driver Infrastructure Improvements

Windows Server 2003 builds on the momentum generated by Windows XP to make more tools available to driver writers, and it significantly toughens the testing and logo certification requirements in order to make the drivers more reliable. Driver writers not only benefit from more tools and education to help them write their drivers, but they also get more feedback and information that allows them to debug their existing drivers and make an updated version available.

10.3.19 HBA API Support

The Storage Networking Industry Association (SNIA) defined a C library API to allow storage management applications to manage Fibre Channel HBAs. The APIs defined include support for querying and setting HBA configuration management, as well as measuring HBA performance statistics.

Although Microsoft and SNIA members both support the HBA API, the approaches differ a little. The SNIA approach, illustrated in Figure 10.8, requires three components:

1. A generic HBA API DLL owned and maintained by SNIA. This DLL exposes a standard interface for the benefit of management applications. At the bottom edge, the DLL interfaces with multiple vendor-written DLLs.

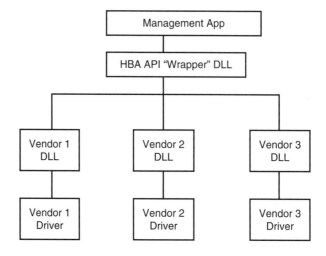

Figure 10.8 SNIA HBA API

2. An HBA vendor-written DLL that plugs into the generic HBA API DLL. This vendor-written DLL makes available management information and interacts with the vendor-written driver using proprietary IOCTLs.
3. A vendor-written device driver for the HBA.

Although this standardization effort has its merits, Microsoft appears to see some problems with this approach, including the following:

■ There is no clear way to manage the distribution and versioning of the proposed dynamic link libraries. This is one more example of a potential DLL hell in which various applications install versions of the libraries and potentially overwrite libraries that other applications have installed.
■ The HBA vendor needs to write not only the device driver and private IOCTL interface to the driver, but also the vendor-specific DLL, and it must potentially modify the wrapper HBA library to handle vendor-specific interfaces to the vendor DLL.
■ It will be extremely hard to test and certify vendor drivers that implement private IOCTLs. For example, how does one verify that the driver code will not result in a buffer overrun situation when bad parameters are passed on the IOCTL call?
■ The architecture appears to be extensible at first sight, but closer inspection reveals that the HBA vendors will be forever chasing the management application vendors to add code that deals with vendor-specific enhancements.
■ The solution does not cater to kernel mode–to–kernel mode communication and management. A management device driver may want to accomplish functionality such as LUN masking before the system completely boots up. With the SNIA solution, the HBA API works only after the system is completely booted up.

Microsoft advocates a slightly different approach, illustrated in Figure 10.9, that consists of the following components:

■ A generic HBA API DLL owned and maintained by SNIA. This DLL exposes a standard interface for the benefit of management applications. At the bottom edge, the DLL interfaces with Windows Management Instrumentation (WMI), the Microsoft implementation of the Common Information Model (CIM), an object-oriented systems management model adopted by both SNIA and the DMTF.

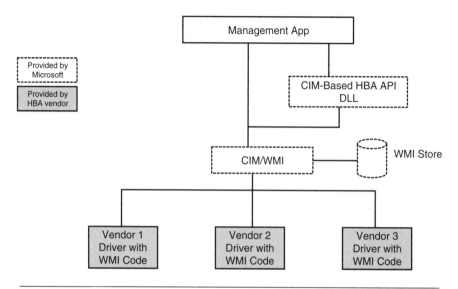

Figure 10.9 Microsoft HBA API

- A vendor-written device driver for the HBA. This driver implements WMI and makes available management and configuration interfaces in the WMI repository. Because WMI is a two-way interface, the driver also implements WMI IRP functionality that allows a management application to set configuration parameters for the driver.
- A mapping DLL written by Microsoft that translates between WMI and the SNIA HBA API interface.

The advantages with the Microsoft approach are as follows:

- All interfaces are standardized, whereas in the SNIA approach, the interface between the generic HBA API DLL and the vendor-written DLL is proprietary for each vendor. The Microsoft approach is consistent with the SNIA adoption of the DMTF Common Information Model.
- A vendor can easily extend an existing WMI class or define a new one and populate management information into that class. Again, this feature just emphasizes the extensibility of the SNIA-adopted CIM model.
- The biggest advantage is that management applications can use either the SNIA HBA API or the SNIA CIM model. Applications

that use the SNIA HBA API still work unaltered, thanks to the WMI code in the driver and the Microsoft WMI-to-HBA mapping DLL.

- The architecture allows a kernel mode component to interrogate the vendor-written driver and take some management action.

Note that the WMI interfaces needed to code the HBA driver shipped with Windows 2000, so device vendors can easily add the required WMI code in their drivers.

10.3.20 GUID Partition Table Disks

Windows Server 2003 has a 64-bit version of Windows that supports the industry standard Extensible Firmware Interface (EFI). EFI is a replacement for the old legacy BIOS that has been a hallmark of the PC industry.

EFI defines a GUID partition table (GPT). *GUID* is short for "globally unique identifier." The exact layout of a GUID table is specified in Chapter 16 of the EFI specification, which is available at http://developer.intel.com/technology/efi/download.htm.

A GPT disk can have 2^{64} logical blocks. The EFI specification uses the term *logical block* for what is commonly termed a **disk cluster**, which is the smallest unit of storage the file system allocates. Because EFI specifies a typical logical block size of 512 bytes, this equates to a disk size of approximately 18EB. A GPT disk can have any number of partitions, just like a dynamic disk. And also just like dynamic disks, GPT disks are self-describing, meaning that all information about how the disk is logically structured is present on the disk itself. And just like Windows 2000 dynamic disks, GPT disks store partition information redundantly to provide fault tolerance. Whereas GPT disks are an industry standard, technically Windows 2000 disks are a proprietary standard. However, there are not too many EFI-based PCs, compared to BIOS-based PCs.

To guard against data corruption when a GPT disk is accessed by a legacy system, GPT disks also have a Master Boot Record (MBR) defined that encompasses the whole disk. Thus the legacy system is prevented from believing that the disk is not partitioned.

GPT boot disks have a new partition defined, called the **EFI system partition**, or **ESP**. This partition contains the files needed for booting the system, such as ntldr, hal.dll, boot.txt, and drivers. The ESP can be present on a GPT disk or an MBR disk, as defined by the EFI specification. The 64-bit Windows Server 2003 requires the ESP to be on a GPT disk.

Another partition of interest is the **Microsoft Reserved partition** (**MSR**). GPT disks prohibit any hidden sectors, and the MSR is used by components that previously used a hidden sector. The MSR is created when the disk is first partitioned, either by the OEM or when a Windows Server 2003 64-bit version is installed. On disks smaller than 16GB, the MSR is 32MB in size. For disks larger than 16GB, the MSR is 128MB in size.

While on this subject, it is worthwhile mentioning that EFI is available from Intel in only a 64-bit version. Although the standard does not prohibit a 32-bit EFI version, no such implementation is on the horizon. Thus the 64-bit and 32-bit Windows versions will have significant differences in their low-level code, as well as boot sequence code.

The 64-bit version of Windows Server 2003 *must* boot from a GPT disk. However, it can access older legacy disks that are not GPT disks (but not boot from them). For the 32-bit version of Windows Server 2003, MBR disks continue to be the preferred disk format over GPT disks.

10.4 Post-Windows Server 2003

Not content to rest on its laurels in terms of storage features added to the Windows NT platform in Windows 2000 and Windows Server 2003, Microsoft continues to build on the momentum with a host of storage features planned for the post-Windows Server 2003 release. These include support for iSCSI and further improvements in storage management infrastructure.

10.4.1 Fabric Virtualization Service

The fabric virtualization service was disclosed briefly at a recent trade show and appears to be an attempt to provide a single interface to manage fabric switches, no matter who the switch vendor is or what the particular model or features of the switch are.

Consider what a storage administrator typically does to accomplish a routine task such as a backup:

1. Create a volume that will serve as a repository for the snapshot.
2. Rezone switches to make this volume visible to the server that is hosting the source volume from which a snapshot is to be created.

Some port manipulation may also have to be done, as well as LUN management at the source server.
3. Create the snapshot.
4. Move the snapshot (e.g., rezoning, LUN reconfiguration) to make it visible to the backup server.
5. Accomplish the backup.
6. Return the snapshot to the storage pool, which involves yet some more switch and LUN configuration.

Typically, the process goes like this: The storage administrator does some manual work, starts some software, does some more manual work, starts some different software, and so on.

The fabric virtualization service, when used in conjunction with the virtual disk service (described in Section 10.3.3) will facilitate full automation of such tasks. The fabric virtualization service has no known time frame for a release, and there is no firm commitment that Microsoft will have such software.

10.4.2 LUN Management

Windows NT is overly aggressive when it comes to handling storage; its philosophy is "see disk, claim disk." Windows spins up every disk it sees to read the partition table and then attempts to mount each file system that it sees. Needless to say, the potential for data corruption is fairly high.

At the time of this writing, LUN masking is available as a feature from third parties (IHVs and ISVs), but not as a built-in feature of Windows itself. One of the problems with these third-party solutions is that there is a chance for the third-party driver or utility software not to be loaded—for example, when a server boots into safe mode. Thus the chances of data corruption still exist. LUN masking is also available as a feature of hardware—for example, RAID boxes or Fibre Channel switches—but the problem with that solution is that the hardware cannot be controlled programmatically. Typically the hardware comes with a graphical configuration utility that can be run remotely.

A future version of Windows NT server is expected to ship with LUN masking implemented in the native driver stack that Microsoft itself ships, and in particular, in the Storport driver at the very minimum.

As per the trial balloons floated at past trade shows (WinHEC), the Microsoft implementation can be expected to have the following features:

- IOCTLs to allow a management application to accomplish and control the LUN masking.
- An inclusion list that can be configured via the IOCTL just mentioned. An inclusion list contains a list of devices that the driver should expose to applications.
- The ability to bypass the LUN masking.[2]

As this book goes to press, Microsoft is believed to be working on implementing LUN-masking capability in the port driver. The advantage of having such functionality in the port driver is that the port driver is always loaded and hence the window of opportunity for nonparticipation in the LUN masking is considerably reduced. The chances of having the wrong port driver loaded are considerably smaller compared to the chances of having the wrong miniport driver loaded as well.

One should not assume that all device vendors are equal in their capability to dynamically configure any port as any kind of port. Some devices have this capability built in and can reconfigure a port on the fly without a reboot or power cycle, but some devices need firmware upgrades or swapping of option cards for the particular port that may require a power cycle.

There is no known time frame or firm commitment for any such software to be released by Microsoft.

10.4.3 iSCSI Support

iSCSI is an industrywide effort to implement block storage over existing network-centric infrastructure. Though iSCSI is not expected to perform on as high a level as other existing storage interconnects, such as Fibre Channel, the focus is on solutions that do not require high performance and can leverage existing network infrastructure. The expected arrival of hardware accelerators for TCP/IP, where some protocol processing

---

2. Without details of the implementation being available, it is difficult to say for certain, but one can expect that a determined kernel mode piece of software may be able to do this. This is not a security risk, because the Windows philosophy is to trust kernel mode software and restrict the ability of people to install kernel mode software, thus allowing a system administrator to install and run only kernel mode software that has been thoroughly tested and can be trusted.

overhead is expected to be moved from the server CPU to dedicated network card hardware, should only help advance the case for iSCSI.

Microsoft has indicated that it is actively implementing iSCSI support in Windows NT. There is no exact release time frame, though the expectation is that Microsoft might release such software after Windows Server 2003, but before the next major release cycle of the Windows operating system.

Figure 10.10 shows the architecture for the Windows NT iSCSI implementation. The iSCSI initiator is implemented as a miniport driver that can work with both SCSIPort and the new Storport port driver.

The discovery DLL tracks all changes dynamically and acts as a single repository for all LUNs discovered through any mechanism, including iSNS (Internet Storage Name Service) client or port notification. The discovery DLL provides an API for management applications to discover new LUNs and, if appropriate, a means for the management application to direct the discovery DLL to perform a login to the new LUN.

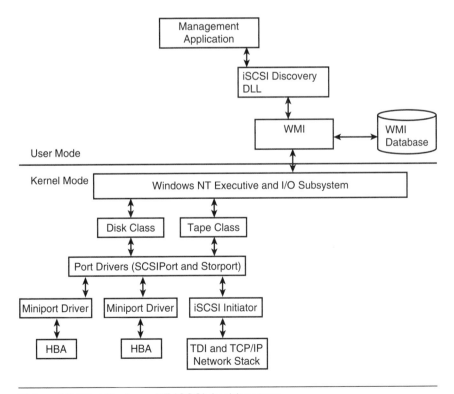

Figure 10.10 Windows NT iSCSI Architecture

Highlights of Microsoft's iSCSI plans include the following:

- To focus on implementing iSCSI on the Windows Server 2003 platform. However, Microsoft will also provide iSCSI code for the Windows 2000 and Windows XP platforms. This code is expected to be available within months of the Windows Server 2003 release.
- To provide code for iSNS server and client.
- To emphasize the use of IPsec as a data protection and security mechanism.
- To focus on iSCSI initiator implementation. There are no current plans to implement iSCSI target on the Windows NT platform.
- To transmit all communication between discovery DLL and iSCSI initiator through WMI.

The port driver also provides a communication path to the HCA miniport, as well as the InfiniBand managers such as the subnet and connection managers. The subnet manager is responsible for managing fabric topology by programming switches and setting host channel adapter (HCA) attributes. The subnet manager also provides a point of confluence for management policies pertaining to access control, performance, and fault tolerance (multipath). The connection manager implements InfiniBand connection-oriented features, as well as policy-based features for failover.

10.4.4 Multipath I/O

Multipath I/O is available for Windows 2000 and Windows Server 2003. Microsoft provides a development kit to vendors, and users can get the complete solution only from vendors. Microsoft is expected to extend the multipath solution to cover removable media (the existing solution works only for fixed hard disks). This explains the shaded portion of the multipath area in Figure 10.5.

10.5 What's Missing?

Microsoft has acknowledged the need for several additional features without yet making any commitment to implement them. This section surveys those features and speculates a bit about their possible future.

10.5.1 SAN Boot

Windows 2000 can be booted from a SAN, but there are many caveats. Microsoft supports SAN boot in a limited scenario. The caveats include the following:

- All hardware and software used must be on the Windows 2000 hardware compatibility list.
- The scenario should not include an FC-AL (Fibre Channel arbitrated loop) environment, primarily because Windows NT kernel has not been modified at all and the delays in an FC-AL environment when the loop is reinitializing can cause kernel timeout errors.
- Windows 2000 needs to have exclusive access to the LUN from which the boot is happening. The required LUN masking must be achieved via switch and HBA management.
- The SAN vendor must be involved in the planning and deployment process and must be the first resource for support issues.
- Having the paging file on a local disk is highly beneficial.
- Most if not all solutions require multipath to be disabled for the duration of the boot process.

Having SAN boot support in the operating system would be highly beneficial. Some better support for latency issues might be one feature. With iSCSI on the horizon, the possibility of a remote SAN boot using a Gigabit Ethernet card is intriguing as well. Of course, having LUN-masking support in Windows NT early in the boot sequence would not be a bad thing to have as well.

10.5.2 Reducing the Layers in the Storage Stack

The Windows NT driver model is highly modular and layered with a view toward providing easy introduction of a new layer as needed. Perhaps the model has been rather too successful in meeting its goal. A typical Windows 2000 server could easily have ten or so drivers between the application and the physical wires. Consider the drivers in the stack:

- The Storport or SCSI miniport driver.
- The Storport or SCSIPort driver.
- The disk class driver.
- The Logical Disk Manager driver, which is really multiple drivers.

- The diskperf driver.
- A virus-checking filter driver.
- The file system driver.
- The file system filter drivers, of which there are more than one. Some examples include the Remote Storage reparse point filter driver, the Single Instance Storage reparse point filter driver, the Symbolic Link reparse point filter driver, and the encrypting file system filter driver.

It might help to see if the functionality of one driver can be subsumed into another driver. Windows XP introduces a limited callback mechanism for filter drivers, and it remains to be seen if this trend is expanded upon. But this is pure speculation for now.

10.5.3 Multipath I/O for iSCSI

The multipath I/O developer's kit does not cater to iSCSI solutions. As the iSCSI market gathers momentum, it remains to be seen what Microsoft does to provide a high-availability and high-performance solution for iSCSI.

10.6 Practical Implications

Microsoft is clearly focused on making Windows an extremely storage-friendly platform. The successive releases of Windows NT described here show rapid progress in this direction. It is clear that Microsoft will play an increasingly important role in the enterprise storage industry.

For persons involved in making purchase decisions, it is worthwhile noting what features are present only in Windows Server 2003 and what features are common to both Windows Server 2003 and Windows 2000. Tracking the ISV or IHV road maps for these two operating systems is also a good idea.

10.7 Summary

The Windows NT platform has made remarkable advances toward becoming an enterprise storage–friendly platform. The Windows NT 4.0 and Windows 2000 platforms more or less stressed improvements in reliability, scalability, and availability. Windows 2003 Server adds more availability features (multipath I/O), performance features (Storport driver model), and a lot more manageability features (virtual disk service, SAN application enabling, SAN-aware mount manager, command-line management interface enhancement). Post-Windows Server 2003, Microsoft will provide a big impetus to iSCSI by natively supporting iSCSI on the Windows platform.

References

Chapter 1

Nagar, R., *Windows NT File System Internals: A Developer's Guide,* OReilly, Cambridge, England, 1997.

Oney, W., *Programming the Microsoft Windows Driver Model,* 2nd Edition, Microsoft Press, Redmond, WA, 2002.

Solomon, D. A., and Russinovich, M. E., *Inside Microsoft Windows 2000,* 3rd Edition, Microsoft Press, Redmond, WA, 2000.

Viscarola, P., and Mason, W. A., *Windows NT Device Driver Development,* MacMillan Technical Pub., Indianapolis, IN, 1999.

Windows Driver Development Kits: http://www.microsoft.com/ddk.

Windows XPSP1 Installable File System (IFS) Kit: http://www.microsoft.com/ddk/IFSkit.

Chapter 2

"Adding Support for More Than Eight LUNs in Windows Server," Microsoft Knowledge Base Article 310072, http://support.microsoft.com/default.aspx?scid=KB;EN-US;Q310072.

ANSI T10: http://www.t10.org.

Porting Miniport Drivers to Storport, http://www.microsoft.com/hwdev/tech/storage/default.asp.

Sawert, B., *The Programmer's Guide to SCSI,* Addison-Wesley, Reading, MA, 1998.

Schmidt, F., *The SCSI Bus and IDE Interface: Protocols, Applications, and Programming,* Addison-Wesley, Reading, MA, 1995.

SCSI Trade Association: http://www.scsita.org.

WinHEC 2001 Enterprise Storage Session: http://www.microsoft.com/winhec/winhec2001.mspx.

Chapter 3

Common Internet File System File Access Protocol, MSDN Web page: http://msdn.microsoft.com/library/default.asp?url=/downloads/list/windevwin.asp.

"How to Enable SMB Signing in Windows NT," Microsoft Knowledge Base Article 161372, http://support.microsoft.com/support/kb/articles/Q161/3/72.asp.

Leach, P. J., and Naik, D. C., "A Common Internet File System (CIFS/1.0) Protocol: Preliminary Draft" [IETF informational RFC, now expired], Internet Engineering Task Force, March 1997, http://www.ubiqx.org/cifs/rfc-draft/draft-leach-cifs-v1-spec-02.html.

Leach, P., and Perry, D., "CIFS: A Common Internet File System," *Microsoft Interactive Developer,* November 1996, http://www.microsoft.com/Mind/1196/CIFS.htm.

Microsoft Settlement Program: Communications Protocol Program: http://www.microsoft.com/legal/protocols.

NFS Version 4 site, maintained by SUN Microsystems: http://www.nfsv4.org.

Pawlowski, B., Shepler, S., Beame, C., Callagahn, B., Eisler, M., Noveck, D., Robinson, D., and Thurlow, R., "The NFS Version 4 Protocol," http://www.nluug.nl/events/sane2000/papers/pawlowski.pdf.

Protocols for X/Open PC Interworking: SMB, Version 2: http://www.opengroup.org/products/publications/catalog/c209.htm.

Shepler, S., "NFS Version 4 Design Considerations," Network Working Group, RFC 2624, June 1999, http://www.ietf.org/rfc/rfc2624.txt.

Shepler, S., Callaghan, B., Robinson, D., Thurlow, R., Beame, C., Eisler, M., and Noveck, D., "NFS Version 4 Protocol," Network Working Group, RFC 3010, December 2000, http://www.ietf.org/rfc/rfc3010.txt.

Storage Networking Industry Association (SNIA): http://www.snia.org.

Windows Driver Development Kits: http://www.microsoft.com/ddk.

Presentations on the SNIA Web Site

CIFS 2000 Conference, various presentations: http://www.snia.org/ education/presentations/cifs_2000.

O'Shea, G., "Operating Systems Case Study Windows 2000 (NT)," http:// research.microsoft.com/~gregos/MScNT.ppt.

Chapter 4

ANSI T11: http://www.t11.org. [The ANSI T11 committee is responsible for all Fibre Channel–related protocols.]

CERN Fibre Channel: http://hsi.web.cern.ch/HSI/fcs. [Interesting information at CERN laboratories High Speed Interconnect pages.]

Clark, T., *Designing Storage Area Networks,* Addison-Wesley, Reading, MA, 1999.

"Fibre Channel," InterOperability Lab Tutorials and Resources (www. iol.unh.edu/training/fc/fc_tutorial.html).

Fibre Channel Industry Association (FCIA): http://www.fibrechannel.org.

Storage Technologies, Microsoft Windows Platform Development: http:// www.microsoft.com/hwdev/tech/storage/default.asp.

Chapter 5

"Evaluator Group Report: An Analysis of the IBM TotalStorage NAS Products 200/300/300Gateway 300" [Persistent Storage Manager architecture], http://www.storage.ibm.com/snetwork/nas/analysis.html.

Griswold, B., "Enterprise Storage," http://www.microsoft.com/winhec/ presents2001/EntStor.ppt.

"I/O Subsystem Enhancements," MSDN Web page, http://msdn. microsoft.com/library/default.asp?url=/library/en-us/appendix/hh/ appendix/enhancements5_33oz.asp.

Moore, G. E., "The Continuing Silicon Technology Evolution inside the PC Platform," Intel, http://www.intel.com/update/archive/issue2/ feature.htm.

NDMP specifications: http://www.ndmp.org/download.

Network Data Management Protocol (NDMP): http://www.ndmp.org.

Open File Manager White Paper: "Preventing Data Loss during Backups Due to Open Files," http://www.stbernard.com/products/docs/ofm_whitepaper.pdf.

Russinovich, M., and Solomon, D., "Windows XP: Kernel Improvements Create a More Robust, Powerful, and Scalable OS," *MSDN Magazine,* December 2001, http://msdn.microsoft.com/msdnmag/issues/01/12/XPKernel/XPKernel.asp.

Storage Networking Industry Association (SNIA) Backup Work Group: http://www.snia.org/tech_activities/workgroups/backup.

T10 and SNIA versions of Extended Copy specifications: http://www.snia.org/tech_activities/workgroups/backup/docs.

Williams, S., and Kindel, C., "Component Object Model: A Technical Overview," MSDN Web page, http://msdn.microsoft.com/library/default.asp?url=/library/en-us/dncomg/html/msdn_comppr.asp.

WinHEC 2002 Conference Papers and Presentations: http://microsoft.com/winhec/sessions2002/default.mspx.

Chapter 6

"Best Practices for Encrypting File System," Microsoft Knowledge Base Article 223316, http://support.microsoft.com/support/kb/articles/Q223/3/16.asp.

Bolosky, W. J., Corbon, S., Goebel, D., and Douceur, J. R., "Single Instance Storage in Windows 2000," http://research.microsoft.com/sn/Farsite/WSS2000.pdf.

"Comparison: Microsoft Logical Disk Manager (LDM) and VERITAS Volume Manager for Microsoft Windows," VERITAS Software Corporation, Mountain View, CA, 2002, http://www.veritas.com/de/produkte/datasht/ldm_vm_vergleich_wp.pdf.

"A Description of the Functions of the Single Instance Storage Filter and the Groveler Service," Microsoft Knowledge Base Article 299726, http://support.microsoft.com/default.aspx?scid=KB;EN-US;Q299726.

"Development Considerations for Storage Applications in Windows 2000,"

Microsoft Corporation, Redmond, WA, 1999, http://www.microsoft. com/windows2000/docs/StorDev.doc.

"Dynamic Disk Configuration Unavailable for Server Cluster Disk Resources," Microsoft Knowledge Base Article 237853, http://support. microsoft.com/default.aspx?scid=KB;EN-US;q237853.

"Dynamic vs. Basic Storage in Windows 2000," Microsoft Knowledge Base Article 175761, http://support.microsoft.com/default.aspx?scid= kb;en-us;Q175761.

"Encrypting File System for Windows 2000," White Paper, July 1999, http: //www.microsoft.com/windows2000/techinfo/howitworks/security/ encrypt.asp.

"How Single Instance Storage Identifies Which Volumes to Manage," Microsoft Knowledge Base Article 226545, http://support.microsoft. com/default.aspx?scid=KB;en-us;Q226545.

"How To: Back Up the Recovery Agent Encrypting File System Private Key in Windows 2000," Microsoft Knowledge Base Article 241201, http://support.microsoft.com/support/kb/articles/Q241/2/01.asp.

"How Windows 2000 Assigns, Reserves, and Stores Drive Letters," Microsoft Knowledge Base Article 234048, http://support.microsoft. com/default.aspx?scid=KB;en-us;Q234048.

"Limitations of Server Clusters," Windows 2000 Datacenter Server Documentation, http://www.microsoft.com/windows2000/en/datacenter/ help/default.asp?url=/windows2000/en/datacenter/help/sag_ mscs2planning_28.htm.

Microsoft storage presentations: http://www.microsoft.com/winhec.

NTFS 5.0, http://www.ccs.neu.edu/home/lieber/com3336/f99/lectures/l11/ ntfs/ntfs5.ppt.

"Reparse Point Support in Windows 2000-Based Clusters," Microsoft Knowledge Base Article 262797, http://support.microsoft.com/default. aspx?scid=kb;en-us;Q262797.

Richter, J., and Cabrera, L. F., "A File System for the 21st Century: Previewing the Windows NT 5.0 File System," *Microsoft Systems Journal*, November 1998, http://www.microsoft.com/msj/defaultframe. asp?page=/msj/1198/ntfs/ntfs.htm&nav=/msj/1198/newnav.htm.

"Software FT Sets Are Not Supported in Microsoft Cluster Server," Microsoft Knowledge Base Article 171052, http://support.microsoft. com/default.aspx?scid=kb;en-us;Q171052.

Solomon, D. A., and Russinovich, M., *Inside Windows 2000*, 3rd Edition, Microsoft Press, Redmond, WA, 2000.

"StorNext File System: High-Performance File Sharing for SAN Environments," http://www.adic.com/ibeCCtpSctDspRte.jsp?minisite=10000 &respid=22372&section=10121.

"Windows and GPT FAQ, Version 1.1," Microsoft Windows Platform Development, http://www.microsoft.com/hwdev/tech/storage/GPT_FAQ.asp.

Chapter 7

The Bluefin Specification and the SNIA Storage Management Initiative (SMI)" http://www.snia.org/tech_activities/SMI/bluefin.

Common Information Model (CIM), Storage Networking Industry Association (SNIA) Web page with links to white papers and presentations: http://www.snia.org/tech_activities/cim.

HBA APIs (Host Bus Adapter Application Programming Interface), Storage Networking Industry Association (SNIA) Web page with links to specifications and reference code: http://www.snia.org/tech_activities/hba_api.

Joshi, N., "Windows 2000 Storage Management Overview," http://www.microsoft.com/Seminar/Includes/Seminar.asp?Url=/Seminar/1033/20000413Win2KStorageNJ1/Portal.xml.

"Removable Storage Management and Windows," Microsoft Windows Platform Development, http://www.microsoft.com/hwdev/archive/storage/RSM.asp.

"Windows Management Instrumentation: Background and Overview," White Paper, November 1999, http://www.microsoft.com/windows2000/techinfo/howitworks/management/wmioverview.asp.

"Windows Management Instrumentation: Provider Programming," White Paper, December 1999, http://www.microsoft.com/windows2000/techinfo/howitworks/management/wmiprov.asp.

"Windows Management Instrumentation Scripting," White Paper, January 2000, http://www.microsoft.com/windows2000/techinfo/howitworks/management/wmiscripts.asp.

Windows Management Instrumentation (WMI) Tutorial: http://msdn. microsoft.com/downloads/default.asp?URL=/code/sample.asp?url=/ msdn-files/027/001/574/msdncompositedoc.xml.

Chapter 8

InfiniBand

Connor, D., "Microsoft Cancels InfiniBand Development," *Network World Fusion,* July 2002, http://www.nwfusion.com/news/2002/ 0730msin.html.

InfiniBand Trade Association: http://www.infinibandta.org.

IP Storage

Clark, T., IP SANs: *A Guide to iSCSI, iFCP, and FCIP Protocols for Storage Area Networks,* Addison-Wesley, Boston, 2002.

IEEE Storage Conference Site: http://www.storageconference.org.

IETF IP Storage Working Group: http://www.ietf.org/html.charters/ ips-charter.html.

IP Storage, Carnegie Mellon University: http://www.ece.cmu.edu/~ips/ index.html.

SNIA IP Storage Forum: http://www.snia.org/tech_activities/ip_storage.

TCP Offload

"Description of NDIS Features in Windows 2000," Microsoft Knowledge Base Article 260978, http://support.microsoft.com/support/kb/articles/ Q260/9/78.asp.

"NDIS 5.0 Overview," Microsoft Windows Platform Development, http:// www.microsoft.com/hwdev/tech/network/ndis5.asp.

"Windows Network Task Offload," Microsoft Windows Platform Development, http://www.microsoft.com/hwdev/tech/network/taskoffload.asp.

Chapter 9

Edelmann, S. "SANworks Secure Path: The Secret of Data Availability," http://www.decus.de/slides/sy2001/vortraege_2504/2d07.pdf.

HP (Compaq) SecurePath: http://www.mcoecn.org/WhitePapers/ COMPAQ-SECURE-PATH.PDF.

Kammer, K. R., "Dell EMC PowerPath: Improving Storage Availability," August 2002, http://ftp.us.dell.com/app/3q02-Kam.pdf.

RAID Web: http://www.raidweb.com/whatis.html.

Multipath

Edelmann, S., "SANworks Secure Path: The Secret of Data Availability," http://www.decus.de/slides/sy2001/vortraege_2504/2d07.pdf.

"EMC PowerPath Enterprise Storage Software: Product Description Guide," http://www.emc.com/products/product_pdfs/pdg/powerpath_ pdg.pdf.

Microsoft Enterprise Storage Presentation, http://www.microsoft.com/ winhec/winhec2001.mspx.

"Multiple-Path Software May Cause Disk Signature to Change," Microsoft Knowledge Base Article 293778, http://support.microsoft.com/ default.aspx?scid=KB;en-us;Q293778.

Storage Technologies: http://www.microsoft.com/hwdev/tech/storage/ default.asp.

"StorageWorks Secure Path, Version 3.0, for Windows NT: A High-Availability Solution for Intel Platforms Product Description," http:// www.compaq.com/products/storageworks/techdoc/storagemgtsoftware/ AA-RL54A-TE.html.

VERITAS White Papers for Windows Products: http://www.veritas.com/ us/partners/microsoft/whitepapers.html.

Chapter 10

"Development Considerations for Storage Applications in Windows 2000," Microsoft Corporation, Redmond, WA, 1999, http://www. microsoft.com/windows2000/docs/StorDev.doc.

"Enterprise-Class Storage in Microsoft Windows 2000," Microsoft Corporation, March 2000, http://msdn.microsoft.com/library/default.asp?url=/library/en-us/dnentdevgen/html/enterstor.asp.

Windows 2000 Storage Services, Microsoft Windows Platform Development, http://microsoft.com/windows2000/technologies/storage/default.asp.

Windows Server 2003, Feature Highlights Sorter Results: http://microsoft.com/windows.netserver/evaluation/features/featuresorterresults.aspx?Technology=Storage+Management.

Windows Server 2003, "Technical Overview of File Services," Microsoft Corporation, July 2002, http://www.microsoft.com/windows.netserver/docs/fileoverview.doc.

Index

389

Also from Addison-Wesley

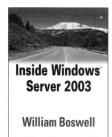

0-7357-1158-5

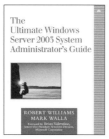

0-201-79106-4

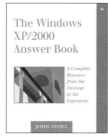

0-321-11357-8

0-321-13345-5

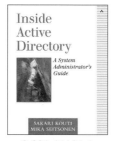

0-201-61621-1

0-672-32125-4

0-201-77574-3

0-201-61613-0

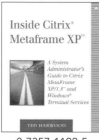

0-7357-1192-5

0-201-61576-2

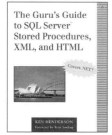

0-201-70046-8

0-201-74203-9

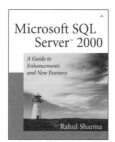

0-201-75283-2

Register
Your Book

at www.awprofessional.com/register

You may be eligible to receive:

- Advance notice of forthcoming editions of the book
- Related book recommendations
- Chapter excerpts and supplements of forthcoming titles
- Information about special contests and promotions throughout the year
- Notices and reminders about author appearances, tradeshows, and online chats with special guests

Contact us

If you are interested in writing a book or reviewing manuscripts prior to publication, please write to us at:

Editorial Department
Addison-Wesley Professional
75 Arlington Street, Suite 300
Boston, MA 02116 USA
Email: AWPro@aw.com

Addison-Wesley

Visit us on the Web: http://www.awprofessional.com